# Battling Miss Bolsheviki

POLITICS AND CULTURE IN MODERN AMERICA

Series Editors: Margot Canaday, Glenda Gilmore,
Michael Kazin, and Thomas J. Sugrue

Volumes in the series narrate and analyze political and
social change in the broadest dimensions from 1865 to the
present, including ideas about the ways people have sought
and wielded power in the public sphere and the language
and institutions of politics at all levels—local, national, and
transnational. The series is motivated by a desire to reverse
the fragmentation of modern U.S. history and to encourage
synthetic perspectives on social movements and the state,
on gender, race, and labor, and on intellectual history
and popular culture.

# Battling
# Miss Bolsheviki

---

## The Origins of Female Conservatism
## in the United States

### Kirsten Marie Delegard

**PENN**

UNIVERSITY OF PENNSYLVANIA PRESS

PHILADELPHIA

Published by
University of Pennsylvania Press
Philadelphia, Pennsylvania 19104-4112
www.upenn.edu/pennpress

Printed in the United States of America
on acid-free paper
2 4 6 8 10 9 7 5 3 1

*Library of Congress Cataloging-in-Publication Data*

Delegard, Kirsten.
Battling Miss Bolsheviki : the origins of female conservatism
in the United States / Kirsten Marie Delegard. — 1st ed.
    p.   cm. — (Politics and culture in modern America)
Includes bibliographical references and index.
ISBN 978-0-8122-4366-6 (hardcover : alk. paper)
    1. Women—Political activity—United States—History—20th
century. 2. Conservatism—United States—History—20th cen-
tury. 3. United States—Politics and government—20th century.
I. Title. II. Series: Politics and culture in modern America.
HQ1236.5.U6D45   2012
305.420973'09045—dc23                                    2011021576

# Contents

# Introduction

This is the story of how a new movement of women changed American politics during the first decade of female enfranchisement. At the end of the seventy-two-year struggle for suffrage, most Americans expected the nation's polity to be remade by new women voters. But they envisioned an entirely different type of transformation from the one forced by a coalition of women led by the Daughters of the American Revolution (DAR) and the American Legion Auxiliary. These women launched the first broad-based, explicitly conservative movement of women in American history. Part of the mission of this new movement was to destroy a critical constituency for progressive causes. In the ten years after the passage of the Nineteenth Amendment—at a crucial moment in the formation of the American welfare state—their actions fundamentally changed how female activists could influence politics. These activists reconfigured the key institutions of women's power between the Nineteenth Amendment and the New Deal. They called into question the vision of social justice that had animated the political activity of middle-class clubwomen since the Progressive Era. They framed domestic reform as an arm of global revolution, banishing the long-standing support for social improvement provided by female voluntary associations. These sustained attacks on female reformers have been described but not adequately explained by historians of this period, who have paid little attention to the "women patriots" behind this campaign.[1] Yet these "invisible" women changed the landscape of American politics for the rest of the twentieth century.

This narrative starts at a moment of heady victory, as female activists rejoiced in the achievement of universal female suffrage. At that moment, politically engaged women believed they stood on the cusp of a new world in which they would work together, in the words of reformer Charlotte Perkins Gilman, "for universal peace, for a socialized economic system that shall make prosperity for us all, for such growth in industry, art and science, in health and beauty and happiness, as the world has never seen." The time had come, according to Gilman, for women to say to men: "you have had your day—you have worked your will—you have filled the world with warfare, with drunkenness, with vice and disease. You have wasted women's lives like water, and the children of the world have been sacrificed to your sins. Now we will have a new world."[2] It was this type of rhetoric that energized many activists, who believed that women were inherently opposed to "war and corruption."[3] They fought for the suffrage on the conviction that once women played an equal role in governance, the nation would look very different. Journalist Rheta Childe Dorr imagined a society in which

> Everything will be as clean as in a good home. Every one, as in a family, will have enough to eat, clothes to wear, and a good bed to sleep on. There will be no slums, no sweat shops, no sad women and children toiling in tenement rooms. There will be no babies dying because of an impure milk supply. . . . No painted girls, with hunger gnawing at their empty stomachs, will walk in the shadows.[4]

In retrospect, it seems hopelessly naive to think that giving women the vote would so thoroughly change American life. But Dorr and other activists had good reason to be optimistic that female enfranchisement would make American government more responsive to the basic needs of its citizens. In the three decades before the Nineteenth Amendment, female activists pioneered lobbying techniques and put them to use in the service of myriad reform campaigns, including votes for women. In these years—which are now seen as a veritable "golden age" of women's politics—civically engaged activists created a female political subculture with settlement houses and women's clubs as its cornerstones. Groups such as the National Association of Colored Women's Clubs, the National Congress of Parents and Teacher Associations (PTA), the National Consumers' League, the Daughters of the American Revolution, and the General Federation of Women's Clubs served as training grounds for middle-class women activists. Women volunteers piloted welfare programs as philanthropic ventures and then used their clubs and organizations to pressure state, local, and national governments to assume responsibility for these programs. Women's political influence surged. But activists perceived their efforts to force municipal reform, enact protective legislation, and craft public health initiatives as selfless missions necessary for the protection of their homes, families, and children. Women "want very little for themselves," declared Dorr. "Even their political liberty they want only because it will enable them to get other things—things needed, directly or indirectly, by children."[5] In seeking to fulfill their "maternal" responsibilities, these activists fundamentally altered the scope of the American state, recasting the welfare of mothers and children as an issue for public policy. At the same time, they carved out a new niche for women in the public sphere, allowing female activists to become respected public authorities on questions of social welfare.[6]

In these decades before the Nineteenth Amendment, female activism became synonymous with reform. Most observers assumed that giving women the vote would boost campaigns to protect maternal and child health and welfare. When critics bemoaned the fact that women would have less time for volunteer work once they were burdened with the franchise, suffrage leader Anna Howard Shaw countered these predictions by promising, "Thank God, there will not be so much need of charity and philanthropy!"[7] Newspapers heralded female enfranchisement as the beginning of a new era for women in politics with cartoons that declared "Enfranchisement Means the Sky's the Limit in Woman's Sphere."[8] Yet in the aftermath of the suffrage amendment, the influence of women reformers plummeted and the millennial social order envisioned by Gilman and Dorr appeared only more remote.

The decade that followed the attainment of the franchise, reformer Grace Abbott complained, was "uphill all the way."[9] "Hardly one of our special bills ever passed in all the eight years I worked in Washington," reflected Elizabeth Hewes Tilton, lobbyist for the PTA between 1922 and 1930. "We labored, we kept the broader faith, Nation-wide action for Nation-wide evils, but we made no headway in the tepid, torpid years."[10] Women reformers found the vote too weak a tool for carving out sweeping social reform. "So far as federal legislation is concerned," reformer and academic Sophonisba Breckinridge observed in the early 1930s, "the cause of Child Welfare . . . has advanced little, if any, since 1921."[11] In the years before the New Deal, she observed, reformers staggered under "the weight of unfinished business."[12]

Why did women's political influence—measured in legislative triumphs— seem to diminish after women won the vote? Or as historian Anne Firor Scott put it: "What happened to the verve and enthusiasm with which the suffrage veterans set about to reorganize society?"[13] Two generations of historians have tried to explain this apparent paradox. Contemporary observers claimed that women were so exhausted after receiving the vote that they abandoned politics for cultural and sexual experimentation.[14] More recent scholarship has demonstrated that this was not the case. Women's interest in lobbying and voluntary politics remained stronger than ever during the 1920s. Well-known labor organizer Mary Anderson, who served as the first director of the Women's Bureau in the U.S. Department of Labor, boasted in 1924 that "American women are organized, highly organized, and by the millions. They are organized to carry out programs of social and political action."[15] What diminished was the ability of female reformers to effect new social welfare policy.[16]

Female reformers faced an array of formidable foes. They had to contend with powerful industrialists, a male medical establishment, and hostile male legislators, who loathed the supposed power exercised by the women's reform coalition.[17] The media fed skepticism about the civic commitment of women citizens, sponsoring debates on the utility of female enfranchisement with headlines like "Is Woman Suffrage a Failure?"[18] Yet these were familiar enemies for the veteran activists, who had learned to navigate the shoals of male-controlled institutions on earlier crusades. More crippling were the divisions that opened among women once they were no longer united by the campaign for the vote. Belief in a sex-based unity had persisted despite entrenched ideological diversity among female activists since the Civil War. In the fifty years before the Nineteenth Amendment, women had been active as anarchists and communists; populists and progressives; racists and civil rights advocates. Rural women, African American women, and immigrant women had contested the efforts of white middle-class women to uplift and educate them in standards of domesticity. Until the passage of female suffrage, however, these conflicts had done little to undermine the dominance of middle-class white reformers in political discourse. Middle-class clubwomen continued to portray themselves as advocates for all women, justifying their political demands by drawing on a universal female moral authority.

The illusion of unity dissolved in the 1920s. During this decade, the conflicts that arose among women slew the chimera of gender solidarity. Immediately after the Nineteenth Amendment, differences stemming from race, class, ethnicity, region, and ideology became impossible to ignore. Female enfranchisement brought new discord. White clubwomen drew protests from African American clubwomen when they refused to help combat the abuses that barred them from voting in the South. A schism also emerged among white activists, who struggled to find consensus on the best way to advance equality and justice for women. The National Woman's Party

(NWP) fastened on the Equal Rights Amendment, which it proposed in 1923 to eliminate all legal disabilities for women. This measure horrified traditional social welfare reformers because it would invalidate protective labor legislation dictating minimum wage and maximum hours for wage-earning women. The split between NWP feminists and traditional reformers widened over the course of the 1920s, prompting journalist William Hurd to observe that "the woman 'bloc' does not tend to become more and more solidified but tends to become more and more disintegrated."[19] These controversies helped to undermine both the hopes and fears associated with women's political power. No longer worried about alienating women voters, Congress perceived little danger in ignoring lobbyists advocating social welfare reforms.[20]

These divisions were demoralizing for many women who had embraced the utopian idealism of the suffrage movement. They would find even more reason to be discouraged, however, as the "woman bloc" came to be regarded as not only divided but also treasonous. Reformers' moral authority was battered by a frontal assault on their patriotism that claimed their efforts to pass reform legislation were part of a Bolshevik plot. Female reformers, according to these charges, had pushed the nation to the brink of revolution. While the accusations had no basis in fact, they left women like Mabel Clare Ladd shaken. The Detroit clubwoman confessed to being "stirred . . . most deeply" by the charge that the League of Women Voters endorsed the legislative program of Soviet Russia. Though she wanted to support child welfare and peace, she was adamant that she could not ally herself "with any organization or disseminate any propaganda which can in any measure be construed as 'Red.'"[21] By the end of the decade, female reform had become linked to global revolution, which placed once-respected reformers beyond the pale of political respectability.

This fear of revolution had its roots in the political changes sweeping the globe. The world was shocked by the 1917 Russian Revolution, which demonstrated the real possibility of Bolsheviks seizing power. Americans had no confidence that their nation was immune from this threat, especially when a wave of domestic unrest hit North America two years after the radical revolution in Russia. Strikes, bombings, and riots racked the country, giving both government agents and private vigilantes a pretext for violent repression. Radicals, labor activists, and immigrants were brutalized and subjected to raids that continued through 1920. Thousands were arrested and hundreds deported. This period is known as the "Red Scare" and is

usually assumed to have ended by 1920, when presidential candidate Warren
G. Harding proclaimed that "Too much has been said about Bolshevism in
America."[22] While government agents did scale back their repression after
Harding's declaration, the end of what is traditionally considered the Red
Scare marked only the beginning of the anticommunist repression experienced by female reformers.[23] The women's "red scare" became obvious with
the publication of the notorious Spider Web Chart in 1924 and continued
without respite through the New Deal. Female reformers found themselves
crippled by attacks on their loyalty and patriotism.

This red-baiting has been observed by historians of this period, who
detail attacks like the Spider Web Chart as evidence of the decade's conservative climate.[24] However, these accounts have done a better job of description than explanation, presenting this hostile climate as an axiomatic
by-product of the hyper-Americanism stirred up by the Great War or the
misogyny of an American military that blamed women for the budget cuts
of peacetime demobilization. Accustomed to defining themselves vis-à-vis
male opponents, female reformers blamed their woes on military authorities. Historians have followed their lead, using War Department documents
to reveal the military's campaign against women associated with the peace
movement of the time.[25]

Yet the actions of a government bureaucracy—even one as powerful as
the War Department—could not have been solely responsible for transforming the political climate for female reformers. This women's "red
scare" received sporadic support from the military. But it was organized
and sustained by a social movement of women, whose historic connections to female voluntary associations made them devastating to reformers.
These women crushed the high hopes that opened the decade. Described
by one activist as a "movement organized for the purpose of destroying
the power of women," this group became the greatest nemesis of female
reformers in the 1920s.[26] They called themselves "antiradicals" and asserted that the women's campaigns for peace and social welfare reform had
opened the door for a Bolshevik-style takeover in the United States. Their
campaign tarred female reform in ways that had implications beyond individual pieces of legislation or particular initiatives to ensure international
peace. They transformed women's institutions, reducing "the churches and
large women's organizations to doing nothing about welfare legislation,"
according to reformer Elizabeth Tilton.[27] Their anxieties about enlarging
the welfare state and shrinking the military in an age of revolution shifted

the trajectory of American reform. Antiradical women created new fault lines that reshaped the landscape of women's politics, transforming the priorities of female voluntary associations and deflating the enthusiasm for social reform among the grassroots women who had provided female policymakers with unwavering support. After a decade of sustained attacks by female antiradicals, female voluntary associations were no longer the wellspring of utopian visions for women activists.

Historians of women have created a rich literature exploring the conflicts among women engendered by race, class, and ethnicity. By contrast, there is scant work on the interplay between conservative women and their politically progressive counterparts. Clubwomen found it impossible to find broad consensus on a legislative agenda in the aftermath of suffrage. By the end of the decade Carrie Chapman Catt concluded that women could not "be joined together for any one purpose because the difference between the reactionary and the progressive is too great to be bridged."[28] But this does not mean that their political paths diverged. The activism of conservative and progressive women remained closely interwoven, like the warp and weft of a cloth. By only looking at the progressive and radical strands historians have missed the larger pattern of the fabric. This history weaves back in the conservative threads that had been left hanging, filling holes in the fabric that had been invisible to earlier historians.

This book explains how conservative women stymied female reformers during their critical transition to full political citizenship. My interest in this topic stems from my personal experience coming of age in another period characterized both by exhilarating optimism and by acrimonious battles. During the 1970s, second wave feminists who were determined to ensure full legal and political equality for women came under attack by conservative women, who demonstrated their ability to undermine the political influence of their liberal and even radical sisters. In the same way in the 1920s, conservative women had succeeded in blindsiding liberal women made confident by years of political success and popular support for their agenda. They engineered headline-grabbing clashes with reformers, which emboldened conservative men who may have initially acquiesced to reform measures in part because they feared the power of women voters. Female conservatives assured them that the majority of right-thinking women did not support disarmament or social welfare measures, giving them license to cast their votes against reform.

In the decade after the Nineteenth Amendment, female antiradicals did more than neutralize once-powerful progressives. They created a new type of activism for women that would continue to shape politics for the rest of the twentieth century. Women had previously supported reactionary causes such as white supremacy or goals that seem conservative in retrospect, such as the prohibition of alcohol. Yet never before had these conservative impulses coalesced into a multi-issue movement. The strict sex segregation of politics meant that women were rarely welcome in male-dominated organizations during the nineteenth century. Before universal female enfranchisement, many women who called themselves conservatives were ambivalent about sustained women's political activism. Having the vote recast political participation for conservative women, who took it as a signal that it was their civic duty to become active in politics. "Whether or not you approved the franchise, it came to you and with it the solemn obligation to use it," argued Anne Rogers Minor, one of the leaders of the Daughters of the American Revolution.[29] Perhaps for the first time, conservative, liberal, and radical women agreed that women, at least those who were white, deserved some measure of political influence. Female enfranchisement set the stage for new battles among these women about how, rather than whether, women should exercise political influence. Working in the same clubs, new conservative activists adopted the strategies for political influence pioneered by female reformers.

While some antiradicals took the Nineteenth Amendment as a new mandate for political engagement, all the women who came to identify themselves as antiradicals framed their activism as a response to the Bolshevik Revolution. Stories emerging from the new workers' republic in Russia outraged conservatives, who popularized stories that depicted a Soviet Union devoted to perverting the traditional family. Many of the founding mothers of antiradicalism probably first heard these stories as testimony before the 1919 Senate Overman Committee, set up to investigate the 1917 Russian Revolution. The committee focused on the fate of women in particular and decried radicals' efforts to obliterate the patriarchal family structure. The myths and rhetoric that emerged from the Overman Committee demonstrate the centrality of gendered imagery to early anticommunism. Witnesses described new Soviet divorce laws that supposedly encouraged men to discard their wives. They recounted the "nationalization" of women and children, claiming that the state had placed children in state institutions to be raised and forbidden women to "belong" exclusively to one man. Bolsheviks, it was said, even forced women to register at the government "Bureau of Free Love" where they were made available to any and all men, regardless of their feelings.

The testimony produced by these hearings was a twisted representation of the suffering generated by the chaos of revolution, civil war, famine, and the American-led invasion of Russia. The so-called "Bureau" was apocryphal. No such office existed. Revolutionary edicts did not rip children from the arms of loving parents. Yet these narratives about victimized women and children gave a moral urgency to a new type of women's activism that gathered steam just as support for working-class radicalism petered out in the United States. Dystopian visions of the Bolshevik gender system were terrifying for women like Grace Brosseau, president general of the DAR. She told delegates at her organization's convention that it was their duty to heed these warnings and protect what she called "the lovely young girlhood of America" by telling "citizens of this country . . . what has happened to women in Russia."[30] This determination to save American women from the fate of their Russian sisters fueled the ascendance of anticommunism. These newly mobilized conservative activists had a clear vision of the consequences of remaining silent: a revolution that would render women destitute and sexually violated.[31]

Although the purported goal of antiradicalism was to prevent a Bolshevik-style revolution in the United States, this movement took shape at a moment when the probability of a radical takeover was remote. By the early 1920s, political repression had pushed American radicalism into its twentieth-century nadir. Yet female antiradicals saw little reason to cheer. They did not believe that the danger of revolution had subsided, even if the number of card-carrying Communists had dropped. Working-class radicals were not the most dangerous agents of revolution for these women. They believed that the most insidious threat was posed by reformers whose legislative agenda was revolutionary in spirit, if not in name. Antiradicals recast federal measures funding prenatal education or regulating child labor as opening wedges for the alleged Bolshevik "nationalization" of women and children. According to one South Dakota woman, reformers are "appealing to women's organizations to support measures to protect children when the real motive is to centralize and nationalize everything and when the Red Revolution comes as they have it planned—the government will have the control of everything such as Russia has today."[32] They viewed international arms agreements as a way to cripple American national security, leaving the nation incapable of resisting a domestic revolution that would bring home the carnage seen in the new Soviet state.

Antiradicalism grew with institutional support from some of the largest women's organizations of the time, most notably the Daughters of the
American Revolution, which had once counted itself as part of the Progressive Era female reform coalition. Only a few years after reformers heralded
the Nineteenth Amendment as the beginning of a new social order, leaders
of the DAR concluded that preventing a radical revolution in the United
States had eclipsed all other goals. By 1925, they had joined forces with the
newly created American Legion Auxiliary to protest the demobilization that
followed World War I. These two groups also enlisted smaller hereditary and
veterans' organizations like the Daughters of 1812 and the United Daughters
of the Confederacy. Bound together by interlocking memberships, these
groups formalized their cooperation in 1925 through the Women's Patriotic
Conference on National Defense (WPCND). Only the ideological agenda of
this organization made it a novelty. The Women's Patriotic Conference on
National Defense was modeled on groups established by female reformers to
promote peace and social welfare measures. It was launched as a response to
the Conference on the Cause and Cure of War and initially mimicked the
educational mission of this group, which was led by Carrie Chapman Catt.
By 1927, the group turned its attention to lobbying and evolved into a conservative version of the Women's Joint Congressional Committee, the "clearinghouse" set up to coordinate lobbying on behalf of female reform after the
Nineteenth Amendment. As the Women's Joint Congressional Committee
waned, the influence of the WPCND waxed in the latter half of the decade.
At its peak it would claim the support of groups whose combined memberships totaled one million women. This group remained vigorous through
World War II, carrying the politics of the first red scare forward into the era
of popular anticommunism.

The groups allied under the rubric of the WPCND remained preoccupied
with countering the women's peace movement, issuing public pronouncements on international diplomacy, troop levels, and military expenditures.
Meanwhile, another group of women viewed the legislative agenda of social
welfare reformers as the most acute threat to national security. The DAR gave
legitimacy to this idea in 1926, when it endorsed the conspiracy theories of
the Woman Patriot Publishing Company (WPPC). This group of former antisuffragists published the *Woman Patriot*, a Washington, D.C.-based publication dedicated to battling the twin menaces of Bolshevism and feminism.
The DAR's alignment with the *Woman Patriot* signaled the organization's
repudiation of its traditional support for social welfare reform as well as its

break with long-time allies in the Women's Joint Congressional Committee. In 1920, it would have been impossible to imagine the leaders of the DAR turning their backs on their organization's long history of support for maternalist legislative measures. By 1927, however, the acrimony between antiradicals and traditional maternalists made it difficult to imagine a time when the DAR and the League of Women Voters had found common cause.

The history that female antiradicals shared with reformers gave them a cultural power, which they put at the service of their new agenda. Grassroots clubwomen accepted the often incredible and inflammatory conspiracy theories of female antiradicals because the women issuing warnings about radical revolution had all the markers of feminine political respectability. When the influential DAR began distributing the polemics of the WPPC, popular support for the social reform agenda collapsed among clubwomen. The WPPC's "petitions" made women wary of associating with even mainstream women's groups. "I want to continue in PTA work," one South Dakota resident declared, "but I cannot see my way clear to work for things un-American."[33]

Female antiradicals scuttled the series of female-sponsored reform measures proposed after the Nineteenth Amendment. Yet antiradicals wanted—and achieved—more than the defeat of key legislation. They envisioned a refashioning of women's politics, a new focus for middle-class women who called themselves patriots. They demanded that women's organizations jettison the entire reform agenda developed over the previous thirty years. Their constant red-baiting dampened enthusiasm for social justice among centrist women's organizations, which had been some of the most important advocates for change since the Progressive Era. By the end of the 1920s women's clubs had buckled under antiradical assaults and dropped their campaigns for progressive legislation. This transformation reached beyond individual organizations to affect the entire female political subculture that had fostered reform and civic engagement since the turn of the century. Conservative women ensured that the whole infrastructure of lobbying groups developed by female reformers was one of the first casualties of the campaign to prevent a Bolshevik-style overthrow in the United States.

The success of conservative women in derailing support for progressive causes among the most prominent women's organizations of the time carried profound implications for the long-term path of American reform. Individual reformers remained politically active through the New Deal, as did left-leaning women's groups like the National Consumers' League and the

Women's Trade Union League, though their membership and vitality declined significantly. Yet enthusiasm for social change would never be revived in more mainstream women's organizations, even by the desperate conditions of the Great Depression. Progressive causes lost some of their most powerful and committed advocates, just at the moment when conditions for meaningful change improved. Women's groups, so vital in driving the reforms of the Progressive Era, were largely absent from the New Deal.

Antiradicals did not destroy the subculture of female voluntary associations. Instead, they reshaped this world, rededicating its key institutions to fresh purposes. Mobilizing through the same sex-segregated organizations favored by female reformers, they used time-tested tactics of education, publicity, and lobbying to advance a new agenda. In addition to supporting a robust military, they envisioned a new patriotic hegemony that would be upheld through carefully vetted textbooks, youth training programs, and restrictions on speech. They advocated new laws requiring that all public officials, especially teachers, take loyalty oaths. They called on politicians to deny recognition to the new Soviet Union. And they fought for the expansion of the federal countersubversion bureaucracy, which had been decimated by scandal at the beginning of the decade. Their advocacy in this area broke new ground for female activists. Responding to what they perceived to be a breach created by the suspension of political surveillance, they immersed themselves in the world of radicalism, struggling to comprehend its ideologies and to monitor the activities of those they saw as its proponents. They refined the tools of investigation and repression that would prove so powerful during the McCarthy years, compiling blacklists that enumerated treacherous organizations and individuals. Women volunteers surreptitiously attended radical meetings, investigated suspicious organizations, and collected subversive literature. They created archives devoted to analyzing and disseminating data on radicalism to house their research. Though they sometimes confronted leftist orators, their efforts were directed mostly at those in power. Radical watching, they discovered, did little to directly reshape the already weakened left in the United States. Those who had confronted violent red squads or embraced revolution after being brutalized by American capitalism were not easily intimidated. Instead, conservative women used their observation to build their expertise, which gave them influence with politicians and other federal authorities whom they lobbied to restart political surveillance operations.

By the New Deal, these conservative women had changed the trajectory of women's politics and American reform. Yet history has been written as though they did not exist. Even though they were the most persistent and effective foes of female reformers, female antiradicals have made only brief appearances in the scores of histories devoted to American reform and the peace movement of the time. When conservative individuals are presented, they always appear divorced from the movement that mobilized them. To be sure, female antiradicals were sometimes difficult to discern because they shared so much with the female reformers who have dominated narratives of this period. They were embedded in many of the same organizations and used the same political tactics as their declared foes. Historians may have expected conservatives to look entirely different from more familiar female reformers. To the contrary, female antiradicals were sociologically indistinguishable from their progressive sisters. They were white, middle-class members of mainline Protestant churches. They had similar levels of education as their progressive counterparts; few were graduates of the "Seven Sisters" colleges but many had some college education. They shared reformers' assumptions about gender roles, the danger posed by unassimilated immigrants, and white racial superiority. And they were motivated by the same sense that they were performing a "special mission" that distinguished them from self-serving male party activists.

Antiradicals shared so much with reformers. But they still left a distinct set of footprints in the archival record. Their influence was etched in the lamentations of reformers; their autonomy bemoaned by bureaucrats in the U.S. Army Military Intelligence Division; their zeal mourned by the maternalist activists of the Labor Department's Children's Bureau; their opinions cited by congressmen voting against maternal and child health programs and government curbs on child labor. They had declared their views to congressmen and newspaper reporters, laid out their agendas during public protests and the annual meetings of hereditary and veterans' organizations that had issued volumes of public proceedings. Their industry overwhelmed me in the national headquarters of the Daughters of 1812 in Washington, D.C., when current-day members of that group opened the closets in their brick townhouse to reveal floor-to-ceiling stacks of material. As my hostesses donned ball gowns for the evening parties that enliven the spring conventions of the national hereditary societies, I sorted through an archival treasure trove of scrapbooks and newsletters. Requesting only that I lock the door behind myself when I finished, they left me to my own devices until late in the night, imagining their Jazz Age predecessors reveling at similar galas.

Female antiradicals were everywhere in the historical record. And the best-known sociological study of the 1920s found that young women—at least in Muncie, Indiana—were actually slightly more likely to support some of the basic premises of antiradicalism than their male counterparts.[34] Yet they have remained largely hidden to researchers, whose range of vision has been traditionally defined by the assumptions of women's history. Even as scholars have explored conflict and diversity among women, this field has continued to be shaped by the unspoken belief that women possess an inherent affinity for demilitarization, an expanded social safety net, and greater social justice. Researchers have also been influenced by the paradigms of social history, which has encouraged scholars to dismantle the hegemonic ideologies that have circumscribed the lives and opportunities of ordinary people. Practitioners of this type of history are drawn almost exclusively from the political left. Traditionally, they have sought inspiration in the radical visions of the past; their scholarship articulated these political alternatives to reveal new possibilities for the present. They also investigated populist movements like the Ku Klux Klan, even though they fall on the far right. But they saw little value in studying more conventional conservatism, an ideology that many of these researchers assumed to be static and ubiquitous. The anticommunism, economic liberalism, and social traditionalism of mainline conservatives was transparent and uninteresting to these intellectuals. They reasoned that ordinary people gave little real support to a type of conservatism that was a simple defense of privilege. Powerful interests may have manipulated working-class men and women into backing conservative causes, but the creed of traditional conservatism remained the ideology of the rich and influential in the minds of most social historians.

In recent years, many researchers have concluded that this simplistic reduction holds little explanatory power. Feminist historians have been at the forefront of efforts to illuminate the ways in which various strands of conservatism, especially those that emphasize the politics of gender and sexuality, shaped twentieth-century politics. The intellectual framework of women's history is being transformed by a growing body of work that analyzes a wide range of women on the right. These examinations of anticommunists, white supremacists, antifeminists, and fiscal conservatives show the complexity of this activist tradition, belying efforts to render conservatives one-dimensional.[35] This excellent work has started to banish deep-seated beliefs about conservative gender politics. Scholars have shown the limitations of depicting conservative mobilizations as backlash phenomena, triggered in reaction to the "real" activism of feminists or progressives. They have demonstrated the danger of dismissing women on psychological grounds, written off as irrational or even unstable for favoring male-dominated causes such as the expansion of the military or countersubversion. According to traditional stereotypes, women join conservative or far-right organizations for so-called nonpolitical reasons, drawn to charismatic leaders or duty bound to follow their male relatives. Conservative women, in this analysis, are no more than pawns.

Antiradicals were no more psychologically unbalanced than their opponents. Women who became conservative activists believed that radical ideologies not only menaced their personal safety but also doomed their domestic relations and religious institutions. Their opposition to radicalism was deeply gendered, for it was motivated by the belief that these ideologies aimed to dismantle the patriarchal protections that provided shelter and care to women and children. Moreover, they were no less political or autonomous than women reformers. Their independence was initially not entirely voluntary: male antiradicals resisted partnership with them out of a deep suspicion of female activists of any stripe, even those who were sympathetic to their views. Throughout the decade, female conservatives tried repeatedly to establish a formal partnership with the military and would have welcomed the legitimacy that would have accompanied such a relationship. Male antiradicals, however, encouraged what they thought was proper female support, but remained hostile to conservative women's attempts to claim power and influence. This hostility forced female activists to invest their energy in sustaining autonomous women's institutions such as the Women's Patriotic Conference on National Defense. Born of discrimination, this female separatism preserved the vitality of their campaign against Bolshevism, demilitarization, and all reforms that could advance radicalism.

It was the analytical tools of social history that allowed me to recognize conservative women's networks in the 1920s. These antiradical activists were hiding in plain sight—in the middle-class women's clubs usually identified with Progressive reform. The story of their political ascendance shows how different kinds of political engagement can grow from the same soil. Similar types of women promoted and fought antiradicalism. In these years, the critical factor in determining whether an affluent woman pursued the unfinished business of the Progressive Era or turned her attention to countersubversion was her reaction to warnings about the Russian

Revolution and the domestic unrest that welled up at the close of World War I. These events transformed some of the most idealistic proponents of women's reform. The experience of working as a war correspondent in "barbarous and half insane" Russia during its revolution altered journalist Rheta Childe Dorr, who seemed to abandon the vision of utopian social transformation that sustained her throughout the suffrage campaign. She did not lose her faith in the importance of women's political engagement, but campaigned for Republicans during the 1920s.[36] Dorr demonstrates how an event on the other side of the world—the Russian Revolution—proved just as consequential as the Nineteenth Amendment in reshaping women's politics during the 1920s.

Dorr was not alone in her transformation. The events she described engendered profound ideological differences among women of the same race, from the same social, educational, and economic backgrounds. The upheaval that roiled women's clubs in the 1920s shows how activism does not automatically grow out of the material experience of class. Social and economic position can produce the ideological basis for activism. Yet scholars have observed for years that it has only limited power to explain the efforts of middle-and upper-class reformers and radicals, who have been lionized for their efforts to create a better society. In contrast, conservatives have been assumed to be simpler creatures, easily defined by their class interests. In fact, both sets of activists believed they were working for the greater good. Class, race, and gender combined to shape the world outlook, political possibilities, and tactics of women on the right as well as the left. No linear formula translated the social consciousness of female conservatives into political commitments. Activism in the 1920s emerged out of an unpredictable alchemy of personal beliefs and fears, experiences, as well as class, race, and sex.

Feminist scholars have reconstructed in rich detail the political subculture of the turn of the twentieth century, which reshaped the American welfare state and encouraged women to achieve tremendous political influence before they enjoyed full citizenship. In the process, they have changed the most basic understandings of politics, which can no longer be reduced to parties, elections, or the deals and pronouncements of elected officials. This book describes the waning days of this once powerful empire, showing how new ideological imperatives balkanized the female dominion of reform into warring states. The chapters that follow trace the rise of antiradicalism, describing how its founding mothers institutionalized their movement while mounting a constant barrage of attacks on women who continued to pursue traditional reform. This story demonstrates how these conflicts banished any vestigial illusion of consensus among female activists and illuminates how painful that process was for women who had come of age politically in the heyday of female reform. It ends with the passage of the Social Security Act of 1935, the most significant piece of social welfare legislation in the twentieth century. Crafted in large part by female policymakers, it was passed without the assistance of broad grassroots support from women's organizations. This measure closed the era in which government policymakers could count on organized, popular support for social welfare reforms from a broad mass of politically engaged women. The Progressive Era political order gave way to a new world of women's politics in which the meanings of female consciousness and womanhood only became more contested. By opening a new space in politics for conservative women, women patriots irrevocably changed the activism of all middle-class women for the rest of the century. The activism of the groups associated with the Women's Patriotic Conference on National Defense created the institutional and ideological framework for later, more populist, manifestations of conservative consciousness, most obviously the Minute Women of the 1950s and the Eagle Forum of the 1970s. Women's activism would never be the same.

Chapter 1

# The Birth of "Miss Bolsheviki": Women, Gender, and the Red Scare

In the winter of 1919, the moral danger posed by Bolshevism was detailed for American newspaper readers by a representative of the U.S. Department of Commerce. After suffering a stint in jail in the new Soviet republic, Roger E. Simmons returned to the United States, where he testified to a crowded Senate hearing room that radical policies had transformed more than factories, farms, and political institutions. He told his audience that it was Russia's women who were suffering most cruelly in the aftermath of the 1917 revolution. He recounted how Bolsheviks had forced women of "frail physique" and "gentle breeding" at bayonet and gunpoint to dig potatoes and wield pickaxes on road gangs. He swore that Red Guards routinely stripped aristocratic women of their clothing in public, one of many indignities that drove "refined" women to suicide. Most lurid were his assertions about the "nationalization of women." Simmons read from a purportedly official decree to illustrate the Bolshevik determination to degrade women, subvert the traditional family, and pervert conventional sexual relations. The diktat proclaimed women "exempted from private ownership" and thereafter "the property of the whole nation." Women were required to present themselves to the authorities, who would then distribute them equally among working-class males, who were granted the "right to use one woman not oftener than three times a week, for three hours." This system, the decree declared, was meant to rectify the inequities of capitalism, which had reserved "the best species of all the beautiful women ... [as] the property of the bourgeoisie." Anyone refusing to succumb to this arrangement would be declared "enemies of the people."[1]

Simmons had been summoned before the Senate Judiciary Committee to illustrate how revolutionary radicalism imperiled women, traditional

gender roles, and by extension civilization itself. His testimony contributed
to a congressional investigation that was charged with documenting the
atrocities of the new revolutionary regime, whose leaders sanctioned mass
murder, desecration of churches, systematic rape of upper-class women,
corruption of children, appropriation of everything from jewelry to land,
and social policies that undermined parental authority and marital bonds.[2]
The Senate focused on reports from postrevolution Russia to demonstrate
why the Bolshevik dogma was, in the words of Secretary of State Robert
Lansing, "the most hideous and monstrous thing that the human mind
has ever conceived."[3] Bolsheviks aimed to destroy more than an economic
system, according to Montana senator Henry L. Myers. They were working toward social and sexual apocalypse, hoping to annihilate "marriage,
the home, the fireside, the family, the corner stones of all civilization, all
society. They have undertaken to destroy what God created and ordained.
They defy alike the will of God, the precepts of Christianity, the decrees of
civilization, the customs of society."[4] Simmons was commended by Senator
Lee Slater Overman for bringing Americans the "real story of the chaos,
anarchism, and immorality that prevail in Russia as a result of Bolshevist
domination."[5] The final report of what came to be known as the Overman
Committee concluded that the radical revolution in Russia had inaugurated
"a reign of terror unparalleled in the history of modern civilization, in many
of its aspects rivaling even the inhuman savagery of the Turk and the terrors
of the French Revolution."[6]

In a nation roiled by labor unrest, the Overman Committee found a receptive audience for its warning of an international radical menace.[7] The
relevance of this message was obvious for American readers, who believed
that their country faced a real threat from Bolshevik-inspired revolutionaries. The Senate Judiciary Committee launched this inquiry after the declaration of the Seattle general strike, which many Americans viewed as an
attempt to start a North American proletarian revolution. Over the decade
that followed, government officials used Bolshevik abuses of women to justify the need for the repression of radicals in the United States, where a wave
of labor protests, vigilante violence, and race riots continued to feed fears
that revolution was imminent. These stories helped recast domestic repression as necessary to shield women and children from the effects of radicalism; they gave moral legitimacy to efforts to crush quests for political,
economic, and racial justice.

Traditional histories of the Red Scare have cast the American response

to the communist revolution in Russia as something of a short-lived national "hysteria" that started in 1917 and petered out by 1920 as government
officials came under increasing scrutiny for civil liberties violations and
war-weary citizens demanded so-called "normalcy."[8] Yet this analysis does
little to explain the experience of middle-class female activists, who found
themselves the targets of red hunts that became increasingly vicious over the
course of the 1920s. Women played complicated roles in the morality play
staged by the Overman Committee. The committee's tale of treachery and
terror cast women as villains as well as victims. It juxtaposed the suffering of
women in the new Bolshevik society with the activism of American women,
whom the committee saw guilty of abetting radicals who were determined
to foment revolution. It singled out women as new agents of radicalism, hidden revolutionaries who were working to transform the United States into a
Bolshevik-style dystopia. Communist leader John Reed bragged to the committee that his revolutionary propaganda campaign was funded by affluent women with radical proclivities, so-called "parlor" radicals. "You know
there are some wealthy women in New York who have nothing to do with
their money except something like that," he said, drawing laughter from the
room in spite of his hostility to the committee's mission.[9]

Reed was not the only one to assert that women were uniquely susceptible to the siren call of radicalism, even if they were particularly vulnerable
to the consequences of revolution. Most often, according to radical hunters,
they were the unwitting dupes of foreign agents, who were bent on destroying
the American social, political, and economic system. "Patriotic and philanthropic citizens have been innocent victims of conniving representatives of
foreign interests and Governments and have been exploited by corrupt and
dishonest elements," the committee's report concluded.[10] In the committee's
interpretation, deluded women had nurtured radical causes through their
influential network of voluntary associations, helping to deliver the United
States to the brink of a proletarian overthrow.

These fears recast middle-class female reformers as political pariahs who
were national security threats on a par with immigrant radicals. J. Edgar
Hoover, head of the Justice Department's new radical division, found John
Reed's boasts credible and contemplated a crackdown on so-called "parlor socialists," whom he defined as rich women who gave money to radical causes.[11] Any harassment by Hoover was overshadowed, however, by an
increasingly vigorous campaign waged by private citizens, who were able
to exert tremendous pressure on female voluntary associations to distance

themselves from progressive causes and philosophies. They cut a destructive wake through women's politics, making female reformers some of the first middle-class Americans to experience the full disruptive power of modern anticommunism. These anxieties about international Bolshevism ultimately transformed the institutions and practices of women's politics in the critical years after suffrage.

Gendered images and concerns continued to animate efforts to suppress domestic subversion long after the Overman Committee wrapped up its investigation. The fear that Bolshevism would destroy the gender conventions and sexual differentiation that defined middle-class life in the United States grew stronger in the decades after the Russian Revolution; leaders responded by developing a foreign policy agenda grounded on the premise that the patriarchal, nuclear family formed the core of American national identity.[12] This assumption would serve as the foundation for later Cold War rhetoric by bolstering those who insisted that Bolshevism would force the United States to wage a holy war to protect traditional domesticity. The "only guaranty" of the home, according to Calvin Coolidge in 1921, was "the American Government."[13] In both the domestic and the international realm, middle- and upper-class Americans saw their country's capitalist system as an ally of traditional domesticity.

### The Russian Revolution and the Global Rise of Bolshevism

The report and testimonials assembled by the Overman Committee were offered to an American public gripped by fear of a Bolshevik takeover. Americans needed little prompting to see the connections between events in Russia and what was happening in their own communities. Witnesses before the Senate Judiciary Committee reinforced these perceptions, illuminating the ties between foreign revolutionaries and domestic dissenters. Communism and radicalism were certainly not unfamiliar to North America. Residents of the United States had simultaneously championed and fought communism from the moment Karl Marx penned his manifesto; workers, employers, and politicians had spilled considerable blood over the redistribution of wealth in the seventy years before the Bolshevik takeover. But the storming of the Winter Palace by Lenin's Red Guards in 1917 marked a turning point for American attitudes. Many Americans had assumed that capitalism would always reign supreme. Yet, around the globe, the world was in flux. The sense that the workers' moment had arrived inspired panic in the United States. Government officials and business leaders intensified their campaign against immigrants, radicals, and dissenters of all stripes. In the aftermath of the Bolshevik Revolution, repression eclipsed any possibility that the victory of radicals in Russia would inspire any transformative political change in the United States.

Russia demonstrated that it took only a committed minority to make a revolution. And American countersubversives asserted that the United States already had a radical cadre determined to see the same kind of political upheaval in North America. They stressed that Slavic immigrants had brought "European" radical ideology and a propensity for violence to North America, along with their unfamiliar languages, food, and dress. Less than a year after the Bolsheviks claimed power in Russia, revolutionary leader Vladimir Lenin fanned these fears when he pleaded with American workers to make his uprising international. In a "Letter to the American Worker" in August 1918, he called on the American working class to rise against its oppressors, an appeal he repeated in January 1919, claiming that Germany was already experiencing a Soviet-inspired revolution.[14] American observers took Lenin's letter as evidence that the United States stood at revolution's door and pointed to the epidemic of postwar work stoppages to demonstrate the seriousness of the situation.

One of the largest of these strikes broke out in February 1919 in the busy port of Seattle. As a stronghold of the Industrial Workers of the World, the city would have been a logical birthplace for a North American revolution. The IWW, one of the most uncompromising of the American revolutionary groups, gained a strong following in the Pacific Northwest during World War I, when workers suffering from stagnating wages and soaring prices were prohibited from striking. IWW militants pushed workers to resist exploitation by trying to take over their plants through work stoppages. "Every strike is a small revolution and a dress rehearsal for the big one," the IWW declared.[15] When workers declared a general strike, business and political leaders assumed that the IWW had prevailed. They warned that Bolshevist-inspired workers had taken control of the city's labor unions and planned to use the city's labor troubles to launch a national uprising.

Sixty-five thousand workers walked off the job that February, staging what became known as the Seattle General Strike. Some workers undoubtedly hoped that the strike would spark the class warfare necessary to produce a proletarian uprising. They plastered the streets with handbills that proclaimed "Russia Did It."[16] Newspaper headlines amplified the threat

posed by the most radical of the strikers: "REDS DIRECTING SEATTLE
STRIKE—TO TEST CHANCE FOR REVOLUTION."[17] Only a minority of
workers were, in fact, inspired by Bolshevism to embrace labor militancy;
most were driven to action by bread-and-butter issues of basic survival. Yet
these legitimate concerns were ignored by business and political elites as
they prepared to crush the strike, which they cast as a prelude to revolution.
Seattle mayor Ole Hanson took the work stoppage as a declaration of war,
rallying Seattle residents as they readied their households for a lengthy siege
by stockpiling food, medicine, water, and guns. Hanson warned that the
protest was instigated by those "who want to take possession of our American government and try to duplicate the anarchy of Russia."[18]

In the face of federal troops and a homegrown Citizens' Committee organized by the business community that pledge to provide "law and order,"
workers maintained impressive solidarity.[19] But their strike collapsed after
only four days. Workers were overwhelmed by pressure from local politicians, federal authorities, and national union leaders to return to work. Yet
the decisive victory of Seattle employers did little to quell anxieties about
revolution, as many observers felt that the port city had only narrowly
avoided becoming the next St. Petersburg. When workers went back to their
jobs, Mayor Hanson reinforced this fear by declaring that "today this Bol-
shevik-sired nightmare is at an end."[20]

The global ambitions of Bolsheviks heightened these concerns. A few
weeks after the collapse of the Seattle General Strike, communists from
all over the world met in Moscow to found the Third Communist International, or "Comintern," to encourage revolutionary movements around
the world.[21] Observers in the United States believed they could discern immediate effects of this meeting. Militant workers shut down one industry
after another. March 1919 saw 175 strikes; April 248; May 388; June 303; July
360; and August 373. In New York's garment industry, 50,000 workers struck
for thirteen weeks. Across town, stage actors walked out. In New Jersey, silk
workers left their jobs in Paterson; woolen operatives protested in Passaic.
Telephone operators struck in New England while building trades workers
suspended construction in Dallas. Streetcar workers in Chicago demanded
better conditions at the same time as marine workers on the Atlantic coast.[22]
In September, the police force in Boston walked out, leaving the city vulnerable to looting and violence. Two days later, hundreds of thousands of steel-
workers walked off the job. Six weeks later, coal miners followed suit. By the
beginning of October 1919, more than 600,000 workers in twenty states were

on strike. By the end of the year, one out of every five American workers had walked off the job.[23]

Although the workers made traditional demands for better hours, wages, and working conditions, opponents condemned them as Bolsheviks. Striking steel workers were beaten and terrorized by vigilantes, state troopers, and newly deputized employees of U.S. Steel. Across the country, local police forces, state militias, and federal troops crushed strikes. While the labor protests ultimately did little to bolster union power in the United States, they demonstrated to many Americans the need for tough action against foreign-born agitators.

Many Americans saw labor militancy as a breeding ground for the kind of political violence that targeted prominent politicians in the spring of 1919. On April 28, a bomb was delivered to Seattle mayor Hanson's office; the explosive was dismantled before it went off. One day later, a maid who opened a package delivered to the home of former senator Thomas W. Hardwick lost both hands when it exploded. The postal service eventually intercepted thirty-four other explosive packages meant for well-known radical foes like Lee Overman, chairman of the Senate committee investigating Bolshevism; attorney general A. Mitchell Palmer; Judge Kenesaw Mountain Landis, famous for sending socialist Victor Berger and IWW leader Big Bill Haywood to jail; Standard Oil tycoon John D. Rockefeller and banker J. P. Morgan; secretary of labor William B. Wilson; antilabor senator William H. King; and postmaster general Albert S. Burleson, who had banned radical literature from the mails. The bombs were designed to arrive at their targets on May 1 to punish officials known for their antiradical sentiments.

Not all such bombs were intercepted. One month later, packages exploded in the homes of the Cleveland mayor, a Massachusetts state legislator, and judges in New York City and Boston. Another bomb was detonated at the abode of a silk manufacturer in Paterson, New Jersey. The most publicized of these incidents took place at the residence of Attorney General Palmer in Washington. The bomber stumbled while planting the explosive; the resulting blast destroyed the entryway and the bomber, leaving only a smattering of body parts (including what seemed to be two left legs) and a leaflet signed by "The Anarchist Fighters."[24] No one else was injured. These acts of terrorism, probably the work of one small anarchist group, stoked fears that revolutionaries were gaining ground in the United States.[25]

A familiar kind of political violence endangered more Americans than anarchist bombers in 1919. Racial massacres terrorized African Americans in Charleston, South Carolina, Washington, D.C., Omaha, Nebraska, rural Arkansas, Longview, Texas, and Chicago. Twenty-five cities and towns were devastated by racial violence that summer, a historic high. Unrestrained by and in some cases aided by local police officers, white mobs entered African American neighborhoods, beating and shooting men and women. In Chicago, black residents fought back, reflecting a new commitment by African American activists to contest white domination. These riots were accompanied by a sharp rise in lynchings that drove home the danger of resisting white supremacy.[26] Conservatives saw these episodes as evidence of African American agitation rather than white vigilantism; they asserted that they were the product of communist promises to upend racial hierarchies. The Comintern gave those anxious about radicalism more reason to red-bait black militants in 1922, when it announced that African Americans were essential to the revolutionary struggle in the United States. Those already on guard felt their worst fears were confirmed. One asserted that radical "nuclei are being established in whatever organizations of negroes are found."[27]

Military and political leaders viewed each clash, raid, bombing, or strike through the prism of revolution. Each new incident reinforced the determination to suppress all dissent that had begun with the American mobilization for the Great War in Europe. The American decision to enter the war had prompted federal officials to enact broad restrictions on freedom of speech, passing statutes that sanctioned the suppression of antiwar publications. The Espionage Act of 1917 banned spying as well as efforts to interfere in any way with the draft; the Sedition Act passed in 1918 made criminal any statements that expressed "contempt" or "scorn" for the American "form of government." Congress also approved the deportation of anarchist aliens.[28] These restrictions were not loosened after the Armistice, thanks to the new anxieties generated by Bolshevik victories. Government officials turned their new tools of repression against all domestic radicals and labor militants, rejecting as illegitimate any efforts to change economic relations in the United States. Attorney General Palmer responded to the unrest of 1919 by reorganizing the antiradical division of the Bureau of Investigation as the General Intelligence Division, appointing J. Edgar Hoover as its head, but this did not satisfy those clamoring for action. In October, the Senate censured Palmer for failing to demonstrate enough force against radicals.

Palmer answered his critics in early November by launching a dramatic new crackdown. It began with the revolutionary Union of Russian Workers, a small group of "atheists, communists and anarchists" who believed in the complete overthrow of all government and the confiscation of all wealth.[29] Local police and Bureau of Investigation agents ransacked the offices, beat members, and detained 250 for further questioning. Hoover soon pressed the army transport ship *Buford* into service to deport 249 supposed revolutionaries to the Soviet Union. These noncitizen aliens included anarchists Emma Goldman and Alex Berkman, long-time residents of the United States. When the "Soviet Ark" deposited its human cargo at a Finnish port, newspaper editorials demanded that the deportations continue. This vision was shared by Hoover, who planned the next set of arrests. On January 2, 1920, Bureau of Investigation agents—assisted by volunteers from the American Legion and local police forces—rounded up 5,000 supposed communists, held them for days without warrants, and denied them the chance to consult lawyers or contact their families. The crackdown climaxed as Hoover argued that membership in any branch of the Communist Party was a deportable offense for alien residents. Thousands of noncitizens languished in jail based on the accusation that they were communists.

Although the "Palmer raids"—as these actions became known—drew widespread protests from civil libertarians and liberal politicians, Palmer was not thoroughly discredited until later that spring, when he warned that radicals had violent plans for the traditional revolutionary holiday of May Day. The country went on high alert as states mustered their militias and cities put their police departments on emergency duty. With guards stationed to protect vulnerable buildings, public leaders ventured out only under the watchful eyes of bodyguards. When the day passed without any civil insurrection, Palmer never recovered his credibility. Moreover, the government campaign against radicals reached a legal impasse later that spring, when first secretary of labor William B. Wilson and then Boston federal court judge George Anderson ruled that being a card-carrying Communist was not grounds for deportation.[30]

The period from 1917 to 1920 saw some of the most intense repression of civil liberties in the nation's history. This campaign drew its moral urgency from a larger propaganda effort, which demonstrated how Bolshevism was antithetical to civilization. The Overman Committee played a key role in communicating this message. The day after the general strike was declared in Seattle, congressional leaders directed the Overman Committee to widen its investigation of German propaganda to include Bolshevism and "all other forms of anti-American radicalism."[31] The Overman Committee served as a forum for publicizing Bolshevik outrages. The Senate committee assembled months of testimony into a final report that concluded that "the activities of the Bolsheviki constitute a complete repudiation of modern civilization and the promulgation of the doctrine that the best attainment of the most backward member of society shall be the level at which mankind shall find its final and victorious goal."[32] These conclusions provided an ideological justification for the efforts by local, state, and federal officials to suppress all manifestations of dissent by demonstrating the urgency of preventing the spread of Russian-style radicalism in North America.

The Overman Committee called one witness after another to present evidence of the way Bolsheviks had stripped away what it viewed as the hallmarks of advanced society, particularly systems of sexual differentiation that designated distinct roles for men and women. By eliminating gendered duties and privileges, the new revolutionary society had reduced its people to the status of racially inferior "savages." Commerce Department representative Roger E. Simmons told the committee that revolutionaries had eliminated the sexual division of labor, forcing women out of the home and into hard, physical labor appropriate only for men. Women, in his telling, were the primary victims of this new revolutionary regime. Yet men were also degraded by this new system, which emasculated males by forcing them to cede their roles as protectors. They were reduced to a brutish state by their inability to prevent their children from starving and their women from being raped.[33]

The most lurid accounts aired by the committee focused on the insatiable and predatory sexuality of working-class male revolutionaries. Another witness, George A. Simons, a superintendent of the Methodist Episcopal Church who returned to the United States in October 1918 after a decade in St. Petersburg, told the committee that these men were suddenly unfettered to pursue their wildest sexual fantasies. Simons recounted how a woman came to him with a disturbing story during his last days in Russia. She was president of his group's Ladies Aid Society and had spent more than twenty-five years as a teacher in one of the country's leading imperial schools. He recalled how she buried her head in her hands as she burst into sobs. "I am sorry I lived to witness all this," she choked out. He tried to comfort her, but she wanted more than solace. "I want you to tell the women of America this," she demanded. On the first floor of her school, which "used to be a palace," she reportedly told him, "these Bolshevik officials have put hundreds of red soldiers, sailors and marines of the red army and the red navy and given orders that in the other half of the same floor the girls of our institute should remain, girls who are from 12 to 16 years." One of the committee members, Senator Josiah Wolcott of Delaware, interrupted the clergyman. "That was not the doing of just an irresponsible crowd of soldiers, or of a soldier mob? That was the arrangement, do I understand you to say, of the Bolshevik officials?" When Simons confirmed this statement, another senator pushed Simons to offer more graphic details. "Of course, that meant that these poor girls were left to the brutal lust of the red guards?" Simons reply was terse: "no doubt in my mind."[34]

With the story of a palace transformed into a sexual torture chamber for the daughters of the elite, Simons evoked a powerful and horrific image of the new Bolshevik society. Under this radical regime, the great institutions of imperial civilization became playgrounds for lower-class brutes to satisfy their basest urges. For counterrevolutionaries, any sexual contact between working-class men and middle- or upper-class women was a violation. It undermined a social order that Americans perceived to be fixed and natural. Stories about breaches of class-based sexual hierarchies sparked fears in Americans who were vigilant in maintaining their own social and caste system, which limited any interracial sexuality to unmentioned but expected liaisons between white men and African American women. Since the radical unrest of the 1880s, revolutionaries themselves had been "racialized" in the American popular imagination: bushy hair, ragged clothing, and wild eyes made radicals easily identifiable as a group distinct from old-stock Americans still loyal to national principles. Stories about revolutionary sexual transgressions thus played on deeply held convictions about race, class, and sex. Sexual fears were critical in triggering the fierce reaction of Americans to the Bolshevik Revolution.

The "Bureau of Free Love" was the most sensational myth of sexual terror to emerge from the Overman Committee hearings. Simmons completed his testimony about the "nationalization of women" by reading from a second decree, supposedly issued by the city of Vladimir in Russia. This edict established the "Bureau of Free Love" to register all women over the age of eighteen in order to make them available to any man, "even without the consent of [the woman], in the interest of the State." Simmons concluded his reading of these proclamations by asserting that "God and morality are unknown to the Bolsheviki, and everything that makes life decent and worth living is in jeopardy if this thing is permitted to go ahead."[35] Although other witnesses challenged Simmons's story, the Overman Committee endorsed the spirit of his account, if not the details. Witnesses sympathetic to the revolution—most notably journalist Louise Bryant—refuted Simmons's claim that Bolsheviks had "nationalized" both women and children by placing children in state institutions and forbidding women to "belong" exclusively to one man. Bryant denounced this allegation as a counterrevolutionary rumor whose origin was obscured by an alleged decree from an anarchist group not sanctioned by the Soviet government.[36]

The Overman Committee conceded that the decrees appeared to be localized and the "central Government has refrained from adopting any such policy in the whole nation." Yet the details about the "Bureau of Free Love" were almost irrelevant to the committee since it concluded that the Soviet government had "promulgated decrees relating to marriage and divorce which practically establishes a state of free love. Their effect has been to furnish a vehicle for the legalization of prostitution by permitting the annulment of the marriage bonds at the whim of the parties."[37] Many Americans found the Overman Committee witnesses more compelling than the complex reality of the new revolutionary society. The testimony before the Committee resonated with Americans because it confirmed their conviction that radicalism sought to annihilate marriage, family, and religion.

Many radicals did envision the end of traditional patriarchy and the beginning of a new social order that would free women from male dependence. These theorists were responding to what they saw as the structural contradictions of capitalism, which forced most women to compensate for low male wages and underemployment by shouldering the double burden of grueling household work and poorly paid waged labor. They called for the state to make women independent and unfettered workers by taking responsibility for domestic work and child care. Soviet policymakers had liberalized divorce laws and promoted revolutionary sexual ideology, imagining a day when all unions would be between comrades, self-supporting and free individuals bound together only by love and mutual respect.[38] Soviet sex radicals sought to disentangle love from the necessities of life. Alexandra Kollontai, the leading light among these freethinking sexual moderns, had envisioned a day when the family would be revolutionized and all children would come under the care of the state.

These radical family theories were never realized in the Soviet Union, which became more socially and sexually conservative than ever after the initial years of the revolution. The state never "appropriated" children; the new nation could not even care for the millions of young Russians orphaned by years of war and famine, much less for children with living parents. Women remained the second-class citizens they had been under capitalism, despite radical ideology that trumpeted gender equality. Just as they had under capitalism, desperate women were forced to barter sex for survival in the radical regime. Soviet employers paid women substandard wages when they could find work, which was difficult in a crippled economy with few provisions for child care. Since many male providers died or disappeared during years of war, upheaval, and food shortages, widowed and abandoned women were left more vulnerable than before the revolution. The edict establishing the "Bureau of Free Love" was twisted by White Russian propaganda; the Soviet state did not prohibit women from being monogamous. Social tumult, not radical ideology, forced women into the streets as prostitutes.[39] Sexual violation of women did not stem from revolutionary edicts.

With the Overman Committee report, however, the myth of the Soviet sex slave became fixed in the imaginations of those anxious about Bolshevism. It confirmed the fear that Bolsheviks were sexual deviants who were determined to destroy the foundations of civilization. Narratives about sexual terror transformed the fight against radicalism into a battle to protect American womanhood. The Overman Committee was only one of many venues used by counterrevolutionaries for the broadcast of these kinds of narratives. Touring Russian émigrés described their revolutionary experiences to groups across the country. Less than a year after the storming of the Winter Palace American publishers began issuing the countless Russian autobiographies that paired descriptions of the horrors of the revolution with nostalgia for Czarist Russia. This literary genre remained popular for decades.[40]

A fixation on the moral danger of Bolshevism provided strong justification for military intervention aimed at defeating the revolutionaries. American troops had entered the Russian civil war in the summer of 1918; they did not leave Siberia until 1920.[41] This invasion fit into a familiar tradition for many Americans, who could call upon a national history of using the violation of women to justify military action and vigilante violence. Only a few years earlier, politicians had described Germans' "rape of Belgium" as a rationale for entering World War I. The wars against Native Americans in the West and Spaniards in Cuba were justified as vindicating the virtues of white women who were supposedly sexually assaulted by enemies of Protestant American values. Southern men, also, had manipulated sexual threats to white women to defend lynchings of African Americans. In the minds of many Americans, the physical rape of women was a potent symbol for the victimization of oppressed people at the hands of dictators. This image of sexual violation allowed Americans to understand these invasions as missions of rescue rather than expeditions to protect economic and political interests.[42]

In the United States itself, domestic repression eased somewhat after 1920. But this was largely because "there [was] little to repress," according to one civil libertarian.[43] The arrests, violence, and deportations had proved devastating to communists, socialists, advocates of racial justice, and labor organizers, crippling radical efforts to address profound social injustices that characterized life and work in the United States. This created a political climate in which "the word 'Liberty,'" according to one Italian American newspaper, "has become a myth."[44] Wartime sedition acts were repealed in 1921 and many political prisoners were released two years later. But the War Department's Military Intelligence Division did not officially cease its surveillance of citizens until 1923. And it was not until 1924, when an investigation revealed that Bureau of Investigation agents had been spying on members of Congress, that lawmakers forced a shake-up of the Justice Department. Attorney General Harlan F. Stone inaugurated his administration by abolishing the Bureau of Investigation's Radical Division and proclaiming an end to all political surveillance. But he then promoted J. Edgar Hoover to the top job at the federal agency, laying the foundation for future red hunts.[45]

The story of the "Red Scare," however, does not end with the dawning of the Jazz Age. While government officials may have temporarily scaled back their assaults on dissenters, this new restraint did not reflect a diminishing concern about Bolshevism. These anxieties did not dissipate; they instead found new outlets over the course of the 1920s. Radical hunters fastened on native-born female reformers as the most worrisome wellspring of domestic subversion. Advocates of reform came under the same fire as self-proclaimed radicals in the wake of John Reed's claim that he enjoyed the financial support of "parlor Bolsheviks." This 1919 comment touched off a storm of commentary on the folly of society women fueling the growth of Bolshevism as a fad. Commentator Helen Wayne mocked the way it was "very unfashionable to be the least bit conservative nowadays, and very, very fashionable to be radical." Politically progressive women, she explained, had rendered themselves vulnerable to those preaching "revolutionary socialism" through "their very idealism, their desire to do the right thing toward people." It was this idealism, she asserted, that would inspire them to "register at one of the new neighborhood leagues or progressive schools or neighborhood centres or welfare councils, all of which have 'uplift' or even if you please, patriotism as their excuse for living, but all teaching quietly some form of socialism between the lines."[46]

Female reformers never completely eclipsed immigrant radicals in the public imagination as agents of subversion. The ideological links between ethnicity, race, and radicalism remained strong. Reformers were never subjected to the same type of persecution as more militant radicals. They were never arrested en masse, held in detention, or deported. Yet their desire to preserve their political respectability made these progressive women more easily intimidated. Many of these women were socially prominent and materially comfortable. This meant that they had far more to lose from social ostracism than working-class radicals. They retained their belief in the American social and economic system, despite feeling pulled to the left by the experience of working for social change. Yet this desire to continue working within the system made these women more threatening for those determined to prevent a revolution. Ralph Easley, head of the National Civic Federation, declared that "educated and criminally sentimental notoriety-seeking women" were actually "infinitely more dangerous and more guilty than are these poor, ignorant foreigners."[47]

Female reformers were being condemned as agents of Bolshevism at a critical juncture for women's politics. Women appeared to be enjoying unprecedented political influence, thanks in part to the hard-fought victory of the suffrage campaign. The Nineteenth Amendment was itself an outgrowth of the wide-ranging political activism of the previous two decades. Female activists were the animating force behind the reforms of the Progressive Era, when they gained a sense of political possibility through campaigns to improve child welfare and clean up cities. During those years, women's clubs and settlement houses taught women the skills they needed for public participation and gave them a framework to identify social problems and pioneer solutions. They also provided a political base for women who realized that voluntary efforts would never eradicate social problems such as child labor, unsafe working conditions, and the financial insecurity that plagued dependent women and children in a capitalist economy. Using the lessons they learned in club and community work, women made powerful appeals to their local, state, and national governments. The welfare state that emerged in the early twentieth century was largely a product of these activists, who worked without the benefit of the vote or the money available to other lobbyists.

The passage of the Nineteenth Amendment gave female reformers hope that they would enjoy greater authority in the decade to come. To harness their new power, suffragists created new institutions to facilitate political participation for neophyte female voters. Once the suffrage amendment passed, the National American Woman Suffrage Association was reincarnated as the League of Women Voters, a nonpartisan group dedicated to encouraging women's political participation. The Women's Joint Congressional Committee (WJCC) was also established in November 1920 to coordinate the federal lobbying efforts of ten of the most important reform-minded women's groups of the time. This coalition included Progressive Era women's organizations like the National Congress of Parents and Teachers, the General Federation of Women's Clubs, the National Consumers' League, and the National Women's Trade Union League. It brokered cooperation between these groups, the Woman's Christian Temperance Union and organizations that emerged around the time of the Nineteenth Amendment, including the League of Women Voters, the American Association of University Women, and the National Federation of Business and Professional Women's Clubs. By 1925, this clearinghouse, as its leaders called it, had the active support of twenty-five women's groups.[48]

As it happened, the Nineteenth Amendment proved to be the apex of women's political influence for the first half of the twentieth century. Female reformers found themselves increasingly isolated by the increasingly aggressive campaign against dissent that began in 1917 and continued through the end of what is traditionally considered the "red scare." By the time they could vote, women reformers found themselves to be some of the lone voices for social change in an increasingly conservative wilderness. This allowed critics to recast them as enemies of American democratic values after only a short honeymoon in formal politics. The WJCC, much heralded as a manifestation of women's new political power, was viewed by critics as the nerve center for a dictatorial "woman's bloc" that was the "most powerful lobby in Washington."[49] Conservative observers saw the evolution of nonpartisan women's lobbying organizations as evidence of radical encroachment. Nathan Miller, the Republican governor of New York, lambasted the League of Women Voters at its own convention in January 1921, calling efforts to organize women voters outside of the two-party system as "a menace to our free institutions and to representative government."[50] Critics like Miller

Figure 1. This 1922 cartoon drives home the premise that middle-class women were uniquely vulnerable to radical ideology. The well-coiffed and modern appearance of an attractive woman hides her status as an agent of Moscow. She pours the poison of Bolshevism into a docile-looking "America," ultimately causing the demise of "American Ideals." Box 1, Helen Tufts Bailie Papers, Sophia Smith Collection, Smith College, Northampton, Massachusetts.

warned that women could vote en masse for an agenda far more radical than any allowed by the two male-dominated political parties. To drive home the danger of following these agendas, conservative pamphlets outlined the parallels between the goals of major women's groups and the Communist and Socialist party platforms.[51] Countersubversive critics asserted that coalitions of female reformers were controlled by a handful of individuals under the influence of dark forces.[52] This small cadre of women leaders, they cautioned, had lined up millions of women in support of legislative measures that would bring Bolshevism home to America. They cloaked these efforts, one conservative explained, to make "the serpent of Socialism sing like an angel of light."[53] Former antisuffragist Margaret Robinson called women lobbyists the secret weapon of communist revolutionaries. "Communists confidently count on the support of women's organizations," she wrote.[54]

Not surprisingly, antisuffragists were most extreme in their denunciations of women voters. "Every time that women have entered the arena of political warfare with men it has been the ultimate signal of decline and decadence. This was true in Rome and Greece and Carthage," asserted the *Woman Patriot*, quoting from a declaration of an antisuffrage activist.[55] The newspaper blamed women voters for opening the nation to violent unrest through their "emasculation of government." By buckling to picketing women's demands for the vote, the antisuffrage publication claimed, the government had sent a message to more violent elements. "Is it any wonder that the Bolsheviki, the radicals, the revolutionists and the mobs question the authority of Government that submits so tamely to any group of agitators who can finance and organize an efficient lobby?"[56]

Two years after John Reed first boasted of his ability to charm wealthy women into supporting radical causes, a mass-circulation women's magazine took up the charge that newly enfranchised women were nurturing domestic subversion. In a series of articles published in 1921 by *The Delineator*, one of the five most popular women's magazines of the time, vice President Calvin Coolidge warned that women's institutions had been infiltrated by subversives. Women's colleges, he wrote, were "the object of adroit attacks by radical propagandists."[57] The American Legion asserted that white women should be subjected to increased scrutiny because left-wing agitators had "changed their tactics," creating links between middle-class women's organizations and the Soviet Union. Rather than "devoting their entire time to the ignorant immigrant," saboteurs had begun "working feverishly through the intelligent, wealthy women who are giving considerable time to club work." Male Legionnaires felt that enfranchised women with radical sympathies were more dangerous than alien subversives. They asserted that "our problem is much more insidious because we have now to deal not with the uneducated, but rather with the best trained minds of the country."[58]

Even though no evidence ever emerged that Moscow had mounted a campaign to recruit American women, anxious opponents of radicalism became convinced that secret agents had manipulated the so-called fairer sex. "Most of those who would destroy the institutions and principles which have carried our government to her present enviable position of world leadership, have directed their attention primarily to the women of America," declared Secretary of War John W. Weeks.[59] The *Woman Patriot* asserted that Marx and Engels considered "woman as the first 'proletariat' and 'oppressed class' before they issued the Communist Manifesto."[60] In 1922, the onetime antisuffragist newspaper presented what it called "proof" that communists had targeted women—a proclamation from the Central Executive of the Communist International enjoining radicals to "make full use of the existing possibilities to convert women into conscious militants."[61]

Many conservatives believed that innate feminine qualities made many women incapable of resisting the allure of radicals. "Women's tender, emotional nature," said General John J. Pershing in an address to the American Legion Auxiliary, "makes her a possible victim for 'the enemy within our gates.'"[62] One former antisuffragist even turned to scripture to demonstrate that women had a long history of both conscious and unconscious betrayal. "It is an old, old story that women are used as dupes and tools for destructive work from the days of Samson's Deliliah [sic] to the Feminist Lobby of today," Anna Moon Randolph asserted.[63] These educated and influential left-wing sympathizers were doubly dangerous, according to one right-wing commentator, because they refused to reveal their subversive allegiances.[64]

Even well-meaning women could be easily manipulated into promoting subversion. Women were "idealistic or sentimental, devoted followers of mirage," according to conservative writer Hermine Schwed. "The master minds among the communists . . . are expert at weaving exquisite mirages to lure visionaries on."[65] Schwed asserted that women were prone to radical manipulation because they would not give deep thought to political decisions.[66] To illustrate her point, Schwed offered an example from her own, more progressive years. In her *Confessions of a Parlor Socialist*, she described her experience of being converted into a radical sympathizer by two Socialists. She came under their sway, she explained, because she had been too lazy to inform herself about the true nature of the ideology. She took "on faith" their idea that "socialism meant a square deal to everyone," since her political tutors concealed their support for the violent abolition of private property. Once she realized the "truth," she dedicated herself to educating other women that her former comrades were sworn to destroy "religion, morality, patriotism, law and order."[67] Although Schwed was able to extract herself from radical snares, most women would not be so lucky. Biology was thus political destiny.

Had it not been for the burgeoning peace movement, anxieties about female voters might have waned as women demonstrated they would not use the ballot box to stage a revolution. But after the Armistice, women embraced the peace movement with enthusiasm. With ten million dead, five million wounded, and a generation of young men buried on the battlefields of Europe, many women had become passionate about making the nation live up to its vow to make the Great War the end to all wars. The pursuit of peace became the most popular issue championed by newly enfranchised women. These activists reasoned that all other reforms became meaningless in the face of global cataclysm.[68] In the early 1920s, activists envisioned a mass movement of women with the vibrancy of the suffrage campaign that would transform military and foreign policy. "Many of us believe that there is nothing that will arouse the crusade spirit which was so inspiring in the suffrage workers like combining to make peace secure," veteran suffragist Grace Johnson told suffrage leader Carrie Chapman Catt in 1924.[69]

A myriad of organizations took up the question of peace. Members of the League of Women Voters were "interested in peace almost to the exclusion of any other topic" for the first two years of women's suffrage, according to one of the organization's leaders. The group condemned war as the "greatest crime against the public welfare."[70] In addition, almost all of the other members of the WJCC—the General Federation of Women's Clubs, the American Association of University Women, the WCTU, the National Federation of Business and Professional Women, and the Parent-Teacher Association—put peace at the top of their agendas in the early 1920s. These groups established internal committees on peace and helped form the National Council for Prevention of War in 1921.[71] The NCPW was facilitating peace efforts among twenty-six constituent organizations by 1922; women's groups, farm organizations, church societies, and peace groups all allied themselves with the organization.[72] Many of these women were attracted to the antiwar cause during the 1920s because they believed that female biology and feminine social qualities made them natural peacemakers. They perceived themselves as nurturers and uncorrupted newcomers to formal electoral politics. They reasoned that this made them uniquely suited to bring about the international reconciliation that men, warlike and cynical, had been unable to achieve.

Women came to dominate the 1920s peace movement, but they certainly were not alone in their determination to end forever the use of trench warfare and poison gas. The industrial efficiency of the killing fields of World War I had left an indelible mark on the psyche of an entire generation. One member of the House of Representatives observed that the people have the "feeling . . . that they want to get away from military matters."[73] The country's dovish mood converged with an isolationist sentiment and a spirit of fiscal conservatism to aid peace activists, who persuaded Congress to slash military appropriations and reject calls for peacetime conscription. In Wisconsin, peace advocates persuaded the state legislature to abolish military training in state universities. The Harding administration even planned a Washington Disarmament Conference in 1921.[74] Thanks in part to peace activists, the military planners' arguments that they needed 150,000 men in uniform went unheeded.

Military leaders blamed their predicament on women peace activists. Secretary of War John Weeks publicly decried these cuts as the work of "silly pacifists," while Major General James G. Harbord, deputy chief of staff, condemned peace advocates who had been swept away "in the enthusiasm of newly conferred suffrage."[75] Embattled military officers feared these early political successes were merely a prelude. Pacifists, according to one officer, were promoting their "propaganda at Wellesley, Bryn Mawr and other colleges with the intent of instilling their views among impressionable girls, so that in the future, should they rear children, they would teach them these pacifist ideals."[76] Military boosters, opponents of female suffrage, and other conservatives saw the "crusade spirit" of the peace movement as treachery. "In all shades of destructive propaganda, striving to mislead the American people in women's organizations, there is none more dangerous than the so-called pacifist movement," warned Margaret Robinson, head of the Massachusetts Public Interests League, a small but influential antisuffrage group in Boston that had turned its attention to broader concerns about radicalism.[77] Supporters of a strong military lumped together all calls for peace. To them, there was no difference between advocates of arms limitation and pacifists.

Those alarmed by the peace movement believed that the real mission of disarmament was to create a defenseless nation vulnerable to a radical take-over. Peace activists, one critic warned, "would have us throw ourselves on the bosom of a loving world—a bosom yet dripping with blood and bursting with hatred and rancor. The Reds and others favor this. They would outlaw war so that we could not resist if attacked."[78] Pacifism, they asserted, was simply the handmaiden of communism and national suicide. The true philosophy of peace advocates, they charged, was "the old socialist doctrine that the bourgeoisie must be disarmed, the proletariat must be armed."[79] Images of women as dupes worked in concert with this charge to recast the women's peace movement as a Trojan horse for a Russian-style insurrection. According to one leading conservative, "some of our very sweetest and best citizens, thoroughly imbued with the highest ideals, have given their aid to this pacifist propaganda of the Russian dictators of the Communist International without knowing or suspecting that they are merely tools of the most cruel and despotic tyranny known in the civilized world today."[80] The *Woman Patriot* argued that communists were "logically letting the Gold Dust Twins, Feminism and Pacifism, do their work. . . . The pinks are all red sisters under the skin."[81]

Opponents of the peace movement painted all women peace activists as un-American or foolish idealists incapable of understanding the gravity of their demands. The most reviled of these activists, however, were the members of the Women's International League for Peace and Freedom (WILPF). Immediately after WILPF's establishment in 1919, conservatives cast it as the wellspring of American radicalism. Over the course of the interwar period, the Military Intelligence Division of the War Department amassed a thick file on WILPF that documented its purported pacifism as well as its supposed radical and foreign sympathies.[82] Secretary of War John Weeks and top-ranking military officials singled out WILPF for condemnation, accusing the group of treason and its members of working to establish communism in America.[83] WILPF drew fire in part for its opposition to chemical weapons, which it considered some of the most heinous tools of modern warfare. Yet this stance alone cannot explain the vitriol the group attracted. The organization was not in truth revolutionary. It did welcome radical members, encouraged study of the economic roots of war, and endorsed "political, social and moral equality between men and women." By definition, however, it was not a communist, socialist, or pacifist group. In fact, WILPF stood squarely at the ideological center of the peace movement. In contrast to the more radical pacifist groups, it required no pledge of nonresistance. While its members collaborated with pacifists to oppose universal military training, they worked for arms limitation as well as disarmament. Its stated goal was expansive: to promote "methods for the attainment of that peace between nations which is based on justice and good will and to cooperate with women from other countries who are working for the same ends."[84]

Military supporters targeted WILPF because it bridged the divide between different elements of the peace movement, attracting mainstream women to a radical-influenced organization. Advocates of nonresistance and class struggle joined WILPF, as did both supporters and opponents of the League of Nations. Some members believed that their role should be educational, while others favored direct action or lobbying. Some of WILPF's most enthusiastic supporters were women who believed in the importance of working to improve international understanding without compromising their nationalist sympathies. Its refusal to hew to ideological orthodoxy helped it attract a broad range of dues-paying women; this approach swelled the group's ranks to 5,000 by May 1923, dwarfing radical pacifist groups. Even with this success in attracting members, the peace group was still small relative to other more broadly focused women's groups of the time. But those who supported a strong military believed WILPF posed a larger threat than its numbers suggested.

Critics claimed that WILPF's true aim was to lead more reasonable American women into the revolutionary fold. Within WILPF, moderate women mingled freely with avowed radicals. Jane Addams's leadership role was especially ominous to its adversaries. The group's international president, Addams was one of the most admired women in America. Her involvement with the peace organization also provided powerful fuel for the anxiety that the nation's most influential women had become acolytes of Soviet-controlled pacifism.[85] WILPF's doctrinal flexibility proved to be a double-edged sword. Its willingness to work with anyone who favored peace through nonviolent social change helped it garner members. Yet by extending this open-door policy to radicals, the group crippled its effort to rebuff charges that its real aim was revolution.

The campaign against WILPF began in large part with the Overman Committee, the congressional investigation that had also exposed the Bolshevik treatment of women. Archibald Stevenson, a lawyer in the New York bureau of the Military Intelligence Division, declared that some of WILPF's leaders were responsible for advancing domestic radicalism. He called on the Senate to mount an official investigation to prove that the opposition to the war voiced by Jane Addams, Emily Balch, and Sophonisba Breckinridge stemmed from their sympathy for Bolshevism. Stevenson's request was taken up by New York State's Lusk Committee, which produced in 1920 the standard reference manual for those determined to combat radicalism. The Lusk report reprinted documents, dossiers of suspicious organizations, and countersubversive allegations; its four volumes spun connections between revolutionary groups and peace activists like Addams and Balch. Although alien radicals' "sedition" and "disloyalty" remained the focus of Stevenson's report, he nonetheless posited some of the first arguments that female pacifism was linked with revolution, implicating WILPF specifically in an international plot against the United States.[86]

As committed peace activists, the women of WILPF were not expecting commendations for their patriotism from conservative Americans. In the years following the Lusk Committee report, however, they were aghast at the lies and slanders they faced. Most egregious in this regard was a thirty-two-page pamphlet published by R. M. Whitney in 1924. Titled *Peace at Any Old Price*, the work vilified WILPF with a mix of facts, lies, and misrepresentations. "Peace at Any Old Price" became an antiradical catchphrase; the inflammatory pamphlet became part of the countersubversive canon that circulated for the next decade.[87] Whitney had been inspired by WILPF's 1923 conference, which, he asserted, put the peace group in a league of its own when it came to subversion. "For complete disloyalty to the United States no public utterances in recent years can compare with this conference, supposedly of Americans," he wrote. The gathering showed that its radical affiliations were beyond dispute, since "the entire conference was dominated by the spirit of Russian Communism, and the words of the speakers left no doubt in the minds of the hearers that Communism—The Third International—which aims at the overthrow of the Government of the United States by force and violence—was the directing force back of the conference." Whitney tied WILPF to international communism by accusing the organization of advocating the abolition of private property. This charge was false. Yet WILPF did advocate the recognition of Soviet Russia and improved relations with Germany. It also did work for the "abolition of the army and navy." It did attempt to uncover the economic causes of war. Yet these efforts did not come at "the behest of the Russian group of Internationalist Communists."[88]

Whitney's most incendiary claim against WILPF was that it encouraged its members to take the "infamous 'slacker's oath'" that pledged women to resist war in every way possible. Women who took the oath would forbid their children to fight for the nation and would refuse to "succor wounded soldiers who fight for their country's safety." While the more radical Women's Peace Society required its members "never to aid in or sanction war, offensive or defensive," WILPF in fact never sought to bind its members with this kind of oath even though some of its more radical members might have supported it.[89] The myth of the WILPF "slacker's oath" was nonetheless explosive and persistent, especially because it played on deep convictions about patriotism, femininity, and civilization. For many Americans, women's highest calling was as mother and nurturer. Women were bound to provide these services unquestioningly to the nation and civilization, raising patriots to defend their country and caring for the weak or wounded. Women's work as mothers provided the foundation for female citizenship; their work as compassionate caregivers was fundamental to civilization. Women who withheld their compassion in times of national crisis were therefore traitors who endangered national security. While pacifists interpreted this type of pledge as a strike against war, which in their minds posed the greatest threat to human life, traditional nationalists saw only their refusal to nurse those in need. Pledge-taking pacifists threatened femininity itself by suppressing the basic female instinct to sustain life. The pledge was more than treasonous. It struck straight at civilization itself.[90]

News of this pledge inspired more than outrage. One woman put her contempt for the pledge into verse. Elizabeth Fries, who was married to the head of the Army's Chemical Warfare Service, wrote a musical response to the peace movement's anthem "I Didn't Raise My Boy to Be a Soldier" entitled "I Didn't Raise My Boy to Be a Slacker." The lyrics were meant to be a father's rebuff of WILPF's alleged oath and went: "My boy will not be skulking in the rear, But go marching to the front, Never heeding Battle's brunt." This verse was followed by a refrain:

Then cheer men cheer
We shall never know the fear
Of the Coward who is the Father of a Coward
But when we're too old to go to the front to meet the foe
We'll be proud we raised the boy to be a soldier.[91]

Whitney's widely circulated charges haunted WILPF for years, despite members' innumerable attempts to refute his charges and explain their positions. Yet even before Whitney's pamphlet, similar attacks had begun to affect WILPF's ability to work with more conservative women's groups. In 1922, the women's "clearinghouse," formed in the wake of the Nineteenth Amendment to coordinate women's political lobbying, responded to the furor by forcing WILPF to leave the Women's Joint Congressional Committee.[92] These same charges sent the General Federation of Women's Clubs and the Parent-Teacher Association fleeing from a coalition to organize peace activism, the NCPW.[93] In both cases, centrist women sought to sever their ties with more controversial organizations in the hopes of preserving their respectable and patriotic reputations.

While the War Department reserved special hostility for WILPF, its officials conflated virtually all female political activity with pacifism. In December 1922, military intelligence chief General Marlborough Churchill asked Major W. H. Cowles to assemble an overview of "pacifist and antimilitary organizations in the country." Cowles replied that sheer numbers made it an "insurmountable" task to compile a comprehensive summary of objectionable groups' activities. The Women's Joint Congressional Committee (WJCC) and the National Council for Prevention of War (NCPW) deserved special notice as the worst of a bad lot, in his opinion. But he issued a sweeping indictment of women's influence. He claimed that the "activities of all women's societies and many church societies may be regarded with suspicion." These groups, according to Cowles, ranged in their sympathies from "a violent red to a light pink."[94]

This blatant antipathy to female political activism did not prevent the War Department from realizing that its aims would be better served if it could cultivate at least some American women as allies. In 1920, the War Department created a new position—director of women's relations—to improve its relationship with the nation's newly enfranchised female voters. Yet the two women who accepted this job were set up for failure. They were given few resources and no military status, which made it impossible to accomplish anything within the all-male, rank-conscious world of the War Department. As a result, the women in this post could do little to curb the constant attacks on women's political organizations by the military, which insisted that women's demands for disarmament were part of a radical conspiracy to destroy the nation. Even the most moderate of peace activists were alienated by the continuing attacks from the War Department.

The first director of women's relations, Mrs. John B. Casserly, lasted only a year. Casserly's successor was Anita Phipps, the articulate and committed daughter of a brigadier general. While Phipps did not approve of the peace movement, she worked through the 1920s to set peace-loving women on a political course that would ensure the nation's security and strength. She believed that the military would gain more allies through reasoned discussions than vicious rhetoric. But Phipps's family background could not compensate for an absence of military status or training, not to mention the inherent limitations of the position itself. Her scant knowledge about either women's politics or military bureaucracy rendered her ineffective both inside and outside the War Department. By appointing Phipps, a woman with little administrative experience and no ties to any of the major women's organizations of the time, the War Department demonstrated the limits of its vision. Phipps shared the War Department's desire to improve its image among women but found herself hamstrung by a constellation of factors. She could overcome neither her alienation from emerging female conservatives nor military leaders' conviction that all politically active women were pacifists. Phipps was a minor player in the political struggles between the War Department and the nation's women. But her tenure at the War Department provides insights into the role that women and gender played in the disarmament debate.

Anita Evans Phipps was thirty-five years old when she became the War Department Director of Women's Relations. Employed for less than a year as a regional director of women's relations, Phipps came from a well-to-do family that included Senator George Evans of Maine. She had been educated at the elite Miss Porter's School in Farmington, Connecticut, a school that provided academic training in science and culture but groomed its students primarily to be wives and mothers. Phipps was part of a significant minority of Miss Porter's students who never married. In other ways she was more typical of her classmates. Few continued their education in college. And though the school counted Alice Hamilton, one of the founders of the field of industrial medicine, among its graduates, Sarah Porter generally discouraged public activism. Those attending Miss Porter's at the turn of the century were less likely to seek careers as professional reformers than were the graduates of elite women's colleges.[95]

For ten years after Phipps finished school, she found golf clubs more compelling than women's clubs. Phipps led a privileged youth. Before World War I, she wrote, her "main claim to fame was . . . I had been twice in the semi-finals of the Women's National Golf Championship and had won several cups in horse-shows."[96] The outbreak of hostilities in Europe raised her civic consciousness. In 1914, she was drawn into war relief work. She first joined an emergency aid group in Philadelphia and eventually signed up for the Motor Corps Division of the Red Cross, rising through the ranks to become director of the Pennsylvania-Delaware Division in 1920.[97] She initially viewed this public service as a short-lived adventure, harboring no long-term drive to pursue a career or become an activist. Her plans were changed by a chance meeting with the army's first director of women's relations, who gave her the opportunity to take a new position as one of her regional directors. "The idea of having a hand in organizing and building up such a unique service was so seductive that I agreed to take it on for a year," she wrote.[98] Less than a year later, she had Casserly's job.

Phipps could draw on little political or administrative experience to ease her transition into the War Department. Perhaps she seemed tractable to those responsible for her appointment. As a political neophyte, Phipps was unprepared for the fierce ideological battles that would consume relations between women and the military in the decade that followed. While she was no friend of antimilitarism, she rejected the strident antiradicalism that was taking shape in the years following the Bolshevik Revolution. This meant that she had no constituency outside the War Department, no grassroots base she could draw on to help her transform the military into an institution more friendly to women. Her family connections to the army and her social prominence could not break down the barriers that kept her marginalized as a female civilian. Although she was appointed at an adequate annual salary of $4,000, she was denied many of the benefits of government service. Until 1926, she was paid from nonappropriated funds, which meant that her first five years of employment did not count toward a federal pension.[99] Her low rank in the War Department was made humiliatingly obvious to the world, she complained, by the "undignified makeshift" of a uniform required by her civilian status.[100]

As War Department liaison to the nation's women, Phipps had little ability to influence military policy. While she remained driven by the conviction that women deserved a role in the military specially tailored to their sex, she found herself unable to stop the War Department's campaign against women reformers. By 1924 she must have realized that she would never gain any real power in a hostile military bureaucracy, when

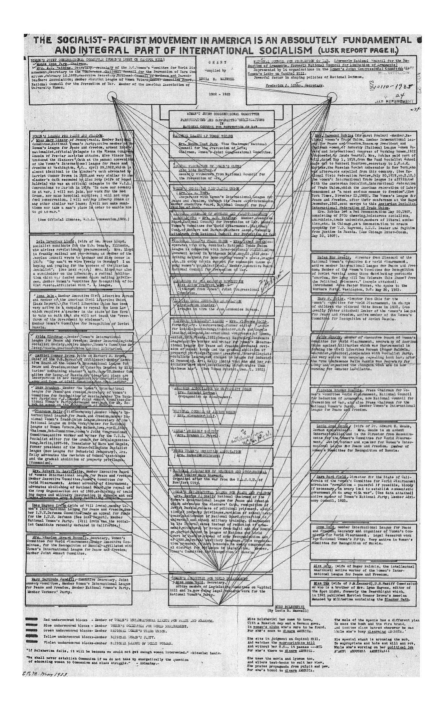

Figure 2. The Spider Web Chart, as originally drawn by Lucia Ramsey
Maxwell. National Archives and Records Administration.

she found herself drawn into to a high-profile fracas between her military bosses and female peace activists that she was helpless to resolve. This conflict grew out of a devastating assault that linked all female activism to revolution. The Spider Web Chart (Figure 2), which was circulated in 1923 and published in 1924, was a diagram of female treachery that linked all middle-class women activists to revolutionary radicalism. It put WILPF at the center of a web of radical conspiracy that enmeshed all of the women's organizations that sought to exert political influence in the new era of female enfranchisement.

The lettering was crude and the typing erratic, but no one could mistake the message. The Spider Web Chart trumpeted to Americans that millions of middle-class American women had become the dupes and agents of Bolshevik revolution. Fifty-two lines of ink on the one-by-two-foot chart connected the names of the country's most prominent women with a conspiracy to sabotage the republic. The crisscrossing lines that lent the chart its name claimed to reveal how pacifism had corrupted most middle-class female reform organizations. Each line denoted a link as vital as an artery, as controlling as a marionette string. Woven together, they were as menacing as strands in the web of some poisonous spider. Activists preaching peace threatened the capitalist nation, according to the hand-lettered banner at the top of the chart, since "the Socialist-Pacifist Movement in America Is an Absolutely Fundamental and Integral Part of International Socialism." The chart became the most notorious attack on female activists during this decade.[101]

The diagram listed sixteen of the largest and best-known women's organizations of the early 1920s in three columns of type. Two umbrella groups, the WJCC and the NCPW, were hubs for ruled pen lines that linked all the groups and thirty individual women. The lines suggested guilt by association, connecting broad-based groups like the League of Women Voters and the Girls' Friendly Society to WILPF and NCPW. The message was that groups formed to facilitate cooperation among women were actually fostering subversion and putting millions of female voters at the service of Soviet agents. The chart turned a broad and diverse political coalition into a sinister conspiracy. The lines etched alarmist visions into the public consciousness that proved impossible to erase. An accompanying poem explained that "Miss Bolsheviki," disguised as a newly enfranchised clubwoman, was in league with immigrant rabble-rousers:

Miss Bolsheviki has come to town,
With a Russian cap and a German gown,
In women's clubs she's sure to be found,
For she's come to disarm America

. . . The male of the species has a different plan
He uses the bomb and the fire brand,
And incites class hatred wherever he can
While she's busy disarming America.

His special stunt is arousing the mob,
To expropriate and hate and kill and rob,
While she's working on her political job
AWAKE! AROUSE! AMERICA!

The chart was first published by Henry Ford's *Dearborn Independent* in 1924. It was accompanied by two articles: "Are Women's Clubs 'Used' by Bolshevists?" and "Why Don't Women Investigate Propaganda?"[102] The articles were signed by an anonymous "American Citizen," but WJCC leaders immediately traced the chart back to the War Department, which had been responsible for so many of the recent attacks on women's organizations. A delegation from the group complained to Secretary of War John Weeks that the chart was "scurrilous, libelous and criminal" and that "twelve million women voters" demanded "redress." They said the chart gave the false impression that the reform groups they represented were connected with WILPF and the NCPW, which were sullied by constant attacks from the War Department.[103]

When women in the WJCC told her about the Spider Web Chart in late 1923, Phipps was horrified. She immediately brought the drawing to the attention of her superiors. Even though the chart was not an official document of the War Department, Phipps warned them they needed to act immediately to smooth the waters and discredit the chart's allegations. To drive home the gravity of the situation, she emphasized the influence of newly enfranchised women. "This Joint Congressional Committee is undoubtedly the most powerful organization of women, not only because the women of the committee are important," she wrote, "but also because they are organized, represent the most powerful of the women's organizations and are in very close touch with Congress." It was in the best interest of the War Department to foster in these defamed women "a friendly attitude toward the Army" since they were "in a position to do very definite work for or against the Army."[104]

Secretary of War Weeks ignored Phipps's advice. Even after a visit from a committee appointed by the WJCC, he remained silent about the Spider Web Chart. This stance intensified protests from the WJCC. In April 1924, Phipps again warned that this stubborn refusal to extend an olive branch was jeopardizing army interests. "The policy of publicly accusing women," Phipps declared in a memorandum to Weeks, was "very harmful to the War Department and has far-reaching consequences." The attacks, she claimed, were uniting moderate and radical women. "A policy of conciliation and education seems to be very necessary at present and will accomplish more for the War Department than denunciation."[105] Military leaders instead intensified their public denunciations of women. The controversy left Phipps isolated and frustrated within the War Department. It also foreshadowed the way the military would continue to resist all efforts by women to wield any kind of political influence in the decade that followed.

In the spring of 1924, Weeks took limited responsibility for the diagram, issuing a terse statement that he had ordered the charts destroyed. At the League of Women Voters' convention in late April, President Maud Wood Park, one of the women on the protest committee, read a letter by Weeks stating his regret that "the charts containing the errors pointed out by your Committee were circulated by any branch of the War Department." Newspapers called Weeks's statement an apology, and women leaders announced that they had been vindicated.[106]

This limited victory enjoyed by female reformers masked the turmoil inspired by the Spider Web Chart. It had driven a wedge into coalitions already fractured by anxieties about Bolshevism. The WJCC responded to the Spider Web Chart by vehemently disavowing any connection with WILPF.[107] That left the groups at the center of the attack, WILPF and the NCPW, to cope with the allegations on their own. Even before the chart was issued, female reformers had shown how sensitive they were to accusations of radicalism. The chart could have never affected them so powerfully if they were not themselves spooked by Bolshevism.[108] These attempts by female reformers to distance themselves from more controversial organizations were meaningless to those alarmed by radicalism, who refused to acknowledge that any ties had been severed. This incident was the first sign to women's organizations that political jockeying could not rid them of radical taint.

Weeks's apology also failed to erase the chart's allegation. Recalling the diagram after its national publication was like trying to capture smoke in a bottle. The factual errors and inflammatory message of the chart stood unchallenged except by the women libeled. The secretary of war refused to issue any additional statements about the chart, and the WJCC never could get the *Dearborn Independent* to publish an apology or retraction.[109] In the meantime, the Spider Web Chart had taken on a life of its own. Two manufacturers' groups, the Associated Industries of Kentucky and New York State, picked up the chart and the accompanying articles and republished them in pamphlet form, blanketing small towns with the diagram to discredit women's groups pushing for restrictions on child labor.[110] For conservative activists, the Spider Web Chart remained gospel.

In the years that followed, the chart inspired activists to spin new webs that were distributed through a growing conservative coalition. In 1927, a retired Cambridge businessman compiled a full-color chart including settlement house founder and WILPF president Jane Addams, government agencies, and even a large number of men. This later chart graded subversive organizations by color; pacifists were classified as yellow, progressives as pink, and radicals as red.[111] The American Legion used these kinds of charts to illustrate its 1933 report on "subversive organizations," and prominently featured Jane Addams in a diagram with the header "Communism in Internationalist-Pacifist Defeatist Organizations."[112] The web motif proved an irresistible way for activists to magnify the dangers facing the United States. Although the WJCC disbanded the committee it had created to refute the Spider Web Chart after the military retraction, the group reconvened a few months later to address new attacks.[113] For the next two decades, women advocates of peace and social justice grew accustomed to seeing their names on diagrams of malicious conspiracies and lists of disloyal Americans.

The women smeared by the Spider Web Chart had assumed that their old-stock American lineage placed their patriotism beyond reproach. The diagram demonstrated that ethnicity and genealogy no longer had the power to absolve women from suspicion. Over the thirty years they had worked as reformers, female activists had become accustomed to enjoying a moral authority engendered by their status as women and political outsiders. They came to expect condescension rather than condemnation. Then the Bolshevik Revolution dramatically changed the global political environment. In the United States, it set the nation on high alert against radicals, creating a sense of alarm that was intensified as bombings, labor unrest, and racial violence rocked the nation in 1919. After arrests and deportations crushed the most militant manifestations of working-class radicalism, newly enfranchised female activists—especially those supporting the popular peace movement—came under increasing scrutiny. The transformative potential of both women's suffrage and the popular peace movement deepened anxieties about social disorder. These concerns recast sexual stereotypes in ways that transformed female reformers from political innocents working for the best interests of their communities into naive dupes susceptible to the evil machinations of dangerous revolutionaries. This revised interpretation of women's political activism made soldiers against subversion as likely to denounce blue-blooded social reformers as red radicals after 1920.

Female reformers shared radicals' concern with unfair working conditions, the exploitation of children, the lack of economic security for most workers in a capitalist economy, and the wasted resources of a bloated military-industrial complex. Conservatives saw this political common ground as evidence of women's revolutionary sympathies. In fact, the targeted women were hardly enemies of capitalism. Most saw reform as a way of buttressing American capitalism and the American political system. But conservative activists increasingly blurred the distinction between reformers and radicals. These slanders did more than inspire a backlash against newly enfranchised women. They constricted the political possibilities for female activists, giving women reformers the dubious distinction of being the first politically mainstream Americans to experience the full destructive power of this new invigorated brand of anticommunism.

As women, gender, and sexuality took center stage in the antiradicalism of the 1920s, women assumed opposing roles in conservative ideology. As reformers and radical dupes, they were the agents of revolution. At the same time, they were held up as the potential martyrs of this same revolutionary radicalism. Forced to endure systematic sexual violation and material privation at the hands of working-class and ethnically undesirable brutes, women devoted to the traditional institutions of home, family, and religion cried out for protection in this antiradical morality play. Any revolution would overturn more than political institutions; all the social structures that gave their lives purpose and protection would be destroyed. These apocalyptic visions gave emotional resonance to the fight against communism for the rest of the century.

The dichotomy between women victims and villains also opened up a political space for a third type of women: conservative female activists.

Conservative women perceived a unique mission. They could spare American women the suffering that would come with the onset of revolution. Only women could undermine the nefarious plots of radical women. Only women could return the vast majority of middle-class women to the political straight and narrow. The salvation of all American women thus rested on their shoulders. Their determination to publicize the plight of communist-inspired suffering and stem the influence of radicalism among middle-class female activists would transform women's politics in only a few short years.

Chapter 2

# The Origins of the Spider Web Chart: Women and the Construction of the Bolshevik Threat

Female reformers saw that single crude drawing—the 1924 Spider Web Chart—as the most devastating attack by male War Department officers on women activists. For the previous two years, peace activists had been locked in battle with the Chemical Warfare Service of the War Department after demanding the abolition of chemical weapons. The leader of the division, Brigadier General Amos Fries, had responded to these calls by accusing the Women's International League for Peace and Freedom and the National Council for Prevention of War of being agents of revolutionary communism.[1] Indeed, when secretary of war John Weeks issued an apology for any chart "circulated" by the War Department, he was tacitly acknowledging that its crisscrossing lines were penned at a desk in the Chemical Warfare Service. Yet even though the Spider Web Chart was conceived in that office, it was not the brainchild of the military brass.

The earlier invectives by Fries, the antisuffragist Weeks, and the rest of the military establishment primed female reformers to suspect the men in the War Department of launching this latest round of abuse. Yet by focusing exclusively on these men, reformers of the time and later historians overlooked the name typed at the top of the document: Lucia Ramsey Maxwell. The indignant targets of this attack refused to believe that Maxwell, a librarian and stenographer in the Chemical Warfare Service, was the real villain behind these allegations. When Maxwell drew the Spider Web Chart, she undoubtedly had the blessing of her old friend and boss, General Fries. But the librarian also drew inspiration for her chart from an entirely female network of conservative activists. While working days in the Chemical Warfare Service library, Maxwell spent her evenings and weekends attending meetings of organizations like the Daughters of the American Revolution (DAR), which was becoming increasingly preoccupied with subversion after the Russian Revolution. By 1924, Maxwell was committed to spreading the message of antiradicalism and warning other women of the peril their nation faced. "It is time for the patriotic daughters of America to be keen and alert to the dangers, internal as well as external, that threaten our country," Maxwell wrote in a private letter in 1922. "The spirit of Bolshevism and Communism is abroad in our land, hissing its hymns of hate and advocating 'Revolution, peaceful if possible, bloody if necessary."[2] Revolutionary radicals, she asserted, were cheering the wildfire spread of female pacifism. Her Spider Web Chart (see Figure 2) for the first time connected the dots of the subversive threat.[3]

In the ensuing furor, Weeks insisted that the clerical worker had made the chart as a private citizen.[4] But reformers of the time believed that women would not attack other women on their own accord. In fact, they scoffed at the idea of women as activists for the right. The women who circulated the Spider Web Chart, wrote Ethel Smith, legislative secretary for the National Women's Trade Union League, were instruments for "men of wealth, economic and political power, men of military rank and prowess" who were fearful of "every woman prominent in public life."[5] Secretary of War Weeks did little to disabuse the chart's victims of this notion; while he alternately endorsed and disavowed the document, he demonstrated little respect for its creator. Maxwell was an outspoken propagandist who articulated the alarm that many women were feeling about global radicalism. Yet she was not recognized for her work because she contradicted popular assumptions about female activism.

Men and women of all political stripes viewed female political engagement as virtually synonymous with Progressive Era maternalism. This type of activism was predicated on the notion that innate maternal instincts drove women into politics, where they worked exclusively to better the lives of women and children. Maternalists' success in carving out a new arena for policymaking focused on child and family welfare made many Americans believe that this was women's sole political activism. Yet maternalism was only one element of a spectrum of political activism embraced by women in the first decades of the twentieth century. They were better known than other women activists, thanks to their ability to build influential institutions, which they used to change the shape of American politics and society. Maternalists hoped that the suffrage victory would enhance their political influence. But they found it difficult to gain political traction in a world that had been changed irrevocably by both the Great War and the Bolshevik Revolution.

The revolutionary drama popularized by the Overman Committee hearings had opened up a new political space for women like Maxwell, who used the dueling images of victimized Russian aristocrats and villainous American reformers to justify their own activism. They mobilized to prevent revolution, casting themselves as the only ones capable of protecting their vulnerable sisters in a battle with "Miss Bolsheviki." These new female antiradicals gave scant attention to the activities of self-declared radicals or Bolsheviks. Instead, they focused on undercutting the women who were demanding a smaller military and a larger social welfare state, which they believed would open the door for radical revolution in the United States. They forced groups like the Daughters of the American Revolution and the General Federation of Women's Clubs to adopt an uncompromising militarism that rejected all reform efforts as dangerous to national security, shattering long-standing alliances within the political subculture dominated by female voluntary associations.

Female antiradicals like Maxwell did not work at the bidding of overbearing male relatives or male superiors, a fact that their female opponents found impossible to accept. They were driven by the same impulse that had inspired their progressive sisters: a desire to protect women and children. In other words, their campaign against radicalism was driven by a desire for self-preservation rather than a self-destructive obedience to patriarchal authority. Women who became conservative activists believed that radical ideologies menaced their homes, churches, and personal safety. Their opposition to radicalism was deeply gendered, for it was motivated by the belief that these ideologies aimed to dismantle the patriarchal protections that provided shelter and care to women and children. In their view, these were the citizens most vulnerable to radicalism's fearsome march.

## The Female Dominion and the Politics of Maternalism

When the Spider Web Chart was published, its creator and her compatriots were still working in the shadow of female reformers. These advocates had demonstrated their ability to reshape American society and politics in the first decades of the twentieth century. Over the course of the Progressive Era, women activists created a network of interconnected organizations and agencies led and staffed by women, which one historian called a "female dominion in the mostly male empire of policymaking."[6] The Children's Bureau, a federal agency established at the urging of child welfare advocates in the Department of Labor in 1912, stood at the pinnacle of this "dominion." It was supported by state-level child welfare agencies, themselves staffed by veterans of the federal bureau. These female professionals claimed authority over child welfare, even while they pushed male policymakers and politicians to assume more responsibility for the health and welfare of mothers and children. The welfare state that emerged in the early twentieth century was in many ways a product of these policymakers, who made powerful appeals to local, state, and national officials to remedy persistent social problems. Their efforts reconfigured the relationship between the individual and the state.

The women who created these institutions would have had few legislative victories, however, without the help of women's voluntary associations like the National Consumers' League, the National Congress of Parents and Teacher Associations (later known as the PTA), and General Federation of Women's Clubs. This coalition of middle-class women's groups essentially became the lobbying arm of the "dominion." In an era before women had the vote, clubwomen perfected the art of pressure group politics. These groups were gateways into politics for middle-class women, forging "the women's sphere into a broadly based political movement."[7] Their leaders used domesticity to frame political activism. They taught rank-and-file members to make the connection between what was considered women's sphere and public life. "Women's place is in the Home," explained suffragist and journalist Rheta Childe Dorr. "But Home in not contained within the four walls of the individual house. Home is the community. . . . And badly [does] the Home . . . need [its] mother."[8] This became the rallying cry for women who decided to change the world. The idea of "social housekeeping" gave cover to women who launched sometimes confrontational campaigns to create new municipal sanitation systems, ban child labor, end lynching, make workplaces safer and healthier for women, and establish parks, hospitals, and schools.

Some of the groups that came to support the maternalist agenda of the Children's Bureau were founded with explicitly political missions, like the National Consumers' League. But even organizations such as the Daughters of the American Revolution and the General Federation of Women's Clubs, that had been established with broader cultural goals, lent their backing to the female reform initiatives of the Progressive Era. These two types of middle-class women's groups were knit together by their overlapping memberships. Women were often active in a constellation of different voluntary associations and pursued the same agenda from multiple contexts. As a result, the "maternalist" politics advocated by the Children's Bureau were embraced by virtually all of the middle-class women's voluntary associations.

The largest and oldest of these groups was the General Federation of Women's Clubs. Local women's clubs—most notably Sorosis and the New England Woman's Club—were started in the immediate aftermath of the Civil War as a way to promote cultural literacy among its members; these groups soon branched out from literature and art to help women to influence civic affairs. Reformers coexisted with conservatives in these myriad local groups, which provided a respectable and even fashionable way for middle-class women to engage politically. These diverse local groups united in a national federation in 1890 in the interest of amplifying clubwomen's influence in public affairs by coordinating efforts to create a "better social order."[9]

Under the motto "Unity in Diversity," the new General Federation of Women's Clubs (GFWC) soon became a powerful vehicle for national reform campaigns.[10] In 1898, the GFWC endorsed an agenda of ambitious social reforms that included adequate schools and an end to employment for children under fourteen; an eight-hour work day for women and children; and the standardization of labor laws throughout the states. Each club was directed to appoint a standing committee to investigate labor conditions in its local community and "secure enforcement of labor ordinances."[11] The national organization urged members to serve as "a 'committee of one' to use all possible influences against anything which dwarfs the minds and bodies of children."[12] Through the first decade of the twentieth century, the group encouraged its members to respond with passionate indignation to what it saw as the excesses and abuses of industrialization. "Probably the most piteous cry which has reached the ears of the mothers of the nation is that which goes up from the little children whose lives are sacrificed to the greed of manufacture," its official history proclaimed in 1912.[13]

The group's desire to protect children waxed through the Progressive years. When the National Child Labor Committee was established in 1904 to spearhead a campaign for tightened regulation, one of the first people to sign up was GFWC president Sarah Decker.[14] The GFWC also sent representatives to Congress to lobby for the creation of the Children's Bureau.[15] The group played an instrumental role in pushing states to provide "mothers' pensions." Government financial support allowed the mothers of young children to avoid working for wages, an issue clubwomen vigorously embraced. By 1920, forty states provided these stipends.[16] The GFWC did not welcome all reforms; the organization did not endorse women's suffrage until 1914.[17]

Another large and prestigious women's organization that endorsed maternalist politics at the beginning of the twentieth century was the Daughters of the American Revolution. The DAR was part of a host of hereditary associations founded in the last decade of the nineteenth century by Anglo-Saxon Americans. Membership in the DAR or the Daughters of 1812, Daughters of American Colonists, Daughters of the Cincinnati, and Colonial Daughters of the Seventeenth Century was a way for women to distinguish themselves from new immigrants.[18] Soon after these genealogical societies were founded, their members were lampooned by the press as buxom, bejeweled, and monied middle-aged women with a fondness for elaborate medals and sashes signifying obscure honors and offices. Yet these women believed they could have a salutary influence on society by preserving select historic sites, buildings, objects, and documents that demonstrated the ideals of their ancestors, the founding fathers.[19] During the first decades of the twentieth century, the organization also lobbied vigorously to ban child labor, which one of its officers described in 1908 as an "evil" that menaced "the institutions the fathers founded."[20] Its members supported the work of settlement houses, international reconciliation, and campaigns for "pure milk."[21] The group reflected these concerns by honoring the work of well-known reformer Jane Addams by granting her a lifetime membership. Until she was expelled for her peace activism, Addams proudly displayed the DAR pin that advertised her association with the hereditary organization.[22]

Female voluntary associations like the DAR and the GFWC were complex institutions, simultaneously conservative and progressive. While politicizing a large swath of middle-class women, they also reinforced class and racial hierarchies. And even as they fought to reform the American polity, these sex-segregated clubs encouraged their members to see their work as removed from male politics.[23] They viewed their work as the antithesis of male maneuvering for money and power. They rendered women's quest for political influence socially palatable by casting their work as a selfless community service rather than an exercise of self-interest.

In practice, the worlds of female and male politics were not as distinct as many activists believed. Nor was the sex solidarity as strong as they asserted. For one, white women's groups would not accept African

American women, who went on to form an entirely separate network of clubs for black women. The blinders of class and race made it difficult for white women to understand the urgency of campaigns that were then undertaken by African American women to end racial violence, especially lynching. They also found it difficult to acknowledge that not all women embraced maternalism as the best solution for social ills. Class, race, region, and ethnicity as well as gender determined which problems women found to be most urgent and the way they chose to address them.[24] For instance, most women agreed that child labor was an evil. But while middle-class women saw mandatory school attendance as the answer to this scourge, working-class women organized to raise their own wages to allow families to survive without their labor. Despite evidence to the contrary, most white middle-class clubwomen retained their belief that immutable sex differences served as a foundation for female solidarity. This theoretical construct left these women ill-prepared to face new female foes in the postsuffrage period, especially women like these antiradicals, who met reformers on their own terrain of sex-segregated clubs.

## The Women's Joint Congressional Committee

The passage of the Nineteenth Amendment left suffragists optimistic that female voters would unite behind efforts to expand government protections for families and children. Journalist and reformer Rheta Childe Dorr responded to the question of "what will women do with their votes?" with the assertion that "social legislation alone interests women."[25] To advocate for these types of measures, middle-class female reformers established a new lobbying organization in November 1920. The Women's Joint Congressional Committee (WJCC) was designed to help women around the country influence politicians in Washington. The WJCC facilitated cooperation among a raft of important middle-class women's organizations, including the National Congress of Parents and Teachers, the General Federation of Women's Clubs, the National Consumers' League, the National Women's Trade Union League, and the Woman's Christian Temperance Union. It also attracted the support of groups that emerged around the time of the Nineteenth Amendment, including the League of Women Voters, the American Association of University Women, and the National Federation of Business and Professional Women's Clubs. Even the DAR joined the WJCC, though it pulled out of the group in 1922.[26] By 1925, this "clearinghouse"—as its members called it—had the active support of twenty-five women's groups and was regarded as "the most powerful lobby in Washington."[27]

The first legislation to win the backing of the WJCC was the Sheppard-Towner Maternity and Infancy Protection Act. This measure was aimed at reducing the nation's infant mortality rate, which was among the highest of twenty developed nations surveyed in 1918.[28] Bureaucrats from the Children's Bureau had drawn up a program with maternal education and state participation as its linchpins. The Sheppard-Towner Act required the federal government to match funds provided by states for health clinics, visiting nurses, classes on nutrition and hygiene, lectures for pregnant women and new mothers. Intended to help women who did not have access to private physicians but open to any woman seeking information, the programs created by the Sheppard-Towner Act were in fact modest. For veteran maternalists like Florence Kelley, however, the measure was still tremendously significant. "Of all the activities in which I have shared during more than forty years of striving," Kelley declared, "none is, I am convinced, of such fundamental importance as the Sheppard-Towner Act."[29] The high hopes of reformers like Kelley seemed destined to ease the legislation into law.

The campaign for Sheppard-Towner showcased the power of newly coordinated women's groups. Though the WJCC's bylaws stated that only five of its constituents were necessary to form a subcommittee to lobby in favor of the bill, the entire coalition worked for it. Endorsements were offered by the GFWC; the League of Women Voters; the Women's Trade Union League; the National Council of Jewish Women; the National Association of Colored Women; the PTA; the National Council of Women; and the Business and Professional Women's Clubs. The DAR also supported the bill and the group's legislative chairman Alice Bradford Wiles urged her fellow members to let their congressmen "know that you and the Daughters of the American Revolution believe in the principles of the bill and wish it to pass."[30] They were joined by many nonmember women's groups, including other groups that would become known for their conservative politics: the Service Star Legion and a Colorado chapter of the Grand Army of the Republic.[31] Even popular women's magazines joined the effort by publishing stories that urged women to take an active interest in the bill's passage. Magazines like *Good Housekeeping, Ladies' Home Journal, Woman's Home Companion, The Delineator,* and *McCall's* supplied women with ready-made petitions to fill out and send to Washington. The maternity act appeared universally popular among women, a fact noted by politicians wary of antagonizing new female voters. "I think every woman in my state has written to the Senator," said one senator's secretary.[32]

Responding no doubt in part to women's enthusiasm for the bill, politicians from across the spectrum claimed it as their own. The platforms of the Socialist, Democratic, and Farmer-Laborer parties called for its passage, while the American Federation of Labor testified on its behalf in congressional hearings. Even Republican presidential candidate Warren G. Harding spoke in its favor. Opinions on the bill were more mixed in the medical community. One of the bill's most powerful opponents was the American Medical Association. Doctors viewed the bill as a challenge to their authority and denounced the power it granted to both social workers and the state. "Medical liberty" groups that favored homeopathic, herbal, and other alternative medical practices opposed Sheppard-Towner for the opposite reason. They feared it would strengthen traditional doctors' hold on the medical system and spread the use of vaccines and other drug treatments.[33] But not all the medical establishment was hostile. The Medical Women's National Association, the National Organization of Public Health Nurses, and the American Child Health Association all threw their weight behind the scheme to bring down the nation's infant and maternal mortality rates.[34]

This overwhelming show of support in 1921 muted the protests of the women who viewed Sheppard-Towner as a pernicious piece of legislation that would endanger the welfare of the nation's mothers and children. The bill's most formidable female opponent was Elizabeth Lowell Putnam, a Boston conservative who came of age politically as a maternalist reformer but would become well known for her campaign against female-driven social welfare reform measures during the 1920s. Her fierce opposition to the welfare state was all the more striking, given her previous wholehearted support of these same measures. As it did with many women of her generation, child welfare first drew this Boston Brahmin into politics. A mansion on Beacon Hill, she was horrified to discover, could not prevent her infant daughter Harriet from dying after drinking "filled" or contaminated milk in 1900. Putnam channeled her grief into an effort to clean up the milk supply. In 1908 she started a campaign through the Woman's Municipal League of Boston to force local government to ensure milk purity. She collaborated with the same group to improve prenatal care, establishing a small clinic in Boston that demonstrated how regular visits with doctors and nurses during pregnancy dramatically improved the health of mothers and babies.

These efforts brought Putnam national and occasionally international recognition as an expert in prenatal care. These credentials helped her become president of the American Association for the Prevention of Infant Mortality in 1918. Putnam's work in infant "hygiene" engendered strong working relationships with the Progressive Era stars of female reform, women who might have been discomfited by her antisuffrage crusading. While they disagreed with Putnam's stance on female enfranchisement, these reformers found common cause with Putnam on child welfare issues and sought her help with publications and studies. She provided both assistance and wholehearted support.[35]

While Putnam and the administrators of the Children's Bureau worked harmoniously through the suffrage campaign, World War I brought a sudden halt to this collaboration. The war absorbed Putnam in a way familiar to many Americans of her time. But Putnam's wartime service was somewhat unusual; she funded a covert program through the state of Massachusetts to keep suspicious individuals under political surveillance. This experience shattered her faith in utopian social improvement schemes. After the Armistice, Putnam returned to child welfare issues with an utterly different agenda. She began to campaign against the legislative reforms championed by the U.S. Children's Bureau. Putnam worked to thwart the Bureau's efforts to fund maternal and infant health education and outlaw child labor, two causes she had previously supported. Once the war drew Putnam into the world of countersubversion, erstwhile allies in the world of female reform became adversaries.[36] Her abrupt reversal was prompted by anxieties about national security, domestic unrest, and international revolution that eclipsed her long-standing concern with public health. By 1921, Putnam was known as a maverick conservative dedicated to diminishing the social welfare state and expanding the internal security state. While her stance on child welfare legislation made her a marginal figure in 1921, her political development foreshadowed broader developments among politically active American women during the 1920s.

In her efforts to defeat Sheppard-Towner, Putnam joined forces with another antisuffragist, Representative Alice Mary Robertson from Oklahoma, who was at that time the only woman in Congress. While Robertson denounced the bill using quotes from the Bible and warnings about "paternalistic government," Putnam's testimony against Sheppard-Towner drew on her expertise in the field of maternal health.[37] The women behind the bill, she claimed, had incorrectly emphasized education over medical care. "In the care of maternity you can not educate a woman to do more than choose a good physician to take care of her," she said. The major causes of death among pregnant and newly delivered mothers, she asserted, were diseases or conditions that needed the attention of trained medical personnel. "You can not instruct an expectant mother how to overcome pelvic abnormalities, prevent postpartum hemorrhage, to prevent infection at the hands of poorly trained nurses, midwives, and physicians, to emerge alive from an attack of pneumonia or typhoid fever occurring at certain stages of pregnancy or to prevent the toll of maternal deaths shortly after childbirth in the case of tuberculous women," she declared.[38]

Putnam had nothing but disdain for the other female critics of Sheppard-Towner, though they shared her background in the antisuffrage movement. Mary Kilbreth led a small band of women associated with the newly formed Woman Patriot Publishing Company (WPPC) in a formal protest of the bill. The WPPC emerged from the National Association Opposed to Woman Suffrage (NAOWS), an organization dealt a killing blow by the passage of the suffrage amendment in 1919. That summer, as the campaign for state ratification charged ahead, Mary Kilbreth was elected president of the fading NAOWS.[39] Kilbreth led a dwindling group of women who fought female enfranchisement well into 1920.[40] Once the Nineteenth Amendment became the law of the land, Kilbreth launched a new career, becoming a spokeswoman for antisuffragists convinced that female enfranchisement would lead to state socialism and profound suffering for women and children.[41] Determined to block social welfare legislation backed by new women voters, Kilbreth became the guiding spirit for a handful of women who transformed the National Association Opposed to Woman Suffrage into the Woman Patriot Publishing Company. She moved the organization's headquarters from New York to Washington, D.C., and declared that the women who had opposed female enfranchisement had a vital role in defending American society against the larger dangers of feminism and socialism.[42] Her new organization, the WPPC, dedicated itself to lobbying and the publication of a newspaper, the *Woman Patriot*, which became the broadsheet of choice for women who identified themselves as conservatives during the 1920s.[43]

Kilbreth's inaugural performance as a lobbyist stood in marked contrast to the eloquent and professional women she opposed. She had prepared the senators for her testimony by sending every member of Congress a letter explicating her objections; her oral testimony was nonetheless tentative and rambling; she refused to discuss what she called the "technical aspects of the bill," demonstrating her unfamiliarity with maternal and child health issues. Inspired by the conviction that this female-driven reform threatened the patriarchal family and laid the groundwork for communist revolution, Kilbreth's objections were difficult for many of the senators to follow. "I am afraid of the socialistic opportunity provided for by this bill, and that it will give an opportunity to destroy the marriage institution," said Kilbreth.[44] Kilbreth's objections were stated more eloquently by Mrs. Albert T. Leatherbee, who spoke on behalf of the Massachusetts Anti-Suffrage Association and later became active in the antiradical Sentinels of the Republic. Any attempt to meddle in the private domestic sphere smacked of radicalism since "Marx and Engels preached destruction of the family, and their followers have never repudiated this teaching," Leatherbee testified. "The family is the core of every Christian State; and it is for these reasons that those who would overturn present Governments consider it the first point of attack. . . . Abolish the family and the whole structure must fall." Radicals, she claimed, did not dare to wage an open attack on the family; instead, they were "beginning with legislation that pretends to benefit the family. They come garbed in sheep's clothing, but their nature is lupine and we must be on our guard."[45] Critics, like supporters of Sheppard-Towner, would never acknowledge that the provisions of this bill were actually quite modest. Free classes, visiting nurses, and clinics for impoverished mothers were unlikely triggers for either the communist revolution feared by Leatherbee or the more modest overhaul of the American political system envisioned by reformers.

As reformers pushed Sheppard-Towner to its final approval in the summer of 1921, the objections of Leatherbee and others carried little weight in this initial debate over the bill. A greater threat was old-fashioned misogyny. Senator James Reed tried to sway his colleagues by ridiculing female reformers. Reading into the record the names of Children's Bureau employees, Reed emphasized their unmarried status. "It seems to be the established doctrine of this bureau that the only people capable of caring for babies and mothers of babies are ladies who have never had babies," he jeered. The Children's Bureau program would mandate that every prospective mother receive a harassing visit from "a bespectacled lady, nose sharpened by curiosity, official chin pointed and keen." These calls would be not only intrusive, but useless, he explained. "I question whether one out of ten of these delightful reformers could make a bowl of buttermilk gruel that would not give a baby the colic in five minutes. [Laughter] We would better reverse the proposition and provide for a committee of mothers to take charge of the old maids and teach them how to acquire a husband and have babies of their own. [Laughter]"[46]

Reformers triumphed over Reed's derision and Kilbreth's warnings. Sheppard-Towner sailed through Congress: the Senate passed it 63–7 and the House of Representatives 279–39. President Harding made it law on November 23, 1921.[47] Supporters of the measure had been forced to make some concessions, however. Some of the oversight was shifted out of the Children's Bureau into the Public Health Service. The measure specifically forbade agents from providing financial support to mothers or entering homes without permission. The bill allocated a portion of the money originally requested and funded only educational programs. Gone were the provisions for medical or nursing care included in the original 1918 version of the bill. Most serious for the long-term survival of the program, the legislation would expire in five years unless it was reauthorized in 1927.[48]

Female reformers saw these compromises as a small price to pay for a major triumph. They focused on the large margin of victory, heralding Sheppard-Towner as the beginning of a new era in which women voters would remake American society and politics with their unselfish use of the franchise. "The enactment of the Sheppard-Towner Maternity Act by the Congress of the United States is the first fruits of women's concentrated, loyal co-operation for public welfare," proclaimed League of Women Voters president Maud Wood Park. "A Congressman, himself opposed to the measure, prophesied: 'The bill will be passed because the women want it and have made their wants felt.'"[49]

The leadership of the GFWC had greeted the passage of Sheppard-Towner with euphoria. Just as Senator Reed was ridiculing women reformers on Capitol Hill, GFWC president Alice Ames Winter strengthened her organization's legislative department and called on the state federations to form legislative councils to facilitate political collaboration among similarly minded women's groups.[50] Yet even at this moment of triumph for female reformers, harbingers of conflict appeared. A renegade clubwoman appeared in Congress to protest the bill and the GFWC's endorsement procedures and testify that support for reform within her organization was far from unanimous.[51] Another clubwoman expressed her objections to the "mischievous" bill privately. "So many of us here were disappointed at the Federation's actions regarding the Maternity Bill," the Massachusetts woman wrote to another opponent.[52] Still more members vowed to draw the line at Sheppard-Towner and lead the resistance within the GFWC to additional reform items.

Maternalist lobbyists believed that these concerns would dissipate once critics observed how the federal program benefited mothers. The measure demonstrated their faith in the traditional institutions of family and home. Sheppard-Towner, according to lobbyist Dorothy Kirchwey Brown, will benefit "the homes suffrage was supposedly to disrupt." She considered it a great irony that antisuffragists, the most ardent defenders of traditional values, supplied "the most virulent opposition."[53]

## Terror and Treachery

In 1921, former antisuffragists like Kilbreth and Putnam seemed like relics from a lost cause. They were in fact harbingers of a new political order, forged by the Bolshevik Revolution and the justification for radical repression offered by the Overman Committee. Popular assumptions about women's political engagement may have blinded female reformers to Lucia Ramsey Maxwell's role as the creator of the Spider Web Chart. But contemporary activists and the scholars who have described them may have also overlooked and dismissed Maxwell because of the novelty of conservative female activism in the 1920s. Distracted by the horrors of World War I, giddy with the excitement of the suffrage victory, and overwhelmed by the enterprise of mobilizing new women voters, reformers probably did not give Maxwell a second look. They would have had little reason to fear a Washington clerical worker. Beyond antisuffragism, which had been rendered obsolete, no tradition of organized conservative women's activism existed in the United States. The Bolshevik Revolution changed all that. In the same way that World War I had been a defining moment for many American women and had inspired millions to prevent all future wars, the Bolshevik Revolution was a watershed for Maxwell and her compatriots. It inspired deep fear in these women, who turned all their energy to halting the global spread of radicalism. In the process they created a rich new political realm for conservative women like themselves.

For most of these women, the Bolshevik Revolution only came home to them in 1919, when widespread domestic unrest seemed to signal that a Russian-style revolt was imminent in the offing in the United States. After the declaration of the Seattle General Strike, the Overman Committee turned its full attention to detailing the consequences of a radical revolution. The Com-

mittee popularized narratives about the suffering of Russian women that justified all efforts to suppress any manifestation of radical dissent. Women like
Maxwell vowed to spare American women the kind of suffering described
during these hearings. They were also determined to avoid this fate for themselves. "When women thoroughly understand how Bolshevism menaces their
sex they will take up arms against it and fight it incessantly to destruction,"
declared Ida Vera Simonton, president of the Women's Military Reserve of
the United States. "Governments so far have been powerless against it, and
it remains for the women to help the Government against this new terror."[54]
Drawing on both the Overman Committee hearings and the Lusk Committee report, Maxwell and other propagandists repeated the "nationalization of
women" myth and warned women that unless they fought back, events in Soviet Russia were a preview of their future.[55] These women saw military force
and vigorous countersubversion efforts as the only sure protection against
the misery and suffering that would accompany a radical overthrow.

The narratives of terror and treachery articulated before the Overman Committee fundamentally shifted attitudes about politics in a host
of women's organizations, most notably the DAR. Even while politicians
declared a return to "normalcy," righteous indignation grew within this
influential hereditary association about "all forms of sovietism, socialism, communism and bolshevism."[56] In 1923, the DAR warned American
women that "the forces of Communism, Socialism, and other forms of
destructive radicalism" aimed not only to level the economic playing field
but to assail "our form of government" as well as "patriotism, religion
and the sanctity of the family and the home."[57] The same year, the group
elected Lora Haines Cook as president general. Cook made antiradicalism the dominant philosophy in the DAR's leadership council. The DAR
leadership came under the influence of conservative propagandist R. M.
Whitney, influential head of the American Defense Society and author of
*Reds in America*. Whitney's 1924 book claimed to illuminate "the present
Status of the Revolutionary Movement in the United States," including the
"numerous connections and associations of the Communists among the
Radicals, Progressives and Pinks." In a section detailing women's work
for communism, Whitney quoted the claim by former antisuffragists that
Carrie Chapman Catt, Jane Addams, and Margaret Dreier Robins directed
an "international feminist-pacifist bloc."[58] Cook declared Whitney's book
a must-read for patriotic women and sent copies to every one of her state
regents and national officers.[59]

Cook's cabinet included women, namely Flora Walker and Grace Brosseau, who would become nationally known for their conservative activism during the second half of the 1920s.[60] During Cook's term, the chair of the society's Publicity Committee was Elizabeth Fries, the wife of General Amos Fries of the Chemical Warfare Service. Fries sought to raise public awareness of her organization's political stance with a 1924 circular letter supporting "adequate defense at all times by land and sea" and pledging "to oppose with all the vigor and strength of their beings any individual or groups of individuals who would substitute for our great institutions of government untried theories and dangerous communist doctrines."[61]

The DAR was the most prestigious female voluntary association to frame the campaign against communism as essential for the well-being of women and children. But it had many allies in this endeavor. Its most important partner became the American Legion Auxiliary, an organization formed in the aftermath of World War I to honor the memory of American veterans. When the group was established in 1921 it was intended to be subservient to the male Legion, which consented to have an affiliated women's organization as long as female members agreed to "render help" to male Legionnaires and not overstep their authority.[62] Membership in the Auxiliary was open to nurses and ambulance drivers who had served in some kind of military capacity as well as the wives, sisters, mothers, and daughters of servicemen. In the decade after the world war, the Legion and its Auxiliary performed charity work to aid veterans and their families and promoted legislation for veterans' benefits. Neither the Legion nor its Auxiliary confined itself merely to veterans' charity. The groups were politically outspoken and pursued a legislative agenda that reflected the acute anxieties of the Red Scare, the fears that defined the political climate in which they were conceived.

By 1925, the Auxiliary had attracted more than 200,000 members and become a mainstay of community life in small towns and cities in every state. It drew civic-minded women who also were active in more-established women's organizations. For example, the second president of the American Legion Auxiliary, Kate Waller Barrett, was not only an officer in the DAR, but also a member of the League of Women Voters and the chairman of the National Congress of Mothers.[63] While it was less exclusive than hereditary societies like the DAR, the Auxiliary was able to maintain a well-staffed headquarters in Indianapolis that could provide ample support for political organizing. And while requirements for membership were different, the Auxiliary and the DAR were brought together in the 1920s by a shared leadership that included Edith Irwin Hobart, who served as president of both the DAR and the American Legion Auxiliary.[64] Almost immediately after the establishment of the Auxiliary, its president challenged her organization's rank-and-file to devote more funds in order to take "a leading part in combating the influences of those who through intent or indifference are a menace to our nation." In 1923, she singled out native-born Americans, faulting them for promoting "the menace rife in the wave of pacifism, social unrest and destructive criticism of our institutions."[65]

Despite the different histories, missions, and memberships of the DAR and the American Legion Auxiliary, the specter of radicalism stirred similar passions within both groups. Their members were convinced that a revolution would be devastating to women and children. They took the testimony offered by the Overman Committee as evidence that a radical takeover would render women destitute and sexually violated.[66] These women were convinced that if radicals assumed power, they would punish anyone who achieved even a modest level of material comfort. They warned that anyone who owned a home, an automobile or a savings account would suffer. As enemies of "civilization and Christianity," radicals hoped to abolish property rights, inheritance, religion, government, and patriotism.[67] Only manual laborers would escape the immediate violence engendered by the abolition of private property. All Americans would suffer, however, once revolutionaries ushered in a reign of terror against the family in order to overthrow traditional domesticity. "The modern savages, the modern Attilas of destruction," according to Maxwell, "are storming the citadel of the Home."[68] The *Woman Patriot* asserted that radicals would destroy the family by "endowing motherhood" so that husbands would no longer be responsible for women and children.[69] In the postrevolutionary society they feared, no man would be free to "live secure with [his] own wife who shall 'cleave to [him] alone'"; parents would be denied the freedom to "watch over, care for, educate and bring up" their children.[70] Once radicals destroyed the institutions most essential to women, home and church, the misery would become acute for those members of the middle and upper class who survived the initial revolutionary purge. These conservative women envisioned a new social order that would no longer honor women's traditional social roles and strip away the customs that provided them with both protection and social authority. They believed that women who supported any form of radicalism were "helping to braid the rope which, if it is ever finished, will surely hang them."[71]

A sense of the precarious nature of their own security drove conservative women to fight radicalism. They believed that capitalism allowed women to devote themselves to the home, ignoring the fact that most working-class women were forced to work for wages. Radicals, they asserted, would make women more vulnerable to the whims of men by undermining the institution of marriage. By this logic, religion and law forced men to protect and care for women. "Feminism and Socialism," asserted antisuffragist Charlotte Rowe, "rob men of their responsibilities and women of their immunities." She warned that "if women are taught to despise and sneer at the mission of womanhood and seek the careers of men, it means the debasement of Christian ideas and the introduction of Socialism."[72] Women bore responsibility for raising children and faced structural inequities that made it difficult for them to earn a living wage in the workplace. Conservative women could not envision a society in which these factors would not limit a woman's ability to be economically independent; they did not relish the idea of being cast on the mercy of an unreliably munificent state. Tales of communist outrages became their rallying cries. In *Red Fog*, Maxwell reported that marriage in Soviet Russia "involves less thought and responsibility than going to the movies. IT IS DEGRADING!" She claimed that women in the Bolshevik state were "tragic in their desire for security instead of freedom."[73]

The success of the Bolshevik Revolution transformed the political outlook of women who embraced a conservative political identity during the 1920s. They built a movement that was bolstered by female enfranchisement, which demanded that conservative women jettison any ambivalence about sustained political engagement. Antisuffragists took this fact to heart and resolved to undermine the claims of progressive women to represent all women. Mary Kilbreth, the last president of the National Association Opposed to Woman Suffrage (NAOWS), vowed to fight the feminist remaking of politics imagined by female reformers. "The best way to have defeated Feminism would have been to have prevented woman suffrage," Kilbreth conceded in 1921. "But . . . Anti-Feminists [cannot] submit to the Sex Revolution simply because suffrage forces have succeeded in crossing a boundary line."[74] Suffragists, asserted Kilbreth, had turned to lobbying in order to "establish vast Feminist Bureaucracies," which could "be used as in the Russian Propaganda System, as channels of Revolution."[75] Kilbreth claimed that "by appointments and the expansion of Federal bureaucracy," women reformers were determined to "obtain a sinister propaganda power far more potent than any legitimate power they could exercise in the polling booth."[76]

The seeming popularity of Sheppard-Towner did not discourage the antisuffragists associated with the *Woman Patriot*. In 1922, the group issued what became a widely distributed manifesto, "Organizing Revolution Through Women and Children," that outlined the philosophy that would shape its newspaper for the rest of the decade.[77] The article focused on the connections drawn by Friedrich Engels between the private family and private property, building on his assertion that revolution would not be complete without the emancipation of women. The *Woman Patriot* reversed Engels's logic, claiming that weakening the patriarchal family structure laid the foundation for revolution. Radicals in the United States, the publication asserted, had decided that "communism can be accomplished as *surely* by poisonous propaganda against the family as by armed uprisings against private property."[78]

According to the scheme explained by the *Woman Patriot*, radicals hoped to undermine the family by eliminating its usefulness as an economic unit; to that end, they promoted the "social 'care for all children, legal or illegal'" and "'endowment of motherhood' so that the 'proleterian' wife becomes 'economically independent' of her 'bourgeois' husband." Though federal programs providing aid to mothers and national laws restricting child labor were designed by reformers to strengthen the traditional family, the *Woman Patriot* countered that such programs disrupted this institution, loosening paternal control as women looked to the state, rather than individual men, for guidance and support. State provisions for women and children, the publication argued, would free former breadwinners to become militant opponents of political and economic exploitation. Once the sanctity of the family had been compromised, private property was no longer safe. "Private property and the private family began together and must stand or fall together," the publication declared, though it failed to elucidate how the disintegration of one would necessarily lead to the destruction of the other. It asserted instead a simple conceptual connection: "the State that takes over the care of a man's *wife and child* will never scruple to take over possession of *his house and lot*."[79]

While a weakened family was a harbinger of revolution, its destruction would be the inevitable outcome of a radical takeover. The recent history of Russia, the *Woman Patriot* claimed, demonstrated that the family would be the first institution attacked by radicals. Inspired by the anti-Bolshevik propaganda popularized by the Overman Committee in 1919, the newspaper took its interpretation of the Russian Revolution from the committee's declaration that "the apparent purpose of the bolshevik government is to make the Russian citizen, and *especially the women and children, the wards and dependents of that government.*" According to the Overman Committee, the revolutionary regime had "destroyed the natural ambition and made impossible of accomplishment the moral obligation of *the father to provide, care for, and adequately protect the child of his blood and the mother of that child* against the misfortunes of orphanhood and widowhood." Throughout the decade, the newspaper kept the spirit of these hearings alive, illuminating the specific horrors of revolution for women and children. The publication reprinted accounts from visitors to the Soviet Union and quotes from "authentic" communist documents to illustrate how women had borne the brunt of the revolutionary fury. One of its most often quoted denunciations of the revolution came from Professor Boris Sokoloff, a Russian socialist who reportedly condemned the new regime's treatment of children. He alleged that children were cared for collectively in Russia, a system he called "positively criminal and worthy of the most savage tribes of the African jungle." Sokoloff, according to the *Woman Patriot*, declared that "the crime knows no parallel in the history of the world. They have destroyed morally as well as physically a whole Russia generation."[80]

In this version of the Bolshevik overthrow, the principal villain was Soviet feminist and sex radical Alexandra Kollontai. In fact, Kollontai was a utopian Marxist and committed revolutionary who strove to improve the lot of women and children. Named as the architect of Soviet family policy, Kollontai routinely drew blame from the *Woman Patriot* for all the devastation, starvation, and suffering caused by years of war, famine, and revolution. In reality, Lenin had chosen Kollontai to head the Commissariat for Social Welfare after the 1917 Revolution. In this position, she mandated state support for mothers and children from the time of conception through the first year of life. Kollontai also demanded a reformed marriage code and legal and political equality for women, principles that the new state quickly espoused. In 1922, under fire from other revolutionaries who were suspicious of her feminism and jealous of her power, Kollontai left the Soviet Union to serve as a diplomat. She lived abroad until the 1940s, returning to Moscow shortly before her death in 1952.[81]

The *Woman Patriot* tied American female reformers to Kollontai, citing a Children's Bureau examination of maternity benefits that referred to a study authored by the Soviet radical. This was clear evidence, according to "Organizing Revolution Through Women and Children," that American reformers had modeled their Russian-style programs on Kollontai's philosophy, even if there was no direct link between the Soviet woman and the Children's Bureau. "Is there an organic connection between Kollontay [*sic*] and the Communists at Moscow and the extreme feminist demands in America," the article inquired, "or are Communism and Feminism, as separate bodies, pulling together in natural conjunction?" Children's Bureau chief Julia Lathrop was baffled by allegations that her policies had been shaped by a woman she did not know. She was forced to turn to the Library of Congress for help in identifying Kollontai.[82]

Using "radical" and "feminist" as synonyms, the publication applied these terms to a host of women who were neither. Well-known social worker Jane Addams, federal Women's Bureau head Mary Anderson, Women's Trade Union League president Margaret Dreier Robins, and the reformist administrators of the Children's Bureau were consciously promoting socialist programs, the article claimed. These leaders were deceiving the majority of American women, who were innocently working as the agents of their own destruction. "Communists cover their revolutionary program today with *flowery language* and beautiful slogans, like 'No More War,' 'Peace and Freedom,' 'Social Welfare,'" the article explained, "so that *women* may be led *to work for Communism* while believing they are working for themselves and their children." Like antiradicals who denounced the peace movement, the *Woman Patriot* claimed that communists were relying on women to lay the groundwork for a new American revolution.[83]

The charges of the *Woman Patriot* obviously echo those leveled against the peace movement at the same time: a few radically inspired leaders with ties to Moscow were leading the vast body of innocent women, who were blindly taking the nation closer to a revolution that carried disastrous consequences for them and their children. Kilbreth's family background makes it somewhat surprising that she identified social welfare activists rather than peace advocates as the most important agents of impending revolution. Reared in an elite New York family, she split her time during the 1920s between her country home in the wealthy summer colony of Southampton, New York, and a small flat in Washington, D.C., that she shared with her brother, John William Kilbreth, Jr., an army officer and Harvard University graduate. As his sister was establishing herself as a lobbyist and propagandist, John was becoming ever more deeply disturbed by plummeting military appropriations, which he feared had ruined the nation's defense.[84] With this intimate connection to the postwar turmoil within the

U.S. military, Kilbreth might easily have gone the way of many women in hereditary and veterans' organizations who shared her fear of revolution but mobilized primarily to neutralize women peace activists. Maintaining that "the only way to establish a Red Dictatorship in this country is to disarm America first," Kilbreth agreed with antiradicals like Lucia Ramsey Maxwell. When Maxwell composed the Spider Web Chart, she dedicated one copy of her diagram to Kilbreth with "appreciation of her work."[85] Yet Kilbreth saw herself primarily as an antifeminist. Believing that feminism paved the way for socialism, and thus revolution, she focused on blocking legislation aimed at women and children that she feared would undermine the sanctity of the family. Also deeply antisemitic and xenophobic, Kilbreth endorsed legislation that choked immigration to the United States to a trickle during the 1920s.[86]

Kilbreth was joined on the board of the WPPC by four other women. From the antisuffrage stronghold of Massachusetts, the board drew a trio appalled by female enfranchisement: Margaret Robinson, wife of a Harvard University botany professor; Katherine Balch, married to a businessman; and Harriet Frothingham, whose husband was a Boston lawyer. From Baltimore, another hot spot for antisuffrage agitation, came antifeminist Cornelia Andrews Gibbs, widow of food-packaging magnate Rufus M. Gibbs.[87] These five women steered the publication's editorial content, most likely depending on frequent contributions from Kilbreth and Robinson, the most prolific writers in the group. The bulk of the newspaper's text, however, was probably composed by J. S. Eichelberger, the newspaper's full-time, male editor, who occasionally testified before Congress, but largely limited his activism to writing at the *Woman Patriot*. Except for Kilbreth, the WPPC board members were either wealthy widows or the wives of professional men, prosperous enough to provide most of the newspaper's financial support. This burden was not inconsiderable since publication costs exceeded subscription revenues by an average of $6,000 a year. Accepting no advertising, the publication also relied on occasional gifts from subscribers and sponsors as well as support from regional groups such as the Massachusetts Public Interests League, the Boston-based women's group whose history paralleled the *Woman Patriot*'s evolution from antisuffrage to antiradical organization during the 1920s. In 1924, Kilbreth claimed a circulation of 3,000 for the *Woman Patriot*, a figure that probably went up in the latter half of the decade.[88] In any case, the publication's core readership was antisuffragists who had turned to antiradicalism after the ratification of the Nineteenth

Amendment. They were women active in the Massachusetts Public Interests League, the Maryland Federation of Democratic Women, and sundry chapters of the Women's Constitutional League.

In their drive to thwart the "feminist program of revolution by legislation," Robinson, Balch, Frothingham, and Gibbs combined their work with the WPPC with leadership of locally based female antiradical organizations.[89] Robinson served as president of the Massachusetts Public Interests League, which also benefited from the prominent support of both Balch and Frothingham. Balch also was an officer of the Sentinels of the Republic, a mixed-sex Massachusetts group well known for vigorous opposition to the child labor amendment and support for the doctrine of states' rights; Frothingham was part of the Advisory Council of the Key Men of America, also a mixed-sex group. The Key Men were headed by well-known antiradical Fred Marvin and were devoted in large part to distributing the former journalist's sensationalist exposés of radical activity in the United States.[90] In Maryland, Gibbs participated in the DAR, while leading the conservative Federation of Democratic Women and the Women's Constitutional League, another antisuffrage turned antiradical organization.[91] Kilbreth's association with the WPPC was best known, but she also worked with the Sentinels of the Republic and the Massachusetts Public Interests League.[92]

The women of the WPPC were ill-equipped to mobilize large numbers of women behind their concerns about social welfare legislation. In the first few years of the decade, relatively few women were prepared to follow the lead of Elizabeth Lowell Putnam and repudiate decades of support for "maternalist" reforms. Many conservative clubwomen, however, did not have the same reserve of goodwill for the peace movement that elicited such passionate enthusiasm after the Great War. They watched with alarm as female activists demanded a diminished military and expanded cooperation with other nations, in the hopes of preserving the world's fragile peace after the armistice. They were convinced that women who demanded disarmament and international reconciliation were simply "tools of the Bolsheviki, the revolutionary radicals and Communists."[93] Pacifists, according to these women, were "gnawing away at the foundations of our Army and Navy. Why? To leave the country defenseless when the social revolutionists get out their rifles."[94]

Antimilitarism had not always elicited such hostility from the groups that would dedicate themselves to neutralizing the women's peace movement. During the first decades of the twentieth century, the DAR followed the lead of other women's clubs on this issue. The group had enthusiastically supported arbitration for the settlement of international conflicts and called on the country to guard against the overemphasis of the military in public schools.[95] In 1915, when Jane Addams founded the Woman's Peace Party—the precursor to WILPF—some of its charter members were also prominent in the DAR.[96] That same year, the chairman of the DAR international peace arbitration committee, Mrs. Henry Cook, reminded members to exercise their special influence as mothers to inculcate resistance to militarism among children. "When we remember that every man who has gone to war or has raised his voice in favor of war is some mother's son, it brings home to us how great has been woman's responsibility for the wars that have been and how great her opportunity for lessening the chances of future wars," she said. Cook had voiced an opinion that would be denounced as subversive by the organization ten years later.[97] Once the United States entered the war, opinion shifted within the DAR to favor universal military training and "adequate" defense. But like most of the other major women's organizations, the DAR again took up peace immediately after World War I, supporting international cooperation and the League of Nations even when the Senate rejected it.[98] In 1921, the DAR played host to the Conference on Limitation of Armament at Memorial Continental Hall in Washington, and endorsed the aims of the gathering.[99]

That same year, however, the president of the DAR "repudiated pacifism and all its visionary folly."[100] President General Anne Rogers Minor encouraged her members to see how what she regarded as the foolish idealism of peace activism was advancing the cause of global revolution. The idea that "all men should have equality of possessions" was a "spirit of evil in our midst" that was growing "under the mask of peace and freedom movements," she said.[101] "Pacifists, socialists, internationalists of a certain type—all are working together" for disarmament, she claimed, since "national defense means safety against the hoped-for world revolution and the dawn of the new day."[102] The next year the convention reiterated its belief in "sane and sound military preparedness against war which is not to be confused with militarism." The women present vowed to do "all in our power to withstand and expose all pacifistic efforts to weaken our defenses under cover of appeals for that world peace which we all desire."[103] Minor and her followers saw military force and vigorous countersubversion efforts as the only sure protection against the misery and suffering that would accompany a radical overthrow.

Conservative clubwomen began to see themselves as the only people who could effectively combat female peace activists. Leaders of the DAR, the Daughters of 1812, the Woman's Department of the National Civic Federation, and the Women's Overseas Service League and the American Legion Auxiliary made the decision to launch a campaign to erase the impression that all women citizens "felt as these radicals and extreme pacifists."[104] Their increasingly strident pronouncements would complement the efforts of the women associated with the *Woman Patriot*, who were already working to undercut the moral authority claimed by female peace activists. After losing their fight to defeat Sheppard-Towner, the publication's board members remained active on Capitol Hill. In 1922, they appeared at a Senate appropriation committee hearing on the War Department budget. Margaret Robinson, president of the Massachusetts Public Interests League, denounced the work of "women pacifists to render our country helpless before attack." Cornelia Gibbs, the secretary of the Maryland-based Women's Constitutional League, called on senators to listen to "real women of this country, who are not pacifists. They are not Socialists. They are not internationalists."[105]

The vigorous militarism articulated by both the DAR and the American Legion Auxiliary during the 1920s fit into the founding mission of these organizations, which included a commitment to honor the patriotism of those who had served in the American military. Both organizations aimed to sanctify the sacrifices of American veterans. Their public tributes were calculated to enhance their own political authority, emphasizing their relationship to proven patriots. Members of hereditary societies declared that they had inherited the qualities that allowed the nation to thrive; the women from veterans' groups, by contrast, contended that they had earned their patriotic credentials by nurturing those who had been willing to make the supreme sacrifice for their country. This construction of female citizenship can be traced back to the Spartan mother described first by Greek philosopher Plutarch and later celebrated by French enlightenment thinker Jean-Jacques Rousseau. Rousseau held Spartan mothers up as ideal citizens, recounting how they were eager to sacrifice their male relatives for military combat. When civic duty called, these women showed no grief at loss of life. They rejoiced only in victory and the honor of service. In the years after World War I, women in veterans' and hereditary groups claimed that their willingness to sacrifice sons, husbands, and brothers for the sake of their country had earned them civic authority.[106] They embraced the image of a sacrificing mother that dominated World War I propaganda, celebrating women who encouraged their sons to enlist in the army, while denigrating those who had resisted military mobilization. Challenging pacifists' attempts to monopolize images of suffering mothers, antiradicals formulated a militant maternalism that demanded a strong military to protect their sons and husbands who served the country.[107] Their vision of the past drove them to embrace an often rigid and reactionary form of patriotism that demanded jingoistic support for American military and political hegemony.[108] History, current events, and a sense of clan loyalty informed the antiradical agenda of these new conservative activists, who sought to defend their ancestors' or loved ones' ideals.

With 150,000 dues-paying Daughters, the DAR was the biggest of the hereditary organizations. Its palatial headquarters in Washington showcased its wealth.[109] Yet the increasingly strident pronouncements of this large and prestigious group went largely unheeded by female reformers until the spring of 1925. Almost exactly a year after the Spider Web Chart made headlines, the DAR shocked the world of women's voluntary associations when it abruptly canceled its contract to rent its auditorium to the National Council of Women. The DAR charged that the venerable, centrist organization had embraced a radical and pacifist-inspired agenda. The NCW was preparing to host its "Quinquennial" gathering, which would bring together 200 women from thirty-six countries who were associated with the International Council of Women (ICW). NCW leaders scrambled to relocate the convention to the Washington Auditorium.[110]

The leadership of the NCW was blindsided by this rejection by the DAR. Before concerns about Bolshevism came to dominate the organization's agenda, the hereditary association had provided as much support for the NCW as more reform-oriented groups like the League of Women Voters or the General Federation of Women's Clubs. For almost forty years before this clash in Washington, both the NCW and its international counterpart, the International Council of Women, had been able to coordinate the activities of a diverse range of politically active women. These groups had been established in 1888 to unite female activists, especially suffragists and temperance workers. From the perspective of moderate reformers like longtime president and Scottish aristocrat Lady Ishbel Aberdeen, the mission of the ICW had remained unchanged since its establishment. In 1925 the International Council was still, in the words of Aberdeen, "a centre round which all women's societies and movements can gather, confer and make the voice of organized womanhood heard regarding various subjects of world interest."[111] The diversity of the NCW had limited its political effectiveness by the early 1920s, but its constituent groups still banded together under the idea that women had a unique contribution to make in public affairs that grew out of their traditional homemaking duties.

NCW president Eva Perry Moore, who was described by newspapers as a "conservative of conservatives," was herself a member of the DAR.[112] After the Spider Web Chart and the accompanying articles in the *Dearborn Independent* accused the NCW of being a hotbed of radical pacifism, Moore decided to make a sharp break with NCW tradition, which held that any group was free to join as long as it treated the other members with respect. She gave in to demands that her organization clean house and expelled WILPF from the Council in 1924.[113] Yet much to her frustration, the purge of WILPF did little to silence the conservative critics of the NCW. One outspoken opponent of the female peace movement went to Capitol Hill to testify that the NCW contained individuals "associated with organizations which are un-American, seditious and dangerous, and whose aims and objects, if carried out, would prove a menace to our Government."[114] Cornelia Ross Potts teamed up with other antiradicals to persuade the House Committee on Foreign Affairs to deny the NCW's request for $10,000 in federal funds. The DAR then deepened the organization's predicament when it called on other self-proclaimed patriotic women to pull out of the umbrella organization.[115]

Moore did everything in her power to appease antiradical concerns, but found herself powerless to prevent new conservative zeal from derailing the international meeting and ultimately destroying her organization.[116] After expelling WILPF, Moore had gone to great lengths to soothe DAR President General Cook and her officers. She even demanded prior transcripts of all the speeches to ensure that no "radical" or "pacifist" speakers would stand behind podiums in the DAR hall.[117] Moore was dumbfounded when her fellow DAR members suddenly rebuffed her efforts to satisfy their demands.[118] "Leadership of women's organizations has not fallen into the hands of radicals," she asserted with some frustration. "The conservative element is so strong in the National Council, that we are constantly urged to be more 'progressive' in meeting radical leaders possibly half way."[119]

The DAR's decision to turn against the NCW signaled that there had been a fundamental shift in the women's politics and placed Moore on the front line of a war she had not anticipated fighting. The outrage of antiradicals quickly drowned out any efforts to conduct the discussions of internationalism and the most effective way to broker peace anticipated by Quinquennial organizers. Conservatives used petitions, letters of protest, and rallies against radicalism to remain in the headlines, keeping their opposition to the ICW's "wholly pacifist program" in the public eye for months.[120] Antiradicals adopted a slash-and-burn approach as they demanded that symbolically important women's institutions demonstrate their patriotic orthodoxy.

When international delegates finally arrived in Washington in early May, the city was tense with anticipation. Any concerns about radicalism or subversion should have been laid to rest when the delegates finally convened with the U.S. Marine Band playing in the background.[121] Although the convention keynote was peace, the program showed the imprint of the veterans' organizations represented in the official U.S. delegation.[122] Far from rejecting the nationalist ideology espoused by antiradicals, convention organizers had arranged pageants to honor the military and remember the war dead. Moreover, when NCW leaders received complaints during the convention that members of the Women's Peace Society were urging delegates to sign the "slacker's oath," which pledged women to refuse to support any aspect of war, they stormed the exhibit hall. After confiscating the offending pledge forms, NCW leaders seized pamphlets condemning war as legalized murder as well as peace literature demanding a halt to all military appropriations and advocating immediate global disarmament. One of the officers claimed to be "astounded" at the discovery of this radical pacifist propaganda from the Women's Peace Union and the Women's Peace Society. Intent on protecting the Quinquennial from giving a "false impression," she joined her fellow officers in pitching the seized leaflets into an impromptu bonfire. There could be no more dramatic proof of the council's determination to avoid being used "as a vehicle for violent pacifist propaganda," according to Mrs. Nathaniel E. Harris, proxy president of the NCW.[123]

The flames of this bonfire, however, did nothing to fuel antiradical confidence in the loyalty and patriotism of NCW leaders. During the last open meeting of the convention, Cornelia Ross Potts convened a rally in the Interior Department, across the street from the site of the Quinquennial. Potts condemned the leadership of the NCW, telling the assembled protesters that the "red flag of Russia ought to be flying over the auditorium."[124] American Legion Auxiliary president Claire Oliphant complained about the foreign domination of the convention and dismissed it as an anti-American "propaganda party" and "a colossal waste of money."[125] Despite Herculean efforts by Moore, antiradicals like Potts and Oliphant prevailed, and they were pleased to take credit for hobbling the NCW. Oliphant boasted that conservatives drove it "on the rocks."[126]

The NCW disintegrated rapidly after the international delegates left Washington. The group's remaining members first tried to maintain some semblance of cooperation, considering a plan in 1926 to eliminate resolutions from its meetings and to focus on "friendly conference over the large and vital problems of American life." But even this basic level of cooperation proved too difficult in the face of conservative hostility. By 1929 only twenty-one women's groups belonged to the NCW, and by the next year all the organizations with strong national memberships had withdrawn. At the very moment the NCW entered free fall, it invited WILPF to return to its ranks.[127] The conflicts over the Quinquennial led to the almost overnight demise of the once-strong NCW.

While the conflict over pacifism and radicalism had been smoldering since the beginning of the decade, women like Eva Perry Moore never imagined that these issues would scuttle her venerable coalition. After all, the American Legion and its Auxiliary had treated the mainstays of the NCW as allies as late as 1924, when the Legion had invited the General Federation of Women's Clubs, the Woman's Christian Temperance Union, and League of Women Voters to a conference designed to coordinate "an aggressive fight to exterminate revolutionary and destructive radicalism and propaganda."[128] Before the Quinquennial, the groups that spearheaded the campaign to expose the disloyalty of the NCW had been some of the biggest supporters of female reform and had even supported women's work on behalf of international reconciliation.

These conflicts were complicated, moreover, by the fact that leaders like Moore remained committed to the basic tenets of established women's organizations like the DAR. Moore shared the hereditary association's conception of patriotism rooted in lineage as much as ideology. The patriotism of peace activists could be judged by the sacrifices of their families for the nation; the advocates of international reconciliation active in her organization had "the more enviable records for gallantry and service in wartime" when compared to their antiradical critics. Moore was unwilling to cede the territory of patriotic sacrifice staked out so aggressively by antiradical women.[129] The worlds of antiradicals and reformers overlapped at so many junctions that it made the conservative mission to quarantine "subversive" women protracted and painful. The tug of war between reformers and antiradicals kept women's organizations in turmoil for most of the 1920s. Women like

Moore were unwilling to walk away from groups in which they had invested decades of support. Yet antiradicals were unbending in their determination to ostracize women like her who refused to repudiate traditional reform activities. As a result, the confrontations between these two groups of women only became more frequent and acrimonious in the years that followed the Quinquennial.

The Spider Web Chart demonstrated that the female reform coalition that had amassed such cultural authority during the Progressive Era was under siege. Female reformers were convinced that they knew their attackers: the military officers who had been leading a crusade against female pacifists, who were determined to reshape the nation's military and foreign policy to ensure long-lasting peace. But the Spider Web Chart was created by a female activist, who used it to rally other women who feared that the United States teetered on the edge of a Bolshevik takeover. Military officers may have encouraged this somewhat unfamiliar type of activism in various ways. But ultimately their mobilization was inspired by images of women rather than entreaties from men. They were moved to action by competing visions of victimized and villainous women. Their fear, anger, and moral passion were stirred by images of women suffering the consequences of Russian radicalism juxtaposed with descriptions of the American dupes who had brought the nation to the brink of revolution. They viewed the ascendance of radicalism in gendered terms, believing that these ideologies menaced social protections for women and children. They united under a new conservative rubric that declared a strong military to be the best guardian of the domestic and religious institutions most important to women. Yet even while they looked to the military to preserve civilization, they believed that women like themselves would play an essential role in this mission of national salvation. Only women could "know what their radical sisters are doing and to warn the public of the menace of their activities."[130]

Female antiradical attacks essentially destroyed the NCW, which endured primarily in name alone after the spring of 1925. The strife in Washington baffled female reformers like Eva Perry Moore, who considered herself a conservative. These traditional club leaders could not foresee that this was only the start of a concerted campaign to marginalize the pursuit of social justice within female voluntary associations. In 1925, these efforts were still somewhat obscured by long-standing assumptions about women's political activism, even after female antiradicals began appearing on Capitol Hill, determined to demonstrate that reformers did not speak for their entire sex. Men and women from across the political spectrum still had difficulty seeing that "maternalism" was not synonymous with women's activism, even though this middle-class movement for reform was only one thread in a rich tapestry of female political engagement during the Progressive Era and beyond. This assumption proved fairly unassailable in the early 1920s, even as new conservatives began to transform the political agendas of well-established groups like the DAR, where the specter of Bolshevism banished earlier visions of a more humane society with robust government protections for women and children. And reformers continued to ignore these new female foes until faced with the fracas surrounding the NCW gathering, which demonstrated that their most challenging foes in the postsuffrage era would be other women. Not just any women, but women like themselves, who had come of age politically in the same type of female voluntary associations, only to repudiate maternalism and peace activism in order to preserve the nation from a growing radical threat.

Chapter 3

# "It Takes Women to Fight Women": The Emergence of Female Antiradicalism

As Claire Oliphant looked out over the auditorium of the Red Cross building on a February morning in 1925, she surveyed what she hoped would be the cadres of a new women's movement. The national president of the American Legion Auxiliary told the women who had gathered in Washington, D.C., for the Conference on National Defense as Peace Insurance that they carried the mantle of heroic female forebears. "Loyal American women have always come to the front in time of a national need with a smile upon their faces and a grim determination to do their part in building Christianity, civilization and the freedom we enjoy," she declared.[1] Oliphant believed that the nation had reached a crossroads. The Bolshevik triumph in Europe inspired unrest across North America; revolution loomed as a real possibility. She had organized this conference to bring together those most capable of preventing the United States from following Russia's tragic path: patriotic women who were cognizant of the Bolshevik menace. In Oliphant's opinion, the best defense against a radical overthrow was a strong military. But she saw the American military establishment as besieged by the women's peace movement. Oliphant called on the women in her audience to challenge these female activists and demonstrate that pacifists did not speak for the entire sex. This was the best way to turn the tide of public opinion against disarmament and international reconciliation.[2] "The women pacifists and women radicals of America," Oliphant said, could only be stopped by their antiradical sisters. "It takes women to fight women."[3]

After the publication of the Spider Web Chart, female antiradicals resolved to instigate highly publicized confrontations with peace activists as a way of distinguishing their own patriotic political engagement. Even before

Oliphant made her address in the winter of 1925, zealous women had already disrupted the conventions of WILPF and the National Conference on the Cause and Cure of War (NCCCW), a moderate women's coalition devoted to examining ways to ensure international peace. These altercations—like the Conference on National Defense as Peace Insurance—were meant to "show that there are women in the United States who believe in those measures for defense which are provided under the Constitution," according to Oliphant.[4] Oliphant's rally undoubtedly helped to galvanize some of the women who would go on to derail the National Council of Women's international conference, turning this global gathering into a public fracas over the proper parameters of female civic engagement. Despite the escalating attacks by female antiradicals, organizers of this international gathering in Washington, D.C., were blindsided. Only later would they realize that the campaign to sabotage their convention was simply one temblor triggered by a larger tectonic shift.

When Oliphant issued her call to arms, female antiradicals were still struggling to bring their movement out from behind the shadow cast by female reformers, whose accomplishments had made women's activism synonymous with maternalist politics in the public imagination. Female antiradicals were determined to set themselves apart from moderate reformers. They had emerged from the same social milieu and had come of age politically in the same women's organizations. But female antiradicals were jolted out of their comfortable routines by the Bolshevik Revolution and the global unrest that followed the end of the Great War. Their staged denunciations of peace activists—which won them national media attention—demonstrated their determination to transform the women's associational culture that had first nurtured their movement.

Oliphant's conference was a watershed for women's politics. It encouraged participating groups to embrace this new vision of conservatism, which had the repression of pacifism and radicalism as its top priority. These organizations went on to create internal committees charged with carrying the work of this movement forward: unveiling radicalism, supporting the foes of revolution within the military and the Department of Justice, and denouncing both the unwitting and conscious agents of Bolshevism among women's organizations. Most notable in this regard was the DAR. The DAR National Defense Committee came to define the political agenda of the entire hereditary association, which worked aggressively to purge supposedly radical influences from the respectable circles of middle-class women's politics. The DAR pushed the ideological center of women's politics to the right. Its efforts kept the world of women's clubs in turmoil for the rest of the decade.

These new institutions would allow female antiradicals to have a sustained influence on public policy. The Conference on National Defense as Peace Insurance attracted delegates claiming to represent one million women.[5] After a one-year hiatus, it reconvened in 1927 under the rubric of the "Women's Patriotic Conference on National Defense." Though it met formally only once a year over the decades that followed, this conference provided a framework for broad collaboration around antiradical political activism. While female reformers blamed the American military establishment for orchestrating the campaign against the women's peace movement, the most devastating attacks were mounted by these new networks of female activists. By establishing the same kinds of structures that had allowed reform-minded women to gain influence, conservative activists challenged assumptions about female political engagement, reshaped the world of women's clubs, and ultimately changed the trajectory of American reform.

## WILPF Under Siege

Female antiradicals had started staging public confrontations with peace activists almost a year before Oliphant made her rousing call to arms. In March 1924, after the publication of the Spider Web Chart, the peace organization WILPF became the target of a group of women associated with the Daughters of 1812, a hereditary association for descendants of the heroes of the War of 1812. WILPF had been denounced by congressional investigations, military officers, and conservative activists for its supposed pacifism and revolutionary ideals. The Daughters of 1812 joined this chorus, issuing a set of resolutions about the group's "ultra pacifism." It accused WILPF of making American women and youth into "slackers" and condemned its efforts to fan the flames of "class warfare" and revolution. The Daughters of 1812 asserted that WILPF had sanctioned "both foreign insult and aggression, leading to war and also domestic strife, riot and bloodshed." A coterie of activists associated with this group resolved to do more than speak out against the peace group. They sought to block the WILPF convention in May. Their goal was to prevent WILPF from furthering its supposedly revolutionary campaign in the city that housed the most sacred institutions of American democracy. They appealed to the police to prohibit the assemblage of peace activists and then demanded that the managers of the hotel reserved by WILPF ban the group from the premises.[6] These demands were rejected.

The ringleaders of this group—Cornelia Ross Potts and Mary Logan Tucker—were not dissuaded. On the eve of the WILPF convention, these descendants "from a long line of fighting, true-blooded Americans" convened a summit to protest pacifism, calling together women representing veterans' and hereditary groups from the District of Columbia. Hardly intimidated, members of WILPF stormed their foes' meeting. The peace activists' hisses and catcalls turned the antiradical rally into what one newspaper reporter called a "'free-for-all' battle."[7] Peace activists seized the floor to proclaim their pride in their Revolutionary War forebears, refuting the antiradical claim that having eighteenth-century patriots as ancestors compelled them to support military preparedness in 1924. Pacifists with impeccable pedigrees asserted that they too were heirs to a patriotism that placed their activism beyond reproach. According to old-stock Americans associated with WILPF, their ancestors would have been proud of their efforts to abolish war. While resisting antiradical attempts to monopolize the authority of genealogy, women peace activists also spun their own narratives of personal sacrifice. Those who had watched family members marching off to war incorporated these experiences in their appeals to abolish the military. By choosing the terrain of patriotism and lineage to fight their battles, female antiradicals and peace activists displayed their similarities as well as their differences.

This clash proved to be a dress rehearsal for the actual WILPF Congress. The peace convention opened on May 1 in a state of siege. Police armed with batons, blackjacks, and pistols stood guard in the Hotel Washington as delegates from twenty-five countries came together to discuss "A New International Order." On hand for the opening ceremony were twelve representatives of the DAR and the Daughters of 1812, their ears trained for the statements that would expose the delegates' doctrine of unadulterated radicalism and subservience to Moscow. Over the next two days, these women listened as speakers advocated outlawry of war, an end to conscription, a ban on chemical weapons, greater influence of women in determining the shape of the international order and popular control of foreign policy. On the third day of the congress, Cornelia Ross Potts, a DAR member and chapter president of the District of Columbia Daughters of 1812, could no longer sit silent. Potts jumped from her seat to interrupt WILPF president Jane Addams. "Do you advocate total disarmament and the slacker's oath?" she demanded, before her voice was drowned in hisses and applause.[8] Addams continued the program without comment. When Potts refused to take her seat, several delegates volunteered to answer her questions in the corridor. The protester led her supporters out of the auditorium en masse, where they began grilling WILPF representatives. The crowd got so combative that hotel detectives dispatched bellboys to break it up. Newspapers reprinted Potts's questions in full, along with her ultimatum to the American members of WILPF to agree to support the country in time of war and pledge to uphold the marriage vow or "get out of this country and sail for Russia or elsewhere, where you may mingle with other deluded people of the earth who have lost their national soul."[9]

This campaign to bar WILPF from the nation's capital garnered extensive media attention for the antiradical logic that linked pacifism to radicalism. When the peace activists adjourned their meeting, Potts called another assembly meant to build on this success. In early July 1924, the National Patriotic Council was born in the District of Columbia's Army and Navy Club, supported by representatives of the American Pen Women, DAR, Daughters of 1812, American Legion Auxiliary and the Massachusetts Public Interests League. Potts intended the Council to be an umbrella group that would draw organizations and individuals of both sexes together "to combat the insidious encroachment of communistic ideas in America and all ultra-pacifistic movements" and "revive in the American born the same unselfish, fervent patriotism which in the early days made us a republic." She hoped the Council would serve as a clearinghouse for information that could be used against enemies of the government. While the organization set a short term goal of fielding inquiries about suspicious individuals and groups, its long term aim was to develop a definitive list of "subversive and near-radical organizations." The Council sponsored speakers, published a newsletter, lobbied Congress and added its name to anti-radical causes, but it never succeeded in mobilizing large numbers of Americans. Although its officers included prominent DAR members and high-ranking military officers, the Patriotic Council remained little more than a soapbox for Potts, who ran the group from her Washington home, organizing regular meetings at the Willard Hotel. The group included both men and women in a period in which most activists felt more enthusiastic about working in single-sex organizations. Potts herself might have had limited patience or talents for organizing a lobbying group. In any case, the Patriotic Council did not become the force Potts had predicted. Still, Potts remained in the public eye, thanks to her sustained campaigns against perceived disloyalty.[10]

Six months after the protests at the WILPF convention, female antiradicals again chose a gathering of peace activists as a forum to broadcast their concerns. Demonstrating that they made little distinction between the doctrine of the reviled WILPF and more moderate peace groups, antiradicals targeted the newly created National Conference on the Cause and Cure of War (NCCCW) for their next assault. Women reformers associated with the League of Women Voters had established the NCCCW in order to bring mainstream, reform-minded women's groups into the peace movement in a way that did not endanger their reputation for patriotism and loyalty. In an effort to deflect attacks from military supporters, leaders of the new coalition specifically barred WILPF and radical pacifist organizations like the Women's Peace Society. In the wake of the Spider Web Chart and the battles at the WILPF convention, the women behind the NCCCW hoped that quarantining these controversial groups would inoculate their organizations from the red taint. Moreover, they tapped former suffragist Carrie Chapman Catt to lead the new group. Catt had already shown she was no pacifist. In 1917, the suffrage leader offered President Woodrow Wilson the services of the National American Woman Suffrage Association for the war effort. This gesture got her drummed out of the New York branch of the Woman's Peace Party, the precursor to WILPF. Following the war she continued to distance herself from WILPF and privately regarded their platform as impractical.[11] Catt envisioned a women's peace movement that could revive the spirit of the suffrage campaign. To this end, she recruited women's social, professional, and reform groups interested in studying the underlying causes of war but chary of direct action campaigns. Keeping WILPF out in the cold, she believed, would stop antiradical attacks. Like the leaders of the WJCC who had expelled WILPF in 1922, Catt assumed that her disavowals of the controversial peace group would make her consortium attractive to conservative women. But antiradicals were intent on purging any hint of internationalism from women's politics and refused to acknowledge Catt's efforts to distance the NCCCW from more radical peace activists. Denunciations of even these moderate peace activists won antiradicals more publicity, giving the new movement a sense of both mission and accomplishment.

Turnout at the first NCCCW meeting showed the strength of women's enthusiasm for peace: 900 delegates assembled in Washington from groups like the General Federation of Women's Clubs, Young Women's Christian Association (YWCA), WCTU, and League of Women Voters. The January 1925 gathering was designed to unite a majority of politically active women in a rational study of world conflict. Catt's goal was political education rather than inspirational mobilization. Hoping to undermine stereotypes of women as sentimental pacifists, Catt called on delegates to offer dispassionate analysis. She wanted them to suppress the evangelical fervor manifested in "emotional appeals made from the floor . . . pouring forth of noble sentiments, pious hopes, fervent dismays over the futility of war."[12] To achieve an appropriately dry tone, Catt recruited mostly male "experts" as speakers. To emphasize that antimilitarism would find no home in the NCCCW, she slated two military officers to speak to the conference. This pragmatic inquiry into the origins of war, according to Catt, was nonideological. "It is not radical, nor is yet conservative," she declared. "It is constructive."[13]

The avowedly moderate tenor of the conference did nothing to dissipate the "hostility everywhere about us," Catt later recalled. Critics descended on the NCCCW with the same vitriolic attacks that had rocked WILPF. "Later it was whispered that our meeting had received money for its expenses from Moscow," Catt complained.[14] Haviland Lund, the woman who had first distributed Maxwell's Spider Web Chart, was among those who monitored the proceedings. The day after the close of the NCCCW, Lund called a meeting of antipacifists to expose what she believed were the subversive underpinnings of Catt's new group. Approximately seventy-five members of the American Legion Auxiliary, the American War Mothers, and the Women's Relief Auxiliary gathered at the New Willard Hotel to hear Lund blame the women's coalition for letting loose a "deluge of propaganda." Lund's denunciations were followed by warnings from a man she identified simply as Captain Harold Spencer. Spencer asked the assemblage of antipacifists to ponder whether the NCCCW was part of a "plan . . . that will mean a destruction of the United States if we don't arouse ourselves."[15] Spencer was, for the most part, preaching to the choir. Yet his charge provoked at least one challenge from the floor. "I am not a pacifist," countered a delegate to the NCCCW from Boston, who also declared her antipathy to socialism. From the perspective of a moderate, she testified, the proceedings of the NCCCW were "fair" and "impartial."[16]

Other participants in the first NCCCW did not share this certitude. This first convention incited turmoil among some of the group's constituents. Catt remembered later that "some of the presidents of the organizations were kept busy placating delegates who did not like the conference nor anything that any speaker had said."[17] Skittish delegates made it impossible to reach consensus over a peace plan. The YWCA protested what it felt was the conference's overly "political" stand, while the WCTU distanced itself from pronouncements hinting of antimilitarism. The General Federation of Women's Clubs refused to line up behind the final report of the meeting, which listed 257 causes of war. The conference was flirting with pacifism in its public declaration, according to the GFWC, by failing to "sufficiently emphasize the need of preparation for security."[18].

A month after NCCCW delegates returned home, the New York state convention of the American War Mothers singled out Carrie Chapman Catt and the NCCCW for special censure when it condemned the women's peace movement.[19] In describing the NCCCW, the president of the American Legion Auxiliary asserted that "extreme pacifist and radical literature" saturated the conference, which was dominated "almost entirely by foreign speakers."[20] These false charges proved impossible for Catt to dismiss. The peace leader was shocked to discover that her moderate and pragmatic conference had been afforded no more credibility than the WILPF convention. Her efforts to distinguish herself from such "radicals" and "subversives" had come to naught.[21] Indeed, moderates ended up exacerbating divisions among women. Moreover, the aggressively centrist stance of the NCCCW produced no great political victories. Although the coalition endured until World War II and eventually encompassed eleven organizations representing five million women, it neither inspired an upsurge in peace activism nor sparked new legislative initiatives to end war.[22]

### The Women's Patriotic Conference on National Defense

In the aftermath of Catt's peace gathering, the president of the American Legion Auxiliary decided that women patriots needed to do more than heckle female peace activists. Claire Oliphant perceived the need for female antiradicals to organize as well as fulminate. This recognition was critical; she was later eulogized as one of the new movement's most important leaders, even though she retreated from the public eye at the end of her tenure as American Legion Auxiliary president.[23] She invited fifteen organizations—including the DAR, UDC, American War Mothers, and Daughters of 1812—to join the Auxiliary in Washington to establish what she initially called the National Defense as Peace Insurance Conference, an event that would allow the New Jersey newspaperwoman to display her skill as a mesmerizing public speaker who could paint vivid images of the perils of pacifism and radicalism.

The February 1925 conference would formalize both the ideological and human connections that knit these groups together, as many women who became animated by antiradicalism belonged to several of the participating organizations. As a coalition took shape out of this meeting, it helped women find more substantial outlets for their concerns than episodic public excoriations of women they deemed treasonous. It would also raise the visibility of antiradicalism. Up until this moment, the movement had been entirely subsumed within women's groups that had only recently embraced the campaign against Bolshevism.

The proceedings of the first national defense conference were scripted to demonstrate why women, especially conservative women, belonged in the public sphere. Conference delegates made an emotional pilgrimage to the Tomb of the Unknown Soldier at Arlington, Virginia. The wreath-laying ceremony mobilized the spirit and image of fallen soldiers to justify women's increased political participation, wrapping the Nineteenth Amendment in patriotic bunting. As "the women most intimately in touch with the great sacrifice you made," Oliphant promised the unknown soldier, "we pledge you that those things for which you gave your life shall live and we will continue in your memory to serve as you served the Nation we love."[24] Moreover, Oliphant laid claim to female citizenship by highlighting the sacrifices made by women in hereditary and veterans' organizations. The nation's wars had required these women to give "of their flesh and blood . . . their very protection." Wars had required services and sacrifices of women that earned them civic authority on traditionally male issues of foreign policy and national defense. The Auxiliary leader reinforced gender stereotypes by invoking traditional female roles. She addressed those paying homage to the war dead as mothers and wives who had been robbed of male protection.[25] Yet she hoped to open new political horizons for her sex. Women themselves needed to recognize, she asserted, that they were full citizens thanks to the vote. This new responsibility brought them the power and responsibility to exercise vigilance against national threats.

Oliphant was able to manipulate assumptions about feminine nationalism in innovative ways that established the legitimacy of a woman's national defense gathering.[26] She worked to disrupt the claim that antimilitarism grew naturally out of the maternal instincts shared by all women, regardless of whether they were mothers. She sought to demonstrate why a weakened military would fail those responsible for giving and sustaining life. The conference, she claimed, would unite women who found common cause through their shared sacrifice, "those women who have known, either in this or past generations, the intimate touch of war."[27] Oliphant invoked the propaganda and commemorations of World War I, which had represented the sacrifices of mothers as the highest form of female patriotic duty. These were the women, she claimed, who were best "qualified to speak on the need for adequate defense as the best method of insuring peace and international justice."[28]

The convention concluded with only a limited commitment to collaboration around carefully defined goals. It produced neither a sweeping platform nor a fiery manifesto. Instead, the delegates called for generous funding for national defense, calling on Congress to raise appropriations to the levels specified by the National Defense Act of 1920. They also demanded the continuation of the Reserve Officers' Training Corps and the Citizens' Military Training Camps.[29] Yet even these cautious resolutions signaled a new era in middle-class women's politics. Until this point, progressive organizations had dominated public policy discussions among women. This antiradical coalition sought to supplant this influence. Leading antiradicals envisioned the convention of "women patriots" as a healthy counterweight to the NCCCW and WJCC. Ultimately it would serve as an institutional base that female conservatives could use to remake women's politics. Besides facilitating political cooperation among female hereditary and veterans' associations, it provided guidance to leaders who sought to translate anxieties about radicalism into a public policy agenda for conservative clubwomen. After a hiatus of one year, this coalition would reemerge as the Women's Patriotic Conference on National Defense (WPCND) in 1927. It met annually into the Cold War, bringing together delegates from member organizations to listen to speeches from other activist women and male military leaders. Participants then reported back to their local chapters to school other women in the proper patriotic positions on national defense and foreign policy.

Oliphant's organization enjoyed long-term success because it conformed to the established culture of women's politics, even as it broke new ideological ground. Oliphant's apocalyptic rhetoric followed the traditions of women's politics, in which leaders normally framed political activism as a righteous crusade.[30] The coalition was designed to destroy the illusion of gender solidarity. But this sex-segregated coalition did not abandon either the institutions or forms of middle-class women's politics, which meant that its meetings felt familiar to veterans of female associational culture. This set the WPCND apart from other efforts to mobilize conservative women. The Republican Party, for instance, sought to co-opt women, without allowing them to influence the direction of the male-dominated party.[31] And the National Patriotic Council, which had been founded by Cornelia Ross Potts at the height of antiradical protests against WILPF to encourage antiradical activism, attempted to bring men and women together in the fight against radicalism.

NCCCW leader Carrie Chapman Catt recognized the familiar structure of this new coalition and sought to portray it as just another meeting of middle-class clubwomen. As part of an effort to contain the disruptive potential of the WPCND, Catt attended the Washington gathering of female antiradicals, nodding congenially for the press as speakers railed against disarmament.[32] Yet antiradicals rejected Catt's efforts to cast the WPCND as a complementary addition to existing women's coalitions. After the conference was finished, the American Legion Auxiliary made it clear that the purpose of the conference was to undermine even moderate peace organizations like the NCCCW. The group denounced the women reformers in the NCCCW as foes, boasting that the WPCND had been "a powerful obstacle in the pathway of the pacifists and radicals."[33]

The first half of 1925 saw another institutional watershed for female antiradicalism. In April, delegates at the national convention of the DAR voted to establish the National Defense Committee, another entity that played an essential role in sustaining and shaping the larger movement of female antiradicalism.[34] The work of this committee would reverberate well beyond the ranks of this hereditary association, especially in the WPCND. The National Defense Committee was created with encouragement from DAR president general Lora Haines Cook, who warned that "under the guise of peace, the radicals are carrying on their work, trying to undermine the Constitution and the foundation of our Government." The committee was assigned to defend the nation from enemies "from without and enemies from within the Republic," especially "Moscow International Communist organizations." Radicals, the founding resolution continued, are "sweeping thousands of unsuspecting pacifists into co-operation with the Communist program, camouflaged as 'measures for peace' for the purpose of appeal, but in reality paving the way for red revolution."[35]

The DAR committee did not get off the ground until the spring of 1926, when Grace Hall Lincoln Brosseau won election as president general. Brosseau earmarked $1,000 in discretionary funds for the work of the National

Defense Committee and appointed her compatriot Flora Walker as chairman.[36] Brosseau, in her mid-fifties at the time of her election, was a native of Illinois and had attended Davenport Business College in Iowa.[37] She recounted later that she had worked as a journalist and writer in Davenport; it remains unclear, however, whether this was a hobby or a paid vocation. In any case, she did not have much time to develop a career. At the age of eighteen, she settled into a life as the wife of an industry baron after marrying Alfred J. Brosseau.[38] Her husband's position as president of Mack Trucks and a leader in the automobile industry kept the couple for many years in Michigan; later they moved to the New York City area, where they maintained residences both on Park Avenue and in Greenwich, Connecticut. Although Brosseau had been active in DAR chapters in the Midwest, she became known in the organization for her work in New York. She headed a committee to improve conditions for immigrants at Ellis Island. Though she favored substantial restrictions on immigration, Brosseau worked to give foreigners a warm welcome. Like the organization she represented, Brosseau viewed as complementary immigration restrictions and programs to assimilate new arrivals. The DAR went to great efforts to reach out and "Americanize" immigrants, to help them shed suspicious foreign customs and ideologies.[39]

Brosseau's generous donations to the DAR also attracted notice. To honor his wife, Mr. Brosseau gave a silver reproduction of the Declaration of Independence to Memorial Continental Hall. The couple also contributed $25,000 to finance Constitution Hall, the auditorium that the Daughters added to their headquarters in 1929. Brosseau's success in raising money for this project helped propel her through the ranks of the organization. This climb culminated in her 1926 election as its national leader.[40]

Although she was wealthy and socially prominent, Brosseau was cut from a different cloth than many previous DAR leaders. She was an ideologue, preferring politics over fashion and organizing over socializing. Grace and Alfred Brosseau used philanthropy to advance the conservative political agenda they shared, granting large sums to educational institutions that met their ideological criteria. During her highly contentious three-year term as DAR president general, Brosseau's work in hereditary and patriotic organizations played an increasing role in her life. Her thirty-year partnership with her husband was disintegrating during this period. In 1930 she filed for divorce, citing "intolerable cruelty" and alleging that her husband had beaten her while she was president general. Although she claimed to have lived happily with her husband until 1928, her dedication to a range of hereditary organizations during the 1920s, especially the DAR, took her away from home for weeks at a time. The DAR may have given her a support network that allowed her to break away from an abusive husband. Or perhaps her long absences took a toll on what had become a troubled marriage.[41]

As her marriage dissolved, Brosseau drew closer to Flora Walker, who became her partner in antiradical activism and an intimate friend. Brosseau first teamed up with Walker in 1923, when both women won national offices in the DAR. Having cut her teeth in the Washington State DAR, Walker joined President General Cook's cabinet as organizing secretary general and worked alongside Brosseau, who remained treasurer general until 1926. Walker immediately began to use her national DAR office as a platform for her concerns about subversion. She delivered speeches on "the Red Menace in America."[42] Walker, who hailed from a comfortable yet more modest background than Brosseau, immediately earned a reputation as a tireless worker and was chosen by Cook to accompany her on national tours of the organization. Energetic and fashionable, with a penchant for stylish dresses and tailored suits, Walker was a charismatic organizer and a powerful speaker. Walker had a more professional bent than women who donated their way to prominence in the DAR. Like many of the women who devoted themselves full-time to female reform organizations during this period, she used the DAR to build a name for herself as an expert on social concerns. For Walker, the question of radicalism overshadowed all other issues in American life.[43]

Walker's focus on Bolshevism most likely grew out of her personal history in Seattle, Washington. In the years surrounding the Great War, this city had been rocked by the rise of working-class radicalism. The local labor movement helped to polarize the region politically when it endorsed the 1917 Bolshevik Revolution. But local militancy reached its apogee with the declaration of a general strike in 1919. As a Seattle resident and wife of a local businessman, Walker witnessed this conflict firsthand. William Walker owned Pantoriam Dye Works and was a member of the city's Chamber of Commerce. This association of local business leaders conspired with government and military officials to mount a campaign of repression against union organizing and radical agitation in their community. News of the impending strike inspired business leaders like Walker to organize a Citizens' Committee to provide "law and order" during the protest. Besides watching her husband work with other business leaders to derail the labor action, Flora must have joined other families in her neighborhood in the race to stock up on food, medicine, water, and guns. Seattle residents were encouraged to treat the walkout like a wartime siege. Once the strike began, women in Flora's situation barricaded their doors against what they believed to be the class uprising outside.[44]

This firsthand experience with working-class militancy may have determined Walker's vocation. The woman leader was certainly influenced by witnessing what she believed to be a city on the brink of revolution. Seattle's labor movement was quickly decimated by the combined efforts of vigilantes, business leaders, and government authorities. Yet even as the immediate threat of revolution receded, Walker began amassing a national reputation for her antiradical zeal. She became identified as a vigorous crusader against all types of radicalism, using the DAR to nurture a larger conservative movement that would allow her to showcase her remarkable organizing talents. By the time Brosseau appointed her chairman of the National Defense Committee in 1926, Walker had settled in the nation's capital permanently. She may have broken with her husband at this point; like her friend Brosseau, Walker was divorced by 1930.[45] This shared experience no doubt drew the two colleagues and friends closer. They vacationed together for years. Walker continued as an antiradical propagandist and organizer in these later years, when she translated the national notoriety she developed as National Defense chairman into a career in conservative politics.[46]

During the summer of 1926, Brosseau and Walker scanned the country for Daughters who could carry on national defense work at state and local levels. The two women were persuasive and tireless organizers; a majority of chapters in Georgia and Michigan, for instance, almost immediately began supporting the work of the National Defense Committee.[47] The Washington headquarters supplied chapters with literature to spread the gospel of antiradicalism. Walker used the local representatives of the National Defense Committee to muster rank-and-file members against "Communism, Bolshevism, Socialism, 'Liberalism' and Ultra-Pacifism." All these "movements" would end civilization if they amassed enough power; their goal was to abolish "government, patriotism, property right, inheritance, religion, and family relations."[48] Once local women had grasped antiradical ideology, Walker pushed them to find practical ways to address the danger. She distributed a questionnaire in 1927 that suggested new avenues for work and inquired, "Has your Chapter made a study of how and through what channels un-American propaganda is being spread through their communities?"[49]

Brosseau and Walker built up the committee at the national level as well. Walker solicited an additional $500 to supplement her initial grant.

Delegates to the annual convention voted to appropriate at least $2,000 for the committee's work in 1927.[50] The next year, the DAR congress assessed a ten-cent levy on every member to fund the committee's work.[51] In 1930, the organization voted to raise this levy to fifteen cents.[52] While the national officers never succeeded in collecting these dues from every chapter, the committee would have had a budget of over $25,000 by 1930 if every member had contributed.[53] The funds that were collected made it possible for the marble-pillared Memorial Continental Hall to become one of the most important nuclei of female antiradicalism. From the office of the National Defense Committee on the National Mall, Walker directed political research and disseminated the committee's findings through correspondence, interviews with the press, and meetings with visitors to the building. She set an intense pace for her volunteers and a growing staff of paid employees who surveyed both radical and antiradical activities.[54] Indefatigable and unflagging in her mission, Walker worked constantly to win new converts, addressing at least one religious, professional, or community group every week.

In the committee's monthly column in the *Daughters of the American Revolution Magazine*, Walker kept members informed about the committee's activities and different themes in the subversive propaganda her workers collected. In addition to gathering reports from rank-and-file members, National Defense Committee workers reviewed books and magazines pertinent to all aspects of radicalism, marking some passages for their files and others for distribution to local chapters. They reproduced radical literature that illuminated the threat of revolution, while also distributing antiradical propaganda that instructed readers in the best ways to prevent a Bolshevik takeover. The committee published pamphlets and wrote radio programs dealing with national defense topics. Its location in the nation's capital made it easier for its workers to lobby Congress; it coordinated letter-writing campaigns designed to influence bills on national defense, immigration, the national anthem, and the flag.[55] Walker described this lobbying in terms intended to reassure congressmen who wanted help from conservative women but worried about ceding too much power to females. "We do not presume to dictate to Congress through our newly acquired privilege at the election booths," she explained. "But we do wish to support Congressmen in obtaining the best possible protection for our homes, our red-blooded American families, our national institutions and our ever-widening commerce."[56]

For her inner council, Walker recruited like-minded prominent women from across the country. The members of the National Defense Committee were not publicly identified, since Walker and Brosseau felt the work and its agents should be kept somewhat covert. But some of the members of the National Defense Committee would become known as outspoken opponents of all forms of radicalism.[57] Helen Gould Shepard of New York, for instance, was a shrewd businesswoman and philanthropist who was part of the inner circle of the National Defense Committee and helped to bankroll its activities.[58] One of the wealthiest women in the United States, Shepard had in 1892 inherited $10 million at the death of her father, railroad baron Jay Gould. After World War I she pushed countersubversion campaigns to center stage in all the organizations in which she was active. Her wealth gave her great influence in the Daughters of 1812 and the National Society of New England Women as well as the National Civic Federation, an organization established before World War I to promote more harmonious relations between labor and capital.[59]

Shepard was serious-minded. She shunned the social whirl of elite New York in favor of charitable projects, which earned her frequent comparisons to Florence Nightingale. Personally overseeing her huge fortune, Shepard tripled her estate by 1927, all the while establishing her reputation as a generous philanthropist and ministering angel to the less fortunate. An evangelical Christian, Shepard gave freely to missionaries and religious groups that adhered to her traditional interpretation of the Bible. But some of her largest gifts were to universities, especially New York University, where she funded the construction of a library and other campus buildings at the turn of the century. Shepard also became renowned as a patron of the military. She bankrolled projects to enhance the comfort and health of soldiers and sailors and donated $100,000 in 1898 to the United States government to support the Spanish-American War. As a token of gratitude, the War Department presented her with a torpedo casing. Shepard placed the munition on the front stoop of the gray turreted castle overlooking the Hudson River that she had inherited from her father.[60]

As it had for so many women who became antiradicals, World War I spawned anxieties about disloyalty and revolution for Shepard. She gave large sums of money to the National Security League during the hostilities.[61] In the postwar period, these acute concerns eclipsed Shepard's earlier focus on philanthropy, although she continued to support innumerable causes.[62] Shepard became known as an outspoken antiradical, whose loathing of pacifist and communist-inspired movements grew out of her conviction that radicals had laid siege to both Christianity and traditional moral values, especially conventional sexual norms.[63] "The subject I have much on my heart," she explained to a DAR member who had requested that she speak at her local chapter, "is the radical propaganda . . . combined with a plea for the Bible message among Americans."[64] She incorporated political crusading into her missionary work, distributing with equal fervor tracts on evangelical Christianity and antiradical broadsides.[65] In addition to becoming a self-taught expert on conditions in the Soviet Union, Shepard studied Russian so she could read radical propaganda for herself.[66]

Shepard fused Christian evangelizing with images of violent efforts by radicals to crush traditional family life and protections for women.[67] She accused women's colleges of harboring professors determined to overturn conventional sexual mores and refused to continue to fund scholarships at the Seven Sisters schools.[68] Her charge during a speech to the Daughters of 1812 that a professor took college students on "sex trips" to learn about "free love and companionate marriage" brought her national publicity that she was eager to avoid.[69] Despite her popularity, Shepard was intent on keeping her righteous rhetoric out of the press. She routinely requested that organizations bar reporters from her talks. Shepard felt that a highly publicized antiradical campaign would mark her for retribution from radicals. In 1926, someone set fire to one of her country homes. Shepard was convinced that Moscow itself had taken notice of her work and singled her out for reprisal.[70]

From North Carolina came Margaret Overman Gregory, the daughter of Senator Lee Overman, who conducted the famous hearings in 1919 to expose the alleged crimes of Bolsheviks during the Russian Revolution. Gregory would win renown among Tar Heels for her crusades against revolutionaries, who she believed had targeted the South in particular.[71] Flora Walker's vice-chairman and right-hand assistant was a woman whose personal experience with Bolshevism had made her into a zealous antiradical. Born in the White House, the granddaughter of Civil War general and president Ulysses Grant, Julia Dent Grant moved from the ranks of the American political aristocracy into European nobility when she married Count Speransky, a Russian nobleman and general in the Russian Imperial Army, in 1899. Grant became Princess Cantacuzene and used her dual identity to make a name for herself after the Russian Revolution, which her husband had fought as a general in the White Army. She returned to the United States and settled as an "exile" in Sarasota, Florida. There she established herself as a staunch American patriot. Cantacuzene published an account of her escape from the Bolsheviks in 1919 and traveled widely to share her experiences in her adopted homeland and enlighten American audiences about conditions under what she called the "criminal" government of Russia. She would go on to lead national defense efforts for other societies affiliated with the Women's Patriotic Conference on National Defense (WPCND), including the American Legion Auxiliary and the Daughters of 1812.[72]

Other hereditary and veterans' organizations that had participated in the first WPCND followed the example of the DAR and established their own internal committees to support the expansion of the military, the defense of what they called American ideals, and the defeat of so-called subversive forces. Although at least one leader of the American Legion Auxiliary had proposed a fund for national defense work in 1923, national defense did not become a standing committee within the organization until 1928. Even then, contributions to the committee's budget were voluntary, unlike the mandatory levy in the DAR.[73] As a result, not even in the American Legion Auxiliary, which had first proposed the WPCND, did the national defense committee achieve the power of Walker's DAR fiefdom.

In other organizations, leadership on antiradical issues was less concentrated than in the DAR. In the Daughters of 1812, for instance, at least three subgroups claimed jurisdiction over the activities supervised by one committee in the DAR.[74] The Daughters of 1812 established its first anti-radical committee in the spring of 1924 in response to the international convention of WILPF. Cornelia Ross Potts headed this Investigation of Propaganda Committee. By early 1927, the organization had decided to add a Loyalty Committee, led by Mary Logan Tucker, another one of the main protesters at the WILPF convention. Tucker's enthusiasm for the military was not surprising since she was the daughter of John Logan, a famous Union general in the Civil War who moved from the battlefield into politics, eventually representing Illinois in both houses of Congress. Tucker was also interested in politics. She served as a leader of the Women's Republican League as well as an officer of patriotic and veterans' groups such as the Dames of the Loyal Legion and the Ladies of the Grand Army of the Republic.[75] Potts and Tucker shared the mantle of antiradical leadership in the Daughters of 1812 with Florine Judik, who was appointed chairman of the National Defense Committee, established around the same time as the Loyalty Committee. The daughter of a financier and lumber wholesaler, Judik followed in her philanthropist mother's footsteps, building a life in Baltimore rich with civic responsibilities. Judik undoubtedly brought social prominence and wealth to the Daughters of 1812 antiradical campaign.[76] None of these women gained the influence and visibility of Flora Walker, however, whose name became synonymous with antiradicalism both inside and outside of the DAR.

## Women and the Military

The 1925 establishment of both the WPCND and the DAR National Defense Committee attracted little notice from traditional female reformers, who probably regarded the new committee and coalition as fresh manifestations of women's long-standing enthusiasm for voluntarist politics. After the Nineteenth Amendment, women streamed into voluntary associations in ever larger numbers, creating new organizations that pursued the time-tested strategy of applying pressure from outside electoral and legislative halls. Antiradicals demanded a new ideological purity in women's associations. But they continued to use this sex-segregated political subculture as the foundation for their campaign, which was premised on the same faith in female distinctiveness that animated the larger network of women's associations that had originally introduced female antiradicals to civic engagement. This same subculture imbued female antiradicals with a desire to remain independent and separate from men in their political work. These conservative women would continue to pursue a separatist strategy, which meant that they sought to do their political organizing in all-female environments, rather than trying to gain traction and influence in male-dominated groups.

Female antiradicals operated independently. But this autonomy grew as much out of necessity as design. Like their liberal and radical sisters, conservative women found ideologically sympathetic men at best undependable allies and at worst dangerous foes.[77] Conservative women were certainly influenced by sympathetic men and many would have welcomed public partnerships with male allies. Indeed, activists within the DAR were able to establish a covert working relationship with some men within the military. But this rapport was frequently broken by military misogyny. Most conservative men, particularly those in the military, refused to establish any kind of public partnership with even their most enthusiastic female advocates. As a result, the bonds between the military and female activists remained tenuous, even as the women's campaign for a strong military grew more vocal and effective. Any alliance between these two parties was repeatedly undermined by army leaders' resolve to keep the American military a male preserve.

Reformers could only guess at the negotiations that took place behind closed doors. They remained convinced that antiradicals were working only at the behest of powerful men and that any attacks by women were fomented by military leaders. DAR president general Grace Brosseau rejected claims that she worked at the direction of male relatives and policymakers, protesting in 1928 "most emphatically that no man or woman during the two years of my administration has dominated me."[78] But Brosseau's protests did little to change perceptions of her work, which were shaped by deeply held assumptions about women's political engagement.[79] Reformers saw themselves as advocates of all women, aligned in opposition to powerful men. As a result, they tended to fixate on the misdeeds of male military leaders rather than rifts with other women. They were especially slow to see other clubwomen as foes. As a result, the new campaign by conservative clubwomen—which retained the trappings and traditions of female associational culture—failed to raise the same kind of alarm bells as the public denunciations of men affiliated with the War Department.

Peace activists of the time were certain that the military had arranged the attacks by female antiradicals on the Washington gatherings of WILPF and the NCCCW. This was a logical conclusion, as the military was conducting its own high-profile campaign against the women's peace movement, and its leaders failed to uphold even a pretense of nonpartisanship. Secretary of War Weeks refused to censure officers like Albert J. Bowley, commandant of Fort Bragg, North Carolina, who denounced WILPF and NCPW as communist inspired. Instead, Weeks demonstrated for the diatribes, calling the brigadier general a "rattling good officer" and declaring that he would not rebuke his officers for speaking the truth.[80] And Bowley was not the sole member of the military who went unpunished. Two years later, in 1926, Assistant Secretary of War Hanford MacNider told the Women's National Republican Club that pacifism had spread so far that "such splendid women as Jane Addams and Carrie Chapman Catt associate themselves with professional agitators" to attack the military. Pacifist ranks were populated with "paid agitators, sentimental sob sisters and Reds who are seeking to undermine our form of government."[81]

Though the War Department was actively hostile to women's peace activism, its leaders did not direct the siege laid by female antiradicals on the Washington peace conventions. Military leaders were undoubtedly heartened to see newspaper headlines proclaiming women's opposition to disarmament and pacifism, yet they were still not ready to take any kind of female activism seriously. The relationship between women conservatives and the military was far more complex than that of master and handmaiden. Their connection would be better described as symbiotic. Female antiradicals developed as activists in the shadow of the military establishment, drawing intermittent inspiration and legitimacy from association with its mission.

When the women associated with the Daughters of 1812 launched their attacks on the WILPF convention, War Department director of women's relations, Anita Phipps, was aghast. WILPF, in her opinion, was led by brilliant, radical women with formidable organizing talents and considerable money. Antiradicals, by contrast, were disorganized and indiscriminate, discrediting "innocent pacifists because of the radical control of some of the ultra-pacifist organizations." She sounded positively progressive when she decried "the wholesale condemnation of organizations which contain a very small minority of radicals or honest pacifists, the lack of discrimination between misguided peace-loving patriots and radicals" as well as "vilifying statements which cannot be proven against individuals." These condemnations were rarely followed by action, in her estimation.[82]

In the wake of the WILPF convention, during the spring and early summer of 1924, members of the Daughters of 1812, the American Legion Auxiliary, the DAR, and the Women's Overseas Service League had contacted Phipps for help in "combating ultra-pacifist propaganda." Phipps established a working relationship with the veterans' organizations, especially the Women's Overseas Service League, a group made up of women who had served overseas with either the military or welfare groups like the Red Cross during the Great War.[83] The group advocated a large professional military, supplemented by volunteers who would assist in running the Citizens' Military Training Camps. At Phipps's request, the women also tried to curry youthful patriotic sentiments by sponsoring an essay contest for girls on the theme "Why a Young Man I Know Should Go to Citizens' Training Camp."[84]

Phipps evinced little faith in the capabilities of those affiliated with the DAR and the Daughters of 1812, however. These women lacked "the same kind of sharpened wits" as pacifists, according to Phipps. They were ineffective crones who were "attempting to meet the enemy's rapiers with broomsticks," she claimed. Members of hereditary societies rarely "engaged in any business or professional work and have not the same kind of trained intelligence as the moving spirits of the organized pacifist societies." Often "fanatically conservative," these women were "deeply patriotic, full of zeal in their desire to combat dangerous propaganda" but ill-informed. She believed that unlike their pacifist sisters, they were not independent activists. "They do not study the question for themselves," she asserted, repeating widely held stereotypes about women on the right, "but take the word of many unauthorized distributors of anti-pacifist information."[85] Some of these criticisms sound harsh, especially from a woman who was not terribly concerned with establishing herself in a profession or earning a living before her tenure in the War Department. In any case, she saw little point in forging a closer alliance with the women most passionate about the need for a robust military. In her analysis, the War Department needed to focus its attention on the women she understood to be sandwiched between peace advocates and their foes. "Between these active factions lie an uninstructed majority of women, many of them emotionally inclined toward the idealism of world peace" yet open to reason, she claimed. "These women are besieged with clever propaganda for radicalism disguised as 'peace' and get very little information on the other side," she complained. "Sincerely peace-loving citizens" were as a result the "innocent tools of a power of which they are totally ignorant." These naïfs needed to be brought into the War Department's camp.[86]

To win the hearts and minds of these moderate women, Phipps proposed that the War Department establish a new, covert committee. This committee would provide guidance to female antiradicals who were "at sea as to how to begin" their campaign to neutralize pacifist influences. A specific strategy for these women could be mapped by an advisory group that would include herself, representatives from the Military Intelligence Division, as well as the operations and training division and the Justice Department.[87] She suggested, in essence, a civilian-military countersubversion task force focused specifically on the women's peace movement. No doubt Phipps believed her relatively moderate views on peace and patriotism would guide this committee. But as a civilian, she would have found herself powerless to prevent such a committee from overreaching its authority to persecute women she felt were loyal, if misguided, Americans. It had the potential to dramatically intensify government repression of women's politics. Phipps's plan also might have dramatically changed the development of female antiradicalism, putting the still-incipient movement under the aegis of a male-controlled military. Eager to demonstrate support, activists likely would have jumped at the opportunity to expand their public authority. They would have eagerly integrated themselves into male administrative hierarchies, especially since they had not yet developed independent institutional structures.

The War Department was eager to cast women progressives as enemies. It proved less receptive, however, to the idea of having like-minded women as its allies. Two divisions within the War Department immediately rejected Phipps's proposal. Colonel J. H. Reeves declared from the Military Intelligence Division (MID) that "as seen from every angle this proposition is loaded with dynamite." Reminding his fellow officers of the controversy over the Spider Web Chart, Reeves asserted that "the War Department would be put to considerably greater embarrassment should [the organizations named in the chart] learn (as they certainly would) that the War Department was officially backing the women's organizations opposing them." Although high-ranking War Department officials had been decrying peace activists in the press, Reeves asserted that "with all its insidious propaganda, the radical and pacifist movement is really a political question in which, however much all military personnel may be concerned as individuals, the War Department as an organization has no business to participate."[88] A colonel in the training and operations division, G. C. Barnhardt, concurred with all Reeves's statements, summarily dismissing Phipps's proposed committee.[89]

Phipps quickly denied that she had intended to endorse particular women's organizations. Her aim, instead, was education, which the War Department was only providing to men and boys, she complained. At the very least, she argued, the War Department needed a committee to coordinate its interactions with women's organizations. Sympathetic groups required information on the army, the Citizens' Military Training Camps, and "radicalism and pacifism." The dire situation allowed no hesitation. "The rapid spread of ultra-pacifism among women seems sufficiently serious to warrant the serious consideration of every department of the Government," she declared. "No opportunity should be lost for the education of women on Army matters so that they will not be misled by specious statements."[90] The War Department leadership was ostensibly wary of the potential political fallout of Phipps's proposal. Yet in rejecting her call for this committee, they were also rebuffing her demand that the army come to terms with women's power. "As the pacifist organizations are being recruited largely from women and as the women's vote is of the same weight as the men's, it is of great importance that instruction should be imparted also to women and girls," Phipps wrote in a memo. Ending the public attacks on peace activists would aid military efforts to curry respect and support. The army, she repeatedly told her bosses, would be best served if it presented a friendlier face to American women.

Phipps's superiors were unmoved by these arguments. They pointed to War Department policy, which had specifically forbidden its intelligence officers from collaborating with civilians in 1922. Two years later, this restriction had been expanded, to prohibit the Military Intelligence Division from conducting any political surveillance of civilians. This ban came in reaction to the gross civil liberties violations that characterized the red raids that opened the decade.[91] Yet these regulations did little to alter the actual practices at MID, which continued to work with civilian groups to undermine the women's peace movement. Since MID was prohibited from disseminating information about civilian groups, Reeves instructed that inquiries about pacifism be referred to "civilian agencies intensively engaged in the anti-pacifist work," naming organizations Phipps had denounced for giving out "sensational and false information" to fuel attacks on peace activists.[92] This policy made some female antiradical groups quasi-official public information organs. MID directed inquiries about the loyalty of WILPF, Jane Addams, or the real nature of the radical threat to the DAR and the Massachusetts Public Interests League.[93]

The War Department also used civilian activists to assemble domestic intelligence reports. In fact, the military became even more reliant on volunteers for information.[94] Throughout the 1920s and into the 1930s, antiradical organizations aided intelligence officers by regularly compiling reports on activists or groups targeted as dangerously subversive. Women in organizations like the DAR synthesized surveillance, reading, and propaganda analysis into reports, which they distributed to parties within the military interested in political intelligence. These documents dramatized the subversive menace, asserting that groups like the Workers Communist Party of America, the Soviet government, and the Communist International were "working hand in hand to destroy our Government, Principles and Institutions."[95] By sharing reports like these with both local military officials and War Department officers, female antiradicals used their knowledge of left-wing politics to establish a relationship with the military.

While some officers welcomed contributions from women, MID files show that they still depended more on male antiradicals for reports. The work of female spies nonetheless gained the respect of some army officers. Intelligence officers accepted all the information women were willing to share, including reports by the National Society of Patriotic Builders of America on antimilitarist campaigns by the Communist Party of America, efforts to undermine the religious faith of the "Negro masses" and movements of Soviet secret agents.[96] Margaret Robinson, the president of the Massachusetts Public Interests League, earned the admiration and notice of officers in Washington with her reports on the public meetings of communists and labor radicals in Boston. A military intelligence officer in that city urged his colleagues in Washington to welcome Robinson when she visited the nation's capital, since his office worked closely with her to "keep tabs" on radical activities in the area. Robinson, he wrote, "has the best library on radicals and radical activities in this Corps Area, and very probably will compare favorably with any in the country."[97] His praise opened the doors of the War Department when she traveled to Washington in January of 1926, where she became acquainted with the men leading the government's official anti-radical campaign.[98]

MID repaid female spies for their reports with official information from its files. MID records show that DAR leaders were privy to reports, documents, and pamphlets from the files of the War Department.[99] Military officers probably also opened their files to the board members of the Woman Patriot Publishing Company as well as other female antiradicals.[100] An investigation commissioned by women progressives to investigate the source of attacks against them concluded that the War Department routinely used "table talk" to barter information about domestic radicalism with both male and female patriotic organizations. No records remain of these informal meetings, which probably were undocumented.[101]

Individual officers laid aside any reservations they had about working with women in order to collect and disseminate information about radicals. But the military hierarchy was hostile to allowing women any kind of public foothold in the War Department. These officers rejected Phipps's proposal on the basis of regulations they felt free to disregard. In the months that followed, Phipps would have to confront the fact that her ideas for combating pacifism among the nation's women would be met with scorn and indifference by her military superiors.

Phipps ultimately hoped to carve out some space for women within the military. Rather than advocating a feminist-inspired equality, Phipps envisioned a women's sphere within the army, where issues that she defined as pertinent to women would be administered by women alone. Phipps had watched the growth of the WPCND with dismay. She believed that female antiradicals were ill-suited to effectively counteract female peace activists. In early 1927 she gave her superiors a plan to develop an alternative to the antiradical coalition: a council of female civilian aides within the military.

Providing women with an official role within the War Department would mean that they would no longer "fanatically demand the dissolution of a ruthless military machine, but will support an adequate army as an acceptable part of national life."[102] She imagined every question that touched on women coming under the control of an entirely female division, headed by a single woman leader. No doubt Phipps imagined herself at the head of this division, but she avoided any discussion of the way these changes would enhance her own power. Instead, she presented them as a way for the army to better utilize the services of women. Though women would reign supreme in the division she imagined, they would not challenge the male dominance of the rest of the military.

Ignoring the sole letter of support from the Woman's Department of the National Civic Federation, the General Staff rejected Phipps's plan for a women's division under her control. It cited costs and the impropriety of having a woman oversee military matters.[103] Colonel John Morgan complained that "it appears that the Director of Women's Relations desires to perfect within the Army an organization of women." This type of division would be dangerous, he protested, as it "would constitute a powerful machine difficult to control and endowed with possibilities of hampering and embarrassing the War Department." Her suggested board of civilian aides might be acceptable, according to Morgan, if it were not under her control. In fact, he suggested, a board of civilian women could be used to replace her altogether, hinting at the growing influence of the women associated with the WPCND. "The women of the country are now well organized and under the intelligent direction of their leaders," he concluded, declaring them "competent to study the subject of National Defense" to reach "their own conclusions as to their duties as citizens."[104]

By the end of the summer of 1927, Phipps was beleaguered within the War Department. She complained that she was forced to shuttle between two offices to perform welfare work and her duties associated with women's relations, an arrangement that made her job impossible.[105] In the meantime, Secretary of War Dwight Davis had concluded that the army had no use for any women professionals. A "salaried employee," he asserted, did not have sufficient "prestige and national character" to represent the War Department to the nation's women.[106] In truth, the War Department would resist any formal, public association with women. This desire to keep all women outside the male fortress of the War Department would serve female antiradicals well in the long term. By concentrating their efforts within the circumscribed world of middle-class women's politics, female antiradicals became far more powerful foes for female progressives than they could have ever been as junior partner in a campaign led by the military. War Department misogyny ultimately helped female antiradicals create a stronger foundation for their activism than any relationship with the military establishment could have provided.

After the publication of the Spider Web Chart, female reformers would find that no amount of capitulation or conciliation could protect them from the vituperation of women conservatives, who blamed middle-class clubwomen for encouraging radical revolution in North America. Antiradicals were incensed by the international reconciliation efforts that followed the Armistice. In their view, anything less than unqualified support for a robust military and vigorous countersubversion campaign constituted treason. While many moderate clubwomen undoubtedly realized that the world had been changed forever by the Bolshevik Revolution, most failed to anticipate how the anxieties it generated would change the landscape of women's politics. Antiradicals believed that ascendant radicalism had rendered the world into a battlefield, in which enemy camps needed to be separated by an impassable no-man's-land. Moderate women leaders were horrified to find themselves targets when they attempted to traverse the area between the trenches. They were infuriated to find themselves in a war they did not declare, with other clubwomen as their enemies.

When reformers and peace activists claimed to speak politically for all women, they made themselves vulnerable to women like Claire Oliphant, whose declaration that it "takes women to fight women" illuminates a pitfall of organizing as women. Yet sex-segregated voluntarist associations continued to be the best way for women of all ideological stripes to influence politics even after the suffrage victory. Antiradicals discovered the difficulties of working within mixed-sex or male-dominated organizations through their troubled relationship with the War Department. While men in the military certainly endorsed the efforts of female antiradicals, they never took their activism seriously, even when they recognized its strategic value. Hostility to female political engagement kept women on the periphery of the military establishment, which meant that antiradical women never developed more than a covert partnership with certain military intelligence officers. Born of discrimination, this separatist strategy preserved the vitality of the female antiradical campaign.

When they found themselves under fire, female reformers resisted the idea that other clubwomen had originated these attacks. They remained convinced that these new foes served as mouthpieces for powerful military men. Even after female antiradicals had laid siege to three different Washington conventions, reformers remained focused on the military's campaign against the peace movement. While they had far more to fear from this new women's coalition, reformers continued to overlook the ascendance of antiradicals. Perhaps they were somewhat perplexed by these newly galvanized conservatives. Their agenda was novel. And their public attacks were discomfiting and broke with tradition in many ways. But the most formidable antiradical organizers probably looked like conventional clubwomen to veteran political activists. Conservatives retained the tactics and structures of established women's club politics. In this way, antiradicalism remained hidden in plain sight during the first half of the 1920s, subsumed within the political subculture of women's associations. Working from within this subculture, these activists would transform women's politics, dividing and polarizing a world that had once enjoyed a more harmonious consensus about the need for social reform. They would shift the focus of well-established women's groups like the DAR, which helped to create new institutions like the National Defense Committee and the WPCND. These new institutions of female activism would ensure that countersubversive stridency would become a perennial feature of women's politics. The crusade against radicalism would continue to alter the institutions of female activism in the second half of the decade, demonstrating the influence and power that conservatives could wield over even the most committed advocates of reform.

Chapter 4

# Stopping the "Revolution by Legislation": Antiradicals Unite Against Social Welfare Reform

In the autumn of 1926, DAR president general Grace Brosseau took an action that would have been inconceivable only five years earlier. Brosseau withdrew her group's long-standing support for maternalist-inspired reform. Since the beginning of the twentieth century, the DAR had followed the political lead of other middle-class women's voluntary groups, operating as part of the lobbying arm of the "female dominion." While the hereditary association was not a leading light of female reform, it had consistently lent its prestige to the legislative agenda conceived by the federal Children's Bureau, advocating for government funding of maternal health programs and legal restrictions on child labor. When the Sheppard-Towner Act first came up for consideration in 1921 the DAR leadership greeted this measure with enthusiasm. Once it was enacted into law, DAR members joined the other women cheering the victory enjoyed by the Children's Bureau.[1] The support enjoyed by this measure—even in this relatively conservative voluntary association—meant that in those early years after female suffrage, the activists associated with the *Woman Patriot* had little audience for its warnings about government programs for the health and welfare of mothers and children.

Half a decade later, the DAR had undergone its own revolution. The establishment of the National Defense Committee within the DAR in 1925 transformed the political priorities of the organization in a way that marked a watershed for women's politics. This subcommittee became the group's political arbiter, demanding that all other concerns be subservient to stopping revolutionary radicalism. Brosseau declared that "the day for filling programs with papers on colonial doorways or the decline in modern art has passed."[2] National Defense Committee chairman Flora Walker asserted that women needed to counteract all "pernicious influences" by checking "their intrusion at your fireside, their invasion of the schoolroom, their usurpation of pulpit and pew . . . for the purpose of overthrowing the present form of the United States Government."[3] This focus on counterrevolution meant that the WPPC's once-marginal conspiracies resonated with leaders of one of the most prestigious women's groups of the time. After years of providing at least passive support for female reform efforts, DAR leaders accepted the charge that seemingly respectable women leaders were masterminding a "revolution by legislation." They began championing the notion that the nation's political and economic system would be destroyed after intrusive social welfare programs weakened the patriarchal family, making the country powerless to prevent a radical takeover.[4] When the DAR embraced the WPPC's logic, it rejected the tenets of maternalist reform that had inspired its leaders to promote measures like the Sheppard-Towner Act and various state and federal initiatives to restrict child labor since the beginning of the twentieth century.[5] This prompted an acrimonious break with the rest of the "female dominion" that undergirded the federal Children's Bureau. The resulting conflicts ultimately destabilized the political world of middle-class clubwomen, whose interlocking voluntary associations had provided institutional support for progressive reform since the turn of the twentieth century.[6]

The WPPC began to develop a wider following during the national debate over a constitutional amendment that would have granted Congress the power to regulate child labor. The measure—which was approved by Congress in 1924 and had nothing to do with global radicalism—was the product of decades of activism by progressive activists in the United States. Yet the proposed amendment stirred fears about Bolshevism among many Americans, allowing the tiny coterie of female activists associated with the WPPC to make the question of communism central to the state-by-state ratification fight. The links they made between "interference" in the family and revolution set the scene for the quick and "bewildering" demise of what reformers had understood to be an "immensely popular measure."[7]

The child labor amendment had its Waterloo in Massachusetts, where voters delivered a crushing defeat to the ratification campaign. Elated by this victory, the women behind the *Woman Patriot* returned to Washington determined to enlist help in preventing additional female reform legislation. Thanks to the National Defense Committee, they found the DAR particularly receptive to their efforts to portray maternalist reform as incompatible with patriotism. WPPC leader Mary Kilbreth reported that the DAR president general had left a 1926 encounter "entirely our friend, apparently willing to be guided, and anxious to actively help."[8] From this point forward, the DAR became a powerful messenger for the WPPC's propaganda. It endorsed what most reformers had dismissed as marginal conspiracy theories.[9] Brosseau agreed to distribute through her organization a WPPC "petition" that argued that radicals hoped to effect revolution by undermining the traditional patriarchal family, the same allegations outlined in the treatise "Organizing Revolution Through Women and Children."[10] The next year, the organization's annual convention condemned the "unwarranted extension of Federal activities" that had created "autocratic bureaucracy, in direct contravention of the American system of government devised by the founders of the Republic." The DAR called on the federal government to drop all activities not "expressly delegated . . . by the Constitution."[11] Brosseau applauded Margaret Robinson, a leader of both the Massachusetts Public Interests League and the *Woman Patriot*, as a patriot "of a high order" who was "deeply interested in the welfare of our country."[12] Most telling, the DAR repudiated its earlier support for the Sheppard-Towner Act, which came up for renewal in 1926.

After the rise of the National Defense Committee, the DAR turned its back on its earlier political life. Initiatives that had earned its endorsement at the beginning of the decade were now denounced as treasonous. This previous history was never acknowledged publicly by the new leadership, which embraced the type of alarmist rhetoric articulated by Flora Walker, who declared that "collectivity and bureaucracy would snatch the child from the nursery and make of it an un-American citizen." She queried delegates at the group's annual convention: "Do you not agree with me that institutional life is never the equal of the home and mother love in the care and development of the child?"[13] The group's leaders gave urgency to these warnings by setting up a program to educate its members about radical philosophies and activities. National headquarters sent prodigious amounts of propaganda to local chapters, where rank-and-file members were urged to supplement these written materials with their own observations of radical organizing in their communities. Analyzing radical activities proved to be a powerful consciousness-raising activity that fed local women's determination to fight subversive influences everywhere. Field missions served as initiation rites for conservative clubwomen, whose confidence in their own expertise imbued them with a new sense of civic purpose.

## Child Labor Amendment

The women behind the *Woman Patriot* were able to turn the ideological tide against maternalist reformers with the debate over the child labor amendment. Child welfare advocates were caught short by the hostility sparked by this measure, having envisioned the decade after female suffrage as a golden age for social welfare reforms. After their success with the 1921 Sheppard-Towner Act, reformers predicted that this "Maternity Act" would inaugurate a wave of female-driven legislation that would transform politics and government. They immediately turned their attention to the problem of child labor, an issue that was familiar to most organized women, who had come of age as citizens in the maternalist politics of "child saving."[14]

Progressive maternalists had identified child labor as inimical to youngsters' health and welfare; they protested that accelerating industrialization sucked ever-greater numbers of children into jobs that broke body and soul. Turn-of-the-century surveys estimated that more than two million children under fifteen were trapped in stultifying and frequently hazardous occupations. Children toiled in coal mines, textile mill spinning rooms, and the broiling furnace rooms of glass factories. With no protection from the weather, children as young as five worked more than twelve hours a day tending and harvesting agricultural crops, shucking oysters, picking shrimp, and processing fruits and vegetables for canning. More easily tired and distracted, children were particularly vulnerable to workplace accidents. Dusty, humid, and dark working environments made them susceptible to tuberculosis and other industrial diseases. Repetitive and strenuous tasks left many with muscular and orthopedic injuries.[15] In 1904, a group of men and women, including Florence Kelley, founded the National Child Labor Committee to publicize the fate of these young workers and illuminate the inadequacy of existing child labor regulations.[16] In 1912, the group proved instrumental in winning federal funds for the establishment of the U.S. Children's Bureau, which would push for greater national restrictions on child labor.[17]

After more than a decade of struggle, these reformers convinced Congress that the social costs of denying children the opportunity to develop their minds and bodies outweighed any economic benefit. In 1916, lawmakers passed the Keating-Owen Act, which was based on congressional authority to regulate interstate commerce. The bill restricted children's labor in industries that sold their products across state lines. Outlawing children fourteen and under from working in mills, factories, and canneries, Keating-Owen also barred those under sixteen from working at night, laboring for longer than eight hours per day, and toiling in mines and quarries. Exempted from protection were the majority of wage-earning children, who worked as street vendors, agricultural hands, domestic servants, or industrial pieceworkers at their families' kitchen tables. The Supreme Court made the nation's experiment with child labor reform short-lived. After only nine months, the justices declared Keating-Owen an unconstitutional extension of the interstate commerce clause.

Reformers did not lose heart. They convinced Congress in 1919 to pass legislation assessing a 10 percent excise tax on the profits of the same establishments regulated by the Keating-Owen law. This act targeted factories employing children under fourteen and levied the tax on mines and quarries employing those under sixteen, as well as establishments in which those under sixteen labored for more than eight hours at a stretch, more than five days a week, or at night. These regulations were immediately challenged in court by Southern textile mill owners. On May 15, 1922, the Supreme Court ruled in the employers' favor. This high court decision launched the campaign for a Twentieth Amendment, which would grant Congress the power to regulate the labor of Americans under eighteen years of age.[18]

The strategy of using a constitutional amendment to eliminate the scourge of child labor quickly won enthusiastic support. The proposed Amendment, known as the child labor amendment, looked headed for certain passage in 1924. Groups on both the right and left endorsed the measure. The reform-minded American Federation of Labor, eleven members of the Women's Joint Congressional Committee, the Federal Council of Churches of Christ in America, and the National Catholic Welfare Council were some of its staunchest backers. Since the start of the decade, the amendment had even gained the endorsement of conservative Massachusetts senator Henry Cabot Lodge, former president Warren G. Harding, and president Calvin Coolidge, as well as more reform-minded Republicans like Herbert Hoover. All the political parties and their candidates for president in 1924 endorsed the amendment. There was little outspoken opposition to child labor regulation outside the Southern textile industry and the National Association of Manufacturers. Although David Clark, editor of the *Southern*

*Textile Bulletin*, had played a key role in bringing the suits that ended the earlier federal regulation, his perennial opposition had failed to sway a majority of congressmen in the past. The protests voiced by Clark on behalf of manufacturers—as well as the arguments of "states' rights" advocates—had been ignored during the previous two debates over federal regulation. Legislators were accustomed to protests from Southern textile manufacturers, other industrialists, and even working-class Americans who depended on their children's earnings for survival. The amendment seemed destined for fast approval.

Then a novel objection was raised in 1924 by the editors of the *Woman Patriot*. In testimony before the House of Representatives Committee on the Judiciary, and more notably, in a petition published in the Congressional Record, the WPPC charged that the amendment was "promoted under direct orders from Moscow." Senator Thomas F. Bayard of Delaware introduced the WPPC petition into the Congressional Record on May 31, 1924, more than a month after the amendment was passed by the House of Representatives with the comfortable majority of 297 to 69. The WPPC petition denounced the amendment as the brainchild of "job hunters" and "high-salaried bureaucrats" as well as "communists and socialists striving to establish governmental control and support of the entire youth of the Nation, which is the basic tenet of communism." The petition warned that the amendment would allow radicals to "'nationalize the children' of America, to remove them from what the propagandists regard as the 'pernicious influence' of the States and the parents, and to compel their surrender to central radical bureaus at Washington." If the amendment succeeded, parents would be discarded; "swarms of Federal agents" would "place the care of every child under control of petty bureaucrats."[19] When this small band of antiradicals weighed in on the question of child labor, the tenor of the debate was changed.

Any kind of "centralized bureaucracy" paved the way for revolution, the petition asserted. Administered by "settlement-house workers disseminating any propaganda they please—socialism, pacifism, or what not," the "uncontrolled, undisciplined, unsupervised" Children's Bureau was especially dangerous. Passage of the amendment would exacerbate this danger. "The power of the chief of the Children's Bureau, under this amendment, would rival that of the soviet feminist chief, Alexandra Kollontay," who had "full control of marriage, guardianship of children, social service, and care of veterans" in revolutionary Russia. "House-to-house and farm-to-farm searches for youthful workers would also furnish an opportunity for propaganda of any kind," the petition concluded. "The enforcement machinery for this amendment would be the greatest engine of propaganda any Federal bureau has ever had."[20]

To demonstrate American radicals' deference to Moscow, as well as the parallels between the Children's Bureau agenda and that of the Communist Party, the petition quoted from supposedly authentic communist documents. The amendment's subversive origins were further demonstrated by its supporters; the petition listed women it claimed to be responsible for the amendment, along with their radical portfolios. The document denounced Florence Kelley as a "socialist" and "translator of Karl Marx," condemned Jane Addams as an "internationalist and pacifist," and lambasted "pacifist" Lillian D. Wald as unfit for public service. The radical associations of Kelley and Addams, as well as Julia C. Lathrop and Grace Abbott, the former and current heads of the Children's Bureau, provided indisputable proof of their subversive intentions. All the women had "been connected with Hull House, Chicago, and with the so-called 'Women's International League for Peace and Freedom,' perhaps the most radical women's organization with American connections."[21]

This petition was the second well-circulated attack on the "women's bloc" in a matter of months. In March, to accompany the Spider Web Chart, the *Dearborn Independent* published a controversial set of articles that used the connections between revolutionaries and reformers to discredit the amendment. "Are Women's Clubs 'Used' by Bolshevists?" argued against the entire maternalist agenda by asserting that women who would "resent being called Socialists or Bolsheviki, are blithely passing resolutions and voting for a program that was inaugurated by Madam Alexandria Kollontay in her Soviet 'Department of Child Welfare.'"[22] This article worked in tandem with the petition from the Woman Patriot Publishing Company, lifting whole sections from the *Woman Patriot*'s antiradical opus "Organizing Revolution Through Women and Children.".

The power of these attacks was not initially apparent as they failed to derail congressional support for the amendment. The Senate passed the measure on June 2, 1924, only three days after Bayard introduced the document into the record.[23] Amendment backers then turned to the task of winning approval from three-quarters of the states. Although they had enjoyed sympathetic press coverage, ample political support among conservative legislators, and a comfortable congressional victory, those committed to the ratification of the child labor amendment knew the state-by-state campaign would be an uphill battle. They were unprepared, however, to find their drive stopped in Massachusetts less than six months later. For it was at the local level that antiradical appeals proved to resonate.

While defeats in Louisiana, Georgia, and North Carolina over the summer came as no great shock, Massachusetts was one of the last places where reformers expected to be stymied.[24] The Massachusetts legislature had petitioned Congress to propose a child labor amendment in February 1924. Both Massachusetts senators backed the amendment, as did the state's Republican and Democratic parties. It had gained endorsement from the sitting governor, Alvan T. Fuller.[25] Home to powerful reform groups, the state had some of the strongest child labor laws in the nation, so the state had the most to gain economically from national legislation. The region's powerful textile industry had been departing to Southern states with lax labor regulations. Yet when the amendment came up for ratification in the state, the legislature put the measure to the voters. It scheduled a referendum to coincide with the November general election.[26]

This window of opportunity gave opposition forces the chance to mobilize. Their campaign was in full swing by September. Amendment advocates assumed that this drive was propelled primarily by Massachusetts textile firms with mills in the South. Employers wanted to protect these factories from increased regulation; low wages in the South could be used as leverage to depress workers' paychecks above the Mason-Dixon Line. Indeed, industry was intent on blocking ratification of the amendment.[27] Yet once it left the relatively safe harbor of Washington, the campaign against child labor was swamped not so much by economic concerns as by fears for home and family. One League of Women Voters activist reflected that "the amendment, long the cherished child of the politically orthodox of both parties," became in Massachusetts "a radical step-child—born and nurtured in Bolshevist Russia."[28] An ideological sea change occurred, precipitated by allusions to communist subversion that quickly overshadowed other more explicitly economic objections to the amendment. As it turned the tide of public opinion, "the friends of the amendment were totally unprepared to combat the flood of distorted propaganda which let loose upon them," according to the *New Republic*.[29]

Despite its vibrant reform tradition, Massachusetts was also a stronghold for female antiradicals who saw the child labor amendment and the Sheppard-Towner Act as the first battles in a war that would determine the future of the nation. The Massachusetts Public Interests League (MPIL), which included WPPC board members Margaret Robinson, Mary Kilbreth, Katherine Balch, and Harriet Frothingham, was the most influential organization for antiradical women in New England.[30] Dedicated to opposing "bureaucratic and socialistic legislation," the philosophy of the MPIL was virtually indistinguishable from that of the WPPC. Established in 1914 to oppose women's suffrage, the MPIL had worked since the ratification of the Nineteenth Amendment to gain recognition as a regional organization for conservative women, attracting about 1,000 members. "The danger of Socialism," the group maintained, has "increased by leaps and bounds" since the end of the war, thanks to "chaotic economic conditions." With leaflets, lectures, and press releases, the MPIL worked—with the help of paid staff—to counter the "foreign propaganda" supposedly flooding the country. From a substantial office on Boston's Newbury Street, the group took aim at "radical legislation, disguised under the misleading title of welfare bills."[31]

The guiding spirit and president of the MPIL was Margaret Robinson, wife of Harvard botanist Benjamin Lincoln Robinson. The daughter of a lawyer, Margaret Louise Casson was born in 1864 in Hennepin, Illinois. As a young adult, Margaret taught music after studying at Illinois State Normal School. Margaret's early years would have been difficult to distinguish from those of reformers Jane Addams and Julia Lathrop. Like Margaret, both reformers came from prominent families in small-town Illinois. All three received similar educations during the same decade. In her early twenties, however, Margaret chose a different path; she embraced the "family claim" Addams had fought to shake off, joining her fortunes with a one-time fellow student at Illinois State Normal School. In June 1887, Margaret married Robinson, a new Harvard University graduate and product of another well-established Illinois family. Less than a year later, Margaret gave birth to their only child, a daughter who died of meningitis at the age of eight. After Benjamin finished his doctorate, the Robinsons moved to Cambridge, Massachusetts, where Benjamin took a position at Harvard University's Gray Herbarium in 1890.[32]

Although he sympathized with Margaret's views, Benjamin was not politically active; his work outside the herbarium was limited to professional organizations. His sentiments are nonetheless noteworthy, since his brother, who followed him to Harvard and later to Strasbourg, was well known for starkly opposing beliefs. James Harvey Robinson was a prominent progressive historian who resigned from Columbia University in 1919 to protest interference with academic freedom. He conceived a new kind of democratically run university; this vision inspired him to found the New School for Social Research. Possible clashes with her brother-in-law may have heightened Margaret's perception that universities were hotbeds of political and social radicalism.[33] In the years before World War I, the concerns ignited by her observations of university life drove Robinson to take action against female enfranchisement. As a well-known antisuffrage writer and speaker, Robinson drew attention to her claims that the suffrage amendment was "fully as much a Socialist measure as a suffrage measure," since it would swell the ranks of voting radicals.[34] Like other forms of radicalism, suffrage was "a blow at civilization itself."[35]

Before the antisuffrage campaign, music had been Robinson's abiding interest; for the rest of her life, all previous passions would be eclipsed by politics. Her style won her the admiration of sympathetic men. A reporter from the *Springfield Union* was relieved to find that Robinson and her compatriots were no "masculine females, devoid of any charm." Implicitly comparing Robinson to female reformers, the journalist characterized her as an "easy, well-poised, tactful" woman who spared her audiences "frenzied oratory." Her political activities had not robbed her of the most important qualities of her sex, this observer noted; Robinson displayed "sure feminine knowledge of an important subject—what to wear and how to wear it."[36]

Margaret Robinson's beliefs, naturally, shaped the warnings issued by the Massachusetts Public Interests League. Public secondary schools, universities, and especially women's colleges all harbored propagandists who encouraged their students to reject God, law, and authority. By demanding "'academic freedom' to teach . . . opposition to government to classes of American boys and girls," radicals of all shades threatened social stability.[37] To make matters worse, the nation's youth had shown itself particularly susceptible to these ideas.[38] Threats were building from other quarters as well. Radical agitators had received a warm welcome from African Americans. "As early as the spring of 1919, the Bolshevists had agents from Moscow at work among the negroes of the South, stirring them to discontent and rebellion against the Government," Margaret Robinson observed in her personal notes.[39]

The groups heading up the MPIL list of potential subversives were middle-class clubwomen. The antiradical group claimed that millions of women associated with large, reform-minded organizations had been unwittingly enrolled in a revolutionary plot. The progressive legislation backed by the WJCC, Robinson explained, has "the enthusiastic support of practically all Socialists and Communists in the country."[40] The group's stance won it praise from conservative observers in Massachusetts who were relieved to find a counterweight for the influence of progressive women. "In these days, when so many women are misled into support of radical 'reform' measures," a conservative Massachusetts newspaper declared, "it is encouraging to find a large, strong organization of women in Massachusetts displaying a different attitude toward legislation and endeavoring . . . to hold State and national legislators to a safe and sane course."[41]

Although Robinson and the MPIL had been fulminating against reform legislation for years, they did not attract significant public attention until they joined the campaign to defeat the Twentieth Amendment. As its first salvo, the MPIL reprinted the petition submitted by the WPPC to the Senate and distributed it in pamphlets. A generous response to its accompanying request for contributions allowed the organization to print thousands of broadsides declaring that the amendment would require parents "to surrender all control of their children," and calling on residents of the Bay State to "be slow in adopting changes urged by adherents of 'soviet Russia.'"[42] The socialist-inspired amendment would allow the federal government unprecedented authority to "control the youth of America as the Communists control the youth of Russia."[43] Not all of the organizations backing the amendment were radical, it conceded, but they were nonetheless advancing the agendas of these dangerous forces. To drive these points home during the antiratification campaign, Margaret Robinson appeared widely to speak against the measure.[44] Repeating the arguments advanced by the WPPC petition, Robinson and the Public Interests League focused the Massachusetts debate on these charges.[45] The group's leadership in the anti-amendment campaign redeemed the female sex for the *Springfield Union*. According to the paper, the League efforts to defeat the measure showed there were women "capable of acting, with unselfish and patriotic motives" and "who know when red means 'Red' and fight it."[46]

Besides serving as a wellspring for antiregulatory propaganda, the MPIL became the largest financial supporter of the ad hoc group formed to spearhead the Massachusetts opposition, the Citizens' Committee to Protect Our Homes and Children. The Committee also received major backing from the Sentinels of the Republic, another group closely allied with the WPPC.[47] Although the Committee was mixed-sex and its president was a man, well-known female antiradicals filled its other top offices, where they shaped the group's tactics and arguments. The secretary, Anne Proctor, was drawn from the leadership of the MPIL. Robinson held a slot on the group's executive committee.[48]

One of the Committee's vice presidents was Elizabeth Lowell Putnam, the maternalist reformer turned Children's Bureau opponent. Before World War I, Putnam's devotion to children's health had spurred her to join the ancillary campaign to end child labor. She retained her membership in the National Child Labor Committee until 1917, after the passage of the Keating-Owen Act.[49] Her opinion on federal regulation had changed dramatically by 1924. "On its face it appears to be a bill for the protection of childhood," she explained. "In reality it is a measure which will go further to injure children than anything which has ever been devised for that purpose."[50]

Even though she had also been an antisuffragist and a member of the MPIL until 1920, Putnam was personally disdainful of the women associated with the WPPC and the MPIL.[51] Putnam undoubtedly made collaboration difficult. But her break with the women associated with the Children's Bureau was prompted by more than personal foibles. By her telling, the work overseeing state-sponsored political surveillance of so-called radicals and immigrants during the war had left her with the sense that powerful forces were corrupting American life. That experience, she told audiences during the campaign, had given her particular expertise "with regard to Socialism, Florence Kelley and the like."[52] The child labor amendment was dangerous, she explained in 1924, because it was a product of the Children's Bureau, which was run by women "from Hull House, with all that implies of sympathy with the enemies of America."[53] But she seemed to reject any government program designed to assist families. "Under the guise of social betterment," she warned, "we are drifting toward a socialistic, even a communistic condition of society."[54] At first glance, Putnam's work on maternal health and political surveillance seem unrelated. Yet recognizing that these missions were overlapping and interlocking reveals how her work suppressing domestic unrest shaped her views on the nascent welfare state.

Putnam did join forces with the women associated with the WPPC long enough to defeat the child labor amendment in Massachusetts. During the ratification fight, the female antiradicals running the Citizens' Committee to Protect Our Homes and Children raised and spent five times more than amendment backers.[55] The group echoed industry claims that additional regulation was unnecessary. Targeting women in particular, the committee also blanketed the state with false warnings that the amendment would prohibit all work—including household chores—for youths under eighteen, condemning them to lives of sloth and vice. If the amendment passed, the committee asserted, states would no longer be able to regulate the labor or education of their youngest citizens. Finally, the measure promised to give unprecedented powers to Congress, an institution filled with politicians who could not be trusted to represent the best interest of the people.

The most powerful argument against the amendment was, however, that it would allow for the "nationalization of children." Taking its lead from the MPIL and the WPPC, the Committee trumpeted the idea that the measure had originated in Soviet Russia.[56] Amendment supporters responded by pointing out that attempts to enact federal child labor regulations predated the Russian Revolution. To further undermine charges of radical influence, ratification advocates repeated the list of the amendment's conservative sponsors like a mantra. After naming the groups that had lined up in favor of ratification, Frank McCarthy of the American Federation of Labor asked in exasperation, "Can you find . . . any who are Bolsheviks or would be destroyers of our government?" But McCarthy and others made little headway against this propaganda.[57]

In early October, in the last month of the ratification debate, the Committee gained a powerful public ally. Even though the prominent Catholic social worker Father John Ryan had been one of the amendment's original proponents, William Cardinal O'Connell came out against the measure. O'Connell claimed it threatened the privacy of the home and parental rights. The cardinal also gave legitimacy to the claim that the amendment was at its root a radical proposition. "The spirit which pervades the whole movement" for child labor regulation, he declared, "is communistic and as such destructive of true Americanism."[58] In laying out the Cardinal's position, the *Boston Pilot* explained that the amendment would substitute "for parental control . . . the will of Congress and the dictate of a centralized bureaucracy, more in keeping with Soviet Russia, than with the fundamental principles of American Government."[59] Massachusetts priests were directed to tell their parishioners to vote "to protect the interests of their children." Endorsements from the National Catholic Welfare Council and the National Council of Catholic Women—given over O'Connell's protests—could not dissipate the pall cast by the cardinal's pronouncement. O'Connell's opposition carried greater weight among the state's working-class Catholics, many of whom were already hostile to government restrictions on their children's labor.[60]

At O'Connell's request, each priest also appointed two women from his parish to attend a rally against the child labor amendment. The assembly was addressed by Lilian Slattery, the head of the League of Catholic Women, who told these representatives of Catholic womanhood that the measure they would vote on in November was the product of "communistic, Russian propaganda." She urged the 600 women to "not give up their homes and children to Congress."[61] For weeks before O'Connell had issued his public statement against ratification, Slattery had been working against the amendment as one of the vice presidents of the Committee to Protect Our Homes and Children. Since female enfranchisement, Slattery and the League of Catholic Women—which claimed a membership of 14,000 and a following of 450,000 women—had been very active in the state's political life. Though founded in 1910 to promote spiritual, cultural, educational, and charitable work among the Catholic women of Massachusetts, the organization had also focused on preserving "true Christian ideals," which in the minds of O'Connell and many of his female parishioners meant bolstering existing gender hierarchies. Efforts to expand women's political, social, and sexual horizons—exemplified by the "new woman"—were the "gospel of the unsexed," in O'Connell's words. "Woman has her place, her capabilities, her aspirations, her duties," the cardinal declared. "None of these are new. They are founded on the very nature of woman and her place in the plan of life."[62] Following O'Connell's lead, the League of Catholic Women campaigned against federal maternal health programs, federal control of education, birth control, the equal rights amendment, and the child labor amendment during Slattery's presidency, which stretched from 1919 to 1932.

This commitment to preserving traditional gender roles made the League of Catholic Women compatible with secular antifeminists. Until the early 1930s Slattery encouraged collaboration between her members, the MPIL, and the *Woman Patriot*, which she credited with revealing for her how the child labor amendment was "aimed at the destruction of our country, our religion and our home." At Slattery's urging, individual parish women's clubs subscribed and collected money to contribute to the WPPC. In 1926, the group featured Margaret Robinson and Mary Kilbreth in its lecture series.[63] This collaboration with the Catholic women of Massachusetts distinguished female antiradicals from groups on the far right, like the women's Ku Klux Klan, which perceived the Catholic Church as one of the most dangerous forces in modern American life. Conservatives, by contrast, saw Catholics as an important bulwark against radicalism. In 1922, the Catholic publication *America* had condemned the Russian Revolution as an "orgy of blood and terrorism." The execution in 1923 of Monsignor Buchkavich, the vicar general of the Roman Catholic Church in Russia, solidified the American Catholic hierarchy's antipathy to the Soviet regime. The Reverend Edmund A. Walsh, an academic at Georgetown University, was a leading critic of the Soviet Union during the interwar years. Walsh waged a propaganda campaign against the Soviet Union, claiming that Bolsheviks had executed 1.8 million of their fellow citizens, including 28 archbishops and 1,400 priests.[64]

While the Catholic Church provided important institutional support to amendment foes, the growing opposition to this measure was not limited to the state's Catholics. In a letter to the editor of the *Springfield Union* on the eve of the referendum, W. S. Palmer railed: "Is it not perfectly apparent that this 'Child' Labor Amendment, if passed, would be an ideal weapon to teach and propagate Bolshevism and Socialism—an opportunity to force these doctrines . . . into every home in the land?" After repeating the WPPC's version of Florence Kelley's and Grace Abbott's supposedly radical personal histories, Palmer warned that these reformers had "thousands of volunteer teachers ready, and the American people would spend millions in salaries to seduce their children to Socialism and destroy their Republic."[65] In a notable reversal that came one month before the referendum, Boston's mayor James M. Curley, the Democratic candidate for governor who had inserted a pro-amendment plank into his party's state platform and had spent the summer speaking on the amendment's behalf, made the surprise announcement that he had decided to oppose ratification. In his statement describing why the amendment menaced American freedom, Curley drew on the logic of the original WPPC petition. "If it be the purpose of Miss Wischenewetski [Florence Kelley], through the Child Labor Amendment, to lay the foundation for a Sovietized United States of America, then it becomes the duty of all persons interested in the preservation of the American Republic to set aside every consideration other than national integrity." Quoting directly from a statement by Utah Senator William H. King that had been distributed by the anti-ratification committee, Curley declared, "this is a Bolshevistic scheme and a lot of good people are accepting it, not knowing the real consequence which will result and the sinister purpose back of the measure."[66]

Curley might have been motivated by his desire to shore up his Catholic support before the next election. But his embrace of the anti-Bolshevist reasoning of amendment opponents demonstrates its potency. It may have proved peripheral to the congressional debate but proved effective in Massachusetts.[67] Commenting on the widespread acceptance of these charges in Massachusetts, amendment advocate Thomas J. Walsh, senator from Montana, observed with frustration that "the most moving arguments in the rejection of the amendment have been arguments that were entirely illegitimate."[68]

Having stoked fears of radical social change, antiratificationists successfully kept public attention focused on revolutionary dangers. When the day of the referendum arrived, an amendment advocate reflected that the choice was clear for most residents: "Massachusetts was asked to vote against the nationalization of children, and Massachusetts so voted."[69] On November 3, 1924, ratification was voted down three to one. For Margaret Robinson, the vote showed that the people of Massachusetts were "not ready to line up with Russia in turning over the labor and education of the young to centralized control."[70] Mary Kilbreth took the victory in Massachusetts as proof that conservative sentiments outweighed radical sympathies among women. The ratification fight, Kilbreth wrote, was "a fair trial of strength between the 'sex-conscious' women's organizations and the normal women of the State." She asserted that the defeat of the amendment in the Bay State showed "that women voters are not sheep to be herded by the fiat of resolutions committees and should dispel the myth of a deliverable 'women's vote.' "[71] In one way Kilbreth was correct; the campaign for the child labor amendment certainly demonstrated the limited national power of the women's reform lobby.

Although the role of the Catholic Church was critical, the Massachusetts Public Interests League, the Sentinels of the Republic, and the Citizens' Committee to Protect Our Homes and Children were credited with the defeat, which proved a fatal blow to the national campaign for the amendment.[72] The *Woman Patriot* also played no small part in repositioning the amendment as a subversive measure; the publication claimed to have distributed over sixty thousand copies of its Senate "petition."[73] Female antiradicals successfully recast public understanding of the measure. Rather than a reasonable effort to bring the social costs of industrial progress into line with broadly held community values, the amendment became a veritable act of treason, a communist-led plot to "nationalize" children and assume control over the home with devastating consequences for women within the traditional family.

The outcome in Massachusetts reverberated through the national ratification campaign. Massachusetts activists joined drives against the amendment in other states, where the same tactics and arguments were successfully repeated.[74] A League of Women Voters activist reported from the Ohio ratification debate that "all those awful arguments about nationalizing the children, interfering between parent and child and federal agents replacing mothers and school teachers were flaunted before us, amidst wild applause from the galleries."[75] The business community also adopted as its own the arguments first put forward by the WPPC, after they proved so effective in neutralizing female reformers. "Manufacturers," observed a special committee created by the WJCC to study attacks on women's organizations, used the allegations published in the *Woman Patriot* to mount "one of the most slanderous, vicious, and mendacious campaigns ever witnessed in the country."[76] In their fight to keep reform at bay for the rest of the decade, industrialists found these ideas to be one of the most powerful tools at their disposal. "This diabolical work of destroying our Constitution and free government by substitutions made in Russia and other foreign workshops is expected to be accomplished through the women's organizations in our country," warned John Edgerton, president of the National Association of Manufacturers at a conference on women in industry in 1926. "The chief instrument to be used is social legislation in the ostensible interest of mothers and children."[77] By the beginning of the 1930s, only six states had ratified the child labor amendment.[78]

Fears that labor restrictions would "nationalize" children did more than doom the ratification campaign for the proposed Twentieth Amendment. They also began to erode support for maternalist politics at the heart of the female dominion. The General Federation of Women's Clubs (GFWC) provides a window on this transformation. The debate over the child labor amendment raised anxieties that began to swamp long-standing support within this organization for restrictions on wage earning by children. The GFWC's position on this issue was challenged by a militant group of clubwomen, who launched a vigorous campaign. Discontent was first evident in Massachusetts, where the state federation of women's clubs invited Henry Lee Shattuck, a prominent opponent of the child labor amendment, to give its members a "safe and sane talk" on child labor in 1923. Member Effie Attwill told Shattuck that the national organization had been "pushing us very hard to take that bill as one of ours for this year but I have been fighting against it and I do not think it will pass the Board as recommended for endorsement."[79] That same year, at the PTA convention, conservative delegates linked the movements for disarmament and regulation of child labor, denouncing both as threats to freedom and public safety. These delegates were easily voted down, but PTA leader Elizabeth Tilton feared resistance would not be as strong within the GFWC.[80] Antiradicals, Tilton warned, had "designs on the General Federation of Women's Clubs and are making some inroads there."[81]

Tilton's fears seemed to be confirmed in 1925, when the GFWC became the second large women's organization to embrace the tenets of antiradicalism. The group passed a resolution asserting that "the plan for destructive revolution in the United States by international communists is not a myth, but a proven fact." Almost identical to the proclamation issued by the DAR that same April, this declaration showed that the GFWC leadership harbored real concerns about radical influences.[82] Antiradical Margaret Robinson predicted that clubwomen would begin to act on these fears and reject the maternalist priorities that had long shaped the political agenda of the group. "As women begin to understand more clearly the real nature of the legislation which the women's lobby at Washington is demanding," she asserted, "many of them are rebelling against such leadership."[83]

Yet in the case of the GFWC, the embrace of antiradicalism did not prompt the organization to jettison its long-standing commitment to social welfare reform. At least at first, the GFWC leadership did not appear to see any contradictions in supporting both intensified countersubversion efforts and new government laws and programs to promote the health and welfare of women and children. The organization remained resolute for female reform, even as it pledged to make a "definite study" of the "danger" posed by radicalism.[84] The GFWC recommended that its members read R. M. Whitney's *Reds in America*, a book detailing the supposed work of American women for communism that was also distributed by the DAR in 1924. The GFWC claim that Whitney's work accurately recounted the spread of "communistic ideas from Russia among us" stunned the other members of the WJCC; in their view, it slandered everyone associated with female reform organizations as "servants of Moscow." They were shocked that the GFWC would endorse an admirer of the *Woman Patriot* and a self-proclaimed enemy of the "international feminist-pacifist bloc."[85]

GFWC's promotion of antiradical tracts did little to satisfy a vocal minority of its members, who were outraged that the national federation did not follow its denunciation of radicals with a rejection of the maternalist legislative agenda.[86] By 1925, the specter of a "revolution by legislation" had fueled a full-blown revolt within the national General Federation of

Women's Clubs. This conservative insurgency might have fizzled without the emergence of an articulate leader, Georgia May Martin, a writer known primarily by her male pen name, George Madden Martin. The daughter of a bookseller and the wife of a successful businessman, Martin spent her life in Louisville, Kentucky, where she joined a group for authors in the early years of the club movement. The support of like-minded women might have helped her launch her fiction-writing career; her first story appeared in *Harper's Weekly* in 1895. Between 1897 and 1935, Martin published eleven novels, becoming less prolific after 1920, when her political involvement deepened. Martin's activist career was complex and riven by contradictions. "Intensely feminine" in demeanor, she always identified herself by her male pseudonym. No advocate of female suffrage, she was an enthusiastic participant in Democratic Party politics. Loyal to this bastion of Southern segregationism, she was also devoted to fighting racial oppression. In 1920, Martin became a charter member of the Committee on Interracial Cooperation; in the 1930s she became a leader of the Association of Southern Women for the Prevention of Lynching. Her desire to eliminate lynchings and improve race relations, however, did not inhibit her support for the philosophy of states' rights.[87]

Martin's belief in states' rights inspired a series of articles published in the *Atlantic Monthly* in 1924 and 1925, detailing her unhappiness with the GFWC's legislative endorsements.[88] Martin objected in principle to federal measures aimed at ameliorating what she saw as local ills, asserting that the content and purpose of the measures were irrelevant. All federal social legislation, especially that creating additional bureaucracies, menaced the freedom of individual Americans by violating the basic principles of the Constitution. Moreover, she claimed that lobbying, a tactic perfected by women's organizations, was incompatible with the tradition of representative government passed down from ancient Greece. By pressuring representatives to support a particular position, women's groups were "tempting the congressman to do evil in violating his own sense of right and wrong."[89]

At fault for the GFWC policies and methods were its rank-and-file members, whom Martin castigated for their ignorance about government, history, and the "fundamentals of economics." As for current events, Martin claimed that she could not carry on a real discussion about the Sheppard-Towner bill or the Ku Klux Klan in her circle of female acquaintances. "In my judgment American women generally are not interested in public affairs, national or local, in the concrete or in the abstract," Martin wrote.[90]

Clubwomen, according to Martin, refused to educate themselves. At the request of leaders, they blithely passed resolutions without discussion, debate, or real understanding.[91] Thanks to the direction they received in women's clubs, moreover, the average female voter was too focused on the "interests of women and children."[92] Her passion for states' rights convinced Martin to become active in the campaign against the child labor amendment. Her objection, she argued, was not against tighter regulation of child labor. "Federal interference," she claimed, would actually delay the eradication of child labor, which had to be addressed at the state level.[93] What disturbed her even more was "the revolutionary purpose within the bill to hand over to Congress powers and duties which under the Constitution belong to the States." A member of the GFWC for thirty-one years, Martin was irked that the influential women's organization was helping to tighten the noose of federal "paternalism."

The national debate over the child labor amendment demonstrated that it was not only Martin who was unhappy about the GFWC's legislative priorities. The president of the Civic Club of White Plains made headlines by denouncing Owen R. Lovejoy, secretary of the National Child Labor Committee, when he spoke to the Westchester Federation of Women's Clubs in New York. Dora Arnold demanded a chance to refute Lovejoy's pro-amendment statements. "Forty-five minutes for Communism and one minute for Americanism," Arnold fumed, after hearing she had sixty seconds to say her piece. She heckled the assembled clubwomen as they resolved in favor of the amendment, warning "this is pure socialism and Communism—the nationalization of children!"[94] Women heard frequent pleas that they reclaim their organization from foreign-inspired radicals. "We read in our Federated Club news that clubwomen will again work against the business interests of our country, work to disintegrate the family by renewing their campaign to pass the most vicious measure ever proposed to a civilized country, the so-called child labor amendment," reported Mrs. Lilla Day Monroe, a writer and speaker from Topeka, Kansas, herself a member of a club associated with the General Federation of Women's Clubs. "Think of the effrontery of the League of Women Voters who would have us go to Russia to learn how to rear our children!"[95] Clubwomen from Florida mounted a more formal protest to the national leadership of the GFWC, presenting a minority report to its governing council. The Southeastern Division of the national organization endorsed this report, which challenged the GFWC's support for the child labor amendment. The response from the GFWC leadership was swift; President Mary Sherman ruled the minority opinion out of order. State federations and individual clubs were forbidden to conduct campaigns opposing measures endorsed by the national federation. "In no other way can the General Federation speak as an organization," she opined.[96]

Martin immediately raised the cry of "clubs' rights" to protest Sherman's decision. She led her Louisville club in drafting a response that asserted "the right of every locality and group within such locality, to decide for itself what is best for it"; the club resolved that it would not be bound by any policy it had not voted to endorse.[97] To publicize their defiance, the women from Louisville sent a delegation to the GFWC's next biennial meeting in Atlantic City, New Jersey, where their protests dominated news coverage of the 1926 convention.[98] Given ten minutes to present their case to the assembled women, the Kentucky women had little visible success in convincing the other delegates to drop their commitment to federal welfare legislation. Ignoring the GFWC's long history of support for such reforms, dissenters argued that since suffrage, unscrupulous leaders had focused on explicitly political activity that contravened the organization's founding principles. "Over-night," Martin claimed, the GFWC "assumed the activities of a political body. Where did the Federation get its authority to do this?"[99]

As Martin launched her campaign to reform the GFWC, her focus on "states' rights" and "club rights" overshadowed references to subversive influences. As her 1921 novel, *March On*, reveals, however, the Louisville writer was not immune to worries about the radical "threat." The book portrayed a hardhearted radical through the eyes of its heroine, a young woman coming of age at the end of the Progressive Era who rejected the lifestyle of her feminist grandmother. The humanitarian Lucy forsook her ambition to make a difference in the world in favor of domestic happiness, marrying the man she loved. Widowed by World War I and soon a mother, Lucy still showed no regrets. Home, family, and country remained her trinity. These values are inverted in a communist she befriended, the brilliant and sinister Eugene Lelewel, a man loyal to a philosophy instead of a country. The ruthless Lelewel demonstrated his willingness to sacrifice his wife and son—whom he treated as mere tools in the fight for internationalism and communism—to political expediency. Never a leftist, Lucy lost all sympathy for radicals when she discovered Lelewel had sunk into the global communist underground, only to resurface to continue fomenting revolution.[100] The "American" values exemplified by Lucy were foreign to underhanded radicals like Lelewel, who would use any means to destroy social harmony for an abstract principle and vast power. Yet the threat posed by Lelewel could be contained relatively easily. While many conservatives of the period feared that radicals had captured the hearts and institutions of middle-class America, the fiction published by Martin at the height of the government red raids portrayed subversives eroding society from its margins. American women, epitomized by Lucy, still retained the values that would sustain the nation.

The longer Martin protested the GFWC, the more prominent the concerns about radicalism expressed in *March On* became for her, especially after she joined forces with other clubwomen determined to expose the radical roots of the GFWC's legislative agenda. New Hampshire clubwoman Grace P. Amsden, an active opponent of the child labor amendment, composed a tract titled "Political Dictatorship in Women's Clubs" in support of the Kentucky dissenters. It was no coincidence, wrote Amsden, that "every Federal measure sponsored this year by our State Federation, under dictation of the General Federation, is a purely socialistic measure, subversive of our Federal Constitution." Rank-and-file club members had no say in the federation's legislative program, according to Amsden. Instead, it was dictated by the WJCC, which was, in turn, controlled by infamous socialist Florence Kelley. Amsden urged organized women to ask themselves: "Is the Women's Lobby, working for the bureaucratic and socialist legislation which is the enemy and destroyer of free government, the true representative before Congress of the Club women of the United States?"[101]

Amsden's pamphlet was distributed by the Massachusetts Public Interests League, which invited the Louisville rebels to speak in Boston. The National Society of Women Builders of America, an antiradical group started by former DAR head Daisy Story, extended a warm welcome to representatives from the Kentucky group in New York; an antiradical meeting in Raleigh, North Carolina, featured Martin as a speaker; the *Woman Patriot* trumpeted the campaign of the dissident woman's club. By the end of 1926, Martin had absorbed at least the rhetoric, and probably the philosophy, of her antiradical supporters. Her club, she told the *New York Times*, was battling "those un-American and unpatriotic forces which . . . are responsible for the mass of paternalistic, socialistic and unconstitutional legislation which . . . is being demanded in the name of organized women."[102]

The leaders of the GFWC stood firm against the rebels. Even with the Louisville dissenters in attendance, the 1926 convention refused overwhelmingly to rescind Sherman's ruling on dissension within the group. Delegates reiterated their endorsement of the doomed child labor amendment as well, despite nay votes from close to one-third of the women attending.[103] The only concession to conflict within its ranks was a cryptic resolution calling on the organization in the future "to guard its Resolutions more carefully."[104] President Sherman tried to short-circuit future controversy about the group's purposes, suggesting its apolitical charter emphasizing "culture" be amended to include an explicit commitment "to promote projects for the betterment of humanity."[105] Little seemed to change in the wake of Martin's challenge to GFWC leadership; the 1926 convention appeared to be a rout for antiradicals. Yet the gathering's official transcript masked how vulnerable the reform mission had become within large, centrist women's organizations. While the group's leadership ultimately quashed the conservative revolt, it could not quell the growing opposition to social welfare legislation harbored by a significant proportion of its membership. The mutiny within the GFWC served as a harbinger for women's clubs of the attenuating support for the female reform agenda.

While the GFWC leadership worked to send opponents of social welfare reform packing, these activists received a warm welcome from the DAR. Immediately after a meeting with Kilbreth in 1926, officers of the DAR began issuing warnings about the "revolution by reform." The group's new antipathy to female reform was traumatic for many clubwomen who remembered its previous political incarnation and had also identified with the mission of the hereditary association. The path charted by Brosseau and her cabinet seemed like a dramatic departure to puzzled clubwomen like Alice Mulford, who wondered "why an old useful organization like the DAR . . . oppose [the Sheppard-Towner Act] so bitterly."[106] Some DAR members pleaded with President General Brosseau to temper her enthusiasm for illuminating the radical influences guiding politically centrist organizations and institutions. "Let us not bring these matters into our program; they are offensive to far too many of us," Mary Miller asserted, closing her letter "with the prayer that the present policies may be abandoned in the Society of the Daughters of the American Revolution, that we may return to our rightful field in which we all belong happily."[107] Brosseau remained steadfast in her support for conservative activism. "Every Daughter of the American Revolution who has sworn to uphold her Constitution is thereby bound to do her utmost to help maintain the institutions of this Government and to be an absolutely loyal citizen," President General Brosseau declared. "If that be politics, then politics is her duty."[108]

Grace Abbott echoed the sentiments of many maternalists when she revealed that "personally it makes me very sad to see patriotism and goodwill on the part of our old American stock—to which I belong on both the maternal and paternal side—diverted to such ends."[109] Female reformers would find it ever more difficult to reconcile their commitment to reform with their sense that they were carriers of a hereditary patriotism. This claim was increasingly monopolized by the DAR, which under the leadership of Brosseau and Walker was determined to destroy the broad coalition that had brought female reformers and social conservatives together.

Women like Abbott and Mulford failed to understand that the mantle of political repression that had settled on the United States in the aftermath of the Bolshevik Revolution had changed sentiments about the welfare state, even within the lobbying arm of the "female dominion." The evolution of the DAR parallels that of Elizabeth Lowell Putnam, the Massachusetts activist whose experience running surveillance programs during the Great War made her see danger in the maternal health programs she had once championed. The National Defense Committee encouraged women to trade maternalism for antiradicalism through an educational program designed to make DAR members into experts on the subversive threat. National headquarters instructed members to study propaganda and gather information about radical individuals and organizations in their communities. DAR National Defense Committee chairman Flora Walker told her followers that "the needs of the hour summon each one of us to action." Her followers joined women from the American Legion Auxiliary, the Daughters of 1812, and the Massachusetts Public Interests League to monitor a huge range of gatherings; they observed groups from the South Dakota League of Women Voters to the Boston Young Communists' Party.[110] By the end of the decade, these women had built an autonomous bureaucracy devoted to collecting and analyzing data on radicalism. They developed networks and systems for watching their enemies and assembled dossiers on people whose political activities, ethnicity, or race aroused suspicion.

These efforts to understand, document, and expose the radical threat supported the DAR leadership's work to transform the political culture of their organization. The kind of intense study promoted by the National Defense Committee made women into ardent antiradicals; surveillance work and propaganda analysis were "consciousness raising" activities that changed women. Once convinced that radicalism was a real threat to their families, women became prepared to support theories they might have once dismissed as marginal. Those who perceived a need for intensified political repression came to see maternal and child health programs through a new paradigm of national peril. Though these measures seemed to have little connection to national security, the reformers behind them became easy targets for the fear unleashed by a preoccupation with revolutionary radicalism. Conservatives argued passionately for an enlarged security state with greater powers to monitor and punish political dissenters. Even as they decried government programs designed to benefit families, they demonstrated that the radical revolution on the other side of the world had not made them wary of an all-powerful state.

The DAR and the American Legion Auxiliary both encouraged their members to undertake vigilante surveillance work. The idea that civilians should take an active role in countersubversion had its roots in World War I, when Americans came to fear that immigrants and radicals would use the war emergency to subvert national security from within. In this tense atmosphere, the minuscule Department of Justice quickly concluded that it could not manage all the countersubversion investigations warranted by the presence of possible alien enemies and the need to enforce new wartime espionage and sedition laws. The federal agency appealed to a group of eager volunteers who worked through the National Security League, the American Defense Society, and most notably the American Protective League (APL) to record and punish every transgression against national security. The APL was the largest of these groups and attracted 250,000 members.[111]

In Massachusetts, Elizabeth Lowell Putnam secretly volunteered her services to the Massachusetts State Intelligence Bureau, where she began by identifying alleged traitors and making maps detailing where immigrants resided.[112] Soon she began volunteering her time and money to expand state surveillance operations; Putnam was named chief of the Women's Auxiliary Intelligence Bureau for the state of Massachusetts in December 1917.[113] Over the next year Putnam recruited a network of women spies to compile reports on suspicious Massachusetts residents. Her work was secret. The women's auxiliary group was not mentioned in public reports of the Intelligence Bureau, and she cautioned her agents to keep their activities quiet. Once she instructed a potential recruit to "burn the letter after reading" to keep their surveillance undetected by "those who are plotting in our midst."[114]

Putnam's efforts were different from the better-known groups because they involved women; Putnam organized her corps of female spies just as the APL banned women from its ranks.[115] No evidence suggests that Putnam's work as chief of the Women's Auxiliary Intelligence Bureau deterred radicals or saboteurs. Putnam's operatives did not uncover any plots to overthrow the government; the only surviving report indicates that her memos on subversion and disloyalty chronicled the violence of wartime nativism and the settling of old scores.[116] Indeed, the whole project of volunteer countersubversion encouraged the most petty and paranoid tendencies of the vigilantes.

The end of the Great War failed to eradicate concerns about domestic subversion. Wartime sleuths took the postwar unrest as evidence that the Armistice had not been recognized by proponents of radical ideologies. Activists like Putnam were eager to put wartime tactics to use in maintaining order in a world in which Bolshevism seemed to be ascendant. They watched with horror as wartime sedition acts were repealed in 1921, political prisoners won their release in 1923, and the federal government announced it would cease political surveillance in 1924.[117] They had little to fear. Pious declarations about political freedom did not mean that the campaign against radicals had been abandoned. Retreating federal agents encouraged local governments to expand their red squads, which recruited volunteers to cooperate with local police to collect information and intimidate dissenters. And despite claims that they had mothballed political surveillance activities, federal agents refused to part with their files. They kept adding to them, optimistically biding their time until more aggressive monitoring of dissenters would receive political sanction.[118]

An ebb in radical organizing left countersubversion agencies plenty of time to reorganize their already voluminous dossiers during the 1920s. Two of the groups most feared by conservatives were struggling to retain followers. The influence and power of the Socialist Party had peaked before World War I; the Communist Party posed no formidable threat during these years, as its members were mired in sectarian disputes that would handicap their efforts to recruit a mass following until the Great Depression. Both of these groups had been crippled by the wide-scale deportations and imprisonments of 1917–1920. Moreover, the number of immigrants coming into the country had slowed to a trickle after the passage of restrictive immigration laws.

Yet antiradicals remained haunted by the memory of the Bolshevik Revolution and the unrest that followed in North America. They refused to be pacified by either the paralysis of the left or the diminishing pool of newcomers. Any period of peace, in their minds, was merely a lull before a larger storm. To meet what they believed to be a waxing threat, these activists immersed themselves in the world of Marxist propaganda, communist rallies, and summer camps for young cadres. They wanted to assemble documentary evidence that would prove that the nation was on the brink of a new civil war. To this end, they collected programs from radical gatherings and reports from meetings observed. They gathered literature from radical meetings and revolutionary headquarters. The DAR organized a brigade of women volunteers to clip both left-wing and conservative newspapers and magazines for references to radical activities. Wealthy antiradical women commissioned translations of foreign language newspapers to sniff out radical activities within immigrant communities.[119] These clippings and pamphlets filled bulging files, which researchers used to create dossiers on organizations and individuals.

Such voluminous documentation of radical ideology, female antiradicals reasoned, would rouse citizens to action. In building support for the National Defense Committee, Flora Walker always quoted at length from supposedly subversive propaganda calling for the abolition of the family and religion or the recruitment of youth for the class struggle. She chose quotes for their shock value, like an excerpt from Alexandra Kollontai's pamphlet "Communism and the Family," which asserted that "the old type of family has seen its day."[120] Authentic propaganda illustrating the bloodthirstiness of the left made real its threat to the American way of life in a way that more general warnings never could. For instance, Walker reprinted portions of a Young Communist League publication that demonstrated the group's intention to "convert" American youth "into class fighters . . . full of conscious hatred of the capitalist system and prepare them when the time comes to fight under Communist leadership for the overthrow of the damnable capitalist system."[121] Wealthy antiradical women and the organizations they supported reproduced and distributed tens of thousands of documents designed to expose radicals' true colors to women skeptical of dissidents' ardor or violent tendencies.[122] Both the Daughters of the American Revolution and the American Legion Auxiliary selected newspapers, pamphlets, placards, and posters and arranged them in exhibits that toured the country.[123] On the premise that targeted organizations would hang themselves with their own words, female antiradicals distributed the propaganda of their sworn enemies much more widely than any of these small left-wing organizations ever could have managed on their own.

Both hereditary and veterans' groups organized their members into propaganda reading groups for antiradical consciousness raising.[124] As part of a program of indoctrination, leaders encouraged women to read and discuss both patriotic and radical literature. These study groups taught women how to recognize dangerous doctrines, helping them to learn the jargon and catchwords that hid subversion from the uninitiated.[125] "This kind of study is not entertaining," asserted Flora Walker. "On the other hand it is often gruesome and repellent. I commend the women upon their willingness to endure discomfort in this connection that they might be better fitted to protect their own families, their communities and even the Nation itself."[126]

The American Legion Auxiliary, the Daughters of the American Revolution, and the Massachusetts Public Interests League used their files to build archives, which they made available for research on radicals. The DAR tried to make its Washington headquarters into a nationally recognized antiradical information center.[127] The location of Memorial Continental Hall in the heart of the monumental city on the Mall was ideal for a civilian countersubversion agency trying to establish itself as part of official Washington. Only a few blocks from the White House, the white marble DAR headquarters on its manicured grounds looked more impressive than the government buildings that surrounded it. The DAR hall was prominently featured in contemporary guidebooks to the nation's capital, making it a perfect venue for educating visitors drawn to the building's colonial relics.[128] Walker set up an exhibit of radical literature in 1927, which remained in place through the Second World War. Women volunteers interpreted this display for thousands of guests annually.[129] These women patriots prided themselves on making their files accessible to the public, claiming that hundreds of people visited their headquarters in Washington for "intensive training" in how to combat the "veritable epidemic of communism sweeping the nation."[130]

Leaders like Walker called on adventurous women to make themselves into field agents for the DAR's countersubversion agency. Women were encouraged to investigate radical activities for themselves and compile information to feed the files of the National Defense Committee. These types of missions were also intended to build grassroots support for antiradicalism; they erased doubts within the organization about the threat facing the nation. In *Confessions of a Parlor Socialist*, Hermine Schwed recounted how eavesdropping on socialist speakers had transformed her from radical sympathizer to antiradical zealot. She claimed that her observations revealed that "our whole country is infested with eloquent speakers . . . who on the one hand are inflaming huge audiences of working people to a Socialist revolution and on the other roundly cursing out Socialism under that name to huge audiences of the employing class, confusing or soothing them as to the likelihood of any revolutionary danger whatever." By her telling, surveillance had provided her with a flash of revelation, when she recognized the barbarity of socialist goals and pledged to fight the advance of radicalism.[131]

Female antiradicals received the most attention when they linked centrist reforms to revolution, especially when they decried the radical influences in middle-class women's voluntary associations. Yet outrage at the supposed treachery of native-born women never erased their xenophobia. MPIL president Margaret Robinson described a Boston meeting that eulogized Lenin as "packed with foreigners, the women dressed in silks and furs." Robinson warned that radical ranks were filled with foreigners who were "enjoying a degree of liberty, comfort and prosperity undreamed of by their parents and grandparents." These newcomers, she observed, were "all eager to overthrow our government and the institutions which have secured them these benefits."[132]

This nativist worldview permeates a story of surveillance told by Helen Stuart, the state Americanization chairman for the Wisconsin American Legion Auxiliary. An encounter with radicals perceived to be "foreign" provided an intoxicating mix of danger and heroism for women like Stuart. She was already a veteran antiradical when she learned in August 1929 that agents of Moscow had literally set up camp in Kenosha, Wisconsin. American radicalism may have been suffering through the doldrums in 1929, but summer camps like the one Stuart discovered were nonetheless common. They were training ground for children, established by communists, socialists, and other radicals to nurture a revolutionary culture among their children. This effort was familiar to Stuart from countless lectures on communist methods and her earlier investigation of a communist school on the banks of Wisconsin's Brule River.[133] A facility to indoctrinate children in radical teachings was the embodiment of danger for women like Stuart.

With insidious enemies working so close to home, Stuart was driven to action. "I felt it my duty to investigate personally," she said. "I found, through a woman in Kenosha who had visited the camp, what was going on, and I got her to take me out there Sunday morning in her automobile." Stuart described how the two walked slowly through the camp, "not wishing to attract attention." But when the women surreptitiously picked up a sign that read "Soviet Defender," Stuart said that a dark and foreign-looking man confronted them and tried to prevent them from leaving with this proof of the camp's radical purpose. She understood her struggle over the sign to be a heroic act in the campaign against communism. In July 1930 Stuart brought the sign to Chicago to buttress her testimony before a congressional committee. Before an audience in the city's Federal Building, she held up the sign as evidence that she had fearlessly defied those working to undermine God and nation.[134] According to a leader of the DAR National Defense Committee, this type of effort to ferret "out seditious enterprises and un-American activities" and expose "explosive propaganda" and "traitorous agitations," showed that female antiradicals could "bravely undertake unpleasant work."[135] These encounters with evildoers galvanized women like Stuart. While their confrontational style was no doubt the luxury of those who could expect their class position to protect them from physical danger, they still saw their activities to be a test of their patriotism and character.

Analyzing the vigilante surveillance campaign undertaken by female antiradicals provides valuable insight into the worldview of these activists; they were desperate to trade liberty for security, especially the freedom of those outside their imagined national community.[136] But it is important to remember that this countersubversion work likely did little to influence the activities of committed revolutionaries. Working-class and radical activists were probably unfazed by interventions on the part of members of the DAR and American Legion Auxiliary. Those who remained active in radical politics during this time were accustomed to facing vigilante violence, police brutality, and politically motivated arrests; they were not likely to be shaken by hostile visits to their meetings, camps, or political headquarters from the women of the DAR, the American Legion Auxiliary, or the Daughters of 1812. "To be an active Communist" at this time "was to expect to be beaten up and jailed," according to historian Ellen Schrecker.[137]

While these field missions changed little on the left, they played an important role in the long-term growth of the right. These activities garnered support for antiradicalism among organized women, who were transformed by their surveillance work and propaganda study. Radical watching and propaganda analysis galvanized female activists who emerged from meetings and reading groups with the sense that their country was in imminent danger. They issued warnings, which were largely ignored by a nation that had decided—at least for the moment—that Bolshevism was less interesting than sexual experimentation. Feeling anxious and marginalized, private intelligence agents became receptive to theories that seemed far-fetched and even paranoid to many of their contemporaries. They accepted the notion that high-minded female reform would beget the revolutionary horrors of Soviet Russia. The women who remained connected to the Children's Bureau were surprised by the growing number of clubwomen who came to see connections between reform and revolution that would recast moderate legislative measures as red-tainted. The most dramatic reversals came from veteran maternalists like Elizabeth Lowell Putnam, who had substantial experience working in the world of female reform and expertise in child and maternal health. From Putnam's perspective, she never lost her commitment to mothers and babies, even as she abandoned allies and causes she had once championed. Like the prenatal clinic she established before World War I, the political surveillance bureau she founded in Massachusetts was dedicated to protecting the most vulnerable members of society. The prenatal clinic could save women and babies from avoidable medical complications, while better political intelligence could spare them the ravages of revolutionary radicals. The information she gathered in this work convinced her that revolution was under way and that female reformers were its handmaidens. Any reformer who visited DAR headquarters would have been aware of the countersubversion work of these female activists. But they probably could not grasp how political surveillance and radical consciousness-raising activities made the threat of "revolution by legislation" seem real to these women.

By 1926, the surveillance campaign had helped to knit together the different strands of female antiradicalism. These activities—along with the more public advocacy associated with the WPCND—joined DAR members in common cause with women from the American Legion Auxiliary and a host of smaller veterans' and hereditary groups. At least in the DAR, this focus on countersubversion opened women to the theories of the WPPC and the MPIL, tiny groups that had little influence in women's club politics in the immediate aftermath of the suffrage amendment. After supplying the key arguments that sank the child labor amendment in Massachusetts, the *Woman Patriot* gained the admiration of these larger women's groups. The political culture fostered by radical watching positioned the WPPC to become an epicenter of propaganda critical in thwarting some of the most important reform efforts between the Progressive Era and the New Deal. While these former antisuffragists never collaborated with the American Legion Auxiliary, women in all these groups began to see themselves as part of a broader conservative movement of women that was animated by a conviction that the nation was in peril.

One large group—the GFWC—struggled to straddle the growing divided between the traditional politics of maternalism and the emergent politics of antiradicalism. By the end of the decade, it would discover how difficult it would be to reconcile these two political agendas. As significant numbers of clubwomen began to trade maternalism for antiradicalism, reformers found their efforts to regulate child labor thwarted yet again. Thanks to Putnam and her allies, female reformers found their claim that they spoke for all women to be undermined at the moment when the franchise promised to finally bring them real political power. Conservative politicians were reassured at the same juncture; the female voter was no longer viewed as a threat, thanks in large part to female antiradicals' activism. "The 1924 Massachusetts advisory referendum on the child-labor amendment alone has surely buried this 'solidarity of women' superstition so deeply that the ghost of the phantom 'solid women's vote' should never more frighten even the most timid candidate," the *Woman Patriot* crowed.[138] Defeat of the child labor amendment in Massachusetts increased the confidence and ambition of foes of social legislation. They would widen their scope after this victory, turning their attention in its aftermath to the institutional framework of middle-class women's politics that had made progressive women such effective champions of social reform.

Chapter 5

# The "Red Menace" Roils the Grass Roots: The Conservative Insurgency Reshapes Women's Organizations

In 1926, antiradical consciousness-raising efforts bore fruit. A conservative insurgency erupted in women's clubs across the country. The polemics and surveillance reports amassed by antiradical groups did not sit collecting dust in the nation's capital. Instead, they were used by antiradical leaders to remake the landscape of women's politics from the ground up. The DAR's National Defense Committee distributed reams of propaganda to its chapters in all corners of the nation. The result was a correspondence course in countersubversion. DAR members were encouraged to fashion themselves into experts on revolutionary radicalism. Mastering this "study material" was more than just an intellectual exercise. It fostered awareness that demanded action. Frances Cone, a DAR leader in South Dakota, declared that "all Americans who are real lovers of our Republic will not sit still and do nothing when they are really convinced of what is going on."[1] This woman patriot was the most outspoken member of a group that mobilized on the northern prairie, where Cone bragged that her chapter had taken "the lead" in rooting out "subversive movements . . . in various South Dakota cities" and showing the people of Huron "the 'Red' menace to our institutions and our form of government."[2] Constant mailings inspired Cone and her compatriots to roil local voters' forums and women's clubs. This new purpose brewed what one League of Women Voters member described as an "antagonistic storm" between traditional reformers and newly zealous antiradicals.[3] Regional LWV leaders instructed their Huron members to keep the "sensational charges" going "back and forth between the League and other organizations" out of the local newspaper. And Huron reformers vowed to keep "quiet for a while" to allow the DAR to "destroy their own organization . . . through such methods." But national leaders of the maternalist coalition soon discovered that it was futile to ignore the insurgency boiling up all over the country.[4]

Dispatches from Washington prompted some newly galvanized conservatives to march directly into the heart of radical politics. They snooped on summer camps and infiltrated political rallies.[5] But most clubwomen gave little time to avowed revolutionaries. These activists chose to attack what they saw as more sinister manifestations of radicalism: the Bolshevik influence on female reform. Frances Cone led her Huron DAR chapter when it came together in the winter of 1927 to pass resolutions condemning the Sheppard-Towner Maternity and Infancy Protection Act and the proposed constitutional amendment to ban child labor. She explained that the innocuous-sounding legislation was an example of "state socialism" conceived by "Red" organizations.[6] Convinced that middle-class reformers had pushed the nation to the brink of revolution, conservative clubwomen in South Dakota and other states lobbied to block key measures assumed to enjoy the support of all women voters. They denounced the type of legislative reform that had won nearly universal support from women's organizations before the Nineteenth Amendment. They used the moral authority they enjoyed as middle-class clubwomen to challenge female reformers, who had built their political influence on their claim to represent all women. By 1926, female antiradicals' grassroots insurgency illuminated the constricting boundaries of the female dominion. Supporters of the Children's Bureau were blindsided by this new nemesis, which blocked the renewal of the Sheppard-Towner Act at the beginning of 1927.

The demise of Sheppard-Towner was a heartbreaking defeat for female reformers. Yet newly mobilized conservatives were not content to prevent the passage of particular bills. They sought to destroy the political reputations of female reformers. They were determined to dissolve the veneer of political respectability enjoyed by female policymakers and lobbyists, championing the idea that there was little difference between female reformers and revolutionaries. "The epithet 'bolshevist' or 'communist'" was used to "discredit both the women leaders and the reforms they seek," wrote reformer Maud Wood Park.[7] The charge first advanced by the Overman Committee—that "important women's organizations" were "peculiarly susceptible to bolshevistic propaganda"—gained an ever-wider circulation, even as public concern with revolutionary radicalism appeared to be waning. A letter to the *Boston Herald* pointed out that they are "continually listening to all sorts of speakers representing bodies with nice sounding names, a great many of which may be traced to Soviet Russia."[8] This type of guilt-by-association logic was deployed with increasing frequency to highlight the radical associations and doctrines of well-respected reformers like Grace Abbott and Florence Kelley. "*Trusted leaders*," well-known antiradical speaker Hermine Schwed asserted in 1927, "have 'sold'" organized women "measures helpful to the Communists—some intentionally like Florence Kelley and others unintentionally."[9]

While these attacks originated from many sources, the DAR's National Defense Committee ensured that no community was left ignorant of the peril posed by Bolshevik-controlled reformers. The group gave urgency and structure to efforts to marginalize maternalists, compiling and distributing six blacklists in 1927 that named organizations and individuals it deemed dangerous to national security. The lists included some of the most prominent and respected women in American life, even some of the hereditary association's own members. The documents provided concrete targets for women who had come to believe that the ascendance of global Bolshevism required female voluntary associations to repudiate progressive politics. They served as operating manuals for self-appointed guardians of political respectability, who declared that the danger of radical revolution necessitated the silencing of political dissenters. "'Hearing all sides' is a slogan used to convert conservatives to radicalism by the subtle method of infiltration," National Defense Committee chairman Flora Walker explained. "By a vision of tolerance one is too often transformed into a victim of tolerance."[10]

## The Reversal of Sheppard-Towner

The importance of this grassroots conservative insurgency became clear when the Sheppard-Towner Act came up for renewal in 1926. Not anticipating any serious problem, Children's Bureau chief Grace Abbott asked Congress to extend funding for Sheppard-Towner when there was still plenty of time remaining in the initial appropriation. The "Maternity Act" had sailed through Congress in 1921 and administrators hoped the program's record of accomplishments would solidify support. The act had funded initiatives to reduce infant and maternal mortality rates by expanding state and local child health divisions. Mothers had demonstrated their desire to take advantage of the clinics and publications it funded; thousands had penned letters of appreciation to the Children's Bureau.[11] Reformers assumed it would be a relatively simple matter to secure the additional congressional action required to keep the measure from expiring in June 1927.[12] They hoped that an extension of the "Maternity Act" would recapture the political momentum they had lost with the defeat of the child labor amendment. Supporters of the Children's Bureau were bitterly disappointed when the Senate denied Abbott's appeal. The political terrain had grown more hostile to maternalists since 1921. In the traditional halls of power, fiscal conservatism reigned more uncontested than ever thanks to the administration of Calvin Coolidge, a self-proclaimed "businessman's government" that made budget reductions and tax cuts for the wealthy its first priority. While the original bill had enjoyed warm presidential support, Coolidge had actively undermined the measure by calling for a two-year extension followed by the "gradual withdrawal of the Federal Government from this field, leaving it to the states."[13] At the same time, potential progressive coalitions in the House and Senate had been split by regional conflicts, while divisions between cities and rural areas also set representatives at odds.[14] For this measure, however, the most dramatic and significant political shifts had occurred in the world of women's politics.

Congressmen opposed to social welfare legislation could draw courage from evidence of waning support for Sheppard-Towner among the nation's women. The Woman Patriot Publishing Company, once the sole women's organization opposed to the bill, had attracted more women to its cause after the defeat of the Child Labor Amendment. "Many of the names mentioned in connection with the sponsorship [of Sheppard-Towner] are alarmingly familiar in connection with other communistic activities," the American War Mothers observed in the summer of 1926 in a resolution the organization sent to Congress. The American War Mothers pledged to mount a "vigorous protest" against the renewal of Sheppard-Towner, since "the next logical step after communizing the child is to communize the mother."[15] One of the leaders of the Daughters of 1812 warned her members of "the viper creeping slowly and surely into the very vitals of our form of government in the insidious form of Maternity Bills, Child Labor Bills, Education, Equal Rights—all communistic—possibly called Socialistic—for it seems a little more respectable—but [it is] one and the same—simply the infant of the Communist Family." Ella Holloway challenged other Daughters of 1812 to repudiate the legislative work of the Women's Joint Congressional

Committee, demanding: "Are you a part of this vast army of twelve million un-American women?" Holloway's group quickly endorsed this effort to defeat the federal maternity bill after she issued her alarm.[16] These women were joined by Lilian Slattery, head of the League of Catholic Women, who traveled from Massachusetts to denounce the legislation before Congress. Slattery repeated the arguments that had proved so potent in defeating the child labor amendment in Massachusetts. "In America we believe that the child belongs to the parent," Slattery declared. "Pagan philosophy says that the child belongs to the State."[17]

While the opponents' ranks swelled, the female supporters of Sheppard-Towner dwindled. The most important defection from the maternalist camp was the DAR, which had been an enthusiastic supporter of the original bill.[18] The GFWC retained its official support for the bill but rebel Georgia May Martin made clear that the group's official stance reflected no organization unanimity. Martin cabled President Coolidge: "MANY CLUBWOMEN OVER COUNTRY OPPOSE MEASURE AND FEDERAL AID IN GENERAL STOP." Attacking the bill in the *Woman Citizen*, the leading journal for female reform, Martin declared that it would set the government up as an "over-parent," creating an "abhorrent" situation. "But then the whole doctrine of Karl Marx is abhorrent to those Americans who prefer a democracy and believe in representative government."[19]

Fresh from their surprise success with the child labor amendment, the bill's female opponents also felt the political winds at their back. When Sheppard-Towner was re-introduced to Congress they put into motion the same plan of attack that had worked so brilliantly with the Child Labor Amendment. They recast the "Maternity Bill," which had been championed as a manifestation of women's new political power, as a bellwether of radical revolution. The downfall of the proposed Twentieth Amendment gave new legitimacy to the most extreme charges of Mary Kilbreth and the WPPC. "It is encouraging to see how alive men now are generally to the underground Communist aspect to these measures which they would have ridiculed a year ago," Mary Kilbreth boasted to Alexander Lincoln.[20] "The campaign against the child labor amendment has done wonders to educate the country," cheered Margaret Robinson, another board member of the WPPC.[21] Antiradicals cast Sheppard-Towner as cut from the same subversive fabric. "It involves the same principle of nationalized, standardized care of children and Federal interference between parent and child which the American people so sweepingly have repudiated in defeating the Federal Child Labor amendment," declared Louisville protester Georgia Martin, quoting verbatim from the *Woman Patriot*.[22]

The WPPC board hoped to replicate its 1924 success, using the Congressional Record to disseminate six years worth of its propaganda to the widest possible audience. It composed another "petition" of the type that proved so effective in sinking the child labor amendment. This thirty-four-page document was introduced into the Congressional Record by Delaware senator Thomas F. Bayard on July 3, 1926. Once part of the Congressional Record, the antiradical diatribe became a "public" document, shielded from libel suits and eligible for subsidized publishing at government printers. Over sixty thousand copies of this attack, the *Woman Patriot* claimed, were sent out postage free.[23] This denunciation of Sheppard-Towner attempted to demonstrate—even more pointedly than the petition against the Child Labor Amendment— the radical roots and purpose of the maternalist agenda.

The "evidence" and allegations of this document were familiar to anyone who had read the *Woman Patriot* or heard its leaders. The petition portrayed the Children's Bureau as the vilest institution in American society, a hub of deception and danger. Spokes connected it to Moscow, Hull House, "international feminists," Friedrich Engels and radical advocates of disarmament. All these influences converged in Washington, where the Children's Bureau had hatched Sheppard-Towner, the child labor amendment, and the proposal to create a department of education. These measures constituted a careful and unified "program of revolution by legislation" that menaced the nation as much as any plot "to overthrow a government by force and violence." Undergirding this legislation lay the proposition that all mothers and children "should be supported by public taxes instead of by individual husbands and fathers." Exhibiting no real regard for the actual health of mothers and babies, the Children's Bureau deceived legislators, exploiting "sentiment for the child" in order to create vast bureaucracies with dictatorial powers.

If granted the muscle it demanded, the federal agency would impose the "feminist phase" or the "worst form" of communism on the nation, the petition predicted. "Put into practice by the Bolsheviks in Russia," this doctrine "makes women and children the wards of the state" and removes "the 'economic foundations' of marriage and of morality." Shifting this responsibility on to the state—"socializing and nationalizing" women and children—carried "incalculable social and moral consequences" that dwarfed any fiscal concerns. Other critics "have seen and exposed the 'economic' fallacies of communism, the dangers of confiscation of property and class war, but they have been almost blind to social, moral, and biological fallacies of communism, the destruction of the family, and the sex-war program and propaganda of Marx and Engels."[24]

The Children's Bureau and all the measures it sponsored originated with Florence Kelley, the petition explained. Working "under the original, direct instructions of Friederick Engels and Karl Marx," Kelley had become the "ablest legislative general communism has produced." The harangue drew circuitous connections between international communism and other important female reformers, namely Jane Addams, Lillian Wald, Grace Abbott, Margaret Dreier Robins, and Carrie Chapman Catt. It made a special effort to illuminate the pacifist and internationalist convictions of maternalist reformers, no doubt a calculated attempt to stir the anger of antiradicals alarmed by disarmament and the supposedly revolutionary agenda of the Women's International League for Peace and Freedom. But the authors of this diatribe returned to the assertion that Kelley had masterminded the alleged revolutionary conspiracy, enlisting "sentimentalists" and mercenaries to push the legislation she chose, but never consulting the women she purported to represent. The lobbyists of the WJCC were Kelley's soldiers who unwittingly furthered radical communism. These women "do as they are told, pass resolutions and lobby Congress as directed, and for the most part know no more about her revolutionary socialist strategy than Napoleon's mercenaries knew of his military strategy." The consequences of allowing Kelley to proceed unchecked were grave, the petition warned. "The Kelley-Engels program proposes to trick our own Representatives to legislate us into communism and make us dig our own graves."[25]

The newspaper's screed had a grain of truth. A powerful and effective lobbyist, Florence Kelley was responsible for groundbreaking social legislation, including the child labor amendment, the Sheppard-Towner Act, and the measure establishing the Children's Bureau. Well known as a passionate reformer, Kelley was also a revolutionary socialist. Kelley was the daughter of an American congressman and had embraced socialism while studying at the University of Zurich, where she met and married a radical Russian physician, Lazare Wischnewetzky. In 1884, Kelley received permission from Engels to translate *The Condition of the Working Class in England in 1844*. Her translation remains the standard version of this work in English. The work was published in 1887, the same year that the couple returned to New York, where they became active in radical politics. In the early 1890s, Kelley remade herself as a child labor reformer after she was expelled from the Socialist Labor Party and forced to flee her physically abusive husband. She came to rely on a web of female allies, drawing support for her reform mission from a network of middle-class women's organizations. Through the Progressive Era and into the interwar period, Kelley's radical views did not prevent her from working effectively with mainstream women's organizations. As the *Woman Patriot* was well aware, she served as a compelling voice for social justice in reform-minded women's groups.[26]

The *Woman Patriot* urged its readers to buy copies of its "petition" in bulk. One thousand copies could be reproduced by the government printers for $23.76 and sent postage free to groups across the country.[27] The DAR followed this advice in November 1926, sending the petition to all of its state leaders. DAR president general Grace Brosseau followed the circular with a plea to "concentrate all our energies toward the defeat of an unconstitutional and vicious law."[28] The DAR chapter in Huron, South Dakota, was one of many groups to take this message to heart. Its members assailed Sheppard-Towner and then went on to assert that "the League of Women Voters was put over on us in a pretty neat way, and it is no wonder that we American women have been so slow to tumble to its background and real purpose."[29] After being labeled "red" during her run for school board, one member of the League of Women Voters complained to the regional office in Minneapolis, "you can readily see that there is no let-up by these women in Huron."[30]

The DAR was undoubtedly just one of the organizations distributing the petition, which had reached all corners of the nation by late 1926.[31] Wildly successful in kicking up fear and confusion, the petition's wide dissemination doomed Sheppard-Towner and menaced the Children's Bureau. "It appears that the argument, backed by the data we now have showing the Federal Education bills, the Child Labor Amendment and the Maternity Act to be interlocked in their origin and purpose, is very inflammatory," Mary Kilbreth reported with satisfaction.[32] As the executive secretary of the League of Women Voters later reflected, "it is the fact that it was printed and circulated as a Government document which made it so particularly damaging and has aroused so much criticism."[33]

The conspiracy outlined by the petition provoked complaints and inquiries that began to dog the Children's Bureau and the organizations affiliated with the WJCC. Usually dismissive of the *Woman Patriot*, Children's Bureau head Grace Abbott was forced to take these charges seriously. Besides responding to voluminous queries from local Sheppard-Towner administrators, Abbott denied the *Woman Patriot*'s allegations in a letter she sent to leading congressmen. On December 11, 1926, Senator Morris Sheppard entered this missive in the Congressional Record.[34] In clear, concise prose, Abbott illuminated the crimes against logic and truth committed by the *Woman Patriot*. The head of the Children's Bureau accused the newspaper of attempting to associate "nonsocialist and noncommunist individuals" with a communist "conspiracy to destroy this Government," by using "a maze of misquotation and irrelevant material." She derided the attacks made on her as an individual, asserting it was "a matter of public record" that she was a registered Republican. "To attempt to build up a theory that I am a communist or a socialist because I believe in national cooperation with the states in reducing the death rate among mothers and babies, or because ten years ago I was supporting votes for women and international organization for the prevention of war is ridiculous as it is untrue," she wrote. Abbott struggled to keep legislators focused on the merits of the maternity bill. "Other examples of unwarranted conclusions and inaccurate statements can be cited," Abbott wrote impatiently, "but most of them have, even if true, no bearing on the question as to whether appropriation for the maternity and infancy act should or should not be extended."[35] These inflammatory charges, however, overwhelmed reasonable objections to the bill, making it impossible for the debate to proceed as Abbott had envisioned. Her energy was drained by an increasingly urgent drive to push fears of a "revolution by legislation" back to the political periphery.

In early January 1927, almost exactly a year after Congress began deliberating Sheppard-Towner's renewal, Senate antagonists of the Children's Bureau brought the debate to a head by launching a nine-day filibuster aimed at discrediting the federal bureau. Senators Bayard of Delaware, James Reed of Missouri, and William H. King of Utah worked as a team to erode Abbott's defense, relying on rebuttals formulated by the *Woman Patriot*. Lauding the patriotic principles of the antiradical publication, the senators drew on testimonials the newspaper had assembled to show that the nation's women opposed maternity legislation and its "Bolshevik ideas." Opponents of the Children's Bureau had demonstrated, Senator King asserted, that "the purpose of this maternity act . . . is not for the benefit of the babes and of the mothers of the country. It is for the conscious purpose of setting up State control of maternity and childhood" as in Russia.[36] The senators demanded not just the defeat of Sheppard-Towner, but the "liquidation" of the federal agency. At midnight on January 12, the Children's Bureau agreed to a compromise that saved its life; the bill extended Sheppard-Towner for two years and then mandated an end to the maternity program on June 30, 1929.[37]

The *Woman Patriot* reported with satisfaction that "the people have finally crushed two of [the Children's Bureau's] great drives for complete centralized power."[38] Antiradicals were not the only ones who cheered the Senate compromise. A *New York Times* editorialist pronounced it a victory for sound government. Promoted by "lay sentimentalists," the achievements of Sheppard-Towner had been "invisible," the newspaper wrote. It bemoaned that Sheppard-Towner's failure would not stop Congress in the future from feeding the "many lips" that would "open longingly for Uncle Sam's magic nursing bottle after 1929."[39] Reformers perceived the repeal as a temporary setback, assuming they would be able to win a reversal in two years, once the political winds had shifted. As Florence Kelley wrote to Grace Abbott, "It seems inconceivable to me that the next Congress should be as bad as this one. I don't believe it can."[40] This proved hopelessly optimistic. Between 1928 and 1932, fourteen bills reappropriating funding for the maternity program failed in Congress.[41] Little did Kelley know that the worst was yet to come.

The *Woman Patriot* vowed not to rest until it saw the destruction of the Children's Bureau. The newspaper declared that "as long as this Bureau lives, its drives for power will continue," since it existed only for socialists seeking "control of all children" and social workers hoping to satisfy their "appetite . . . for jobs."[42] Mary Kilbreth worked to capitalize on her long-awaited victory to intensify pressure on maternalist reformers. "With the DAR with us, the War Mothers, the Daughters of 1812," she wrote fellow WPPC board member Katherine Balch, "I believe we can at last fight a properly prepared campaign."[43] Her new allies continued distributing the latest WPPC petition, along with a call for the immediate elimination of the Children's Bureau. Bills to abolish the Children's Bureau were introduced in the House and Senate in late February and early March 1927.[44]

Old and new allies of the *Woman Patriot* used the logic and language of the newspaper's petition to justify the elimination of the Children's Bureau. The Sentinels of the Republic, the Massachusetts Public Interests League, as well as the Women's Constitutional Leagues of both Maryland and Virginia sent resolutions to Congress demanding the eradication of "this nest of communistic propaganda." The Daughters of 1812 accused the agency of broadcasting "Socialist propaganda for maternity benefits, children's doles, government guardianship of children and compulsory registration of expectant mothers, hostile to American civilization, and intolerable to a self-respecting free people." Through "bureaucratic despotism" the nation had been driven to the brink of radical revolution, the hereditary organization claimed, since "the only justification for such bureaucratic supervision of homes and children is in a Communist State, where governmental guardianship of all children is a necessary sequence to the Communist program to abolish marriage and destroy the family, as in Soviet Russia." The North Carolina DAR joined the Maryland and New Jersey branches of its organization in denouncing the bureau; the Tar Heel Daughters averred that "persons of extremely communistic views" persuaded Congress to establish the Children's Bureau, which "developed into an effort to obtain control of State health departments in matters relating to maternity, infancy and childhood."[45]

Independently of these groups, Boston antiradical Elizabeth Lowell Putnam capitalized on her personal connections and reputation as a maternal and infant health expert to press for the elimination of the Children's Bureau, which she claimed had actually exacerbated maternal mortality rates and succeeded only "in giving a great many jobs to a great many people." In private correspondence to a Florida clubwoman, she also charged that "there has been an undoubtedly too close connection between the Children's Bureau and the Communist Government of Soviet Russia." Her statements were hotly disputed by Washington reformers, but her opinions were seconded by Hannah Schoff. Schoff was an early president of the National Congress of Mothers and Parent-Teacher Associations and a likeminded conservative who first gained prominence in Progressive Era maternalist politics. In an address to the Sentinels of the Republic in early 1927, Schoff declared that "it is absolutely unnecessary that there should be a Children's Bureau" since "its work is subversive of all we want in the lines of health or in the lines of human betterment."[46]

Besides issuing public condemnations, Putnam also covertly plotted how best to destroy what she called the "useless" and "vicious" bureau. "I am gunning to be made chief of the Children's Bureau, in order that I may get that Bureau abolished without antagonism to the President from the women of the country," Putnam confided to Dr. Tagliaferro Clarke of the U.S. Public Health Service. She told President Coolidge of her plan, which he rejected as politically unfeasible; she claimed, however, that there was "no opposition from him personally."[47]

The WPPC petition continued to inflame passions about the revolutionary consequences of reform. Carrie Chapman Catt attested that the antiradical document set Americans abuzz. "Scared groups of men and women from Maine to California have discussed its awful import with many an 'Oh,' 'Ah,' and 'How Terrible!'" she recounted.[48] Requests poured in to the Children's Bureau from organized women and their local leaders who hoped to educate themselves about the facts of the dispute.[49] "One of our parent advisers, calling upon mothers last week, found a most intelligent college woman seriously confused concerning the information put out through the 'Sentinels of the Republic' in reference to the Sheppard-Towner bill and the Children's Bureau," one woman related from Minneapolis in 1928.[50] Grace Abbott tried to neutralize these charges by distributing the refutation she had published in the Congressional Record. Local health officials in every state welcomed this authoritative rejoinder. "I shall be glad indeed for some of the thunder which that reprint from the *Congressional Record* contains," wrote Mrs. Jean T. Dillon, director of the West Virginia Division of Child Hygiene and Public Health Nursing. "It is hard to understand what possesses a group such as the one behind the 'Woman Patriot' to make them circulate such statements."[51]

In addition to distributing the WPPC petition, the DAR also sought to disseminate the conspiracy theories dogging the "woman's bloc" in other ways after the defeat of the "Maternity" bill.[52] The hereditary association devoted one entire evening during its 1927 national convention to exposing the radicals within the female reform establishment.[53] Opening the Thursday night program was Margaret Overman Gregory, a member of the National Defense Committee who, like her father, Senator Lee S. Overman, was well known for fighting radicals in her home state of North Carolina.[54] Gregory echoed the wary tone of Grace Brosseau's opening address, which had urged delegates to question the background and aims of anyone who sought their endorsement. The president general cautioned that women needed to know "who are the members of the group; what are their affiliations and have they demonstrated conformity to true American ideals?"[55] The evening ended with "Subversive Forces," an address that unmasked the dangers facing the nation. This vituperation against women reformers was delivered by Captain George Darte. Darte was a professional antiradical associated with the Military Order of the World War, an antiradical veterans' association for officers who served in World War I. The orator singled out Jane Addams and others associated with the peace movement for especially vicious condemnation. Yet he did not spare advocates of social welfare measures. "Prominent in" the WJCC "is one Mrs. Florence Kelley (formerly Wischniwetsky) [sic], an ardent Socialist," Darte explained. "This group is much interested in the Child Labor Amendment and the Maternity Act—both Socialistic stories unto themselves." The system of lobbying devised by the WJCC served revolutionary ends, according to Darte, since "*the bloc system is exactly what the Communists and Socialists are depending upon here in their hope for future control of our own legislative program!*" This evil loomed near and demanded immediate resistance. "The world—our own land—is suffering from socialism in action! Make certain it gains no firmer foothold!"[56] Darte appealed to women to "protest against radicals or liberals speaking in your club, schools, or churches." He rallied them to future action: "Be unafraid to challenge those whom you know are disloyal!"[57]

Discreetly watching the proceedings was the chief of the Women's Bureau, Mary Anderson, who had been sent by her fellow reformers to observe the DAR convention. "The Daughters," Anderson reported, "cheered" these speeches "to the echo." One delegate from New York was so inspired that she "stood up and moved that all these speeches be printed so that they could distribute them . . . as a warning to the citizens of the United States of the persons and organizations carrying on Red propaganda. It was carried by unanimous vote," Anderson reported. When the gavel came down at eleven o'clock, one of the other representatives from the WJCC, Marian Parkhurst, rushed to the president general's office to protest these slanders. In the executive suite, Parkhurst stumbled into a convocation of the fifty-woman National Defense Committee, which invited her in to present her objections. This committee grilled the lobbyist until the wee hours of the morning.[58] The next day the DAR called on the federal government to drop all activities not "expressly delegated . . . by the Constitution."[59] Thanks to Parkhurst's interview with the National Defense Committee, however, the most "vicious resolutions which were proposed have been suppressed," concluded Anderson. Still, she confided to Valeria Parker, "I felt so sorry for [Children's Bureau chief] Miss Abbott this morning. While a person of course tries not to take it too seriously, at the same time it does hurt, and the fight is so much harder."[60]

At this most disheartening moment, the staff of the Children's Bureau was enervated by the task of repeatedly refuting ridiculous allegations. Their responses to these antiradical calumnies were mechanistic; they quietly countered lies with correct information, marshaling statistics they hoped would neatly prick antiradical balloons.[61] They appeared exasperated by the illogical nature of the attacks, as they strove to return the debate to terra firma. "'The child belongs to the parents!' has frequently been a slogan in the fight against the child hygiene movement," a press release from the bureau conceded in 1928. "A true statement, surely, but quite irrelevant."[62] Though in 1929 Grace Abbott confessed her "shock" at hearing her Bureau was "an avenue for the distribution of communist propaganda," she was resigned to ride out these attacks. "It is a libel which, if it were directed to an individual, action would be possible although perhaps not wise."[63] Issuing occasional low-key and colorless rebuttals, Abbott tried to avoid bringing additional political pressure to bear on her agency. A veneer of professionalism masked any feelings of outrage; Abbott and her colleagues allowed themselves no public flashes of anger or bitterness. The weapons of choice for these bureaucrats were dry memoranda on maternal and infant mortality rates and official publications peppered with discreet denials of any connection to Soviet sex radical Alexandra Kollontai.[64] Grace Abbott displayed no passion to rally grassroots women to her defense; in retrospect, however, her instinct to duck and cover rather than rise and fight may have been wise. The agency managed to weather this firestorm.

The Children's Bureau policymakers displayed none of the fury demonstrated by Carrie Chapman Catt, who ripped into the WPPC petition, proclaiming that if it contained "any truth at all, it is buried so deep that an excavating expedition would be needed to find it." Her comic tone belied the seriousness with which she regarded the motives and tactics of those associated with the *Woman Patriot*. "You, Gentle Reader, can campaign against any group that disagrees with you, if you will stoop so low, by mobilizing lies, hate and malice and getting it into the [Congressional] *Record*," she told subscribers of the *Woman Citizen*. One of the most moderate of the decade's reformers, Catt waxed eloquent in her defense of Grace Abbott and the maternalist agenda, labeling the WPPC petition a "conglomeration of lies and innuendo."[65]

In the weeks following the DAR convention, the leaders of the WJCC focused on persuading Brosseau to discard plans to reprint and distribute Captain Darte's address. "That speech was so full of misstatements and misrepresentations that I know you would not be willing to have the Daughters of the American Revolution responsible for the spreading of such injustice," Ethel Smith counseled Brosseau.[66] Brosseau rebuffed WJCC overtures, refusing to meet or discuss the charges leveled by Darte and other speakers. The maternalist reformers were dumbfounded by this reaction; despite the group's escalating attacks, they never expected to see a former member of the WJCC so solidly in the camp of their enemies. "It distresses me," wrote Helen Atwater, chairman of the WJCC, to Grace Brosseau, "to think that your organization, to which many of my friends belong and for which I have had a real respect, may play into the hands of some of our common opponents by allowing zeal to outrun discretion." The hereditary organization could be damaged by these attacks, since it "has been so-closely associated with the Women's Joint Congressional Committee," Atwater told Brosseau. "Many individual members of the Daughters of the American Revolution are also members of constituent organizations of the Women's Joint Congressional Committee and as such not out of sympathy with the Committee."[67]

Yet reformers who tried to broker a peace were rebuffed by this growing rebellion. The state leader of the New Jersey DAR rejected the suggestion that she sit down with representatives from the League of Women Voters, declaring simply that her organization was on "record as opposed to legislation which aims in one way or another toward centralization of our government."[68] Leaders of the LWV were forced to concede that attacks by DAR officers and individuals are "widespread in the states" and have "in some instances been directly damaging to League organization."[69] The LWV decided to fight fire with fire. It adopted a confrontational tone exemplified by a pamphlet titled "Who Are the Patriots?" The circular juxtaposed the civic service of individuals "attacking the reputations of those who have devoted their lives to making better living and working conditions for women and children" with activists "working to preserve the race by protecting women in industry, and to safeguard our children against the evil effects of child labor so that they may have the opportunity to grow up healthy, intelligent American citizens." With these records in mind, the New Jersey LWV demanded, *who are the patriots?*"[70] The Minnesota LWV responded with less passion than humor, putting on a "minstrel show" that featured the tune "Blame It on the Reds," which at least one League activist dedicated mentally to the DAR.[71] Pamphlets, skits and counterattacks did little to neutralize the zeal of these newly mobilized conservatives. "Attacks of one form or another keep us busy most of the time," admitted League of Women Voters president Belle Sherwin.[72]

## The DAR Blacklist

Any hope at reconciliation between traditional maternalists and ascendant antiradicals was quashed in early 1928 when press reports confirmed

Figure 3. This cartoon illustrated Carrie Chapman Catt's condemnation of the campaign to discredit the Children's Bureau and the female voluntary associations that supported its agenda. *Woman Citizen*, June 1927, 10.

what many reformers had long suspected. The DAR had been distributing "blacklists" that named as revolutionary conspirators over 200 prominent men and women and hundreds of organizations sympathetic to female reform. DAR member Helen Tufts Bailie stepped forward, along with several other members of the hereditary association, to reveal that in the spring of 1927, the group's national headquarters had distributed the lists to chapters all over the country. The intention was to provide local antiradicals with a Who's Who of subversive politics.[73] Bailie had been disturbed when her chapter received the blacklists naming many people she respected, including the Reverend E. Talmadge Root, the husband of a fellow member.[74] She was also emboldened by a denunciation of the hereditary association penned by Carrie Chapman Catt, who attacked the DAR for disseminating literature claiming that 250 American organizations had put themselves at the service of Russian Bolsheviks. In "Lies-At-Large," published in the *Woman Citizen* in 1927, the peace activist and former suffrage leader ridiculed these charges, claiming that "it is safe to say that in the women's organizations listed as dangerous and deceitful, even Diogenes with his lamp could not find a Bolshevik. Whoever says they are red, *lies*."[75] "An Open Letter to the DAR" was even more blistering. The campaign by the DAR, Catt concluded, "has made slanderous, mendacious and brutal attacks upon thousands of Americans who never saw a Bolshevik in their lives," and it created "a veritable wave of hysteria."[76]

After Catt's impassioned missive, Bailie organized a Committee of Protest, a group of fourteen like-minded members who objected to the increasing dominance of antiradicalism within the organization. These women released a letter to DAR president general Grace Brosseau that outlined their unhappiness with the organization's censorship campaign. In early April 1928, Bailie released the DAR blacklist to the media to prove that the organization had systematically targeted widely respected Americans.[77] At the same time, she mailed to sister DARs a pamphlet titled "Our Threatened Heritage" that detailed the blacklisting system and condemned the antiradical philosophy that undergirded it.[78] In this pamphlet, Bailie charged that the DAR had been hijacked by superpatriots, who allowed other antiradical organizations, namely the Massachusetts Public Interests League, the Industrial Defense Association, and the Key Men of America, to dictate its policies. "The humiliating fact is that we have been duped," she wrote. "Our officers are not really our pilots . . . Fellow members, I appeal to you to throw off this foreign domination so at variance with our ideals."[79]

The blacklists laid bare the DAR's comprehensive campaign against peace activists, liberal clergymen, and social reformers. Its blacklists included some American luminaries, including a number of the hereditary association's own members. All the leading lights of liberal social causes as well as organizations advocating any degree of reform earned a place in this rogue's gallery. Settlement house founder Jane Addams, suffragist Carrie Chapman Catt, Children's Bureau head Grace Abbott, lawyer Clarence Darrow, editor William Allen White, Rabbi Stephen Wise, and even several DAR members were among those labeled "socialist," "pacifist," "radical," or "in-

ternationalist." The lists accused the federal Children's Bureau, the League
of Women Voters, and the PTA of working consciously or unwittingly with
groups the DAR deemed revolutionary. These included the American Civil
Liberties Union, Women's Trade Union League, and more radical organizations affiliated with the American Communist and Socialist parties.[80] Pacifists and other opponents of military preparedness, along with advocates
of the League of Nations and the World Court, made up the bulk of individuals and organizations singled out for condemnation. But advocates of
child labor laws, social insurance, and better industrial relations also found
themselves in the "subversive" column. Some were condemned for their own
purportedly "radical" agendas; others simply for their solidarity with "internationalist" movements that had the sympathy of most reformers of note
during the 1920s. Groups like the PTA were included because they supported
"measures that are contributing to socialistic legislation," in the words of
Emily Hurd, DAR National Defense chairman for Massachusetts.[81]

Coverage by national publications such as the *Literary Digest*, the *New
York Times*, *Harper's Magazine*, and the *Nation* contributed to a national
clamor over the irony of the descendants of American revolutionaries cur-
tailing free speech.[82] For many observers, it was "peculiarly dramatic and
humorous that an organization which sets out to worship the revolutionaries of a century and a half ago should join in a crusade of religious persecution against those who dare to criticize anything American today."[83] But
this controversial political mission also earned plaudits for the DAR. One
woman wrote to the *Boston Daily Advertiser* that she was "not a D.A.R. but
I wish to express my profound agreement with their attitude regarding persons whose aims are opposed to the real welfare of the nation." The dangers
of "a handful of tyrants riding rough shod over the cowering masses; streets
flowing with the blood of the best citizens" outweighed any other concerns,
she concluded. "Certainly it is no time for Pacifists, Communists and socialists, whether calling themselves Christian or infidel, to be encouraged
to spread their pernicious doctrines."[84] The DAR's campaign was also applauded by men eager to undermine assertions of women peace activists
that advocacy of pacifism, disarmament, and internationalism grew organi-
cally from their roles as mothers and nurturers. "The women of the United
States are not cowards or defeatists," said a Washington editorial defending
the organization. "American mothers who bear a double burden whenever
there is war, are determined that this country shall never again be caught
unprepared if they can prevent it."[85]

Figure 4. This cartoon played on the charge by Kansas editor William Allen White that the DAR had become an acolyte of the Ku Klux Klan. This image reflects the belief of many critics of antiradicalism, who believed that new female conservatives were subservient to male members of the far right. Cartoons re DAR Blacklist folder, Box 1, Helen Tufts Bailie Papers, Sophia Smith Collection, Smith College, Northampton, Massachusetts.

Drawn by Harry Bressler for The New Leader.

Figure 5. This was one of the many cartoons and commentaries that
lampooned DAR members during the blacklist controversy. It depicted
current day members of the hereditary association as comically clueless
about the revolutionary legacy they purported to cherish. Cartoons re
DAR Blacklist folder, Box 1, Helen Tufts Bailie Papers, Sophia Smith
Collection, Smith College, Northampton, Massachusetts.

The DAR was certainly not the first organization to distribute a blacklist; Archibald Stevenson, a lawyer employed by the War Department's Military Intelligence Division, had delivered a similar, though much smaller list
to the Overman Committee in 1919.[86] National DAR leaders may have put
together their particular version by drawing on already existing lists. One
DAR leader in Massachusetts attributed the hereditary organization's list to
Harriet Frothingham, one of the directors of the *Woman Patriot*.[87] Although
the DAR blacklists were amateurish in the way they garbled the names of

Figure 6. All the cartoons that commented on the DAR blacklist linked femininity to patriotism. Cartoonists ridiculed both protesters and antiradicals by portraying them as dowdy, unattractive and hysterical spinsters. Cartoons re DAR Blacklist folder, Box 1, Helen Tufts Bailie Papers, Sophia Smith Collection, Smith College, Northampton, Massachusetts.

some organizations and listed others that no longer existed, they helped to make attacks against political dissenters more systematic and more relentless. By early 1928, at least eight blacklists were being distributed to local activists by both men's and women's national antiradical organizations.[88]

DAR officials handled the blacklist controversy by alternately denying the existence of the lists and defending the national organization's right to

Figure 7. The blacklist earned the DAR praise as well as condemnation. The hereditary association's anti-radical campaign demonstrated the organization's heroic patriotism in the minds of some Americans who were fearful of radicalism. Cartoons re DAR Blacklist folder, Box 1, Helen Tufts Bailie Papers, Sophia Smith Collection, Smith College, Northampton, Massachusetts.

"guide" local chapters.[89] Denials flew in the face of overwhelming evidence of the blacklist's existence and ample testimony that it was distributed as an easy-to-use guide for muffling so-called subversives, not just for selecting patriotic speakers for chapter meetings. Both officers and rank-and-file members admitted distributing and using the lists.[90] In tandem with their release, the National Defense Committee had also intensified pressure on rank-and-file DAR members to become active in the campaign against radicalism. Flora Walker and her co-workers asked chapters to evaluate whether "radical or subversive movements or activities" were hampering "constitutional government and in the maintenance of American ideals" in their local communities.[91] The group also distributed and endorsed pamphlets that might as well have been blacklists, such as "The Common Enemy" and "Who Is Back of the Pacifist Movement Opposing National Defense." These DAR-approved publications pointed the finger at organizations such as the American Association of University Women, the League of Women Voters, and the YWCA.[92] The National Defense Committee offices at Memorial Continental Hall distributed an arsenal of antiradical propaganda playing on these same themes to DAR chapters and interested nonmembers. Free copies of leaflets like "Communist Corruption of Youth" and "The Truth About the Red Movement" were piled on the tables in the group's national headquarters for tourists who visited the monumental building in Washington, D.C.[93] In addition, the National Defense Committee urged chapters to subscribe to all the major antiradical publications, such as Fred Marvin's *Daily Data Sheets* and the *Woman Patriot*, that hammered on the culpability of "pinks," especially women reformers, in advancing Moscow's agenda.[94] Even if the organization stopped sending true blacklists to chapters after the national controversy in 1928, it continued producing and distributing pamphlets that served the same purpose.[95]

The blacklists were part of a widespread effort by conservative activists to limit speech they viewed as dangerous. From the earliest days of this conservative women's movement, female antiradicals relished the challenge of silencing speakers whose views they opposed. Their national organizations provided vital support for these efforts by sending "data" that grassroots activists could use to petition government officials, ministers, and school authorities.[96] And antiradical evangelists thundered from podiums across the nation about the dangers of giving forums to "clever minds . . . seeking to undermine our social, political and economic system."[97] A lecture tour undertaken by Lucia Ames Mead—the seventy-year-old grande dame of peace activism—shows how the development of an institutional framework for female antiradicalism helped to bring pressure to bear on political dissenters. The coordinated attacks on Mead demonstrated what antiradicals hoped to accomplish with the blacklists.[98]

Antiradicals prepared for Mead's lecture tour of the southeastern United States well before she left home. In late August 1926, Ida Floyd White, state regent of the Florida DAR, sent a circular letter to Rollins College president Hamilton Holt warning that although Mead proposed to lecture at the college on "harmless subjects," "authentic" information gathered by the DAR demonstrated that she belonged to organizations promoting "socialist and radical ideas," "pure communism," and the "famous 'slacker vow.'" Mead's long history with movements "alien to the hearts and minds of every red-blooded American man and woman" made her a dangerous speaker, White wrote, especially for youth "who are always susceptible, to hearing a speaker who may implant in their minds false ideas and ideals."[99] The aim of these accusations was twofold. Antiradicals obviously hoped to deter organizations who might have invited Mead to speak. But they were also designed to expose Mead as a dangerous radical. White explained to President Holt that Mead's respectable exterior was deceiving, since "many radicals work under clever disguises and we must be alert." To left-wing peace activists Mead seemed moderate, even reactionary. But she was a revolutionary in the eyes of conservative crusaders like White, who were unimpressed by the fact that she had been a member of the DAR.[100]

These accusations were not new to Mead, who had been one of the women featured in the original Spider Web Chart and had already experienced serious problems securing invitations to lecture.[101] She responded to allegations of radicalism with plainly worded denials. "I am not a socialist and never have been . . . I am not 'an advocate of the Pacifist oath for women' and never have been," she wrote in a letter to the editor in 1924.[102] But Mead's reassurances about her intentions did not stem the flow of cookie-cutter accusations from conservative activists. The data sent out by national antiradical organizations provided local activists with readymade scripts for grassroots harassment. The dossiers prepared by national organizations like the DAR rested on the classic propaganda techniques of guilt by association and hyperbole. In Mead's case, censors offered her associations with allegedly radical individuals and organizations as proof of her subversive intent. Grassroots activists usually accepted this prepackaged documentation of revolutionary radicalism on faith, and no amount of argument or "facts" could convince them that the information was false.[103]

Mead left Boston in mid-November 1926 for scheduled lectures in Virginia, North Carolina, and Georgia. While her visit to Virginia went smoothly, she was ambushed in North Carolina by a group of antiradicals led by DAR regent Margaret Overman Gregory. Alarmed by what she called "the invasion of communistic activities in the South," Gregory, a conservative Democrat, had established herself as a leading Tar Heel antiradical in the years leading up to Mead's visit.[104] Gregory warned that North Carolina was "the target of the most desperate efforts of the Soviet propagandists seeking the overthrow of the American government and planning for a Red Russian invasion of the South."[105] During her tenure as state leader of the DAR, Gregory organized a series of meetings with Daughters around the state to rally the descendants of soldiers to demonstrate their "martial blood" by rising to fight the dangers that she had revealed to them. These female warriors had responded by targeting the Greensboro Open Forum, an institution dedicated to promoting free speech and sponsoring speakers with a variety of different viewpoints. The censors of the North Carolina DAR pressured the organization to sanitize its speaker's roster of suspected reds.[106] Mead's visit gave Gregory another ideal opportunity to muster her troops, who joined forces with the American Legion and its Auxiliary.

Gregory had prepared for the visit by working with DAR president general Brosseau to assemble information about the peace advocate. Gregory and her followers attended Mead's appearances en masse and prevented her from delivering addresses in Charlotte and Salisbury.[107] Once Mead left North Carolina, she continued to be beset by civilian censors. Mead was barred from podiums in Atlanta, where antiradicals persuaded administrators at Agnes Scott College and Emory University to cancel her lectures.[108] As was almost always the case when antiradicals tried to censor speakers, however, these cancellations sparked other community groups to open their doors to the banned speaker. The Ministers' Association and the Liberal Christian Church each gave her the chance to address their members.[109]

Contemporary observers and historians have concluded that Mead capitalized on the turn of events during her southeastern tour, using opposition to rally supporters of peace and free speech. These attacks gave the movement for free speech symbols to mobilize against and an impetus to push for more explicit legal protections for First Amendment rights.[110] But although Mead may have prevailed in the battle against antiradical censorship, that does not mean that she won the war. When the peace activist left Atlanta, she was pursued by DAR and American Legion members who cited her scuttled speeches in Atlanta as proof of her radical credentials. Mrs. John Landrum, a DAR leader in Greenville, South Carolina, used news of Mead's canceled lectures, along with information she had received from her organization's headquarters in Washington, to convince club leaders that Mead was too radical for Greenville. The New Englander's appearance in the South Carolina town was canceled after a coalition of antiradicals proclaimed that Mead could "teach the South nothing of patriotism" because she stood for "pacifism, communism, socialism and equality of the negro."[111]

Antiradicals were also waiting for Mead when she returned north of the Mason-Dixon Line. In early 1927, on the eve of a scheduled lecture in Boonton, New Jersey, a leading DAR member named Helen Baldwin charged Mead with "playing the Communist game," sparking a dispute that escalated into a nationally publicized courtroom drama.[112] The 1926–27 Communist Party-led textile strike in nearby Passaic provided a dramatic backdrop for the libel trial, lending urgency to accusations of radicalism for those who felt that the militant labor campaign provided ample proof of the clear and present danger of subversion. Under cross-examination from leading civil liberties lawyer and ACLU president Arthur Garfield Hays, Baldwin asserted that propaganda circulated by the DAR National Defense Committee provided irrefutable evidence that reformers like Mead and Jane Addams harbored radical agendas and subversive affiliations. A New Jersey court refuted Baldwin's claim in a decision that was hailed as a major victory for progressive activists. But Lucia Ames Mead and most of the other people appearing on the witness stand in New Jersey remained at the top of blacklists circulating at the end of the 1920s. The scent of subversion clung to Mead. For the rest of her career, her public appearances were plagued by blacklist-waving hecklers.[113] The censorship campaign stripped Mead of the protection of middle-class respectability, which in turn had a chilling effect on the causes she and other banned speakers supported. The campaign by the DAR to silence dissenters was designed not just to censor unpleasant ideas but to expose hidden subversives, especially articulate old-stock women who did not fit nativistic stereotypes about working-class foreign radicals.

After protesting Mead's tour of North Carolina in 1926, DAR members in the Tar Heel State kept working to close the Greensboro Open Forum and tried to convince leaders in Raleigh that Sherwood Eddy, a Protestant pacifist and leader of the YMCA, was unsafe to appear before American audiences.[114] Female antiradicals in Milwaukee, Wisconsin, successfully prevented a representative of the National Council for Prevention of War (NCPW) from speaking at an Armistice Day program in November 1929. Wisconsin state regent Mrs. James F. Trottman explained that the DAR barred Miss Eleanor Brannan's address from St. Paul's Episcopal Church because Brannan "represents an active organization that wants to remove all protection from our country."[115]

## Choosing Sides

In April 1928, dissenting Daughter Helen Tufts Bailie and the other protesters brought their campaign against the blacklists to the DAR annual convention in Washington. Kansas representative Eleanor St. Omer Roy, who had helped Bailie organize the protest campaign, faced down a hostile audience from the speaker's podium, enduring hisses when she revealed that she was also a staff member of WILPF. St. Omer Roy introduced resolutions that affirmed the right of chapters to choose their own speakers and demanded that chapters be allowed to vote on political positions taken by the national organization. When the vote was taken, the resolutions were defeated by a standing vote of more than 2,000 delegates. At every turn during the convention, the suggestions of the Committee of Protest were repudiated by the rest of the DAR. The 4,000 women packed into the galleries and on the convention floor clapped and cheered when President General Brosseau defended the antiradical agenda with a ringing call for the DAR to lead the revival of "Americanism" and the annihilation of "destructive ideas regarding home, religion and Government."[116] The DAR National Board of Management signaled its enthusiastic support for the antiradical policies of Brosseau and National Defense chairman Walker by passing an additional resolution praising the women for their "courageous" work "to maintain American ideals." Despite the assertions of Bailie and the other protesters that the majority of the DAR was apathetic, rather than sympathetic with regard to the organization's National Defense Committee, the response of the women at the 1928 Continental Congress showed that the antiradical campaign was wildly popular among the Daughters most deeply involved with the national organization.[117]

Only a few days after the close of the convention, nineteen Daughters prominent in the national organization filed charges with the organization's National Board of Management, accusing Bailie of conducting "herself in a way calculated to disturb the harmony and injure the good name of the national society." In a closed hearing in which both sides were represented by lawyers, Bailie presented her case to the fifty-woman National Board. The DAR officers ruled unanimously against Bailie and expelled her from the society on June 22. The Board went on to expunge other protesters from their ranks, conducting hearings on the membership of another prominent dissenting Daughter, Mary P. Macfarland. Macfarland, who was a Republican Party activist and a leading member of the American Association of University Women, League of Women Voters, and New Jersey Federation of Women's Clubs, had distributed her own pamphlet in the spring of 1928 protesting the organization's antiradical policies. The National Board of Management tried Macfarland on the same charges as Bailie; when she refused to appear in Washington, they sent her official word of her expulsion in autumn 1928. While Macfarland announced that she was pleased with her expulsion since the decision would give her a chance to devote her full energies to the "blacklisted" organizations, Bailie kept fighting. She appealed her expulsion at the Continental Congress in 1929, but delegates upheld the ruling of the National Board.[118]

As the summary expulsion of Bailie showed, the leaders of the DAR had little patience for renegade members who fought the organization's embrace of antiradicalism. DAR chapters in Kansas, Massachusetts, Rhode Island, Connecticut, California, Michigan, Ohio, and Oregon divided after receiving the blacklist, with some members banding together to protest to the national organization.[119] Brosseau ignored these complaints. She turned the tables on the dissidents, telling defenders of free speech it was "unpatriotic for American citizens who enjoy the freedom and blessing of country to advocate its disarmament" and "'subversive' to foster internationalism."[120] Another leader summed up the official stance of the organization when she asked, "If some of these people don't like the policies of the D.A.R., why don't they get out?"[121] In hindsight, the better question might be, why did so many reform-minded women stay in the group after it started to embrace an activist agenda of antiradicalism? By the time of the blacklist controversy, a clear philosophical divide had been established in women's politics. Nonetheless, as a Raleigh, North Carolina, columnist observed, progressive and antiradical women were "unfortunately, often mixed up in the same organizations."[122] The blacklist controversy revealed that the constituency for women's antiradical and progressive politics was nearly identical. At the beginning of the decade, it would have been difficult to predict exactly which middle-class women would embrace the new conservative agenda.

Though it is difficult to judge just how many DAR members held progressive sympathies, the organization's own blacklist declared that at least some of its most well known members were dangerous radicals.[123] One prominently blacklisted member, Jane Addams, might have resigned by the time the organization had publicly labeled her dangerous. In earlier years, however, Addams, the international president of WILPF, had astonished her friends by frequently displaying a DAR pin advertising her lifetime membership in the organization.[124] Reformers like Margaret Dreier Robins, the long-time president of the Women's Trade Union League, clung to the assumption that most members of the DAR shared the worldview of the WJCC. "Surely you and Mrs. Park and I and many others of our group know individual members of the DAR to whom we can go with a plea for fair play."[125] The blacklist affair revealed even more women unsympathetic to organized antiradicalism who clung to membership in the DAR, such as DAR protester and WILPF staff member Eleanor St. Omer Roy. A charter member of the DAR in her home town of Fort Scott, Kansas, St. Omer Roy emphasized that in 1928, well after antiradicalism had become a priority of the national leadership, she was still "intensely proud" of her founding role in the organization.[126] Protest leader Bailie refused to give up her membership and had to be expelled from the organization, a fate she shared with Macfarland. Other progressive women also stayed in the DAR after antiradicalism came to dominate its activities. Dr. Valeria Parker, a prominent social welfare worker who had served as director of the National League of Women Voters, National Congress of Teachers and Parents, and the National WCTU, as well as honorary president of the National Council of Women, remained in the DAR until 1930 even though all the organizations she led had been blacklisted.[127]

Well into the 1920s, individual women maintained multiple allegiances that complicate efforts to draw definitive boundaries between the old politics of maternalism and the new politics of antiradicalism. Many moderate women chose to work in a borderland between the two political blocs, picking sides only when forced. A survey based on a sampling of DAR members taken around the time of the controversy revealed that slightly more than one-fourth of all Daughters also belonged to the General Federation of Women's Clubs. The GFWC was not itself on the DAR blacklist, but DAR pamphlets accused its leaders of aiding the communist cause because until 1928 the organization worked for social welfare legislation. While the survey did not note the number of DAR members who belonged to WILPF or other peace groups, it claimed that close to 8 percent of the membership also belonged to the League of Women Voters, PTA, or American Association of University Women, all blacklisted organizations.[128] Not surprisingly, progressive allegiances were most pronounced among the women who joined Bailie's group of dissenters.[129]

Women who called themselves antiradicals in 1928 not only belonged to the same organizations as those who saw themselves as supporters of reform, they also came from the same social and economic class. They held in common many racial and ethnic prejudices, political party affiliations, and social mores.[130] Even blacklisted DAR members were repelled by what they interpreted as encroaching societal degeneracy, for they shared notions of sexual and social propriety with antiradical women. Mount Holyoke president Mary Woolley, for example, railed against the young woman who "frightens her family by her radicalism" on social questions, reads light novels, goes to movies, and participates in "petting parties," trends she feared were epidemic among American college students.[131] Blacklist protester Bailie bemoaned the "terrible goings on of young people—drunkenness, promiscuity, flat contempt for their elders."[132] Middle-class clubwomen who came of age before World War I were equally uncomfortable with the culture of sexual experimentation embraced by Jazz Age youth.

Middle-class reformers and antiradicals were also both horrified by radicalism. Lucia Ames Mead denounced the "atheistic Russian communists" in the lectures targeted by antiradical censors, while DAR critic Carrie Chapman Catt asserted that she "abhor[red] the Communists and their program as genuinely as any living person."[133] Catt and Mead were not alone. DAR protester Macfarland supported the military and her son in the ROTC, dismissed pacifism, and advocated measures to brook subversion in the form of "restraint upon any organizations which seek to undermine our institutions."[134] Helen Tufts Bailie wrote that she wished she "could boil Trotsky in oil, and Lenin too."[135] Opposition to radicalism made women more rather than less susceptible to attacks by their conservative sisters. Unlike avowed radicals, they were determined to hang on to political respectability and to work within centrist women's groups with broad constituencies. Their difficulty came in charting a political path that was both countersubversive and progressive.

In the immediate aftermath of the Nineteenth Amendment and the Armistice, many women who campaigned for disarmament or appropriations for Children's Bureau programs papered over widening fissures separating them from antiradicals with a tissue of social conservatism and a belief in hereditary patriotism. Women like Bailie, Macfarland, and St. Omer Roy, who were alienated by antiradicalism, nonetheless remained believers in

what they called the true "ideals" of the DAR.[136] Central to their understanding of the DAR's mission was the notion that descent from Revolutionary soldiers obligated women to uphold their ancestors' mission. St. Omer
Roy asserted that her ancestors "left me a heritage of patriotism, of loyalty
to those ideals for which my country was founded, of pride in my nation,
which is known as 'the home of the free and the land of the brave.'"[137] DAR
women of all stripes asserted the elitist view that descendants of the nation's
founders were most qualified to protect the founding principles and traditions of the country. Both Grace Brosseau and Helen Tufts Bailie, who kept
her ancestors' relics and records in her apartment to show to journalists, felt
that they had a special relationship with the nation's founders.[138] "I shine
with reflected glory," Bailie remarked, when her DAR chapter commended
her for being a descendant of Revolutionary War heroine Anne Adams
Tufts.[139] The devotion of female reformers to this concept allowed many of
them to live with antiradicalism's ascendance within the organization for
most of the decade.[140]

Women who operated in the middle ground between antiradicalism and
progressivism were attracted to organizations like the DAR because they
supported their assumptions about the relationship between patriotism and
race, class, and ethnicity.[141] By tugging at the strings of class and nationalistic
prejudice, the DAR reeled in advocates of disarmament and children's health
programs who thought that people outside the Anglo-Saxon elite were gaining too much power and influence. The organization's emphasis on elaborate
ritual, beautiful clothes, and wealth satisfied members' craving for elite status. Especially before the blacklist controversy, the DAR drew women who
espoused complex and seemingly contradictory political ideologies.

Helen Tufts Bailie, for instance, was in some respects progressive. She
was a member of WILPF, a liberal Unitarian and a defender of Sacco and
Vanzetti.[142] The Boston woman was a passionate supporter of "liberty of
conscience and freedom of speech," which she considered part of "the very
spirit which brought our Nation to birth."[143] In her mind, these were classic
American values, but they situated her on the ideological left in the interwar
period. Yet at the same time she shared the social conservatism of many
Daughters who embraced antiradicalism. Bailie railed against the DAR's
antidemocratic practices and accused it of becoming a "Ku Klux Klan of
women," but she herself was hostile to the people targeted by the Klan.[144]
Bailie was a downwardly mobile, old-stock American whose husband was
a struggling entrepreneur in the wicker furniture business. Even though

her husband's roller-coaster business ventures put her middle-class status in constant danger, she was disdainful of those outside elite white circles.[145] Bailie dismissed Jews, whom she cast as social climbers, called African Americans "coons," and described Irish Catholics as "big glossy mutts . . . all four feet in the public trough."[146] Even though her own husband was an immigrant from Ireland, she feared "the polyglot mass of freshly made Americans" would corrupt "the institutions that invited them." She revived her lapsed membership in the DAR in 1925 after a parade marking the 150th anniversary of the battle of Bunker Hill convinced her that Irish Catholics had taken over patriotic celebrations in her hometown, making her feel like one drop in a "Hibernerian bucket." Civic celebrations could be trusted only to pedigreed patriots. "Evacuation Day," she wrote, "is to them more for St. Patrick than for the evacuation of Boston." Bailie's return to the DAR came just months after she joined WILPF.[147]

Bailie's social views were not representative of all reformers. But she did share them with the other prominent critic of the DAR in this period, Carrie Chapman Catt, who denounced unrestricted suffrage that gave old-stock Americans no more power in the public realm than illiterate immigrants. In calling for tests to weed out voters who could not demonstrate a command of "American values," Catt resurrected the nativist rationale for women's suffrage. She proclaimed that "the blood of the very men who devised and created American democracy" flowed in the veins of newly enfranchised women, "yet they have stood powerless beside the polling booths while illiterate men, often only a few years in this country, have been voting in blocks against them."[148] Bailie and Catt's conservative views on class and ethnicity provide clues as to why so many moderate women simultaneously could have supported both reform-minded and antiradical organizations in the 1920s.

Even women who were hounded by female antiradicals shared their persecutors' idea that a distinguished lineage legitimized their activism. Lucia Ames Mead touted her patriotic credentials vocally; in fact, she had been a member of the DAR. When under attack, Mead portrayed herself as an old-stock American who epitomized the antithesis of a dangerous or violent radical; she undercut any attempts to portray her as a firebrand by mentioning her great-grandfather who had fought in the American Revolution.[149] Like Bailie and Catt, Mead was not shy about using stereotypes about foreign radicals to make her own positions as palatable as possible, in the process reinforcing the widespread nativism that made antiradicalism so acceptable to many Americans. Although the links between immigrants and

Figure 8. In this cartoon, Carrie Chapman Catt ridiculed the notion that female reformers were promoting revolution. This picture played on the assumption that old-stock Americans could be easily distinguished from genuine radicals, who were ethnically distinctive. Note the figure of the bearded radical. *Woman Citizen*, June 1927, 11.

radicalism were still strong in the public imagination and her background made some observers dismiss the charges of radicalism against her, Mead did not sway veteran antiradicals. They saw her as evidence that subversion had eaten right to the core of America.[150]

Women like Helen Bailie, Mary Macfarland, and Eleanor St. Omer Roy fought to reform the DAR because its concept of hereditary patriotism was critical to their consciousness as activists.[151] But they ultimately interpreted the ideals they had inherited from their ancestors in ways that led them far from the antiradical agenda and the censorship campaign. "As descendants of the Founders of the Republic," one group of protesting Daughters wrote in 1928, "we feel that we should hold a higher vision of tolerance toward the opinions of sincere persons and should cultivate a more intelligent patriotism."[152]

Antiradicals were determined to draw a distinction between constructive civic engagement and subversion. This desire produced the blacklists, which were designed to put into place "a clear cut cleavage between un-American subversive forces and the constituents of our patriotic societies."[153] The blacklists simply deepened the widening rift between reformers and antiradicals, especially after DAR leaders rebuffed protests with calls for heightened vigilance against radicalism. Instead of backpedaling to appease offended progressives, Brosseau preached that antiradicalism was the one true faith for respectable women. "For the protection of all our lives and our precious possessions THERE ARE NOT TWO SIDES, and anyone who wants to argue on the other side is in grave danger of being misunderstood," she asserted.[154] Antiradical intransigence created a gulf in middle-class women's politics between conservative and reform-minded activists that became too wide for most women to bridge. Women reformers who had been willing to overlook the earlier attacks on female peace activists were no longer able to ignore the divisions.

Given the rigidity of antiradicals, many of those who maintained their belief in female reform eventually left organizations like the DAR. After the blacklist revelation, DAR chapters in New Haven, Connecticut, Crawfordsville, Indiana, and Highland Park, Michigan, saw large-scale defections.[155] Some socially prominent members made their departures as public as possible.[156] Those who had previously maintained a pride in both their colonial ancestry and their achievements as reformers suddenly perceived a new chasm separating them from self-proclaimed conservatives. They ultimately accepted the antiradical declaration that countersubversion, internationalism, and female-driven reform could not coexist within the same organization. By the end of the decade, anti-radicals and progressives still shared socioeconomic background and social world. Yet they had become distinct groups, separated by ideology.

The decade following the Bolshevik Revolution was marked by efforts to mandate political conformity in the United States. A tide of legislation attempted to curtail any expression of dissent, as states passed a barrage of sedition laws, legislated flag saluting for students, and required that teachers and public servants swear loyalty oaths.[157] With its blacklists and other efforts to mobilize grassroots demonstrations against social welfare reform, internationalism, disarmament or radicalism, the DAR played a key role in nurturing this culture of political repression. It needs to be recognized for its outsized role in making the years between the Great War and the Great Depression into what Democratic Party activist Emma Guffey Miller called the "age of intolerance."[158]

The hereditary association disseminated blacklists that were meant to impose a new orthodoxy on middle-class women's politics; they were intended to delineate new boundaries of political respectability for women accustomed to working freely within the broad subculture of female voluntary associations. Publication of these lists brought on a storm of denunciation, which cast the DAR as a group for toothless and hysterical political reactionaries. But even the most outraged critics failed to grasp the power and significance of this campaign. It fundamentally changed the political culture of women's clubs. They underestimated the breadth and scope of the group's countersubversion efforts, which paired images of revolution abroad with warnings about radicalism in North America to jolt otherwise comfortable women into entirely new patterns of political engagement. Packages of clippings, pamphlets, and speeches incited fear and anger in ordinary clubwomen, who resolved to squelch manifestations of subversion in their communities. This new breed of female political activist took greatest pride in her assaults on reformers and peace activists. She eagerly fomented warfare within the ranks of female voluntary associations.

The antiradical smear campaign took its power from the myriad connections that linked women reformers to their new female foes. Advocates of progressive causes proved to be particularly susceptible to attacks from former allies, with whom they shared social mores, class and racial assumptions, and a history of club work. Even after the attacks by female antiradicals on the peace movement and associated organizations intensified after 1925, middle-class white women activists of all ideological stripes had continued to be bound together. A common activist history, memberships in the same organizations, and shared ethnic and class prejudices kept these women operating in the same political world, even as ideology was pulling them apart. Magnifying once-hidden differences among women from similar backgrounds, the DAR's blacklists served as the final nail in the coffin for long-standing alliances, an ineluctable sign that women who had considered themselves natural allies were now enemies. The vitriol of these encounters makes it difficult to remember how much new conservatives had in common with traditional reformers.

This history not only gave potency to conservative attacks on individual activists, it also made formidable the antiradical campaign against the maternalist legislative agenda. During the first two decades of the twentieth century, the links between organized women and reform were cemented in the public consciousness, reinforced by activists who asserted that their desire to curb child labor and fund programs to improve the health of mothers and children grew out of a feminine predilection for caregiving and housekeeping. As emissaries from the world of female voluntary associations, conservative women were welcomed into debates about maternalist legislation. Since social welfare policy was an accepted site for female policy agency, these women had the ear of male politicians considering the merits of this type of legislation. It was easy for them to undermine the claim that it was desired by all female voters. Over the course of the decade, conservative women sought to fashion themselves into national experts on the radical menace. Yet it was in the traditionally female arena of social welfare policy rather than the male realm of countersubversion that antiradical activists were able to win their most significant political victories.

Female antiradicals condemned the women's movements for peace and legislative reform as extremist in the hopes of laying claim to the vital center of a reconstituted women's politics. Instead, this struggle for the political center created warring camps that replaced the more harmonious spectrum of activism in the prewar female dominion. Three decades before grassroots anticommunism reached its zenith, anxieties about disloyalty and subversion determined the course of women's politics in the postsuffrage era, setting up divisions between women that would persist through the end of the Cold War. These new rifts were the most enduring legacy of the ascendance of female conservatism during the 1920s.

# Chapter 6

# The Legacy of Female Antiradicalism

By 1929, many civically engaged women had accepted a central tenet of anti-radicalism. The WPPC petition and the DAR blacklists had popularized the idea that social welfare legislation had been created by radical leaders promoting "a program dictated by Moscow, by the leaders of the Russian communist party."[1] According to this logic, a federal mandate to regulate child labor and the public health programs funded by the Sheppard-Towner Act would force "the federal dictation of our children, education and religion as in Soviet Russia."[2] These assertions seemed ludicrous to traditional reformers, who found it "discouraging to find how many people will believe anything."[3] Most dispiriting was the deep imprint these charges had made on female voluntary associations. The specter of global revolution eclipsed the civic pride that many clubwomen had once derived from improving health care and working conditions for society's most vulnerable members. This shift carried ominous institutional consequences for the "female dominion" of reform.

The antiradical campaign forced female voluntary associations to abandon the moral vision that had guided their political activism since the last decade of the nineteenth century. These ideals had bound together a raft of middle-class women's clubs into a distinct female political subculture, inspiring these groups to expand their scope beyond self-improvement and sorority to support a wide range of reforms during the Progressive Era. Women's clubs were the critical institutions in this world, mobilizing their members to translate social concern into political action. They devised ways for women to influence politics without having the franchise. They pioneered lobbying tactics that pressured those in power to expand the scope of government activities to encompass tasks traditionally relegated to female volunteers. Women's clubs were complex institutions, simultaneously conservative and progressive. A far cry from radical, club membership was an eminently respectable way for middle-class women to express particular gender, class, and racial identities. Yet even while they reinforced class and racial hierarchies, these clubs managed to politicize a large swath of middle-class women. Clubs, in the words of one scholar, forged "the women's sphere into a broadly based political movement."[4]

Women's clubs played a critical role in recasting the American social contract, bringing grassroots pressure to bear on state and federal governments to make human welfare—once considered a subject merely for private concern—into a matter demanding public policy.[5] They allowed middle-class women in the United States to play a role in state building unequaled in other countries. In many ways the limited welfare state that took shape in the United States before 1930 owed its existence to these types of female voluntary associations. These female activists sought to improve family life and motherhood, putting their efforts into reforms that addressed the needs of women and children. These groups facilitated campaigns to clean up city streets, demand bans on child labor, battle lynching, and create public health programs to improve child and maternal health.[6] But they helped their members situate their concerns within a larger critical framework, using the exploitation of women and children to illuminate the cruelty of unregulated industrialization and urbanization.

The antiradical campaign against female-driven social welfare legislation fundamentally changed the role of women's clubs. National leaders of female voluntary associations came under pressure from their own members to renounce the "socialistic program" that had given these groups a "black eye."[7] Once-popular reform legislation made grassroots women uneasy. One member of the South Dakota LWV, Mrs. Fred Hoffman, explained that her support for maternalist measures had always been tepid. Now that this legislation and the groups that supported it were under constant attacks from the DAR in her community, she called on her national organization to send reinforcements to fight the conservative activists, since "it is useless for individual members like myself to try to do anything." She had given up. "I am through fighting now. . . . Personally, I never have been in favor of some of these measures, but worked for them through a sense of loyalty to the organization," she confessed.[8]

This rejection of progressive reform marked the end of an era for women's clubs in the United States. While the federal Children's Bureau was able to weather the antiradical offensive of the late 1920s, the broad-based women's movement for social welfare that had brought this agency into existence proved less resilient. Anxieties about radicalism, reform, and revolution vitiated the political zeal of many female voluntary associations, neutralizing them as a force for progressive change. Once "social housekeeping" became patriotically suspect, leaders who were determined to enact social reform and transform the political system lost their grassroots base. They buckled under antiradical assaults, capitulating to demands that their group drop their campaigns for progressive legislation. By 1929, the largest groups had defected from the Women's Joint Congressional Committee, the reform-minded coalition set up to leverage women's influence in Washington after female enfranchisement. Faded was the hope that the reform-minded women's coalition could make traditional power politics more democratic and responsive to women and children. By the time the economic disaster of the Depression inspired fresh interest in government programs that could ensure the health, welfare, and safety of American citizens, female voluntary associations had forgotten their once-proud commitment to this type of social justice reform.

While female antiradicals cheered as they viewed the changed landscape of women's politics, they were not content simply to watch the destruction of existing institutions. They created new structures to support the mobilization of conservative women, most notably the Women's Patriotic Conference on National Defense, which the DAR and the American Legion Auxiliary revived in 1927. This conference had initially been conceived in 1925 as a symbolic show of support for a strong military; when the coalition reconvened two years later, its focus had shifted to political action. In the decades that followed, the WPCND would provide a logistical and ideological framework that would guide the lobbying efforts of the women's groups that had embraced the antiradical mission. While the DAR withdrew from the WPCND in the 1930s, both groups remained vibrant into the Cold War. And the DAR continued to nurture conservative activists, playing an instrumental role in launching the political career of Phyllis Schlafly, who became the best-known American female conservative of the twentieth century. The hereditary association championed her message of popular anticommunism, which she ultimately fused with antifeminism to usher in a new era for the American right.[9]

## Female Reform Under Siege

Reform leaders were slow to acknowledge that this conservative mobilization endangered the whole institutional framework of female reform politics. As they fielded reports of a conservative backlash among civic activists, leaders remained optimistic, unable to imagine a future in which women's groups would no longer be the standard-bearers for a more humane society. By 1927, however, they did recognize the need for a coordinated response to antiradical attacks. To this end, the WJCC reconstituted its committee on attacks, which pledged to analyze the source and nature of the assaults on women's organizations and distribute this information in order "to combat derogatory statements whenever and wherever made." This six-woman committee released a first draft of its report in April 1927.[10] Analyzing the rhetoric and content of the calumnies, the group concluded that no matter the issue, "the method of attack is much the same. It is charged that the legislation is un-American; that it seeks to break down the Constitution; that it originated in Moscow; that it is paternalistic; and that it is supported by socialists and communists, pacifists and feminists, frequently with the implication that these names are indistinguishable." The report saddled the *Woman Patriot* with almost exclusive blame for these slurs, tracing the trajectory of its attacks from the 1922 article "Organizing Women and Children for Revolution" to the 1926 Senate petition. The committee emphasized that the five women leading the WPPC bore sole responsibility for what had become classic documents in the antiradical canon. Their propaganda had "no authority behind it" and would have "no importance" if it had not been "seized upon and circulated" by enemies of the WJCC. In the committee's view, these fabrications were cruel attempts to bludgeon "patriotic men and women who believe in safeguarding the public health from the very beginning of life," protecting "motherhood and infancy," and ending the "commercial exploitation of young children."[11]

Some of the most damaging charges were dissected in a point-counterpoint style that illuminated fallacies and flawed logic. The committee summoned official Children's Bureau publications to debunk allegations that the agency had distributed the writings of Soviet sex-radical Alexandra Kollontai. To quash assertions that the child labor amendment and other legislative reforms originated in Soviet Russia, it named these measures' most conservative backers. To vanquish rumors that women lobbyists drew on huge sums to fund their campaigns, it explained the WJCC treasury held no more than $200. To address the reproach that member organizations were forced to support legislation they had not endorsed, it elucidated how constituents were not barred from campaigning according to their consciences. To refute criticism that women's groups refused to poll members before setting legislative priorities, the report drew on a document supposedly revered by antiradicals, explaining that these groups had "patterned their constitutions as far as practicable after the Constitution of the United States, thereby setting up . . . representative systems of government."[12]

The WJCC special committee advised its members to react promptly and vigorously to attacks, since "experience" had shown it was "unwise" to let them go "uncorrected." Though usually "absurd," antiradical myths would persist without "careful and painstaking replies." Public rejoinders were especially important in preventing "members of the accused organizations" from being "misled by accusations against the work of their officers." The report called on all the leaders of the groups associated with the WJCC to learn the "simple statements of fact with which the falsehoods may be refuted" and laid out a detailed strategy to coordinate efforts to combat future assaults and compile information about them.[13]

Despite this trenchant analysis, female reformers were hobbled by their unwillingness to stand in solidarity. Even the report from the WJCC's committee on attacks instructed members to use the report "on their own responsibility." Mounting a publicly coordinated defense might exacerbate attacks by reinforcing the sense that the WJCC was a monolith, coalition leaders decided. As a mere clearing-house for legislation, moreover, the coalition was "not authorized to answer charges made against member organizations or to defend measures supported by them."[14] The coordinated antiradical offensive against the female reform coalition quickly overwhelmed these timid and disjointed defenses of the WJCC.

The WJCC made sporadic efforts to match the support local antiradicals were receiving from their national leaders. For instance, the coalition sent reinforcements from Washington to North Carolina in 1927, when antiradicals announced a meeting meant to expose the nefarious politics of the GFWC. In Raleigh, a group of female antiradicals associated with DAR leader Margaret Overman Gregory had invited Georgia Martin to air her grievances against the GFWC. To the audience gathered at the Sir Walter Hotel, the leader of the Louisville rebellion excoriated the women's lobby for encouraging "bureaucratic, paternalistic and hence Socialistic" legislation. Emma Bain Swiggett and Kate Trenholm Abrams responded by organizing a countermeeting to take apart Martin's allegations. "If anything 'revolutionary' is going on," Abrams declared, "then the men started it with their advocacy of federal aid for business, agriculture, good roads, and so on." The appearance of national leaders did little to stem attacks on female reformers in North Carolina, however. Only two days after the Raleigh meeting, women from the Greensboro DAR accused the head of the North Carolina PTA, Bulus Swift, of being an "atheist," a slander she denied immediately. These DAR members linked Swift's alleged irreverence to the degeneration of the Greensboro College for Women, which they claimed was "a hotbed for Communism."[15]

By 1928, the League of Women Voters was the only member of the legislative clearing-house actively resisting antiradicals. As recommended by the WJCC's special committee on attacks, the League had adopted a defiant stance, assembling a "Defense Kit" that helped its local branches cope with ongoing defamations of the organization's patriotism. The packet included information about the League and the WJCC useful in exposing antiradical lies and correcting widely circulated distortions. Although it never pursued the idea, the League also explored bringing a libel suit against the DAR.[16] It instituted a much slower endorsement process, but remained true to the legislative agenda embraced by the WJCC at the beginning of the decade.[17]

Although the PTA remained associated with the WJCC, it could no longer match the League of Women Voters' commitment to legislative reform. The organization's resolve to support social welfare measures still appeared strong in 1927, when national legislative chairman Elizabeth Tilton encouraged members to not be "intimidated by name-calling or ridicule." That year, the group passed a resolution that defended the "constructive work" of the Children's Bureau and reendorsed the child labor amendment. Yet self-improvement soon became paramount over politics within the growing organization; members were urged to focus on "sound health, mastery of tools, technics and spirit of learning, useful citizenship, and wise use of leisure."[18] The group had laid aside its concern with social change by the time PTA president Minnie Bradford asserted, in 1930, that most of the problems of children could be solved by the education of mothers rather than political or social transformation.[19] Several years later, Elizabeth Tilton recounted how the officers of the PTA had consciously rejected federal legislation as the organization's main focus. "Mrs. Reeve wrote me that my policies were out of touch with the Board, that a narrowing in policy had begun and that the women decided that a few women ought not to make decisions for the many," she remembered and dismissed these arguments as antiradical propaganda. Support for legislative reform within the PTA, she asserted, had been a victim of the campaign "to get the women's organizations out of the large child welfare issues, like prohibition, the child labor amendment, etc."[20] The PTA's commitment to legislative reform was gone by the onset of the Great Depression.

Antiradicals viewed association with the WJCC as a political litmus test, demanding that women's groups prove their patriotism by cutting ties with the reform coalition. "If you find that you . . . are being counted at hearings before Congress as swelling the ranks of the women demanding pacifist or socialist legislation, do not quietly withdraw without letting any one know your reasons," Margaret Robinson told delegates at the Women's Patriotic Conference on National Defense in 1927. "Band yourself together with other like minded women, and demand that your *organization* withdraw from the radical affiliations."[21] The WJCC was sapped of its strength and vitality as groups succumbed to this call.

The first to pull out of the WJCC was the Woman's Christian Temperance Union, one of the oldest and largest women's organizations of the time. At the time of its exit in 1927, the group cited insufficient interest in prohibition on the part of the other members. For most of history, however, the WCTU had maintained a broad agenda; its membership had thrived under its "do everything" policy. Though conceived as a temperance group, the WCTU was in fact a broad-minded reform organization. Most of its departments, in fact, had been concerned with other issues. Juggling the concerns of a large and diverse membership as Prohibition came under intensifying scrutiny, it may have decided that the liabilities outweighed the advantages of being associated with the red-tainted coalition. The Girls' Friendly Society flirted with the idea of following in the WCTU's footsteps, but progressive activists were able to defeat an internal drive to cut ties to the WJCC. The most serious blow to the WJCC came in 1928, when the General Federation of Women's Clubs decided to get out.[22]

The conservative insurgency within the GFWC played a key role in unmooring the group from the larger mission of female reform. When first faced with the challenge led by Georgia May Martin, the Kentucky clubwoman, the national leadership of this coalition of women's clubs appeared steadfast, refusing to jettison its thirty-year record of lobbying for social welfare legislation. At their 1926 convention clubwomen endorsed the renewal of the Sheppard-Towner Act, which was set to expire the next year.[23] The following year, the GFWC expelled Martin's Louisville club.[24] Yet these actions did little to quell the revolt.

The WPPC petition, in particular, stirred agitation among rank-and-file clubwomen that state health officials reported they had difficulty containing.[25] Unhappy clubwomen broadcast their displeasure with the organization's progressive politics in myriad ways, including protest meetings. Clubwoman Dora Arnold teamed up with Haviland Lund, one of the first promoters of the Spider Web Chart, to host a meeting in February 1927 that promised to expose the "Congressional Woman's Lobby at Washington" and "the real driving power back of much of our legislation which is Socialistic and Communistic." The women attracted thirty listeners to Arnold's Greenridge Inn in White Plains, New York, where they paraphrased the WPPC's petition.[26]

Yet even as the GFWC national leadership appeared to be united behind maternalist reform, the organization demonstrated it was coming under the sway of antiradical activists. Soon after banishing the Louisville club, the GFWC issued a pamphlet calling on members to fight U.S. recognition of Soviet Russia. GFWC President Sherman, whom Georgia Martin had accused of promoting "socialist" legislation, also urged clubwomen to combat radicalism at the grass roots. "I am asking you now to make your own investigations as to the extent of communistic activities in your community," she wrote. "Turn the searchlight of intelligent and sustained investigation upon your schools, your churches, and your community gatherings, for it is among our young people, even among our young children, that the communists are working steadily and persistently."[27] This pronouncement set the tone for a series of GFWC-issued bulletins that began in 1927 to summarize "Bolshevik Activities in the United States."[28] The language of President Sherman and these newsletters echoed that of the DAR and the American Legion Auxiliary, reflecting the fears of clubwomen who did not join the "Louisville rebellion" but were nonetheless active in antiradical causes on a local level. Condemnations of peace activists and disarmament were especially loud from clubs in New York and Illinois, generated in part by the many DAR members who were also members of the GFWC.[29] The group's departure from the WJCC was just the first sign it would end its collaboration with female reformers.

The defection of the GFWC meant that American reform lost an important wellspring of popular support. Over the previous thirty years, this large, centrist organization had served as a training ground for legions of female political activists. But the GFWC's ability to represent and mobilize a broad ideological spectrum of women was a double-edged sword. Its size gave it considerable political clout. At the same time, its diverse membership made it vulnerable to internecine battles. Women who emerged as antiradicals in the 1920s were just as likely as female reformers to have been introduced to women's politics by their local club. As a result, women on both sides of the growing ideological divide claimed this organization as their own. As the largest and oldest group active in the female reform coalition, the GFWC had both practical and symbolic importance to antiradicals determined to banish traditional reform work from the respectable circles of women's politics. The GFWC found itself on the front lines between antiradicals and reformers struggling for the heart and soul of women's politics. By the end of the decade, antiradicals would have full control of the national organization. The GFWC served as a bellwether for the transformed political priorities of female voluntary associations.

Large, mainstream women's groups like the WCTU, PTA, and GFWC proved most vulnerable to antiradical pressure. As they capitulated to antiradical demands that they abandon national legislative reform, these types of groups crippled the broader efforts to bring progressive political influence to bear on politicians and bureaucrats. In just a few short years this new movement had dismantled much of the broader institutional framework that had nurtured three decades of coordinated female reform work. Some organizations, most notably the League of Women Voters, the National Consumers' League, and the Women's Trade Union League remained steady in their commitment to social welfare reform. The latter two groups benefited from the new power of the labor movement; but for the League of Women Voters, it became increasingly difficult to find allies willing to share in the work of sustaining a broader women's movement. When antiradicals discredited female reform, propelling it beyond the pale of political respectability, they also eviscerated the organizations that had placed this type of political work at their core.

## New Structures for Conservative Mobilization

In the winter of 1927, female antiradicals began touting new institutions they hoped would supplant the waning WJCC as a commanding force in national politics. Conservative women envisioned an alternative coalition that could provide policymakers with the views of "patriotic" women on questions of national defense. To this end, the American Legion Auxiliary and the DAR invited thirty-three women's groups to Washington, D.C., for a revived Women's Patriotic Conference on National Defense.[30] Like the 1925 version of this alliance, this congregation was intended to refute "the claim of the women pacifists that they represented the women of the United States," in the words of Adalin Macauley, president of the American Legion Auxiliary.[31] Yet these delegates came to Washington also prepared to chart a course of action and pledged to "take up the gauntlet women pacifists have thrown down," according to Macauley.[32] While the first iteration of the WPCND had featured primarily male "experts," this conference was a place where women activists could take the podium.[33]

The WJCC served as a blueprint for this new conservative organization. The conservative women borrowed the structures and tactics pioneered by female reformers, in the hopes of coordinating their own lobbying efforts. Like the WJCC, this coalition of women patriots never had a large budget or an independent membership. Its mission was to encourage the antiradical activities of member organizations. Conference officers relied on the constituent organizations to muster financial resources and womanpower for specific projects.[34] Delegates elected a standing committee that encouraged member groups to work together on various legislative issues and to keep national defense issues in the public view.[35] This team was responsible for sustaining the coalition between meetings, determining the conference program, and collecting dues assessed on the participating organizations according to their size.[36]

Constituent organizations pushed their members to lobby politicians, encouraging them to write letters informing congressmen of the sentiments of "loyal" American women on immigration, national defense, and the cultural symbols of patriotism.[37] Women associated with the WPCND testified at congressional hearings, where they spoke as representatives of both their individual organizations and the larger coalition of women patriots. Quoting WPCND resolutions, they championed "The Star-Spangled Banner" as the national anthem and argued against further immigration as well as the naturalization of immigrants identified as pacifists.[38] The WPCND also served as a venue for leaders to share practical strategies and intelligence about their common enemies. For instance, at the 1929 conference, Walker and Oliphant conducted a workshop for the delegates on "methods to be adopted by women's groups in combating pacifist propaganda." Part of the 1933 conference was devoted to instructing delegates how to be most effective in influencing congressmen.[39]

Delegates set the tone for this political engagement at the inaugural meeting of the reconstituted WPCND, when they approved a "specific program of action" designed to protect "home and government."[40] Their first priority was an increase in military expenditures for the "protection of our sons and grandsons," gendered language that couched their appeal in maternal terms. They called for an expansion of airpower and a naval building campaign that would bring the United States fleet up to the maximum allowed by the 1921 Washington Conference on the Limitation of Armaments.[41] They also insisted that the Chemical Warfare Service, which had been pilloried by peace activists, be preserved as an essential element of American national defense.[42] In articulating these demands, they positioned themselves as mothers protecting their progeny from other women's efforts to disarm the nation.

They justified another initiative by casting themselves as moral guardians of American youth, another traditional role for women. They asserted that young people were particularly vulnerable to radical influences. Imbuing these future leaders with "love of country and respect for its laws" was vital, they declared, "for the future safety . . . of these great United States of America."[43] Evidence abounded, in their eyes, that Americans needed schooling in the ways of patriotism. "Pacifist, socialist, communist and radical organizations seeking to overthrow the government of the United States," they declared in their resolutions, are "endeavoring in every way to persuade boys in our colleges to resist military training and education, to teach disrespect for the flag and national ideals . . . [and] to persuade the youth of America to take the so-called 'slacker's oath.'" Like women, young people were an apt target for radicals since they had not yet internalized conservative respect for authority and tradition; as blossoming citizens they needed training "to reverence God . . . to defend the institutions of Government, to venerate our national patriotism," and "to respect traditions of nationalism."[44] For more than a century, women had justified their presence in public life by claiming responsibility for the moral and political development of children. By emphasizing this issue, female antiradicals were placing their activism within the framework of traditional women's expertise.[45]

The delegates approved a program to inculcate patriotic principles in children and young people. This could only be achieved, they asserted, by reshaping the political culture of the schoolroom and public life. Identifying school textbooks as one of the most important vehicles for transmitting political philosophy, female antiradicals decried those who wrote history that minimized the "heroism of battles," refused "to recognize our warrior patriots who have fought and died for the life of the nation," and substituted "for our patriotic expressions radical-pacifist slogans calculated to stress internationalism in place of nationalism."[46] The women pledged to address this situation by demanding that their local schools adopt a history textbook called *The Story of Our American People*, which they endorsed as a "true and accurate history of our nation's life." The delegates also promised to eliminate teachers who evangelized for "atheism, disrespect to the flag and opposition to the Constitution of the United States." This purge would be achieved through laws that required teachers to swear "loyalty" oaths.

Female antiradicals believed that young Americans would be inoculated against subversive doctrines if they embraced cultural symbols that encouraged patriotism, loyalty, and respect. They thus called on Congress to raise the symbols of American patriotism to iconographic levels. They demanded greater reverence for the flag. And they endorsed the campaign to have "The Star-Spangled Banner" adopted as the country's official national anthem. Composed by Francis Scott Key at Baltimore's Fort McHenry during a battle of the War of 1812, the song had been named the anthem of the U.S. army and navy and was widely seen as the appropriate musical selection for official occasions and patriotic gatherings. But "The Star-Spangled Banner" had no official status as the national song, which prompted a campaign by Ella Holloway, a wealthy Baltimore widow prominent in the Daughters of 1812 and the DAR. The WPCND endorsed Holloway's efforts in 1927, when she told conference participants that legal protection for the song would encourage youthful veneration of proper American ideals and heroes.[47]

These two goals—increasing military strength and filling the hearts of young Americans with patriotic ardor—converged in their efforts to protect two military programs targeted by peace advocates, the Citizens' Military Training Camps and the Reserve Officer Training Corps. Both the CMTC and the ROTC provided young men with military training, which female antiradicals declared was "of inestimable value" in preparing them "for citizenship, leadership and to uphold the standards of our nation."[48] Not only could these recruits swell the ranks of the armed forces in times of national crisis, they argued, but the training would also render them masculine and mature and thus capable of repelling corrupt philosophies. In 1928, delegates added calls for tightened immigration restrictions and continued opposition to diplomatic recognition of the Soviet Union to their list of concerns. After that, the WPCND agenda remained fundamentally unchanged until World War II.[49]

Despite the entreaties of the women associated with the Woman Patriot Publishing Company, the group never took up the campaign against maternalist legislation that animated so many grassroots antiradicals. When

Margaret Robinson addressed the delegates at the 1927 convention, she told the assembled women that communists—by which she meant Florence Kelley, though she refrained from naming names—planned to destroy the American political system by manipulating women into supporting federal legislation. "Who would suspect," she asked, "that the 'Maternity Act' or the 'Child Labor Amendment' were anything but measures for the benefit of mothers and children?" Clubs that claimed the allegiance of conservative, right-minded women, she told the delegates, had become the most dangerous agents of national destruction. "I would be willing to stake almost anything I possess, except my wedding ring," she asserted, "that a large proportion of us are members of organizations whose legislative committees follow the leadership of a woman trained by the founders of Communism in Europe, to work for the overthrow of our form of government."[50]

Robinson's inflammatory rhetoric failed to incite the delegates. The coalition of hereditary and veterans' groups remained silent on the question of social welfare legislation. The conservative group was probably prevented from embracing Robinson's position by the American Legion Auxiliary, one of the main sponsors of the conference, which continued to support a conservative maternalist agenda. The Auxiliary flirted with repudiating maternalism in 1927, when its annual convention passed a resolution undoubtedly aimed at the Children's Bureau. The Auxiliary condemned as "evil" what it described as "the system of bureaucracy which is threatening to nullify local self-government" and registered its unease with "the growing tendency of the Federal Government to take over and exercise responsibilities properly belonging to the individual States."[51] This isolated resolution might have been the work of dissident members, who certainly came under the sway of the *Woman Patriot*. But the group never embraced the view that social welfare reform was synonymous with radical revolution.

As the closing gavel sounded in 1927, WPCND delegates dispatched messengers to deliver their platform to Congress, the president, and the secretary of war, a practice that became an annual tradition.[52] But in the years that followed, the activism of this group was largely ignored by leaders in the War Department, who remained preoccupied with ensuring that the American military remained an all-male bastion. While female antiradicals imagined themselves as the lobbying arm of the military establishment, they never developed the kind of close rapport or symbiosis that female reformers had with leaders of the Children's Bureau.

## Women and the Military

Those offended by the intolerant nationalism and strident militarism of antiradicals never believed that these women patriots sustained autonomous organizations, insisting that the inspiration for antiradical activism "undoubtedly came to the D.A.R. managers from military and naval officers." According to Helen Tufts Bailie, the DAR member who challenged the ascendance of antiradicalism within her hereditary association, the women's group had become simply a "cat's paw" for these powerful interests.[53] Journalist Norman Hapgood claimed that the DAR and the Daughters of 1812 were only "sporadically active when stimulated by the Military Order of the World War or some more hysterical post of the American Legion."[54] Historians have largely accepted this interpretation that conservative activists were only dupes or scribes for powerful men.[55]

Yet most female antiradicals had little to do with military leaders or antiradical men. Their political world was defined by the female subculture of women's organizations. They lobbied local, state, and national leaders at the direction of female leaders. Autonomous women's organizations were the most dependable source of support for these activists, who found male allies to be mercurial and suspicious of female activism, even when it served their most cherished political goals. Like their counterparts on the left, female antiradicals found men to be problematic political allies.[56] Only a handful of committed antiradicals were able to develop any kind of satisfying collaboration with the military leaders who should have been their most sympathetic allies. This means that even more than their counterparts on the left, they were forced to rely on an all female network of voluntary associations to sustain their activism.[57]

Female antiradicals received scant assistance from Anita Phipps, the War Department employee charged with the task of finding a way to make American women sympathetic to the priorities of the military establishment. Phipps had little sympathy for the conservative movement that grew out of these convictions. Not herself an activist, Anita Phipps had no ties to the world of women's politics that predated her tenure as director of women's relations.[58] Without a visible and vocal following that could apply pressure from the outside, Phipps was not able to win power and influence for women within the military. Women's groups provided her with only tepid support, perhaps because ideologically she insisted on inhabiting what was increasingly a no-woman's-land between the camps of antiradicals and reformers.

Phipps's political inexperience, isolation from networks of female activists, and determination to lobby for a strengthened military from an ideological middle ground all made her the wrong person to broker cooperation between women and the military. She was unable to harness the alarm female antiradicals felt about women pacifists and put it at the service of the War Department. In trying to secure a foothold for women within the War Department, Phipps was also handicapped by the basic misogyny of most military officers. The same narratives about female treachery that mobilized conservative women to fight radicalism among middle-class women made conservative men loath to accept these activists as equal partners. Men both inside and outside the War Department were convinced that all women were handicapped by an attraction to pacifism that was almost biological in nature. Their disdain for all women made effective cooperation impossible, even with some of their most enthusiastic supporters. Phipps had already witnessed this in 1927, when her superiors rejected her plan to establish a council of female civilian aides within the military. For a brief period in 1929, the War Department seemed to reverse this decision; Secretary of War Dwight Davis summoned representatives from representatives from thirteen women's organizations to confer with him. In February of that year, he issued invitations not only to groups like the DAR and the American Legion Auxiliary, which had for years expressed support for the War Department's policies, but also to the General Federation of Women's Clubs, which had only recently repudiated maternalist politics and moderate internationalism. He also reached out to groups that had remained steadfast advocates of reform, like the League of Women Voters, the American Association of University Women, and the National Federation of Business and Professional Women's Clubs. Despite their history of conflict with the War Department, representatives of these groups were eager for an "opportunity for patriotic service."[59] Ten days later virtually all of the women selected by Davis traveled to Washington at their own expense. "I did not know what the meeting was called for," wrote Mary Spence, president of the American War Mothers, afterward, "but felt that Mr. Davis would not ask me to come from Milwaukee, Wisconsin, unless it was important."[60]

Spence and the others were surprised to hear that they had been selected to help the secretary of war choose a council of nine female civilian aides. This group, they learned, would provide the War Department with support and advice from a feminine perspective. Davis told them that the new council was intended to allow women to exercise their "proper influence in connection with national defense policies." While they would serve in essentially the same capacity as male civilian aides, their sphere of influence would be limited to the "human side of Army life," he explained; "purely military" issues would remain off-limits. Like male civilian aides, the women would be led by a female chief aide; she would preside over a group that would represent all nine of the army's corps areas and would be responsible for educating women's groups about the War Department's mission. To distinguish them from male military professionals, these aides would receive no perquisites from their service.[61] Davis named Bettie Monroe Sippel, a DAR member and the conservative president of the General Federation of Women's Clubs, as chief aide.[62] Before adjourning, the women chose a subcommittee responsible for collecting nominations for the council and agreed to meet back in Washington in mid-March.[63] Immediately after the February meeting, Sippel assured the secretary of war that he would "find the women of this country enthusiastic supporters of your plan for a close cooperation between themselves and the army."[64]

This plan proved short-lived. Davis had called Sippel and the other women into his office during his last week as secretary of war. His successor, James W. Good, refused to embrace the new group of advisers. When the committee of five women returned to the War Department less than three weeks later to meet with the new secretary of war, they were informed that their appointment had been canceled. "This postponement," Good wrote the women on the nominating committee, somewhat belatedly, "was not due to any lack of interest on my part." The delay was necessary, he maintained, since "misunderstandings have arisen" concerning the plan to appoint women as advisers.[65]

Immediately after its first meeting, this council of female aides had aroused deep opposition from all quarters. The War Department heard first from its traditional critics. The National Council for Prevention of War decried the creation of the female civilian aides as an attempt to dampen the enthusiasm for peace within reform-minded women's organizations.[66] But objections to the proposal also poured in from the army's most enthusiastic backers. This ensured that the council would never make it off the drawing board.[67]

Female antiradicals were most vigorous in their denunciations. Davis had offended the leaders of hereditary and veterans' organizations when he had appointed Bettie Monroe Sippel as chief civilian aide. Representatives of the

DAR, the American Legion Auxiliary, and the American War Mothers could not fathom how the secretary of war would expect them to accept direction from Sippel. Although Sippel was a member of the DAR and would emerge as a committed antiradical in the years that followed, as president of the GFWC she had presided at the Conference on the Cause and Cure of War which they derided as "opposed to National Defense policies."[68] They were stunned that the War Department seemed dismissive of the years that they had spent leading the charge on the issue of national defense. "It is not necessary to call to the attention of the Secretary of War that the DAR collectively and individually have demonstrated their policy of cooperation with the War Department in times of both war and peace," Flora Walker, National Defense chairman of the DAR, wrote. "We wish to continue this cooperation but feel we should find it difficult to collaborate with certain organizations or individuals, holding views widely divergent from ours on the subject of National Defense."[69] Mary Spence, the national president of the American War Mothers, remained deferential, if pointed, in her protest. "I felt that a Secretary of War would not appoint any one whom he thought was going to work against the War Department and the protection of our country."[70]

Phipps had convinced former Secretary of War Davis that Sippel was most appropriate for this leadership position, since she headed up what was probably the largest women's organization of the time. Since beginning her work as director of women's relations, Phipps had asserted that the military could not afford to ignore powerful women's groups, even those that had shown sympathy for what she believed were pacifist doctrines. Moreover, she had developed a deep distaste for the confrontational tactics of female antiradicals. By following her recommendation and appointing Sippel, however, the War Department slighted the strongest backers of a large and respected military. "Each of our organizations has been a member of the Women's Patriotic Conference on National Defense, whose resolutions and programs have been in keeping with American ideals and strongly supporting adequate National Defense in all its phases," leaders of the American Legion Auxiliary, DAR, and American War Mothers protested to the secretary of war.[71]

Secretary of War Good also heard rumblings from powerful civilian men with close ties to the army, who had caught wind of the women's council. Male activists were outraged at the prospect of women winning formal recognition from the military. While outside the military hierarchy, male civilian aides still assumed that any connection to the military required gender-specific virtues. Feminizing these positions would be an affront to the men who had already volunteered for duty, they claimed. "I am perfectly certain that if this title is conferred upon women it will become impossible to get the right sort of men to serve—even if some of those who are now Civilian Aides do not resign in disgust," wrote George Wharton Pepper, a former Republican senator from Pennsylvania, to the new secretary of war. "I for one shall feel seriously embarrassed if it turns out that positions urged upon he-men are being tendered also to ladies, however charming and patriotic."[72] Female civilian aides would undermine the clear dichotomy between male warriors and female home-keepers. Serving the military, even as civilians, signified male virility and courage in the minds of men like Pepper; they were determined to preserve this association.

Integrating women into the War Department would compromise American martial spirit, male aides argued, since women could not resist pacifism's siren song. Writing from Milwaukee, Wisconsin, one aide complained that he had witnessed women's efforts to "abolish the National Guard and all military training in the University and schools in this state." Women's leadership of the peace movement, Wheeler P. Bloodgood declared, disqualified all members of the sex from holding any position of responsibility within the military. In addition, women were handicapped in patriotic service by pettiness and poor judgment. "It has been my experience that almost invariably serious and difficult complications arise the moment women are given equal powers with men in connection with the direction of organization work that relates to the Citizens' Army," Bloodgood wrote.[73]

In the opinion of these protesters, the military was asking for trouble by denying the natural fact that war planning was for men. John Holabird of the Military Training Camps Association, a male voluntary organization that supported the army's training efforts, explained that the appointment of female aides would lead to "confusion" and would drive many "distinguished men" away from doing their patriotic duty.[74] These boosters believed that the military should be preserved as a masculine domain. "The men of this country . . . do not expect the women to take part in wars on the firing line," Wheeler Bloodgood asserted. "Until women are subject to military service on the same basis as men, they cannot expect and should not be given equal authority, either in organizations for preparedness, or in fighting units."[75] No doubt such critics also feared that women would derive power from serving the military; women might then exert this newfound authority well beyond the confines of the War Department.

Male activists ignored the deep differences between female "patriots" and their foes that loomed so large in the minds of female antiradicals. As these reactions showed, male antiradicals were deeply suspicious of any female activists, even those who shared their concerns. Male activists, conscious of the common wisdom that held women to be naturally peace-loving, had tried to enlist sympathetic women to provide ammunition for their war on women peace activists. They hoped to cloak their activities in female moral authority, encouraging women to pass supportive resolutions. But they hoped that women would leave the official work of the campaign against radicalism to men. Many men in the American Legion, for instance, had opposed the establishment of an Auxiliary on the grounds that former soldiers should be the only ones to turn their military service into political capital. Like many men of their time, Legionnaires regarded all women's activism with a mixture of fear and resentment, convinced that it had the potential to promote sex antagonism. The women in the Auxiliary frequently tried to reassure the Legionnaires by emphasizing their roles as "handmaidens" to true heroes, mobilizing only to further an agenda determined by men.[76]

Although they remained deferential to male authority, female antiradicals chose to ignore the admonitions of their male allies. They defied calls from antiradicals like Vice President Calvin Coolidge to concentrate on their duties as Republican mothers and patriotic educators.[77] As caregivers to patriots, conservative women reasoned, they were entitled to civic authority. Female enfranchisement also conferred, in their eyes, a "sacred duty" to take public stands against women who used assumptions about female purity and innocence to evade censure for treasonous actions.[78] Leaders of the American Legion Auxiliary justified their activism in almost penitent terms. They committed themselves to fight pacifist propaganda as compensation for the sins of their sisters, confessing "with deep shame" that "most of this propaganda and subversion of patriotic ideals of our country, comes from organized groups of women."[79] But they were unapologetic about their desire to speak on questions of national defense and national security, topics that had traditionally been seen as the exclusive province of men.

The committee designated to choose the female aides never reconvened. And the controversy engendered by this scuttled plan administered the coup de grâce to Anita Phipps's ailing career. After the demise of the council, her supervisors further narrowed her field of operations; she was confined almost exclusively to the "welfare work" of the War Department. Putting energy into other projects was futile, she groused. No one was interested in her opinions regarding relations between women and the military. Any further studies, she complained bitterly, would be "a waste of time" since those "submitted in the last few years have been filed and no further action taken on them."[80] Although poor health forced Phipps to take an extended leave of absence in 1930, she made a final appeal to the secretary of war to either give her the power to do her job or to dispense with her entirely.[81] Assigned to clarify her duties, Brigadier General Albert Bowley proved sympathetic to her complaints, concluding that if given proper support, she could provide valuable services.[82] But in 1931 a new chief of staff, General Douglas MacArthur, overrode these recommendations from the personnel division, tersely declaring to the secretary of war that Phipps's duties were of "little military value."[83] Phipps was stripped of her responsibility for women's relations. Her salary was slashed as she was forced to take a new post as coordinator of war department welfare activities. When Phipps left the War Department about a year later, her job was eliminated. Almost immediately, the army seemed eager to forget that it had ever had a director of women's relations.[84]

Like their liberal and radical sisters, conservative women found ideologically sympathetic men at best undependable allies and at worst treacherous foes. Yet even as it rebuffed women, the War Department also encouraged some of the activities of female antiradicals. The Military Intelligence Division provided activists who studied and tracked radicals with covert endorsements instead of public acknowledgments; women like Flora Walker embraced this cooperation as a chance to glean confidential information and enhance her authority as an expert on antiradicalism. Walker drew on her group's unauthorized partnership with certain military intelligence officers to claim "the confidence of government authorities."[85]

Although it may seem odd that these women enthusiastically supported a military establishment that excluded women and ranked their volunteer efforts only second best, the military's hands-off policy left the female antiradical campaign free from restrictions that might have dampened their passion. With autonomy from the formal military hierarchy, conservative women leaders were free from supervision to interpret the support of male officers however they saw fit. Female antiradicals collaborated with the War Department and invited officers to endorse the WPCND. In the long run, the military had no way of controlling female antiradicals, who funded all of their own activities and held no official status within the government. A public partnership would have represented a short-term victory for female antiradicalism, but it ultimately might have stifled the conservative women who gave antiradicalism its passion and intensity. Their separate sphere helped the movement continue to mobilize women and extend its political influence.

### The New Landscape for Women's Politics in the New Deal

By the early 1930s, the millennial joy that had opened the age of female enfranchisement was a distant memory.[86] Female reformers were confronted by the hard facts of this new political reality when the presses for the *Woman's Journal*, formerly *Woman Citizen*, rolled out their last issue in 1931. This feisty publication had provided a platform for female reform since its establishment in 1870. In recent years it had been supported by a subsidy from the League of Women Voters, which decided in the early years of the Depression that the newspaper's subscribers were no longer the League's most vigorous activists.[87] Relieved, perhaps, by the enfeebled state of its traditional enemies, the *Woman Patriot* closed down in December 1932. That same year, socialist reformer Florence Kelley died; three years later, peace activist and settlement founder Jane Addams succumbed to cancer. The death of these giants in the field of progressive reform marked the end of an era. In the years that followed, female antiradicals would be forced to redirect their energies against a new generation of enemies.

Female antiradicals won a notable victory in 1931, when Congress voted to adopt "The Star-Spangled Banner" as the national anthem. This legislation defied critics who protested that Key's lyrics glorified war and his melody was difficult to sing and unsavory in its origins. The tune had apparently been appropriated from a barroom ballad of the Anacreontic Society, an eighteenth-century London drinking club. Antiradical leader Ella Holloway scoffed at these complaints. "The anthem for the service must be the anthem for the people," Holloway had asserted.[88] The Baltimore activist was enraged by those who would substitute at official gatherings "America the Beautiful" for "The Star-Spangled Banner," which she considered patriotic poetry. According to Holloway, "The Star-Spangled Banner" was a sacred expression of the highest values of American civilization. It had the power, she believed, to rouse respect for past military service and banish pacifism and radicalism. The drive to win official recognition for "The Star-Spangled Banner" was part of a larger effort by antiradicals to create a cultural landscape that supported their interpretation of American nationalism. The

Depression and the social upheaval that attended the prolonged economic crisis only confirmed the antiradical conviction that the nation needed symbols that would instill their brand of patriotism in all Americans.[89]

At least initially, the national emergency engendered by the Depression seemed to soften antiradical militance. In 1932, Edith Scott Magna, the newly elected DAR president general, removed Flora Walker as head of the National Defense Committee. In 1933, Magna pulled the organization out of the Women's Patriotic Conference on National Defense, claiming that the group's Constitution forbade it to identify with another organization. Citing a need to keep "the D.A.R. for the D.A.R." and pursue a "constructive" program of "patriotic education," Magna called on her members to resist the overtures of "other groups" that would "have us operate under their titles, rather than our own."[90] The group also recruited Eleanor Roosevelt, documenting her genealogy and paying her fees for a lifetime membership.[91]

The shake-up in the DAR did little to dampen antiradical zeal, however. Many members of the hereditary association continued to support the WPCND, participating under the aegis of other groups. While the antiradical coalition never regained the broad following it had enjoyed when the DAR was sponsoring its activities, it remained vigorous through World War II, sustained by the backing of the American Legion Auxiliary.[92] And Walker remained active in the DAR, combining her work in the hereditary association with new duties as the executive secretary of the American Coalition of Patriotic Societies, a mixed-sex group she remained associated with until at least 1956.[93] The DAR continued its robust financial support for the National Defense Committee, which remained the arbiter of DAR legislative priorities. Under the guidance of this powerful committee, the Daughters lobbied against the recognition of Soviet Russia and in favor of legislation requiring teachers to take oaths of allegiance, maintaining that "anti-American influences are being exerted through the schools."[94]

Moreover, the woman who took the helm of the DAR National Defense Committee, Florence Hague Becker of Connecticut, proved no less committed to an antiradical agenda than Walker. Becker asserted that the activities of her members "do not cease with words—they carry on further with deeds." She told national delegates to the group's 1933 convention that chapters had reported "investigation of Communist and Socialist organizations in their towns" as well as their work in "controlling or suppressing them." In one community the group convinced the Board of Education to ban "un-

The Beacon-light of Patriotism

Figure 9. This cartoon illustrates the DAR's steadfast commitment to antiradicalism during the Great Depression, which was forcing many Americans to reconsider their opposition to unfettered capitalism. *Daughters of the American Revolution Magazine* (November 1932).

American meetings"; in another town, the DAR rallied neighbors to round "up its communistic element" and show "them to the gates."[95]

In 1935, the *New York Times* revealed that Becker had endorsed Elizabeth Dilling's *The Red Network*, an anti-Semitic attack on the Roosevelt administration. *The Red Network* explained the dangers of communism and listed hundreds of organizations and thousands of individuals engaged in what Dilling believed was a vast atheist, Zionist plot. Besides comparing Franklin Roosevelt to Karl Marx, the book used an alphabetical blacklist to classify the League of Women Voters and the Women's Trade Union League as "red."[96] Dilling had dedicated this book to the DAR, which earlier had distributed her pamphlet, "Red Revolution, Do We Want It Here?" to its chapters. The organization also made sure its members had copies of *The Red Network*, which drew the group into another public relations storm.[97] But Becker's public praise for *The Red Network* was no black mark in the eyes of most DAR members. In 1935, Becker won the office of president general in a landslide victory over a supporter of Franklin Roosevelt.[98] Moreover, when the House Un-American Activities Committee (HUAC) was established in 1938, the head of the DAR appeared before the committee to endorse its efforts to expose the communist infiltration of American institutions.[99]

The stridency of the DAR was cheered by the GFWC, where enthusiasm for antiradicalism replaced an earlier relish for reform. The same year that the GFWC separated from the WJCC, it elected DAR member Bettie Monroe Sippel president. The federation of women's clubs then followed the political trajectory established by the DAR. The GFWC became increasingly preoccupied with subversion under Sippel's leadership. She had revealed her own sympathy to antiradicalism when she affiliated herself with the International Committee to Combat the World Menace of Communism, an organization that counted leading female antiradicals like Flora Walker, Grace Brosseau, and Margaret Robinson in its ranks. Women's clubs associated with Sippel's national federation established committees on "citizenship" and "Americanism," which worked to combat "subversive movements" in communities around the nation. And like the DAR, the GFWC also distributed Dilling's outrageous book, *The Red Network*. National officers of the GFWC urged club program chairmen to use the book as a guide for avoiding speakers who disseminated "subversive propaganda," including those who say "there is no communist menace." Defending the free speech of these dangerous individuals, according to the chairman of the GFWC's Department of Education in 1936, was simply an attempt to "intimidate our less informed citizens."[100]

Even as the GFWC and the DAR became ever-more staunch champions of the politics of antiradicalism, the desire for progressive social change remained strong among the women associated with the Children's Bureau. After fighting off the antiradical onslaught in 1927, female reformers rose to defend the Bureau again in 1930. Female activists prevailed when President Herbert Hoover attempted to transfer the responsibilities of the Bureau to the Public Health Service. Antiradical attacks could not breach the defenses of the Children's Bureau, nor could they extinguish the reforming spirit of its leaders. And when the economic collapse of the 1930s opened the door for the New Deal, maternalist reformers were prepared to take full advantage of this political sea change. They pursued reforms from the Progressive Era through the New Deal, rooting the achievements of one era in the dreams of another.[101]

Many of the programs envisioned by Progressive Era reformers became part of the Social Security Act of 1935, the cornerstone of the American welfare state. The Social Security Act grew under the leadership of Secretary of Labor Frances Perkins, a veteran of the Consumers' League of New York who had emerged from a network of female reformers. In shaping the Act, Perkins collaborated with Grace Abbott and Katharine Lenroot, who took over administration of the Children's Bureau from Abbott in 1934. After leaving the Children's Bureau, Abbott retained significant influence in Washington policymaking circles. She was one of four women to join President Roosevelt's Advisory Committee on Economic Security, which was charged with developing a comprehensive social security program. Abbott and Lenroot drew up programs for children during the New Deal, working with Perkins to restore funding to Sheppard-Towner style maternal and infant health programs. The three women made other proposals that inspired little controversy: new services for disabled and neglected children and federal funding for mothers' pensions, which became known as Aid to Dependent Children or simply "welfare." As part of the Social Security Act, this program enshrined the practice of federal aid to the states so reviled by antiradicals.

In some respects the Social Security Act was the culmination of more than thirty years of advocacy by female reformers. The successes of the 1930s, however, came in spite of the waning power of female reformers. They were only possible because of the cataclysm of the Great Depression. The collapse of the banking system, shuttering of industry, and unprecedented unemployment shook the assumptions of many Americans, allowing the administration of Franklin D. Roosevelt to craft a new relationship between individuals and government. Without the radical protests inspired by the decade's economic disaster, reformers could have never mustered enough political influence to win passage of these long-sought measures.

Even at this moment of supreme satisfaction, scars were obvious from antiradical attacks, which, according to historian Linda Gordon, had left Children's Bureau administrators "perpetually anxious." Discarding Sheppard-Towner's efforts to reach all women, regardless of income, the Social Security Act institutionalized means testing in federal welfare programs, in part because reformers wanted to avoid the kind of controversy that had dogged them in the past. As a result, the major welfare program for women and children stigmatized its recipients. Means testing ultimately made it impossible for Aid to Dependent Children to build the kind of broad constituency enjoyed by Social Security, for instance. As a result, it was easily assailed, undermining the ability of the American welfare state to ensure social justice for women.[102]

Three years later, in 1938, Perkins, Abbott, and Lenroot also drafted vital sections of the Fair Labor Standards Act. Besides regulating workers' hours and setting a minimum wage, this legislation banned child labor, providing an anticlimatic end to the campaigns for labor legislation that had begun early in the century. By 1940, with the exception of national health insurance, the social welfare reforms that women's groups had sought since the Progressive Era had been achieved by the New Deal. Equally important, this legislation was upheld by the Supreme Court in 1941.[103]

The New Deal ushered in reforms long championed by women and elevated veteran female reformers to leadership positions within the federal government.[104] But the sweeping reforms of the Roosevelt administration did not revive the political institutions that had nurtured these activists and measures for so many decades. Emptied of their ardor for reform by the early 1930s, women's clubs never recaptured their earlier vibrancy or political influence. The Depression revived other progressive social movements. Radicals energized communist and socialist organizations, farmers' associations, groups devoted to racial justice, and labor unions. All these movements demanded greater social justice and a more equitable distribution of wealth. Women's clubs, in contrast, remained largely silent on questions of progressive reform.[105]

A few female voluntary organizations deemed revolutionary by anti-radicals—the National Consumers' League, the Women's Trade Union League, and the League of Women Voters—continued agitating for labor legislation, health programs, and government income supports for families during the New Deal. But these smaller organizations could not mobilize the millions of women affiliated with more centrist groups. No movement coalesced, for instance, to champion government relief for impoverished mothers, a demand made by women's clubs during the Progressive Era. The federal government inaugurated Aid to Dependent Children at the behest of women employed in the federal bureaucracy, not a coalition of powerful women's groups. Individual women like Grace Abbott and Katharine Lenroot remained prominent advocates for government health programs and labor legislation and emerged as some of the central architects of the New Deal. But women's clubs no longer served as fulcrums for national legislative reform. It was individual female reformers rather than larger organizations who did the critical work of carrying the campaigns of the Progressive Era into the New Deal.[106]

At their moment of greatest triumph, these female policymakers who were embedded in the federal bureaucracy found they could no longer call on their political base for support. Progressive social welfare reform lost the grassroots advocates so vital to its advance in the past, a fact that went largely unnoticed at a moment when the possibilities for dramatic social change seemed rosier than ever. This loss seemed inconsequential, obscured by the power of female bureaucrats, the growth of radical politics, and the new vibrancy of labor activism. The Depression had put the concerns of female reformers back on the political map. The women's clubs that had promoted these concerns for more than two decades, however, had moved to the periphery.

The Roosevelt administration provided another outlet for women's energies, welcoming their contributions inside the burgeoning federal bureaucracy in the early 1930s. Yet their newfound foothold within the federal government proved impermanent. Without the grassroots support provided by female voluntary associations, the influence and autonomy of the Children's Bureau diminished. After the passage of the Social Security Act, oversight for the new programs concerned with the health and welfare of children was given to the Social Security Board. The Children's Bureau was relegated to an advisory role, as public policy issues concerning children moved into the hands of male bureaucrats. No longer able to fall back into its traditional symbiosis with the club-based female reform movement, the Children's Bureau became more vulnerable than ever. Calls for its elimination resurfaced before the end of the Roosevelt administration.[107] Other bureaucracies that had welcomed women reformers at the beginning of the New Deal also became increasingly male-dominated. As women departed, they were not replaced by other women, in part because groups outside the government no longer groomed and promoted new candidates. The decline of the "woman's bloc" thus ultimately inhibited the ability of female reformers to remain influential in government reform circles even through the end of the New Deal.

Since the nineteenth century, separate female institutions have encouraged both intimate friendships and professional networks that enhanced the effectiveness of women's activism and heightened their political influence.[108] Sex-segregated institutions have played a vital role in sustaining women's activism on behalf of a broad range of causes.[109] Autonomous women's organizations were as important to activists on the right as the left. Actually, in the early twentieth century they were more critical, as female reformers were able to gain power and influence in male-dominated institutions during the period between the Progressive Era and the New Deal. As they entered government agencies, however, progressive women gave up many of the benefits of a separate female sphere without gaining substantial power and influence in these male worlds.[110] By contrast, women on the right did not have the same opportunities to contribute publicly to male-dominated bureaucracies. With the exception of the War Department's Anita Phipps, who did not even consider herself an antiradical, conservative women remained circumscribed in the world of female voluntary politics, using the WPCND, the National Defense Committee of the DAR, the Woman Patriot Publishing Company, and myriad other committees within hereditary, veterans', and former antisuffrage organizations to influence public policy. These mainstays of female antiradicalism kept conservative activism vital through the New Deal, continuing to groom grassroots leaders who sustained the women's campaign against communism until it could blossom in the fertile soil of the Cold War.

# Epilogue: From Antiradicalism to Anticommunism

The women who embraced the Spider Web Chart as a blueprint for activism reshaped politics in the United States. As they wrested control of established institutions from traditional reformers in the decade after enfranchisement, they redrew the map of women's politics, balkanizing an empire that had once been united under the flag of social improvement. As they drew new political boundaries, they divided women who had once worked together in the same world of female voluntary associations, where unspoken assumptions about class and racial superiority had bound together ideologically diverse club-women. By the New Deal, the antiradical campaign had established a separate political domain for conservative women, who found common cause in their determination to halt the global advance of radicalism. Anchored by powerful institutions—the WPCND, National Defense Committee of the DAR, and American Legion Auxiliary—this sphere would nurture a new generation of female activists who would call themselves anticommunists.

The modern crusade against communism that began in the aftermath of the Bolshevik Revolution crescendoed through the Cold War. Growing tensions with the Soviet Union provided the backdrop for a flood of government reports and popular books warning Americans of the invisible army of communist spies and agents in their midst. This new anticommunism had a populist tone that mobilized scores of ordinary citizens to guard against foreign agents. Its champions saw evidence of subversion in the nation's most important institutions and worked to expunge radical influences from schools, libraries, and government bureaucracies. They sustained the belief that female reform organizations were particularly susceptible to subversion, even recycling the rhetoric of the 1920s about the sinister goals of the "women's bloc." In 1948, the diminished WJCC drew the fire of conservative publicist Lucille Cardin Crane, who resuscitated the allegation that this female political coalition had duped women into supporting "socialist" measures. She wrote "Packaged Thinking for Women," a pamphlet published by the National Industrial Conference Board, that outlined a Cold War version of the antiradical Spider Web Chart. In this later attack on middle-class female reformers, the State Department replaced the Children's Bureau as the villainous government authority that was manipulating ten million gullible women into lobbying on behalf of policies that would ultimately bring their demise.[1]

The groups that had built female antiradicalism into a social movement stood ready at the end of World War II to provide grassroots organizers for anticommunist campaigns. The DAR, the American Legion Auxiliary, and the WPCND used their national networks to mobilize women who fought the global rise of communism in their local communities. While female antiradicals had been preoccupied with influencing the legislation of national public policy in Washington, D.C., anticommunist women focused on rooting out subversive influences closer to home. Influenced by the nation's vigorous embrace of domesticity after World War II, grassroots anticommunists used new family values to frame their civic work, justifying their political engagement as an extension of their homemaking and mothering roles. These mostly suburban women took advantage of their flexible schedules to canvass voters and mimeograph political pamphlets between diaper changes, car pools, and cooking.[2] Across the political spectrum during these years, women were the "doers" in their communities, the social glue that sustained the kinship and friendship networks. Like their counterparts in the civil rights movement of the time, anticommunists put these networks at the service of their political work, drawing friends and relatives into this mission of national salvation. In a pattern familiar to their progressive counterparts, these women ceded visible leadership positions to men.[3] As in the African American freedom struggle, it was women who did the footwork of organizing their communities, making anticommunism into an effective grassroots movement that shaped all aspects of American life in the 1950s and 1960s.

For some women in this period, it was difficult to reconcile their desire to play an active role in civic life with what they perceived to be their proper roles as wives and mothers. This conflict reshaped the tactics of the American Legion Auxiliary, which became increasingly ambivalent about the symbolic and practical importance of maintaining a single-sex antiradical bloc. Twenty-five years after Auxiliary leaders convened the first meeting of the WPCND, the group decided to abandon this strategy in favor of emphasizing collaboration with likeminded men. In 1950, female hereditary and veterans' groups teamed up with the American Legion in its All-American Conference to Combat Communism, and two years later, the Auxiliary withdrew from the WPCND. It declared that it could no longer endorse resolutions that mandated activism. The conference interfered, leaders explained, with their organization's role as helpmeet to the Legion. They had no right to work independently with other women's groups to set a political agenda; they needed to concentrate entirely on following the lead of the Legion, putting all their energy into advancing its platform. The next year, the Auxiliary reorganized the conference as the Women's Forum on National Security, designed to educate rather than mobilize delegates. This nonactivist version of the WPCND met annually until 1981.[4]

The DAR, by contrast, refused to cede any autonomy. Its leaders were galvanized by the Cold War preoccupation with subversion and made anticommunism more central to the organizational mission. The hereditary association continued to have its political priorities determined by the National Defense Committee and was instrumental in cultivating a new generation of Cold War activists. The best-known woman to emerge from this society was Phyllis Schlafly, "the sweetheart of the silent majority" from Alton, Illinois. Schlafly became the most famous conservative woman of the twentieth century, earning national recognition for her leadership of the campaign against the Equal Rights Amendment in the 1970s.

The ERA would have altered the nation's Constitution to include the promise that "equality of rights under the law shall not be denied or abridged by the United States or by any State on account of sex." Schlafly launched the campaign to block ratification of this amendment, positioning herself during the struggle that followed as a housewife and political outsider. Yet she was hardly a political neophyte. She brought to this battle a wealth of skills and experience developed over decades as a grassroots anticommunist organizer. Known for her expertise on the traditionally male subjects of the Soviet Union, national security, and international arms limitation agreements, she was backed by an enthusiastic following that she had cultivated through her decades of leadership in sex-segregated organizations. Women from the National Federation of Republican Women and the DAR were drawn to her charisma; she channeled their outrage into a conservative insurgency that would challenge the nation's political establishment. This mobilization from the right would ultimately reinvigorate the Republican

Party, making it the standard-bearer of a conservative populism that would dominate the last decades of the twentieth century.[5]

Schlafly became known as a Republican Party activist in the 1950s. She ran for an Illinois congressional seat in 1952 at the urging of local party leaders, who were drawn to the uncompromising conservatism of the twenty-seven-year-old new mother.[6] As a Republican candidate in a heavily Democratic district, Schlafly lost her election bid. Undaunted, she remained active in party politics, convinced that the Republican Party was an effective vehicle for fighting communism, though she was always suspicious of blind partisanship. Her uncompromising stridency put her at odds with the party hierarchy, which she viewed as serving politics over principle. She spent her career pushing the party to rededicate itself to the conservative principles she cherished. She championed her anticommunist agenda from the margins of the party, as both ideology and gender excluded Schlafly from her party's leadership circle.[7]

Schlafly's career demonstrates the continued importance of autonomous women's organizations in nurturing conservative female activism. Schlafly assembled her following of like-minded women from both the National Federation of Republican Women and the DAR. Unfettered by any association with male leaders discomfited by female activism, the DAR gave Schlafly more enthusiastic institutional support than the Republican women's group, which emphasized party unity over ideological purity. In contrast, the DAR had only deepened its commitment to anticommunism with the onset of the Cold War, which was undoubtedly one of the reasons Schlafly was drawn to the Alton, Illinois, chapter of the group in the early 1950s.[8] She immediately assumed a leadership role, serving two terms as chapter regent before moving into the state leadership of the organization, where she worked as Illinois state chairman of National Defense, Illinois state recording secretary and editor of the state yearbook.[9] The hereditary association gave Schlafly the platforms she needed to organize against communism, rallying women to save the "Republic . . . from the fires of Communism which have already destroyed or enslaved many Christian cities."[10] In her search for "ten patriotic women in each community," Schlafly maintained an intense writing and speaking schedule.[11] She composed monthly columns for the *DAR Magazine* and edited the *National Defender*.[12] She was a popular presence at DAR meetings all over Illinois, where she became known as an engaging orator capable of translating complex conservative philosophies into rousing polemics. Schlafly's warnings echoed those issued by National

Defense Committee founder Flora Walker. The midwestern activist rallied listeners with her message that the United States was "in a life-and-death struggle" with radicals who "expect to destroy our Church, our country, our freedom, the institution of the family, and everything else we hold dear."[13] The Illinois DAR allowed Schlafly to disseminate this message to a regional audience in the early 1960s, when it sponsored a weekly syndicated radio program called *America Wake Up* featuring her discourses on national security issues.[14]

The DAR was crucial in helping Schlafly develop a loyal following, which she tapped in 1964 to disseminate *A Choice Not an Echo*, a self-published pamphlet that would change the course of that year's presidential election. Her fans proved essential to the success of this volume, which was publicized through word of mouth and distributed entirely through grassroots networks. A populist attack on the eastern elite, the book electrified grassroots conservatives with the charge that the Republican Party's secret "rulers" were internationalists who refused to nominate candidates who would be tough against domestic subversion and political corruption. Schlafly argued that Barry Goldwater was the best candidate for president since he would "not pull his punches to please the kingmakers."[15] The book, which introduced Schlafly to a national audience for the first time, gave Goldwater the edge he needed to secure the Republican presidential nomination.[16]

To the chagrin of Republican Party leaders, Schlafly continued to mobilize fellow conservatives in the aftermath of Goldwater's defeat to support small government and a vigorous national defense against external and internal enemies, especially communists.[17] She showed no interest in feminism.[18] That changed in 1971, when Schlafly was invited to speak about the proposed Equal Rights Amendment. A brief examination of the measure convinced her it posed a danger to women, who would suffer the tyranny of an enlarged government bureaucracy if it was enacted, losing any special protections and privileges they enjoyed for the sake of equality.[19] Schlafly's epiphany marked a turning point for the American right. The seasoned anticommunist would meld her traditional concerns about subversion with new fears about feminism and changing gender roles to create an explosive new strain of conservatism that would roil the nation for the next thirty years. Her polemics on gender roles and family life won her an entirely new level of public renown. She became an overnight sensation for her warnings about the sexual Armageddon facing the United States, wielding a political authority she had never been able to muster as a pundit and policy expert on the traditionally "male" subjects of arms limitation and Soviet aggression.

Schlafly's realization came too late to slow the initial progress of the ERA, which was overwhelmingly approved by Congress in March 1972. At this point the amendment was widely regarded as an innocuous piece of "women's" legislation whose time had come, much like the Sheppard-Towner Act of the early twentieth century. Within the first year, thirty states had ratified the amendment, and in March, 1973, Representative Martha Griffiths predicted that "ERA will be part of the constitution long before the year is out."[20] Like the Child Labor Amendment fifty years earlier, the ERA appeared to be unstoppable. And just like the measures targeted by anti-radical women in the 1920s, the ERA would be defeated by newly mobilized conservative women determined to "not permit these women's libbers to get away with pretending to speak for the rest of us."[21]

Schlafly provided the ideological underpinning for this new women's movement with a widely reprinted antifeminist manifesto that rebutted the feminist logic behind the campaign for the ERA. Her 1972 "What's Wrong with 'Equal Rights' for Women?" harked back to the polemic of the WPPC that first linked anticommunism to antifeminism. "The family," wrote Schlafly, "is the greatest single achievement in the entire history of women's rights. It assures a woman the most precious and important right of all—the right to keep her own baby and to be supported and protected in the enjoyment of watching her baby grow and develop." She asserted that women's liberation was "superficial sweet-talk" designed "to win broad support for a radical 'movement.'" American women already enjoyed tremendous privileges thanks to the "great American free enterprise system" that had freed them from "backbreaking 'women's work.'" Feminism was "a total assault on the role of the American woman as wife and mother, and on the family as the basic unit of society." She enjoined her readers to "not let these women's libbers deprive wives and mothers of the rights we now possess."[22]

Women answered Schlafly's call. In September 1972, Schlafly launched STOP-ERA (Stop Taking Our Privileges), a loosely configured national group designed to spur grassroots activism against the amendment.[23] The group quickly received backing from the DAR, which announced its opposition to the ERA in 1973.[24] Local antiratification groups received no financial support or tactical directives from the national antiratification group. Instead, grassroots women received regular updates on the fight against the ERA through the *Phyllis Schlafly Report*, which provided tactical advice and talking points to a rapidly expanding readership during those years.[25] Schlafly had populist instincts absent in her antiradical foremothers. A new kind of conservative leader, she opened a new era for American conservatism by incorporating emerging anxieties about sexuality into old warnings of the traditional anticommunist right.

Neither STOP-ERA nor Schlafly's Eagle Forum, which she called "the alternative to women's lib," ever had the membership of the National Organization of Women.[26] Yet this campaign confounded feminists who were blindsided by these female opponents, fifty years after female reformers were flummoxed by a parallel challenge by women determined to undermine their moral authority. Their logic bewildered their opponents, who found themselves overwhelmed by the passion and outmaneuvered by the organizational power of the antiratification campaign. Feminist hostility to Schlafly—who came to personify antifeminism—helped to make the conservative leader into a cultural icon. At the apex of her personal fame, she agreed to join the national leadership of the DAR, filling the post first created by Flora Walker. She began her first of five terms as chairman of National Defense in 1977.[27]

Most political observers believed that Schlafly's followers had virtually no chance of preventing the ratification of the amendment. But these conservative women defied predictions over the next decade. Their arguments carried emotional resonance with state legislators, who sympathized with pleas to save "the difference" between women and men by blocking the ERA.[28] The tide turned decisively against the ERA in 1977, when antifeminists used the International Women's Year Conference to link the amendment to abortion and gay rights. By 1979, the amendment still had not won support from the thirty-eight states required for ratification. Congress passed a three-year extension, but ERA supporters were able to make little headway. In fact, five states rescinded their initial endorsement.[29] The deadline for ERA ratification passed on June 30, 1982.[30]

Feminists responded to this defeat by redoubling their efforts to erase discriminatory laws and practices; the ERA campaign quickly faded from public memory. Yet it left behind a deep imprint on American politics. Schlafly's followers remained active in politics after their victory, animating campaigns that pivoted on the preservation of traditional gender roles in the years that followed. These women were instrumental in turning the GOP to the right, ensuring that Ronald Reagan, an avowed conservative, won the party nomination and then the presidential election of 1980. His tenure in the White House marked the ascendance of a new conservative populism that dominated the last decades of the twentieth century.[31]

The conservative groundswell that swept Reagan into the White House can be traced to the antiradicalism of the 1920s, when women patriots first articulated a conservative political identity. These Jazz Age conservatives created an institutional and ideological infrastructure that endured through most of the twentieth century, sustaining conservative ideals and nurturing activists like Schlafly who would popularize the theories advanced by female antiradicals. Yet almost a century later, women on the right are still treated as a novelty and assumed to be dupes for powerful men. This history demonstrates that conservatism is not the province of men. Women have been the backbone of mobilizations on the right, organizing their communities to circle the wagons against radical influences for most of the twentieth century.

The Nineteenth Amendment proved to be a Pandora's Box. Suffragists had expected that giving women the vote would usher in a new era of female political engagement. None of them envisioned it would inspire an entirely new strain of activism that would transform some of the most powerful institutions in women's politics. While it remade the terrain on which women activists operated, antiradicalism also encouraged activists to practice politics in time-tested ways. Exposing subversion became a moral crusade not unlike the female reform campaigns of the nineteenth century.[32] For women who believed that they served as the nation's conscience, the campaign against communism was a battle against evil, a sanctified mission that transcended politics as defined by men, which they believed to be tainted by horse-trading and jockeying for personal enrichment.

No less than women on the left, conservative women struggled to be integrated as full citizens into government bureaucracy, elected bodies, political parties and a broad range of policy debates. Antiradical women exercised political influence by appropriating the strategies of female reform leaders, using popular women's groups to mobilize grassroots activists. While they challenged the moral vision that had guided middle-class women's clubs since the 1870s, their new strain of activism did little to enlarge the scope of female policymaking. Male policymakers, bureaucrats, and politicians resisted their attempts to play more than symbolic roles in debates on national security and countersubversion, forcing female activists to create autonomous institutions to support their more substantive work on these issues. They found they could exercise the most political influence in the realm of social welfare policy, a policymaking sector established by female reformers as a site appropriate for womanly intervention. Gender assumptions essentially relegated them to this circumscribed political arena, where they became locked into competition with other women for power and influence. Traditional reformers regarded antiradicals across a deep ideological gulf. Yet this fissure did not separate the political fortunes of these two groups of women. Conservatives discovered they had the power to shape the ways in which their female foes could claim and wield power. The story of antiradicalism shows why the history of women in American politics cannot be understood without a close analysis of conservative activism.

This analysis underscores an insight already familiar to feminist scholars. Autonomous women's groups appear to have been the best way for women to achieve political influence in the United States during the twentieth century. During the thirty years leading up to the Nineteenth Amendment, reformers had reshaped the American state by using female voluntary associations to bring grassroots pressure to bear on male politicians and policymakers. These groups rooted their authority in their claim to advocate for all women. But this powerful organizing tactic also had its perils. The history of twentieth-century female conservatism demonstrates that organizing in this way makes activists vulnerable to challenges from other women. The success of maternalist reformers at the beginning of the twentieth century opened the door for battles over the right to speak for the sex, triggering an intense campaign by women conservatives to undercut the political authority of their female opponents. Long before the rise of second-wave feminism, conservative women established an adversarial relationship with liberal women that changed the landscape of women's politics and the trajectory of American reform. Fifty years later, liberal feminists found themselves stymied by a parallel movement of grassroots antifeminists, who captivated audiences with their assertions that they were the true voice of American womanhood. The power struggles chronicled here illustrate both the political potential and the pitfalls of using female solidarity as a foundation for organizing, a paradox that will continue to bedevil politically active women well into the twenty-first century.

# Acronyms for Archival Sources

Alexander Lincoln Papers: Alexander Lincoln Papers, Schlesinger Library

Bailie Papers: Helen Tufts Bailie Papers, Sophia Smith Collection

Barrett Collection: Kate Waller Barrett Collection, Manuscripts Division, Library of Congress, Washington, D.C.

Catt Papers: Carrie Chapman Catt Papers, Manuscripts Division, Library of Congress, Washington, D.C.

Children's Bureau Records: Records of the Children's Bureau, RG 102, NARA

DAR Blacklist Controversy Papers: DAR "Blacklist" Controversy Papers and the Palo Alto Chapter of the Daughters of the American Revolution Collection, Department of Special Collections, Stanford University Libraries, Palo Alto, California

DAR *Proceedings*: *Proceedings of the . . . Continental Congress of the National Society of the Daughters of the American Revolution*, published annually

Helen Gould Shepard Collection: Lyndhurst, Tarrytown, New York

The Papers of Hannah Clothier Hull, 1889–1958, microfilm edition (Wilmington, Del.: Scholarly Resources Inc., 1991)

La Follette Papers: Belle Case La Follette Papers, La Follette Family Collection, Manuscripts Division, Library of Congress, Washington, D.C.

LOC: Library of Congress

LWV Papers: Papers of the League of Women Voters, *1918–1974*, microfilm edition (Frederick, Md.: University Publications of America, 1985)

Mary Anderson Papers: Mary Anderson Papers, microfilm edition, WTUL Papers

Maud May (Wood) Park Papers: Maud May (Wood) Park Papers, Woman's Rights Collection, microfilm edition, *Women's Studies Manuscript Collection from the Schlesinger Library, Radcliffe College*, series 1, *Woman's Suffrage*, part D, *New England* (Frederick, Md.: University Publications of America, 1993)

Maud Wood Park Scrapbooks: Maud Wood Park Scrapbooks, Schlesinger Library

Mead Papers: Papers of Edwin Doak Mead and Lucia Ames Mead, 1876–1936, microfilm edition (Wilmington, Del.: Scholarly Resources, 1991)

MID Correspondence: Military Intelligence Division Correspondence, 1917–1941, Records of the War Department General and Special Staffs, RG 165, NARA

MPIL Collection: Massachusetts Public Interests League Collection, Massachusetts Historical Society, Boston

NARA: National Archives and Records Administration, Washington, D.C.
RG 80: Records of the Department of the Navy
RG 102: Records of the Children's Bureau
RG 107: Records of the Office of the Secretary of War
RG 165: Records of the War Department General and Special Staffs
RG 175: Records of the Chemical Warfare Service
RG 407: Records of the Adjutant General's Office
NCF Collection: National Civic Federation Collection, Rare Books and Manuscripts Division, New York Public Library
NCPW Collection: National Council for Prevention of War Collection, SCPC
NYPL: New York Public Library
Putnam Papers: Elizabeth Lowell Putnam Papers, Schlesinger Library
Schlesinger Library: Schlesinger Library, Radcliffe College, Cambridge, Massachusetts
Schwimmer-Lloyd Collection: Schwimmer-Lloyd Collection, Rare Books and Manuscripts Division, New York Public Library, New York
SCPC: Swarthmore College Peace Collection, Swarthmore College, Swarthmore, Pennsylvania
Senate, *Overman Committee Report*: Final Report, U.S. Senate, Committee on the Judiciary, *Report and Hearings on Brewing and Liquor Interests and German and Bolshevik Propaganda*, 66th Cong., 1st sess., 1919
Senate, Protection of Maternity: U.S. Senate, Committee on Education and Labor, Protection of Maternity, 67th Cong., 1st sess., April 25, 1921 (Washington, D.C.: Government Printing Office, 1921)
Shattuck Papers: Henry Lee Shattuck Papers, Massachusetts Historical Society, Boston
Sophia Smith Collection: Sophia Smith Collection, Smith College, Northampton, Massachusetts
Tilton Papers: Elizabeth (Hewes) Tilton Papers, Schlesinger Library
WILPF-U.S. Section: Women's International League for Peace and Freedom Collection, microfilm edition, part 3, U.S. Section, SCPC
WJCC Records: Records of the Women's Joint Congressional Committee, microfilm version, Manuscripts Division, Library of Congress, Washington, D.C.
WTUL Papers: Papers of the Women's Trade Union League and Its Principal Leaders, microfilm edition, Schlesinger Library

## Additional Acronyms

*AHR*: *American Historical Review*
APL: American Protective League
CMTC: Citizens' Military Training Camps
DAR: Daughters of the American Revolution
ERA: Equal Rights Amendment

GFWC: General Federation of Women's Clubs
ICW: International Council of Women
IWW: Industrial Workers of the World
LWV: League of Women Voters
MID: Military Intelligence Division
MPIL: Massachusetts Public Interests League
NAOWS: National Association Opposed to Woman Suffrage
NCF: National Civic Federation
NCCCW: National Conference on the Cause and Cure of War
NCMPTA: National Congress of Mothers and Parent Teacher Associations
NCW: National Council of Women
NSDAR: National Society of Daughters of the American Revolution
NSNEW: National Society of New England Women
PTA: Parent-Teacher Association
ROTC: Reserve Officers' Training Corps
UDC: United Daughters of the Confederacy
WILPF: Women's International League for Peace and Freedom
WJCC: Women's Joint Congressional Committee
WPCND: Women's Patriotic Conference on National Defense
WPPC: Woman Patriot Publishing Company

# Notes

## Introduction

1. Nancy F. Cott, *The Grounding of Modern Feminism* (New Haven, Conn.: Yale University Press, 1987); J. Stanley Lemons, *The Woman Citizen: Social Feminism in the 1920s*, 2nd ed. (Charlottesville: University of Virginia Press, 1990); Jan Doolittle Wilson, *The Women's Joint Congressional Committee and the Politics of Maternalism, 1920–30* (Urbana: University of Illinois Press, 2007).

2. Charlotte Perkins Gilman, "The New Mothers of a New World," *Forerunner* 4 (June 1913): 145–49; quoted from *Charlotte Perkins Gilman: A Nonfiction Reader*, ed. Larry Ceplair (New York: Columbia University Press, 1991), 249.

3. William H. Chafe, *The Paradox of Change: American Women in the Twentieth Century* (New York: Oxford University Press, 1991), 25.

4. Rheta Childe Dorr, *What Eight Million Women Want* (Boston: Small, Maynard, 1910), 328.

5. Ibid., 322.

6. Molly Ladd-Taylor, *Mother-Work: Women, Child Welfare and the State, 1890–1930* (Urbana: University of Illinois Press, 1994), 74–103, 167–96; Lemons, *The Woman Citizen*, 153–80; Robyn Muncy, *Creating a Female Dominion in American Reform, 1890–1935* (New York: Oxford University Press, 1991), 93–123; Paula Baker, "The Domestication of Politics: Women and American Political Society, 1780–1920," *AHR* 89, 3 (June 1984): 620–47; Karen J. Blair, *The Clubwoman as Feminist: True Womanhood Redefined, 1868–1914* (New York: Holmes and Meier, 1980); Anne Firor Scott, *Natural Allies: Women's Associations in American History* (Urbana: University of Illinois Press, 1991); Anne Firor Scott, *The Southern Lady: From Pedestal to Politics, 1830–1930*, 2nd ed. (Charlottesville: University Press of Virginia, 1995); Seth Koven and Sonya Michel, "Womanly Duties: Maternalist Politics and the Origins of the Welfare States in France, Germany, Great Britain, and the United States, 1880–1920," *AHR* 95, 4 (October 1990): 1076–1108; Kathryn Kish Sklar, "The Historical Foundations of Women's Power in the Creation of the American Welfare State, 1830–1930," in Seth Koven and Sonya Michel, eds., *Mothers of a New World: Maternalist Politics and the Origins of the Welfare States* (New York: Routledge, 1993), 43–93; Nancy A. Hewitt, "Varieties of Voluntarism: Class, Ethnicity, and Women's Activism in Tampa" in Louise A. Tilly and Patricia Gurin, eds., *Women, Politics, and Change* (New York: Russell Sage, 1990),

63–86; Suzanne Lebsock, "Women and American Politics, 1880–1920," in Tilly and Gurin, eds., *Women, Politics, and Change*, 35–62; Mari Jo Buhle, *Women and American Socialism, 1870–1920* (Urbana: University of Illinois Press, 1981), 49–94; Deborah Gray White, *Too Heavy A Load: Black Women in Defense of Themselves, 1894–1994* (New York: Norton, 1999).

7. Quoted in Cott, *The Grounding of Modern Feminism*, 100.

8. Political cartoon from *Rocky Mountain News*, September/October 1920, quoted in Cott, *The Grounding of Modern Feminism*, 84.

9. Quoted in Ellen Fitzpatrick, *Endless Crusade: Women Social Scientists and Progressive Reform* (New York: Oxford University Press, 1990), 210.

10. Quoted in Clarke A. Chambers, *Seedtime of Reform: American Social Service and Social Action, 1918–1933* (Minneapolis: University of Minnesota Press, 1963), 2.

11. Sophonisba P. Breckinridge, *Women in the Twentieth Century: A Study of Their Political, Social and Economic Activities* (New York: McGraw-Hill, 1933), 264.

12. Ibid., 269.

13. Anne Firor Scott, "After Suffrage: Southern Women in the Twenties," *Journal of Southern History* 30, 3 (August 1964): 298–31, quote 318.

14. William E. Leuchtenburg, *The Perils of Prosperity, 1914–1932*, 2nd ed. (Chicago: University of Chicago Press, 1993); Frederick Allen Lewis, *Only Yesterday: An Informal History of the 1920s* (New York: Harper, 1931).

15. Quoted in Cott, *The Grounding of Modern Feminism*, 99.

16. Cott, *The Grounding of Modern Feminism*; Nancy F. Cott, "Across the Great Divide: Women in Politics Before and After 1920," in Tilly and Gurin, eds.,*Women, Politics, and Change*, 153–76; Lemons, *The Woman Citizen*; William H. Chafe, "Women's History and Political History: Some Thoughts on Progressivism and the New Deal," in Nancy A. Hewitt and Suzanne Lebsock, eds., *Visible Women: New Essays on American Activism* (Urbana: University of Illinois Press, 1993), 101–18.

17. Ladd-Taylor, *Mother-Work*, 169; Muncy, *Creating a Female Dominion*, 124–57; Lemons, *The Woman Citizen*, 153–67; Joseph B. Chepaitis, "Federal Social Welfare Progressivism in the 1920s," *Social Service Review* 46, 2 (1972): 213–29; Breckinridge, *Women in the Twentieth Century*, 257–74.

18. Cott, *The Grounding of Modern Feminism*, 101–5.

19. Quoted in ibid., 114.

20. Lemons, *The Woman Citizen*; Cott, *The Grounding of Modern Feminism*; Chafe, *The Paradox of Change*.

21. Mabel Clare Ladd to Mrs. Maud Wood Park, March 12, 1924, Frames 768–69, Reel 4, Part 3, Series A, National Office Subject Files, 1920–1932, Papers of the League of Women Voters, microfilm ed. (Frederick, Md.: University Publications of America, 1985) (hereafter LWV Papers).

22. Quoted in Leuchtenburg, *Perils of Prosperity*, 81; see, for example, Eric Foner, *The Story of American Freedom* (New York: Norton, 1998), 177.

23. Kim E. Nielsen, *Un-American Womanhood: Antiradicalism, Antifeminism, and the First Red Scare* (Columbus: Ohio State University Press, 2001).

24. Cott, *The Grounding of Modern Feminism*; Lemons, *The Woman Citizen*; Wilson, *The Women's Joint Congressional Committee*.

25. Joan M. Jensen, "All Pink Sisters: The War Department and the Feminist Movement in the 1920s," in Lois Scharf and Joan M. Jensen. eds., *Decades of Discontent: The Women's Movement, 1920–1940* (Boston: Northeastern University Press, 1983).

26. Mrs. Fred Hoffman to Mrs. R. E. Cone, Huron, South Dakota, n.d., Frames 888–89, Reel 9, Part 3, Series A, National Office Subject Files, 1920–1932, LWV Papers.

27. Elizabeth Tilton to Mrs. Moulton, n.d. Folder 250, Box 9, Elizabeth (Hewes) Tilton Papers, Schlesinger Library, Radcliffe College, Cambridge, Massachusetts (hereafter Tilton Papers).

28. Quoted in Cott, *The Grounding of Modern Feminism*, 259.

29. Anne Rogers Minor, "Why I Am a Daughter of the American Revolution," June 12, 1930, quoted in Christine Erickson, "Conservative Women and Patriotic Maternalism: The Beginnings of a Gendered Conservative Tradition in the 1920s and 1930s" (Ph.D. dissertation, University of California, Santa Barbara, 1999), 30.

30. Annual Message of the President General, Mrs. Alfred J. Brosseau, *Proceedings of the Thirty-Sixth Continental Congress of th National Society of the Daughters of the American Revolut*ion (April 18–23, 1927): 21–22.

31. Elizabeth Barney Buel, "Socialist Propaganda in the United States," Connecticut Daughters of the American Revolution, 1925. Reel 40, Vol. X, scrapbook, Schwimmer-Lloyd Collection, Rare Books and Manuscripts Division, New York Public Library (hereafter Schwimmer-Lloyd Collection); Mrs. William Sherman Walker, "Keep Yourself Informed About Radicalism," *National Republic*, July 1925, 25; Address of Mrs. William Sherman Walker, Ohio State Conference, March 16, 1927, Folder: Publications—D.A.R, Box 1, Helen Tufts Bailie Papers, Sophia Smith Collection, Smith College, Northampton, Massachusetts (hereafter Bailie Papers)

32. A. N. Hoy, Huron, South Dakota, to National PTA, Washington, D.C., December 12, 1926, Folder 248: Congress of Mothers, correspondence, 1926, Box 9, Tilton Papers.

33. Ibid.

34. Robert S. Lynd and Helen Merrell Lynd, *Middletown: A Study in Modern American Culture* (New York: Harcourt Brace, 1929), 200–201.

35. For women on the far right, see Kathleen Blee, *Women of the Klan: Racism and Gender in the 1920s* (Berkeley: University of California Press, 1991); Nancy Maclean, *Behind the Mask of Chivalry: The Making of the Second Ku Klux Klan* (New York: Oxford University Press, 1994); Nancy Maclean, "White Women and Klan Violence in the 1920s: Agency, Complicity and the Politics of Women's History," *Gender and History* 3, 3 (Autumn 1991): 285–303; Laura McEnaney, "He-Men and Christian Mothers: The America First Movement and the Gendered Meanings of Patriotism and Isolation-

ism," *Diplomatic History* 18 (1994): 47–57; Glen Jeansonne, *Women of the Far Right: The Mothers' Movement and World War II* (Chicago: University of Chicago Press, 1996); Kathleen M. Blee, "Reading Racism: Women in the Modern Hate Movement," in *No Middle Ground: Women and Radical Protest*, ed. Kathleen Blee (New York: New York University Press, 1998), 180–98. For conservative women after World War II, see Lisa McGirr, *Suburban Warriors: The Origins of the New American Right* (Princeton, N.J.: Princeton University Press, 2001); Michelle Nickerson, *Mothers of Conservatism: Women and the Post-War Right* (Princeton, N.J.: Princeton University Press, 2012); Donald T. Critchlow, *Phyllis Schlafly and Grassroots Conservatism: A Woman's Crusade* (Princeton, N.J.: Princeton University Press, 2005); Mary C. Brennan, *Wives, Mothers, and the Red Menace: Conservative Women and the Crusade Against Communism* (Boulder: University Press of Colorado, 2008); Lisa Kay Speer, "'Contrary Mary': The Life of Mary Dawson Cain" (Ph.D. dissertation, University of Mississippi, 1998). A body of work on earlier conservative women has emerged as well. See Sonya Michel and Robyn Rosen, "The Paradox of Maternalism: Elizabeth Lowell Putnam and the American Welfare State," *Gender and History* 4, 3 (Autumn 1992): 364–86; Elna C. Green, "From Antisuffragism to Anti-Communism: The Conservative Career of Ida M. Darden," *Journal of Southern History* 65, 2 (May 1999): 287–316; Manuela Thurner, "'Better Citizens Without the Ballot': American Anti-Suffrage Women and Their Rationale During the Progressive Era," *Journal of Women's History* 5, 1 (1993): 33–60; Susan E. Marshall, *Splintered Sisterhood: Gender and Class in the Campaign Against Woman Suffrage* (Madison: University of Wisconsin Press, 1997); Catherine E. Rymph, *Republican Women: Feminism and Conservatism from Suffrage Through the Rise of the New Right* (Chapel Hill: University of North Carolina Press, 2006); Karen Cox, *Dixie's Daughters: The United Daughters of Confederacy and the Preservation of Confederate Culture* (Gainesville: University Press of Florida, 2003); Francesca Morgan, *Women and Patriotism in Jim Crow America* (Chapel Hill: University of North Carolina Press, 2005); Nielsen, *Un-American Womanhood*; June Melby Benowitz, *Days of Discontent: American Women and Right-Wing Politics, 1933–1945* (DeKalb: Northern Illinois University Press, 2002); Erickson, "Conservative Women and Patriotic Maternalism."

36. Rheta Childe Dorr, *A Woman of Fifty* (New York: Funk and Wagnalls, 1924), 341.

Chapter 1. Birth of "Miss Bolsheviki": Women, Gender, and the Red Scare

1. "Bolshevism Bared by R. E. Simmons," *New York Times*, February 18, 1919, 12.

2. Final Report, U.S. Senate, Committee on the Judiciary, *Report and Hearings on Brewing and Liquor Interests and German and Bolshevik Propaganda*, 66th Cong., 1st sess., 1919 (hereafter *Overman Committee Report*).

3. Quoted in John Lewis Gaddis, *Russia, the Soviet Union, and the United States: An Interpretive History* (New York: Knopf, 1978), 106.

4. Quoted in Peter G. Filene, *Americans and the Soviet Experiment, 1917–1933* (Cambridge, Mass.: Harvard University Press, 1967), 67.

5. "Bolshevism Bared by R. E. Simmons."

6. Senate, *Overman Committee Report*, xxxi–xxxii.

7. Kim E. Nielsen, *Un-American Womanhood: Antiradicalism, Antifeminism, and the First Red Scare* (Columbus: Ohio State University Press, 2001).

8. The classic account of these red purges is Robert K. Murray, *Red Scare: A Study in National Hysteria* (New York: McGraw-Hill, 1955). The assumption that the Red Scare ended in 1920 has permeated the historical literature; see William E. Leuchtenburg, *The Perils of Prosperity, 1914–1932* (Chicago: University Chicago Press, 1958); Robert L. Friedheim, *The Seattle General Strike* (Seattle: University of Washington Press, 1964), 175; Alan Dawley, *Struggles for Justice: Social Responsibility and the Liberal State* (Cambridge, Mass.: Harvard University Press, 1991); M. J. Heale, *American Anticommunism: Combating the Enemy Within, 1830–1970* (Baltimore: Johns Hopkins University Press, 1990), 60–78; Filene, *Americans and the Soviet Experiment*; Stanley Coben, "A Study in Nativism: The American Red Scare of 1919–1920," *Political Science Quarterly* 79, 1 (March 1964): 52–75.

9. Statement of John Reed, Senate, *Overman Committee Report*, 592.

10. Senate, *Overman Committee Report*, xlix.

11. Quoted in Richard Gid Powers, *Not Without Honor: The History of American Anticommunism* (New York: Free Press, 1995), 27–28.

12. Elaine Tyler May, "Commentary: Ideology and Foreign Policy: Culture and Gender in Diplomatic History," *Diplomatic History* 18, 1 (Winter 1994): 71–78.

13. Calvin Coolidge, "Enemies of the Republic: They Must Be Resisted," *Delineator*, August 1921, 42.

14. Powers, *Not Without Honor*, 18.

15. Quoted in Powers, *Not Without Honor*, 18–19.

16. "Seattle Calmed by Quick Action of Authorities," *New York Times*, February 9, 1919, 1–2.

17. Quoted in Murray, *Red Scare*, 65.

18. Quoted in Powers, *Not Without Honor*, 19.

19. Dana Frank, *Purchasing Power: Consumer Organizing, Gender and the Seattle Labor Movement, 1919–1929* (Cambridge: Cambridge University Press, 1994); Friedheim, *The Seattle General Strike*; C. B. Bagley, "William S. Walker," in *History of Seattle: From the Earliest Settlement to the Present Time*, vol. 3 (Chicago: S.J. Clarke, 1916).

20. Quoted in Murray, *Red Scare*, 64.

21. Gaddis, *Russia, the Soviet Union, and the United States*, 105–11.

22. Murray, *Red Scare*, 111.

23. Murray, *Red Scare*; Joshua Freeman et al., American Social History Project, "Wars for Democracy," in *Who Built America? Working People and the Nation's Economy, Politics, Culture, and Society*, vol. 2, *From the Gilded Age to the Present* (New York: Pantheon, 1992): 258–64; Nell Irvin Painter, *Standing at Armageddon: The United States, 1877–1919* (New York: Norton, 1987), 344–80.

24. Murray, *Red Scare*, 68–81; Powers, *Not Without Honor*, 22.

25. Powers, *Not Without Honor*, 22.

26. Painter, *Standing at Armageddon*, 344–80.

27. R. M. Whitney, *Reds in America* (New York: Beckwith Press, 1924), 193; see also General Albert J. Bowley's warning that a "negro revolution" was imminent in North Carolina in 1924, since "these Soviet emissaries have subsidized some of the yellow Negroes who have more sense than the others, and have brought about the movement north in preparation for a black revolution." Quoted in Oswald Garrison Villard, "What the Blue Menace Means," *Harpers Magazine*, October 1928, folder 13, box 1, DAR "Blacklist" Controversy Papers and the Palo Alto Chapter of the Daughters of the American Revolution, Department of Special Collections, Stanford University Libraries, Stanford, California. Another example of race-baiting antiradical propaganda can be found in Elizabeth Barney Buel, "Socialist Propaganda in the United States," Connecticut Daughters of the American Revolution, 1925, Reel 40, Vol. X, Scrapbooks, Schwimmer-Lloyd Collection; Powers, *Not Without Honor*, 58; Gaddis, *Russia, the Soviet Union, and the United States*, 105–11; Robin D. G. Kelley, *Hammer and Hoe: Alabama Communists During the Great Depression* (Chapel Hill: University of North Carolina Press, 1990).

28. Eric Foner, *The Story of American Freedom* (New York: Norton, 1998): 177.

29. Murray, *Red Scare*, 196.

30. Leuchtenburg, *The Perils of Prosperity*, 80; Murray, *Red Scare*; Painter, *Standing at Armageddon*; Powers, *Not Without Honor*; Dawley, *Struggles for Justice*.

31. Nielsen, *Un-American Womanhood*, 14.

32. Senate, *Overman Committee Report*, xli.

33. Gail Bederman, *Manliness and Civilization: A Cultural History of Gender and Race in the United States, 1880–1917* (Chicago: University of Chicago Press, 1995), 25.

34. Senate, *Overman Committee Report*, 146–47.

35. "Bolshevism Bared by R. E. Simmons."

36. Statement of Louise Bryant, Senate, *Overman Committee Report*, 475. The "nationalization of women" myth was first reported in the *New York Times* in October 1918. The Overman Committee hearings, however, played a critical role in disseminating this story. See Filene, *Americans and the Soviet Experiment*, 46; Nielsen, *Un-American Womanhood*.

37. "Senators Hear Woman Defend the Bolsheviki," *New York Times*, February 21, 1919, 5; "Reds Defended Before Senators," *New York Times*, March 6, 1919, 4; "Senators Tell What Bolshevism in America Means," *New York Times*, June 15, 1919, 40.

38. Wendy Z. Goldman, *Women, the State and Revolution: Soviet Family Policy and Social Life, 1917–1936* (New York: Cambridge University Press, 1993).

39. Ibid.

40. Display Ad for Maria Botchkareva, *Yashka: My Life as Peasant, Officer and Exile*, *New York Times*, March 2, 1919, 84; see also, for example, Aleksandr Mikhailovich, *Once a Grand Duke, by Alexander, Grand Duke of Russia* (New York: Cosmopolitan Books, Farrar and Rinehart, 1932); Sofiia Karlovna Buksgevden, *Before the Storm* (London: Macmillan, 1938).

41. David S. Foglesong, *America's Secret War Against Bolshevism: U.S. Intervention in the Russian Civil War, 1917–1920* (Chapel Hill: University of North Carolina Press, 1995).

42. Susan Jeffords, "Commentary: Culture and National Identity in U.S. Foreign Policy," *Diplomatic History* 18, 1 (Winter 1994): 91–96.

43. Civil libertarian quoted in Foner, *The Story of American Freedom*, 179.

44. Quoted in Foner, *The Story of American Freedom*, 177.

45. Quoted in Robert Justin Goldstein, *Political Repression in Modern America: From 1870 to the Present* (Cambridge: Schenkman, 1978), 176; for a general account of the retreat of these federal agencies from political surveillance see 174–77; Frank J. Donner, *The Age of Surveillance: The Aims and Methods of America's Political Intelligence System* (New York: Knopf, 1980), 42–47; Roy Talbert, Jr., *Negative Intelligence: The Army and the American Left, 1917–1941* (Jackson: University Press of Mississippi, 1991), 221–25; Joan Jensen, *Army Surveillance in America, 1775–1980* (New Haven, Conn.: Yale University Press, 1991), 194–200. David Williams goes beyond the rhetoric of the FBI to describe how the agency continued collecting information on so-called subversives, albeit in much smaller volumes. See David Williams, "'They Never Stopped Watching Us': FBI Political Surveillance, 1924–1936," *UCLA Historical Journal* 2 (1981): 5–28.

46. Helen M. Wayne, "Radicalism as a Fashionable Pose," *New York Times*, March 9, 1919, 76. For more condemnation of "parlor Bolsheviks," see Gertrude Atherton, "Time as a Cure for Bolshevism," *New York Times*, March 16, 1919, 74.

47. Speech by Ralph Easley, October 20, 1919, New York City, Metropolitan Club, Folder: Bolshevism, Box 99, National Civic Federation Collection, Rare Books and Manuscripts Division, New York Public Library (hereafter NCF Collection).

48. The two other founding groups were the National Council of Jewish Women and the American Home Economics Association. See Dorothy E. Johnson, "Organized Women as Lobbyists in the 1920s," *Capitol Studies* 1 (Spring 1972): 41–58.

49. Quoted in J. Stanley Lemons, *The Woman Citizen: Social Feminism in the 1920s*, 2nd ed. (Charlottesville: University of Virginia Press, 1990), 56.

50. Quoted in Nancy F. Cott, *The Grounding of Modern Feminism* (New Haven, Conn.: Yale University Press, 1987), 107.

51. Anna Moon Randolph, Women's Constitutional League, Virginia, 1926, "Parallels for Thinking Men and Women, Are State and Federal Governments Adopting Measures of Socialists and Second International?" Frame 000475–479, Container 27, Reel 17, The Papers of Carrie Chapman Catt, Microfilm edition, LOC Manuscripts Division; Hermine Schwed, "The Strange Case of Mrs. Carrie Chapman Catt," August 1927, Folder: Carrie C. Catt, Box 1, Bailie Papers.

52. "Are Women's Clubs 'Used' by Bolshevists?" *Dearborn Independent*, March 15, 1924; "Communism in Government," published by the Daughters of the American Revolution, Muncie, Indiana, 1926, Folder: Publications—DAR, Box 1, Bailie Papers; Schwed, "The Strange Case of Mrs. Carrie Chapman Catt."

53. "Army Fights Women's Societies Because They're in War on War," *New York*

*World*, June 10, 1924, Frame 397, Reel 2, Vol. 4, Maud Wood Park Scrapbooks, Schlesinger Library, Radcliffe College, Cambridge, Massachusetts (hereafter Maud Wood Park Scrapbooks).

54. Margaret C. Robinson, "The Responsibility of Being Led," reprinted from *Dearborn Independent*, May 23, 1925, Folder: Publications—Massachusetts Public Interests League , Box 1, Bailie Papers.

55. "Political Embroilment Means Degradation of Womanhood," *Woman Patriot*, September 6, 1919, 2.

56. "Wanted—Men for Government Jobs," *Woman Patriot*, October 11, 1919, 2.

57. Calvin Coolidge, "Enemies of the Republic: Are the Reds Stalking Our College Women?" *Delineator* (June 1921): 4–5, 66–67. Reed originally made his charge during the Overman Committee hearings. See *Overman Committee Report*, vol. 2, 2758.

58. Quoted in Marcus Duffield, *King Legion* (New York: Jonathan Cape, 1931), 195.

59. File 10261–201, 2, John W. Weeks, Secretary of War to Mrs. Helen R. Bamberger, League of American Pen Women, Military Intelligence Division Correspondence, 1917–1941, RG 165, Records of the War Department General and Special Staffs, National Archives and Records Administration (NARA), Washington, D.C. (hereafter MID Correspondence)

60. "Organizing Revolution Through Women and Children," *Woman Patriot*, September 15, 1922.

61. "All Communist Parties Organizing Women," *Woman Patriot*, October 1, 15, 1922, 16.

62. "Legion Auxiliary Elects Its Officers," *New York Times*, September 23, 1927, 625, Folder: Schwimmer-Lloyd Collection scrapbooks, topic series, women: militarization of, Undated–1916–1930, Box N188, Militarization, n.d.–1916–1941, Morgue Files: Women, Schwimmer-Lloyd Collection.

63. Randolph, "Parallels for Thinking Men and Women."

64. Schwed, "The Strange Case of Mrs. Carrie Chapman Catt."

65. Hermine Schwed, "How They Put It Over in Clubs," from "The Truth About the Red Movement," pamphlet reprinted from *Iron Trade Review*. Folder: Pamphlets—DAR and related matters, Box 1, Bailie Papers.

66. Nancy Cott cites studies done by political scientists during the 1920s that found that a majority of eligible women voters were "politically uninformed and unambitious." Cott, *Grounding of Modern Feminism*, 102.

67. Hermine Schwed, *Confessions of a Parlor Socialist, Told by Herself* (Washington, D.C.: National Association for Constitutional Government, 1922).

68. Charles DeBenedetti, *Origins of the Modern American Peace Movement, 1915–1929* (Millwood, N.Y.: KTO, 1978); Carrie A. Foster, *The Women and the Warriors: The U.S. Section of the Women's International League for Peace and Freedom, 1915–1940* (Syracuse, N.Y.: Syracuse University Press, 1995); Harriet Hyman Alonso, *Peace as a Women's Issue: A History of the U.S. Peace Movement for World Peace and Women's*

*Rights* (Syracuse, N.Y.: Syracuse University Press, 1993); Harriet Hyman Alonso, *The Women's Peace Union and the Outlawry of War, 1921–1942* (Knoxville: University of Tennessee Press, 1989); Susan Zeiger, "Finding a Cure for War: Women's Politics and the Peace Movement in the 1920s," *Journal of Social History* 24 (Fall 1990): 69–86; Cott, *The Grounding of Modern Feminism.*

69. Quoted in Zeiger, "Finding a Cure for War," 74.

70. First quote by Maud Wood Park, from Dorothy M. Brown, *Setting a Course: American Women in the 1920s* (Boston: Twayne, 1987): 64; second quote from DeBenedetti, *Origins of the Modern American Peace Movement*, 94.

71. For information on the popularity of peace among large women's organizations in the 1920s see Cott, *The Grounding of Modern Feminism* and Lemons, *The Woman Citizen.*

72. According to Charles DeBenedetti, the number of organizations affiliated with the National Council for Prevention of War fluctuated between seventeen and forty-three in the early 1920s, largely because of attacks from antiradicals, both inside and outside the military. See DeBenedetti, *Origins of the Modern American Peace Movement*, 88; Frederick J. Libby, *To End War: The Story of the National Council for Prevention of War* (Nyack, N.Y.: Fellowship Publications, 1969).

73. Quoted in Walter Millis, *Arms and Men: A Study in American Military History* (New Brunswick, N.J.: Rutgers University Press, 1981), 242.

74. Foster, *The Women and the Warriors*, 46; Cott, *The Grounding of Modern Feminism*; DeBenedetti, *Origins of the Modern American Peace Movement*; Lemons, *The Woman Citizen.*

75. Robert D. Ward, "Against the Tide: The Preparedness Movement of 1923–1924," *Military Affairs* 38 (April 1974): 59; Cott, *The Grounding of Modern Feminism*, 247.

76. James Justice to the Assistant Chief of Staff, G–2, Subject: Pacifism in Schools and Universities, October 26, 1923, File 10110–2473, 13, MID Correspondence.

77. Quoted in Vance Armentrout, "The Red Brand," a series of articles originally appearing in *Louisville (Kentucky) Courier Journal*, March 24–31, 1929, Women's International League for Peace and Freedom Collection, microfilm ed., U.S. Section (hereafter WILPF-U.S. Section), Frame 340, Reel 33, Swarthmore College Peace Collection (hereafter SCPC), Swarthmore College, Swarthmore, Pennsylvania.

78. "Pacifists and Women Subject Sewall Address to DAR of Maine," March 19, 1924, Folder: NCPW Attacks, D.A.R., Mostly Clippings, Box 494, National Council for the Prevention of War Collection (hereafter NCPW Collection), SCPC.

79. Hermine Schwed, text of speech, reported by Office of Naval Intelligence, file 10110–1935, 6, 7, MID Correspondence.

80. Melvin M. Johnson, "'Red, White and Blue' or 'Red, Pink and White,'" reprinted by the DAR, New Jersey Society, March 15, 1928, Folder: Publications—DAR, Box 1, Bailie Papers.

81. "'Both Pacifists and Reds' There Is a Bit of Red in Every Pink," *Woman Patriot*, January 15, 1927, 16.

82. File 10110–1935, MID Correspondence.

83. Joan M. Jensen, "All Pink Sisters: The War Department and the Feminist Movement in the 1920s," in Lois Scharf and Joan M. Jensen, eds., *Decades of Discontent: The Women's Movement, 1920–1940*, (Boston: Northeastern University Press, 1983); Jensen, *Army Surveillance in America*, 198–99; "Army Fights Women's Societies Because They're in War on War"; Leonard L. Cline, "Others Carry on War Department's Attack on Women," *The New York World*, June 8, 1924, Vol. 4, Frame 398, Reel 2, Maud Wood Park Scrapbooks; "The War on the Peace Seekers," *New Republic*, July 2, 1924, Subject Files: Women's Organizations, attacks on, Container 28, Frame 000023, Reel 18, Catt Papers; Mrs. Mead to Secretary of War Weeks, April 12, 1923, Folder: BCL Research Materials, Against Militarism, Container D32, Belle Case La Follette Papers, La Follette Family Collection, Manuscript Division, Library of Congress, Washington, D.C. (hereafter La Follette Papers); "Says Fries's Critics Are Led by Moscow," *New York Times*, April 5, 1923; "Anti-War Council Denies Red Taint," *New York Times*, April 14, 1923.

84. Quoted in Foster, *The Women and the Warriors*, 39.

85. Foster, *The Women and the Warriors*; "Miss Jane Addams Denies Slacker Oath," *Washington Post*, April 27, 1924, 8.

86. Allen F. Davis, *American Heroine: The Life and Legend of Jane Addams* (New York: Oxford University Press, 1973), 252–54; Foster, *The Women and the Warriors*, 36; Murray, *Red Scare*, 98–102; New York State Joint Legislative Committee Investigating Seditious Activities report, *Revolutionary Radicalism: Its History, Purposes and Tactics, Report of the Joint Legislative Committee Investigating Seditious Activities* (Albany, N.Y.: J.B. Lyon, 1920).

87. Richard Merrill Whitney, *Peace at Any Old Price: Annual Conference of the Woman's International League for Peace and Freedom, Held in Washington, D.C., March 13th to 16th, 1923* (New York: Beckwith Press, 1923). Copies of the pamphlet can be found in many places. See for instance, Frame 7, Reel 39, WILPF, U.S. Section, Microfilm edition; Frames 198–216, Reel 4, Mary Anderson Papers, microfilm ed. (hereafter Mary Anderson Papers), Papers of the Women's Trade Union League and Its Principal Leaders (WTUL Papers), Schlesinger Library, Radcliffe College, Cambridge, Massachusetts.

88. Whitney, *Peace at Any Old Price*.

89. Foster, *The Women and the Warriors*, 39.

90. Whitney, *Peace at Any Old Price*.

91. "I Didn't Raise My Boy to Be a Slacker," Words and Music by Mrs. Amos A. Fries, Distributed by the Reserve Officers Association of the United States, copyright 1924, Elizabeth C. Fries, Folder: Fries, Amos A. Gen. 1923–24, Box: Attackers, American Coalition, Jung, Harry, Special Attacks Collection, SCPC; "Mrs. Fries Writes Song, Reply to 'slacker Oath,'" Folder: NCPW Attacks, American Legion Clippings, Box 492, NCPW Collection; Susan Zeiger, "She Didn't Raise Her Boy to Be a Slacker: Motherhood, Conscription, and the Culture of the First World War," *Feminist Studies* 22, 1 (1996): 7–39.

92. Minutes of the Meeting of the Women's Joint Congressional Committee, May 1, 1922, Frame 603, Reel 3, Records of the Women's Joint Congressional Committee, microfilm version, Manuscripts Division, Library of Congress (hereafter WJCC Records).

93. Lemons, *The Woman Citizen*, 215; Florence V. Watkins, NCMPTA to Tilton, December 12, 1922, Folder 245; Confidential circular from Florence Watkins, NCMPTA, April 5, 1923; Florence V. Watkins to Tilton, April 4, 1923, Folder 246, Box 9, Tilton Papers.

94. Churchill to Major William H. Cowles, December 14, 1922; Cowles to Churchill, December 19, 1922, File 10110–2491, MID Correspondence; Jensen, "All Pink Sisters," 211.

95. Anita Phipps, autobiography, Archives of Miss Porter's School, Farmington, Connecticut (hereafter Phipps autobiography). My thanks to Shirley Langhauser, archivist, for this information; Louise L. Stevenson, "Sarah Porter Educates Useful Ladies, 1847–1900," *Winterthur Portfolio* 18, 1 (Spring 1983): 39–59. After the death of Sarah Porter, her school was rocked by conflict between two competing leaders. Phipps followed the exodus led by the headmistress, finishing her education at Briarcliff Manor in Briarcliff, New York.

96. Phipps autobiography.

97. AG 201, Phipps, Anita E., Memorandum for the Chief of Staff; Subject: Former Status of Miss Anita E. Phipps, October 25, 1940, File: Civilians 301–600, Box 36, General Correspondence, 1932–42, RG 107, NARA; Resume for Miss Anita Phipps; W. G. Hann to Anita E. Phipps, March 18, 1921, File 9835, Box 55 (9835 to 9919), Numerical File, 1921–42, War Department General Staff, RG 165; Phipps autobiography.

98. Phipps autobiography.

99. AG 201, Phipps Memorandum for the Chief of Staff; War Department Abstract of Official Record of Civilian Employee, Anita Phipps, Personnel file of Anita E. Phipps, Civilian Division, United States Office of Personnel Management, St. Louis, Missouri.

100. Mattie E. Treadwell, *U.S. Army in World War II: Special Studies—The Women's Army Corps* (Washington, D.C.: Department of the Army, 1954), 11–12.

101. Copies of the original Spider Web Chart can be found in several places. See Frame 223–4, Reel 4, Mary Anderson Papers; Microfilm Reel M10–M15, Schwimmer-Lloyd Collection scrapbooks, references to Rosika Schwimmer, vol. 4, European and American Press, Schwimmer-Lloyd Collection; reproduced as part of Armentrout's "Red Brand" series; file 10110–1935, 24, MID Correspondence.

102. The *Dearborn Independent* was an appropriate venue for the national debut of the Spider Web Chart. The *Independent* had published the Protocols of the Elders of Zion in 1920 and seemed to embrace conspiracy theories of different types during this period. See Powers, *Not Without Honor*, 48–49. According to Will Irwin, *Ladies' Home Journal* gave the chart serious consideration, but eventually decided that the women who submitted the chart and accompanying articles—Mrs. Haviland Lund—

could not be trusted. Will Irwin to Arthur Charles Watkins, National Council for the Prevention of War, February 10, 1925, Folder: NCPW Attacks, Spider Web Chart, Box 497, NCPW Collection. The real author of the chart, Lucia Ramsey Maxwell intervened to stop publication in the *Chicago Tribune*. File PF51440, Major Mark Brooke, "Memorandum for file with Major Brooke's memorandum of January 14, 1923, re Mrs. Haviland Lund," January 19, 1923, Box 4071, MID Correspondence; "War Department Poster Withdrawn," *New York Sun*, April 25, 1924, File 10110–1935, MID Correspondence; "Weeks Recalls Army Poster," *Milwaukee-Wisconsin Journal*, April 25, 1924, Vol. 4, Reel 2, Maud Wood Park Scrapbooks; Frames 679–80, Minutes of the Meeting of the Women's Joint Congressional Committee, April 7, 1924, Reel 3, WJCC Records.

103. Special Committee, Women's Joint Congressional Committee, Maud Wood Park, Frances Fenton Bernard, Cora M. Baker, to Secretary of War John Weeks, April 2, 1924; Special Committee, WJCC, to Weeks, April 14, 1924; Weeks to Maud Wood Park, April 16, 1924; Memorandum for General Fries, J. L. Hines, April 15, 1924, File: AG 061.3, Box 1: AG 000.73 to AG 201.6, Security Classified, Office of the Adjutant General Central Files, 1917–25, RG 407, NARA; "War Department Poster Withdrawn"; Minutes of the Meeting of the WJCC, April 7, 1924. See also "Weeks Recalls Army Poster," Frame 317; "War Dept. Heeds Poster Protest," *Buffalo Evening News*, April 25, 1924, Frame 320; "'Scurrilous' Slur by War Department Aide Charged by Mrs. Park," *Rochester New York Herald*, April 26, 1924, Frame 316; "Pacifist Tendency Promises Trouble," *Buffalo Evening News*, April 26, 1924, Frame 324, all in Vol. 4, Reel 2, Maud Wood Park Scrapbooks; Letter to the Club Women of Massachusetts, Alice Stone Blackwell, "A Slander Quashed," May 9, 1924, Maud May (Wood) Park Papers, Woman's Rights Collection, microfilm ed., Women's Studies Manuscript Collection from the Schlesinger Library, Radcliffe College, Series 1, Woman's Suffrage, Part D: New England (Frederick, Md.: University Publications of America, 1993), Reel 44, Frame 1071 (hereafter Maud May (Wood) Park Papers); "What Women Voters Want, The League of Women Voters' Convention," Buffalo, N.Y., *Woman Citizen*, May 3, 1924, 11; Carrie Chapman Catt, "Poison Propaganda," *Woman Citizen*, May 31, 1924, 14, 32–33; "Would Add 6,000,000 to Nation's Voters," *New York Times*, April 26, 1924, 8.

104. Memorandum for the Assistant Chief of Staff, G–2 by Miss Anita Phipps, Director of Women's Relations, "Subject: Possible action of the Women's Joint Congressional Committee on Statements made by Mrs. Haviland Lund, which concern the War Department," January 10, 1924, PF51440, Box 4071, Military Intelligence Division, War Department General Staff, RG 165.

105. Memorandum for the Secretary of War from Miss Anita Phipps, Subject: Information regarding visit of Mrs. Maud Wood Park to the Secretary of War, April 10, 1924, File: AG 061.3, Box 1, Office of the Adjutant General, Central Files, 1917–1925, Security Classified, RG 407.

106. Special Committee, WJCC, to Weeks, April 2, 14, 1924; Weeks to Maud Wood Park, April 16, 1924; Memorandum for General Fries, J. L. Hines, April 15, 1924; "War Department Poster Withdrawn"; Minutes of the Meeting of the WJCC, April 7, 1924;

"Weeks Recalls Army Poster"; "War Dept. Heeds Poster Protest"; "'Scurrilous' Slur by War Department Aide"; "Pacifist Tendency Promises Trouble"; Blackwell, "A Slander Quashed"; "What Women Voters Want"; Catt, "Poison Propaganda"; "Would Add 6,000,000 to Nation's Voters."

107. Special Committee, WJCC, to Weeks, April 2, 1924; Blackwell, "A Slander Quashed."

108. Even the DAR did not escape the Spider Web at first, as it was included on the first draft of the chart. See File 10110–1935, 24, MID Correspondence; Carrie Chapman Catt to Jane Addams, May 27, 1924, Frame 104, Reel 39, WILPF-U.S. Section, Microfilm Edition; Marguerite Owen to Mrs. William G. Hibbard, May 26, 1924, Frames 893–4, Reel 3, Part 3, Series A, National Office Subject Files, 1920–1932, LWV Papers.

109. File 10110–1935, 35, John Weeks to Mrs. Maud Wood Park, May 2, 1924; File 10110–1935, 34, Frances Fenton Bernard, Maud Wood Park, Cora M. Baker, WJCC, to John Weeks, April 22, 1924; File 10110–1935, 32, Amos Fries to Captain J. H. Bogart, April 23, 1924; MID Correspondence; Amos A. Fries, Memorandum for the Deputy Chief of Staff, April 28, 1924; WJCC Special Committee to John Weeks, May 9, 1924, File: AG 061.3, Box 1, Security Classified, Office of the Adjutant General Central Files, 1917–25, RG 407; Minutes of the Meeting of the Women's Joint Congressional Committee, May 12, 1924, Frames 682–85, Reel 3, WJCC Records; "Editor's Note," Frame 751, Reel 4, Part 3, Series A, National Office Subject files, 1920–1932, LWV Papers, 1918–1974.

110. Cline, "Others Carry on War Department's Attack on Women"; see also Alice Lloyd to Mary Anderson, April 21, 1924, Frames 258–59; Mary Anderson to Alice Lloyd, April 24, 1924, Frames 261–62; and "Kentucky Group Sent Members Pamphlet," *Louisville Courier-Journal*, March 31, 1929, Frame 383, Reel 4, Mary Anderson Papers; Armentrout, "The Red Brand,", Frame 340–45; Catt to Addams, May 27, 1924.

111. Cott, *The Grounding of Modern Feminism*, 249–50; Davis, *American Heroine*, 263–64; "The Spider Web," compiled and printed by Chas. Norman Fay, Cambridge, Mass., Folder: NCPW Attacks, Spider Web Chart, Box 497, DG 23, NCPW Collection; Mrs. Joseph T. Bowen to Charles Norman Fay, January 24, 1927, Folder 17, Box 5, Frame 793–95, Reel 42, Series C, Correspondence, WILPF-U.S. Section. This chart was supposedly distributed by the DAR or at least its chapters in Iowa. "DAR 'Yellow List' Cites Degrees of Radicalism," *Des Moines Tribune-Capital*, April 17, 1928, Microfilm Reel M10-M15, Schwimmer-Lloyd Collection scrapbooks, references to Rosika Schwimmer, vol. 4, European and American Press, Schwimmer-Lloyd Collection.

112. "Legion Lists Noted Figures as 'subversive,'" *Chicago Daily News*, January 23, 1933, Folder: American Legion, (2) Box: Attackers—American Legion—National—Local Branches, American Legion material on peace, Special Attacks Collection, SCPC.

113. Frame 242, Executive Committee, January 7, 1925, Reel 2, Part 1, Meetings of the Board of Directors and the Executive Committees: Minutes and Related Documents, 1918–1974, LWV Papers.

Chapter 2. The Origins of the Spider Web Chart: Women and the
Construction of the Bolshevik Threat

1. Joan M. Jensen, "All Pink Sisters: The War Department and the Feminist Move-
ment in the 1920s," in Lois Scharf and Joan M. Jensen, eds., *Decades of Discontent: The
Women's Movement, 1920–1940* (Boston: Northeastern University Press, 1983); Joan
Jensen, *Army Surveillance in America, 1775–1980* (New Haven, Conn.: Yale University
Press, 1991), 198–99; Frame 397, "Army Fights Women's Societies Because They're in
War on War," *New York World*, June 10, 1924; Frame 398, Leonard L. Cline, "Others
Carry on War Department's Attack on Women," *New York World*, June 8, 1924, Vol.
4, Reel 2, Maud Wood Park Scrapbooks, Schlesinger Library; Frame 000023, "The
War on the Peace Seekers," *New Republic*, July 2, 1924, Subject Files: Women's Or-
ganizations, attacks on, Container 28, Reel 18, Catt Papers, Microfilm version, LOC;
Mrs. Mead to Secretary of War Weeks, April 12,1923, Folder: BCL Research Materials,
Against Militarism, Container D32, La Follette Papers; "Says Fries's Critics Are Led by
Moscow," *New York Times*, April 5, 1923; "Anti-War Council Denies Red Taint," *New
York Times*, April 14, 1923.

2. Lucia Ramsey Maxwell to Lucia Ames Mead, March 13, 1922, Folder 7, Box 54,
Reel 43, NCPW Collection.

3. As librarian of the Chemical Warfare Service, Maxwell collected information
on supposedly subversive movements, focusing in particular on radicalism within
women's organizations. The Spider Web Chart was an attempt to marshal all her data
in a clear and succinct fashion. Her effort to track and document radicalism foreshadowed later work by antiradicals like Flora Walker, who built up elaborate bureaucracies
for gathering information about radical individuals and organizations. See PF5 1440,
Memorandum by Major Mark Brooke, General Staff, Office of the Chief of Staff, January 19, 1923, Box 4071, MID Correspondence; PF 51486, Maxwell to Graham, April 14,
1926, MID Correspondence; Memorandum from Lucia R. Maxwell to General Amos
A. Fries, December 19, 1921, File 001/1005, Box 9, Correspondence 1918–1940, Chemical
Warfare Service, RG 175; Letters from Mrs. Haviland Lund to J. Mayhew Wainwright,
June 2, 8, 11, 1922, File: Women's Organizations, Box 193, 080: "Military Training" to
080 "Women's Motor Corps," Central decimal files, 1917–25, RG 407, NARA.

4. Carrie Chapman Catt stated the widespread conviction when she wrote, "these
charges have come from the War Department itself, and have been spread by war
officers." See Carrie Chapman Catt, "The Lie Factory," *Woman Citizen*, September
20, 1924, 10, 24–25. Historians of women accepted the interpretation that the Spider
Web Chart was the product of a military establishment hostile to women peace activists. See Jensen, "All Pink Sisters" and Jensen, *Army Surveillance in America*, 198–99.
Nancy Cott modifies this interpretation slightly, showing that the Chart attacked
feminists in particular in *The Grounding of Modern Feminism* (New Haven, Conn.:
Yale University Press, 1987), 249. In his discussion of the Spider Web Chart, J. Stanley Lemons focuses on the way it vilified social welfare reformers. See Lemons, *The

*Woman Citizen: Social Feminism in the 1920s*, 2nd ed. (Charlottesville: University of Virginia Press, 1990), 214–17.

5. Ethel Smith, "Organized Women and Their Program," Frame 295–307, Reel 4, Mary Anderson Papers.

6. Robyn Muncy, *Creating a Female Dominion in American Reform, 1890–1935* (New York: Oxford University Press, 1991), xii.

7. Paula Baker, "The Domestication of Politics: Women and American Political Society, 1780–1920," *AHR* 89, 3 (June 1984): 638.

8. Rheta Childe Dorr, *What Eight Million Women Want* (Boston: Small, Maynard, 1910), 327.

9. Sophonisba P. Breckinridge, *Women in the Twentieth Century: A Study of Their Political, Social and Economic Activities* (New York: McGraw-Hill, 1933), 19; Mildred White Wells, *Unity in Diversity: The History of the General Federation of Women's Clubs* (Washington, D.C.: General Federation of Women's Clubs, 1965).

10. Breckinridge, *Women in the Twentieth Century*, 19; Wells, *Unity in Diversity*; Karen J. Blair, *The Clubwoman as Feminist: True Womanhood Redefined, 1868–1914* (New York: Holmes and Meier, 1980).

11. Breckinridge, *Women in the Twentieth Century*, 21–22; Kathryn Kish Sklar, "The Historical Foundations of Women's Power in the Creation of the American Welfare State, 1830–1930," in Seth Koven and Sonya Michel, eds., *Mothers of a New World: Maternalist Politics and the Origins of the Welfare States* (New York: Routledge, 1993), 64.

12. Quoted in Walter I. Trattner, *Crusade for the Children: A History of the National Child Labor Committee and Child Labor Reform in America* (Chicago: Quadrangle Books, 1970), 34.

13. Sklar, "The Historical Foundations of Women's Power," 64.

14. Trattner, *Crusade for the Children*, 65.

15. U.S. House Committee on Expenditures in Department of Commerce and Labor, *Establishment of a Children's Bureau*, 61st Cong., 2nd sess., April 13, 1910.

16. Seth Koven and Sonya Michel, "Womanly Duties: Maternalist Politics and the Origins of the Welfare States in France, Germany, Great Britain, and the United States, 1880–1920," *AHR* 95, 4 (October 1990): 1094; Sklar, "The Historical Foundations of Women's Power," 64.

17. Wells, *Unity in Diversity*, 34.

18. Between 1890 and 1900, at least seventy hereditary organizations were founded by people who traced their ancestry back to the early years of the republic. See Margaret Gibbs, *The DAR* (New York: Holt, Rinehart, 1969), 21. See as well Wallace Evans Davies, *Patriotism on Parade: The Story of Veterans' and Hereditary Organizations in America, 1783–1900* (Cambridge, Mass.: Harvard University Press, 1955); Lucile Evelyn LaGanke, "The National Society of the Daughters of the American Revolution: Its History, Policies, and Influence, 1890–1949" (Ph.D. dissertation, Western Reserve University, 1951); Francesca Morgan, "'Home and Country': Women, Nation and the

Daughters of the American Revolution, 1890–1939 (Ph.D. dissertation, Columbia University, 1998).

19. LaGanke, "The National Society of the Daughters of the American Revolution," 498; Breckinridge, *Women in the Twentieth Century*, 45. In contrast, the Daughters of 1812 had about 4,000 members in 1922. Annual Message and Report of the President National, Mrs. Clarence F. R. Jenne, *National Society United States Daughters of 1812 News-letter*, April 25, 1922.?

20. DAR *Proceedings of the Seventeenth Continental Congress* (April 20–25, 1908): 542–50.

21. Ellen Starr Brinton, "The DAR Reaches Middle Age," Folder: Ellen Starr Brinton, Unpublished works, DAR, Box 2: Writings and Research, Ellen Starr Brinton Collection, SCPC; see "Daughter's Revolution," *Time*, May 14, 1928, Folder: Clippings, D.A.R., Box 1; Florence G. Adams to Mrs. Bailie, June 13, 1928, Folder: Correspondence—Adams to H.T.B., 1928–29, Box 2, Bailie Papers; Viola C. Reeling to McCulloch, January 23, 1929, Frame 286, Catherine Waugh McCulloch segment of the Mary Earhart Dillon Collection, Reel E17, Series 1, Part E, Women's Studies Manuscript Collections, Schlesinger Library.

22. Brinton, "The DAR Reaches Middle Age"; Jane Addams, *The Second Twenty Years at Hull House: September 1909 to September 1929, With a Record of a Growing World Consciousness* (New York: Macmillan, 1930).

23. Baker, "The Domestication of Politics"; Blair, *The Clubwoman as Feminist*; Koven and Michel, eds., *Mothers of a New World*; Anne Firor Scott, *Natural Allies: Women's Associations in American History* (Urbana: University of Illinois Press, 1991); Anne Firor Scott, *The Southern Lady: From Pedestal to Politics, 1830–1930*, 2nd ed. (Charlottesville: University Press of Virginia, 1995); Louise A. Tilly and Patricia Gurin, eds., *Women, Politics, and Change* (New York: Russell Sage, 1990), 63–86; Leslie K. Dunlap, "The Reform of Rape Law and the Problem of White Men, 1885–1910," in Martha Hodes, ed., *Sex, Love, Race: Crossing Boundaries in North American History* (New York: New York University Press, 1999), 352–72; Ruth Bordin, *Women and Temperance: The Quest for Power and Liberty, 1873–1900* (Philadelphia: Temple University Press, 1981); Allen F. Davis, *Spearheads for Reform: The Social Settlements and the Progressive Movement, 1890–1914* (New Brunswick, N.J.: Rutgers University Press, 1967); Molly Ladd-Taylor, *Mother-Work: Women, Child Welfare and the State, 1890–1930* (Urbana: University of Illinois Press, 1994); Muncy, *Creating a Female Dominion*; Mary E. Odem, *Delinquent Daughters: Protecting and Policing Adolescent Female Sexuality in the United States, 1885–1920* (Chapel Hill: University of North Carolina Press, 1995); Kathryn Kish Sklar, *Florence Kelley and the Nation's Work: The Rise of Women's Political Culture, 1830–1900* (New Haven, Conn.: Yale University Press, 1995).

24. Mari Jo Buhle, *Women and American Socialism, 1870–1920* (Urbana: University of Illinois Press, 1981); Ardis Cameron, *Radicals of the Worst Sort: Laboring Women in Lawrence, Massachusetts, 1860–1920* (Urbana: University of Illinois Press, 1993); Eileen Boris, "The Power of Motherhood: Black and White Activist Women Redefine the 'Po-

litical,'" in Koven and Michel, eds., *Mothers of a New World*, 213–45; Noralee Frankel and Nancy Shrom Dye, eds., *Gender, Class, Race and Reform in the Progressive Era* (Lexington: University Press of Kentucky, 1991); Glenda Gilmore, *Gender and Jim Crow: Women and the Politics of White Supremacy in North Carolina, 1896–1920* (Chapel Hill: University of North Carolina Press, 1996); Linda Gordon, "Black and White Visions of Welfare: Women's Welfare Activism, 1890–1945," *Journal of American History* 78 (1991): 559–90; Jacquelyn Dowd Hall, "Disorderly Women: Gender and Labor Militancy in the Appalachian South," *Journal of American History* 73 (1986): 354–82; Nancy Hewitt, *Southern Discomfort: Women's Activism in Tampa, Florida, 1880s–1920s* (Urbana: University of Illinois Press, 2001); Evelyn Brooks Higginbotham, *Righteous Discontent: The Women's Movement in the Black Baptist Church, 1880–1920* (Cambridge, Mass.: Harvard University Press, 1993); Tera Hunter, *To 'Joy My Freedom: Southern Black Women's Lives and Labors After the Civil War* (Cambridge, Mass.: Harvard University Press, 1997); Paula Hyman, "Immigrant Women and Consumer Protest: The New York City Kosher Meat Boycott of 1902," *American Jewish History* 70 (1980): 126–40; Stephanie Shaw, *What a Woman Ought to Be and to Do: Black Professional Women Workers During the Jim Crow Era* (Chicago: University of Chicago Press, 1996); Rosalyn Terborg-Penn, *African American Women and the Struggle for the Vote, 1850–1920* (Bloomington: University of Indiana Press, 1998); Deborah Gray White, *Too Heavy a Load: Black Women in Defense of Themselves, 1894–1994* (New York: Norton, 1999).

25. Dorr, *What Eight Million Women Want*, 315.

26. Alice Bradford Wiles, Chairman, National Committee Legislation in United States Congress, National Society Daughters of the American Revolution to Mrs. Maud Wood Park, February 6, 1922, Frame 91; Park to Wiles, February 10, 1922; Park to Anne Rogers Minor, President General, DAR, November 1, 1920; Park to Minor, November 26, 1920; Minor to Park, November 6, 1920, Frames 431–34; Wiles to Mrs. Watkins, July 1921, Frame 25; Wiles to WJCC, December 1, 1921, Frame 36, Reel 1, WJCC Records.

27. Quoted in Jan Doolittle Wilson, *The Women's Joint Congressional Committee and the Politics of Maternalism, 1920–30* (Urbana: University of Illinois Press, 2007), 1; Dorothy E. Johnson, "Organized Women as Lobbyists in the 1920s," *Capitol Studies* 1 (Spring 1972): 41–58; Charles Selden, "The Most Powerful Lobby in Washington," *Ladies' Home Journal*, April 1922.

28. Lemons, *Woman Citizen*, 154; Ladd-Taylor, *Mother-Work*, 170.

29. Quoted in Josephine Goldmark, *Impatient Crusader: Florence Kelley's Life Story* (Urbana: University of Illinois Press, 1953), 93.

30. Alice Bradford Wiles, "Report of the Chairman of Committee on Legislation in U.S. Congress," *Daughters of the American Revolution Magazine*, April 1921, 236.

31. U.S. Senate, Committee on Public Health and National Quarantine, Protection of Maternity and Infancy, 66th Cong., 2nd sess., May 12, 1920, 39; Ladd-Taylor, *Mother-Work*, 170; Lemons, *The Woman Citizen*, 153–80.

32. Dorothy Kirchwey Brown, "The Sheppard-Towner Bill Lobby," *The Woman*

*Citizen*, January 22, 1921, 907–8; Lemons, *The Woman Citizen*, 158; Ladd-Taylor, *Mother-Work*, 170.

33. Ladd-Taylor, *Mother-Work*, 173; Lemons, *Woman Citizen*, 165; "The Maternity Bill," *Capitol Eye*, October 1921, 3–12.

34. Lemons, *The Woman Citizen*, 154; Ladd-Taylor, *Mother-Work*, 170.

35. For instance, Lillian Wald, a settlement worker at Henry Street Settlement in New York, shared Putnam's interest in infant "hygiene" and like Putnam, became one of the original backers of the Children's Bureau; Lemons, *The Woman Citizen*, 154; Elizabeth Lowell Putnam to Senator Henry Cabot Lodge, April 10, 1914, Folder 511, "Children's Bureau, 1912–1929," Box 30, Elizabeth Lowell Putnam Papers, Schlesinger Library (hereafter Putnam Papers); Sonya Michel and Robyn Rosen, "The Paradox of Maternalism: Elizabeth Lowell Putnam and the American Welfare State," *Gender and History* 4, 3 (Autumn 1992): 364–86.

36. Putnam resigned from the American Child Hygiene Association in October 1922 after they, in her words, "got in such close cahoots with the Children's Bureau that they kicked me off the executive committee in order to keep Grace Abbott on." Putnam was angry about this turn of events. "They have slighted me nobly," she asserted. Elizabeth Lowell Putnam to Mr. Andrew, March 8, 1929, Folder 288, Box 16, Putnam Papers.

37. Statement of Miss Alice M. Robertson, U.S. House, Committee on Interstate and Foreign Commerce, Public Protection of Maternity and Infancy, 67th Cong., 1st sess., July 12–16, 18–23, 1921, 230–34; "The House Discusses the 'Maternity Bill,' " *Capitol Eye*, October 1921, 5.

38. House Committee on Interstate and Foreign Commerce, Public Protection of Maternity and Infancy, 67th Cong., 1st sess., July 12–16, 18–23, 1921, 148–66.

39. "Fight on Suffrage Goes On," *New York Times*, July 3, 1919; Eleanor Flexner and Ellen Fitzpatrick, *Century of Struggle: The Woman's Rights Movement in the United States* (Cambridge, Mass.: Belknap Press of Harvard University Press, 1996), 300–317.

40. "Antis to Continue Fight on Suffrage," *New York Times*, September 18, 1919, 8; "The Need of Further Organization," *Woman Patriot*, October 23, 1920, 4.

41. Miss Mary G. Kilbreth, "The New Anti-Feminist Campaign," *Woman Patriot*, June 15, 1921, 2–3. Many antisuffragists linked female enfranchisement to socialism. See Elna C. Green, "From Antisuffragism to Anti-Communism: The Conservative Career of Ida M. Darden," *Journal of Southern History* 65, 2 (May 1999): 295.

42. "National Association Moves to Washington," *Woman Patriot*, October 9, 1920, 2.

43. Ibid.; Kilbreth, "New Anti-Feminist Campaign," 2–3; "Antis Will Renew Fight," *New York Times*, May 2, 1920, Section 8, 2; "Fight on Suffrage Goes On"; Flexner and Fitzpatrick, *Century of Struggle*, 300–317; Ladd-Taylor, *Mother-Work*, 169; Muncy, *Creating a Female Dominion*, 124–57; Lemons, *The Woman Citizen*, 153–67; Joseph B. Chepaitis, "Federal Social Welfare Progressivism in the 1920s," *Social Service Review* 46, 2 (1972): 213–29; Breckinridge, *Women in the Twentieth Century*, 257–74.

44. Brown, "The Sheppard-Towner Bill Lobby"; Statement of Mary G. Kilbreth, U.S. Senate, Committee on Education and Labor, Protection of Maternity, 67th Cong., 1st sess., April 25, 1921, 9.

45. Statement of Mrs. Albert T. Leatherbee, Senate, Protection of Maternity, 52–57.

46. "The Maternity Bill," Speech of Hon. James A. Reed, Appendix to Congressional Record, 67th Cong., 1st sess., vol. 61, June 29, July 21, 22, 1921, 8759–69; "Why They Fought Their Senator," Woman Citizen, December 2, 1922, 11, 25.

47. Chepaitis, "Federal Social Welfare Progressivism," 217; Ladd-Taylor, Mother-Work, 174.

48. Ladd-Taylor, Mother-Work, 174–75; Lemons, The Woman Citizen, 158–59; Muncy, Creating a Female Dominion, 105–6.

49. Press Statement by Mrs. Maud Wood Park for the General Federation of Women's Clubs' Magazine, December 28, 1921, Frame 714, Reel 44, Maud May (Wood) Park Papers.

50. "A Powerful Army Against Corrupt Politics," Woman Citizen, July 2, 1921, 9.

51. Statement of Mrs. Fred Manville, Senate, Protection of Maternity, 67–68.

52. Mrs. Josiah Hatch Quincy to Mrs. Putnam, March 4, 1922, Folder 306, Box 17, Putnam Papers.

53. Brown, "The Sheppard-Towner Bill Lobby."

54. "Plans to Halt Bolshevism," New York Times, April 13, 1919, 22.

55. Address of Mrs. William Sherman Walker, Ohio State Conference Daughters of the American Revolution, Columbus, March 16, 1927, Folder: Publications—DAR, Box 1, Bailie Papers; Mrs. William Sherman Walker, "Keep Yourself Informed About Radicalism: Indifference of Americans to Danger Is a Direct Contribution to the Strength of the Reds and Their 'Cause,'" National Republic, July 1925, 25.

56. DAR, Proceedings of the Thirty-Third Continental Congress (April 14–19, 1924): 541.

57. DAR Proceedings of the Thirty-Second Continental Congress (April 1923): 157.

58. R. M. Whitney, Reds in America (New York: Beckwith Press, 1924), 177–82.

59. Gibbs, The DAR, 108.

60. Flora Bredes Walker, who would become chairman of the DAR National Defense Committee in 1925, initially was organizing secretary general in Cook's administration. Cook's treasurer general was Grace Hall Lincoln Brosseau, who would succeed Cook as president general and become a well-known antiradical.

61. Memo from Publicity Committee, National Society, Daughters of the American Revolution, Mrs. Amos A. Fries chairman, 1924, Folder: NCPW Attacks, DAR, 1924–1938, Box 494, NCPW Collection.

62. Frank Ernest Hill, The American Legion Auxiliary: A History, 1924–34 (Indianapolis: American Legion Auxiliary, 1935), 62; Mrs. O. D. Oliphant, "We Are Just the Same Women Serving You," January 12, 1925, before the American Legion in Indianapolis, American Legion Weekly, January 30, 1925.

63. Hill, *American Legion Auxiliary*, 62–63; Kate Waller Barrett Collection, Manuscripts Division, Library of Congress, Washington, D.C. (hereafter Barrett Collection).

64. Edith Irwin Hobart, who had been president of the American Legion Auxiliary in 1922, was elected DAR president general in 1929. At least three presidents of the American Legion Auxiliary were also members of the DAR during the interwar period: Kate Waller Barrett, Mrs. Robert L. Hoyal, and Mary Virginia Miller Macrae. See Gibbs, *The DAR*, 139.

65. Vye Smeigh Thompson, *History, National American Legion Auxiliary* (1921–1924) (Pittsburgh: Jackson-Remlinger, 1926), 63.

66. Elizabeth Barney Buel, "Socialist Propaganda in the United States," Connecticut Daughters of the American Revolution, 1925, Reel 40, Vol. X, Scrapbooks, Schwimmer-Lloyd Collection; Walker, "Keep Yourself Informed About Radicalism"; Address of Mrs. William Sherman Walker, Ohio State Conference, March 16, 1927, Folder: Publications—DAR, Box 1, Bailie Papers.

67. Fred Marvin, "The Common Enemy," Box 1, Bailie Papers; Address of Mrs. William Sherman Walker, Ohio State Conference, March 16, 1927, Folder: Publications—DAR, Box 1, Bailie Papers.

68. Bonnie Busch and Lucia Ramsey Maxwell, *The Red Fog* (Washington, D.C.: National Patriotic League, 1929), 74.

69. "Organizing Revolution Through Women and Children," *Woman Patriot*, September 15, 1922.

70. Melvin Johnson, "Red, White and Blue' or 'Red, Pink and White,'" reprinted by Daughters of the American Revolution, New Jersey, March 15, 1928, Folder: Publications—DAR, Box 1, Bailie Papers.

71. Hermine Schwed, "How They Put It Over in Clubs," from "The Truth About the Red Movement," pamphlet reprinted from the *Iron Trade Review*. Folder: Pamphlets—DAR and related matters, Box 1, Bailie Papers.

72. "Political Embroilment Means Degradation of Womanhood," *Woman Patriot*, September 6, 1919, 2.

73. Busch and Maxwell, *The Red Fog*, 88.

74. Kilbreth, "The New Anti-Feminist Campaign."

75. Ibid.; "Antis Will Renew Fight."

76. Kilbreth, "The New Anti-Feminist Campaign."

77. For an example of the pamphlet, see "Organizing Revolution Through Women and Children," frame 190; for its distribution, see "Propaganda Against Our Women's Organizations, Who Is Madame Kollontai?" Frames 310–11, Reel 4, Mary Anderson Papers. A special committee of the WJCC complained that it had been distributed widely, generating many of the myths about the women's coalition. See Summary of Report of Special Committee, Signed by Mrs. John D. Sherman, et al., Frames 1032–53, Reel 44, Maud May (Wood) Park Papers. Other antiradicals, most notably Mrs. Haviland Lund, lifted wholesale from the piece for their own propaganda. See J. S. Eichelberger to Mr. W. J. Cameron, March 21, 1924, Frames 229–31, Reel 4, Mary Anderson Papers.

78. "Organizing Revolution Through Women and Children." For Engels's argument, see Friedrich Engels, *The Origin of the Family, Private Property, and the State* (New York: International Publishers, 1972, 1942).

79. "Organizing Revolution Through Women and Children."

80. Ibid. For the conclusions of the Overman Committee, see Senate, *Overman Committee Report*.

81. Barbara Evans Clements, *Bolshevik Feminist: The Life of Aleksandra Kollontai* (Bloomington: Indiana University Press, 1979).

82. Linda Gordon, *Pitied But Not Entitled: Single Mothers and the History of Welfare, 1890–1935* (New York: Free Press, 1981), 93.

83. "Organizing Revolution Through Women and Children."

84. Mary Kilbreth to Rossiter Johnson, April 30, 1922; Mary G. Kilbreth to Rossiter Johnson, September 24, 1922, Folder: Kilbreth, Mary G., 1919–1922, Box 4, Rossiter Johnson Collection, Rare Books and Manuscripts Division, New York Public Library; "John William Kilbreth, Jr.," *Who's Who in America* 11 (1920–1921): 1594; Mr. and Mrs. John W. Kilbreth, *New York Social Register, 1901* 15, 1 (1900): 241.

85. "'Both Pacifists and Reds,'" *Woman Patriot*, January 15, 1927, 15–16; Norman Hapgood, ed., *Professional Patriots* (New York: Albert and Charles Boni, 1928), 103. Cornelia Gibbs also shared this view and appeared before a Senate appropriations committee in 1922 to demand higher appropriations for the military.

86. In letters to Alexander Lincoln, Kilbreth condemned "slum-bred, curly-haired Jews" who, she asserted, were "so hungry and voracious to seize our nation." See Kilbreth to Alexander Lincoln, January 11, 1935, Folder 30, Box 5, Alexander Lincoln Papers, Schlesinger Library (hereafter Alexander Lincoln Papers). Kilbreth was not unique in her antipathy to Jews; liberal and conservative Americans shared her anti-Semitism. Linda Gordon analyzes how progressive reformers of this period believed that "Jewishness" was synonymous with a predetermined set of personal characteristics, many of which were negative. Kilbreth's prejudice, however, meshes with her conspiratorial worldview and sounds qualitatively different from that of her progressive counterparts. See Gordon, *Pitied But Not Entitled*, 85–87.

87. For 1922 Board of Directors, see Mary Kilbreth to Dear Sir, October 16, 1922, Folder 3, Massachusetts Public Interests League Collection, Massachusetts Historical Society, Boston (hereafter MPIL Collection); Barrett Collection; "Robinson, Benjamin Lincoln," *Who's Who* 14 (1926–1927): 1630; "Frothingham, Randolph" and "Balch, John," *Boston City Directory*, 1925, Massachusetts Historical Society; Cornelia Andrews Gibbs file; Rufus Macqueen Gibbs file, Dielman-Hayward Files, Maryland Historical Society, Baltimore.

88. In comparison, the liberal publication the *Nation* claimed a circulation of about 30,000 during this period. See Peter G. Filene, *Americans and the Soviet Experiment, 1917–1933* (Cambridge, Mass.: Harvard University Press, 1967), 289. "A Bazaar for 'The Woman Patriot,'" *Woman Patriot*, September 15, 1921, 2; "'something Different' in Bazars," *Woman Patriot*, December 1, 1921; "The Patriot Bazar," *Woman Patriot*,

December 15, 1921; Kilbreth to Rossiter Johnson, June 11, 1922; Kilbreth to Johnson, January 2, 1923; Kilbreth to Johnson, September 17, 1929, Folder: Kilbreth, Mary G., 1919–1922, Box 4, Rossiter Johnson Collection; Bentley W. Warren to Starling Childs, December 11, 1925, Folder 2, Box 1; Kilbreth to Alexander Lincoln, November 25, 1934, folder 28, Box 5, Alexander Lincoln Papers; For description of the structure of the WPPC, see Mary G. Kilbreth, U.S. House Committee on Foreign Affairs, Relief for Women and Children of Germany, 68th Cong., 1st sess., February 13, 1924; also see Statement of Miss Mary G. Kilbreth, U.S. House, Committee on Education, Proposed Department of Education, 70th Cong., 1st sess., May 2, 1928, 472–73; and To Create a Department of Education and to Authorize Appropriations of Money to Encourage the States in the Promotion and Support of Education, 68th Cong., 1st sess., June 4, 1924, 740–48.

89. Kilbreth, Proposed Department of Education, 473.

90. Advisory Council for the Key Men of America, Folder: Publications—Key Men of America, Box 1, Bailie Papers.

91. Cornelia Andrews Gibbs file, Dielman-Hayward Files; Statement of Mrs. Rufus M. Gibbs, Senate, Protection of Maternity, 38; "Maryland Democratic Women Denounce Maternity Act," *Woman Patriot*, December 15, 1923, 8. According to a 1929 version of the Constitution of the Woman's Constitutional League of Maryland, this organization was dedicated to preserving the "principals of the Constitution and the Bill of Rights," which were threatened by "direct assault" and "indirect evasion . . . in the name of socialism, feminism, or in the name of humanity." Specifically, the organization pledged to fight jury service for women and "all measures tending to centralize power in the Federal Government." U.S. Senate, Subcommittee of the Committee on the Judiciary, Equal Rights Amendment, 70th Cong., 2nd sess., February 1, 1929, 62–63.

92. Mary Kilbreth, "Let Us Play the Game," MPIL, Folder 14, "Child Labor Amendment, Important Papers, 1924–25," Box 2; Minutes from a 1923 meeting, Folder 1, Box 1, both in Alexander Lincoln Papers.

93. "Sees Pacifist Menace," *New York Times*, April 4, 1924, 34.

94. Buel, "Socialist Propaganda in the United States."

95. LaGanke, "The National Society of the Daughters of the American Revolution," 125, 128.

96. Ellen Starr Brinton, "An Unwritten History of the DAR," Folder: Ellen Starr Brinton, Unpublished works, DAR, Box 2: Writings and Research, Ellen Starr Brinton Collection, SCPC.

97. Mrs. Henry L. Cook, quoted in LaGanke, "The National Society of the Daughters of the American Revolution," 135.

98. Gibbs, *The DAR*, 101; LaGanke, "The National Society of the Daughters of the American Revolution," 474.

99. Anne Rogers Minor, "A Message from the President General," *Daughters of the American Revolution Magazine* 55, December 1921, 688 and November 1921, 621; Mrs. William N. Reynolds, Chairman, Committee on International Relations,

Daughters of the American Revolution to Edward N. Denby, Secretary of the Navy, February 16, 1922; Denby to Reynolds, February 25, 1922; "Disarmament Conference at Washington," Committee on International Relations, National Society Daughters of the American Revolution, File: 3809–959:138 fg, Box 10, Secretary of the Navy General Correspondence, 1916–1926, Records of the Department of the Navy, RG 80, NARA.

100. Minor, "A Message from the President General," December 1921.

101. DAR *Proceedings of the Thirty-Second Continental Congress*, 15.

102. Ibid., 17.

103. DAR *Proceedings of the Thirty-Third Continental Congress*, 412–13.

104. For quote, see Mrs. O. D. Oliphant, "Rallying for National Defense," *American Legion Weekly*, August 21, 1925; John Weeks to Miss Wetmore, Woman's Department of the National Civic Federation, April 29, 1922; John Weeks to Mrs. John Francis Yawger, Daughters of the American Revolution, May 16, 1922; John Weeks to Mrs. Clarence F. R. Jenne, National Society United States Daughters of 1812, May 20, 1922; Anna M. G. Stevens, Connecticut Daughters of the American Revolution, to the Secretary of War, October 16, 1922; John Weeks to Mrs. Anna M. G. Stevens, File 2045–674, 61, 98, 107, 128, 134, Military Intelligence Division Correspondence, 1917–1941, Records of the War Department General and Special Staffs, RG 165; DAR *Proceedings of the Thirty-First Continental Congress*, 215; Edwin Denby to Maude Wetmore, Chairman, Woman's Department of the National Civic Federation, April 25, 1923, File 3809–959: 251, Box 11, General Correspondence, 1916–1926, Records of the Navy, RG 80; DAR *Proceedings of the Thirty-Second Continental Congress*, 365. Around the same time, the League of American Pen Women also condemned the activities of organizations it described as "unpatriotic and directed against preparation adequate to insure our national defense." John W. Weeks, Secretary of War, to Mrs. Helen R. Bamberger, Chairman, Authors' and Publishers' Committee, League of American Pen Women, File 10261–201, 2, Military Intelligence Division Correspondence, 1917–1941, RG 165; Memorandum for Assistant Chief of Staff, G–1, by Anita Phipps, Subject: Report on trip to Chicago and Camp Custer, June 27, 1923, File 5281, Box 5, Numerical File, 1921–42, G–1 (Personnel), War Department General Staff, RG 165.

105. Anita Phipps to Mrs. Koyle, November 16, 1921, File 231.35, Papers Re-Women's Relations and Hostess Service, U.S. A, Box 1700, Central Decimal files, Bulky Files, 1917–1925, RG 407, NARA; Statements of Mrs. B. L. Robinson, Mrs. Rufus M. Gibbs, Mrs. Leo Fallom, and Miss M. G. Kilbreth, U.S. Senate, Subcommittee of the Committee on Appropriations, War Department Appropriation Bill, 1923, 67th Cong., 2nd sess., April 24, 1922.

106. Jean Bethke Elshtain, *Women and War* (New York: Basic Books, 1987), 62–71.

107. "For Immediate Release," press release from Mrs. Nobel Newport Potts, Frame 53; "Borah Denies He Will Speak at Peace Meet," *Washington Herald*, April 29, 1924, Frame 63, Reel 39, WILPF—U.S. Section, Microfilm Edition; "Peace Women Cause Row in 1812 Daughters Meeting," *Washington Post*, April 28, 1924, 1; "Women

in Uproar over Peace Gathering," *New York Times*, April 28, 1924; Susan Zeiger, "She Didn't Raise Her Boy to Be a Slacker," *Feminist Studies* 22 (Spring 1996): 7–39.

108. See constitution of American Legion Auxiliary in Thompson, *History, National American Legion Auxiliary*, 56.

109. LaGanke, "The National Society of the Daughters of the American Revolution," 498; Breckinridge, *Women in the Twentieth Century*, 45. In contrast, the Daughters of 1812 had about 4,000 members in 1922; Jenne, "Annual Message and Report of the President National."

110. Eva Perry Moore to Hannah Clothier Hull, President, WILPF, December 6, 1924, Frame 644, Reel 40, WILPF, U.S. Section; Cott, *The Grounding of Modern Feminism*, 256; Jensen, "All Pink Sisters," 215; "Women of 36 Lands Will Confer Here," *Christian Science Monitor*, April 21, 1925, Folder: 1925 Research Material Suffrage, Women's Suffrage, Container D36, La Follette Papers.

111. Quoted in *Women in a Changing World: The Dynamic Story of the International Council of Women Since 1888* (London: Routledge, 1966), 52.

112. "Women of 36 Lands Will Confer Here."

113. Eva Perry Moore to Mary Anderson, March 28, 1924, Frame 236; Mary Anderson to Mrs. Philip N. Moore, March 21, 1924, Frame 227; Anderson to Moore, June 8, 1924, Frame 283; Anderson to Spencer Gordon, March 24, 1924, Frame 332; Ethel Smith to Anderson, April 3, 1924, Frames 244–48; Alice Lloyd to Anderson, April 21, 1924, Frames 258–59, Reel 4, Mary Anderson Papers; Eva Perry Moore to Amy Woods, Women's International League for Peace and Freedom, April 21, 1924, Frames 632–33; Eva Perry Moore to Amy Woods, WILPF National Secretary, September 13, 1924, Frame 637; Eva Perry Moore to Members of the Executive Committee, Frame 646, Reel 40, WILPF-U.S. Section.

114. Presentation to House Committee on Foreign Affairs, Washington, D.C., January 20, 1925, Folder: National Patriotic Council Attacks 1925, Box: Attackers, National Civic Federation, Sentinels of the Republic, Special Collection: Attacks, SCPC.

115. Eva Perry Moore to Hannah Clothier Hull, President, WILPF, December 6, 1924, Frame 644, Reel 40, WILPF, U.S. Section; Cott, *The Grounding of Modern Feminism*, 256; Jensen, "All Pink Sisters," 215; "Peace Groups Strife Renewed in Two Centers in Capital," January 20, 1925; "Mrs. Potts Hits 'Reds,' Mostly Russian in U.S.," Folder: NCPW Attacks, National Patriotic Council, Mrs. Noble Newport Potts, Box 496, DG 23, NCPW Collection; Presentation to the Committee on Foreign Affairs of the House of Representatives, Washington, D.C., January 20, 1925, Folder: National Patriotic Council Attacks 1925, Box: Attackers, National Civic Federation, Sentinels of the Republic; "Mrs. Potts Assails Peace and Freedom League," *Washington Post*, Folder: Attackers, Daughters of the American Revolution, Clippings about the DAR, Box: Attackers, Daughters of the American Revolution, Material about 1924–1938 Blacklists, Special Attacks Collection, SCPC; "World Peace Issue Threatens Rift in Women's Council," *Washington Post*, May 9, 1925, 1; "Threatens to Leave Council of Women," *New York Times*, May 9, 1925, 3.

116. "Women of 36 Lands Will Confer Here."

117. "Anger over DAR Action Flames in Women's Council," Folder: 1925 Research Material Suffrage, Women's Suffrage, Container D36, La Follette Papers.

118. Eva Perry Moore to Hannah Clothier Hull, President, WILPF, December 6, 1924, Frame 644, Reel 40, WILPF, U.S. Section; Cott, *The Grounding of Modern Feminism*, 256; Jensen, "All Pink Sisters," 215; "Women of 36 Lands Will Confer Here."

119. Mrs. Philip N. Moore to Mr. W. J. Cameron, Editor, *Dearborn Independent*, May 21, 1924, Frame 288–90, Reel 4, Mary Anderson Papers.

120. "New England Women Protest 'Pacifist Talk,'" *Washington Post*, May 8, 1925, 4; "Women Outline World Peace Steps," *New York Times*, May 13, 1925, 3; "War Mother Makes Bitter Attack on Council of Women," *Washington Post*, May 13, 1925, 2; "World Peace Issue Threatens Rift in Women's Council," *Washington Post*, May 9, 1925, 1; "New Attack Is Made by Women Critics on World Council," *New York Times*, May 3, 1925, 1; *New Republic*, May 13, 1925, 303; "U.S. Women Oppose Resolution Data as League Propaganda," *Washington Post*, May 4, 1925, 1; "Heated Discussion of League Foreseen for Quinquennial," *Washington Post*, May 3, 1925, 2; "Peace Groups Strife Renewed in Two Centers in Capital," January 20, 1925; "Mrs. Potts Hits 'Reds,' Mostly Russian in U.S."; "Patriotic Body Veils Charges," Folder: NCPW Attacks, National Patriotic Council, Mrs. Noble Newport Potts, Box 496, DG 23, NCPW Collection; Presentation to House Committee on Foreign Affairs, Washington D.C., January 20, 1925, Folder: National Patriotic Council Attacks 1925, Box: Attackers, National Civic Federation, Sentinels of the Republic; "Mrs. Potts Assails Peace and Freedom League," *Washington Post*, Folder: Attackers, Daughters of the American Revolution, Clippings about the DAR, Box: Attackers, Daughters of the American Revolution, Material about 1924–1938 Blacklists; "Mrs. Catt Defends Motives Inspiring Quinquennial Here," May 1, Folder: Catt, Carrie Chapman, Answers, 1924–1927, Box: Attacks, Attacks on WIL, 1924–39, Attacks on Jane Addams, Lucia Ames Mead, etc., Special Attacks Collection, SCPC; "Super Patriots Continuing Attacks on Women," May 13, 1925, Press release from National Women's Trade Union League, Frame 419, Reel 67, WTUL Papers; Lucia Ames Mead, "The International Council of Women," *Unity*, June 8, 1925, 247, Box 15: Lucia Ames Mead Printed Articles, 1922–1936, Reel 10, Papers of Edwin Doak Mead and Lucia Ames Mead, 1876–1936 (Wilmington, Del.: Scholarly Resources, 1991), microfilm ed. (hereafter Mead Papers).

121. "Hoover Welcomes Women Delegates in Peace Speech," *Washington Post*, May 5, 1925, 1.

122. In the U.S. delegation, Mrs. Flo Jamison Miller represented the National Woman's Relief Corps and Mrs. O. D. Oliphant represented the American Legion Auxiliary. The American War Mothers did not have a delegate. The Ladies of the Maccabees, which seemed sympathetic to antiradical concerns even though it was not a veterans' organization and had not participated in the Women's Patriotic Conference on National Defense, was also represented in the official U.S. delegation. See "Women Here Today from 36 Countries for World Council," *Washington Post*, May 2, 1925, 2.

123. "Women Destroy Pacifist Tracts at Quinquennial," n.d., Folder: 1925 Research Material Suffrage, Women's Suffrage, Container: D36, La Follette Papers; "See Rising Tide of League Support," n.d., Folder: Catt, Carrie Chapman, Answers 1924–1927, Box: Attacks, Attacks on WIL, 1924–39, Special Attacks Collection; "Quinquennial Tea Guests' Exclusion Disturbs Morale," *Washington Post*, May 7, 1925, 1; "Mrs. Catt Resents Attitude Toward Women's Council," *Washington Post*, May 8, 1925, 1; Cott, *The Grounding of Modern Feminism*, 257.

124. "Women Outline World Peace Steps," *New York Times*, May 13, 1925, 3; "War Mother Makes Bitter Attack on Council of Women," *Washington Post*, May 13, 1925, 2.

125. "Council of Women Forget Discord at Farewell Banquet," *Washington Post*, May 14, 1925, 1; "Defends Loyalty of World Council," *New York Times*, May 14, 1925, 3.

126. Oliphant, "Rallying for National Defense."

127. Breckinridge, *Women in the Twentieth Century*, 84–85; First Report of the Committee on Inquiry, with Suggested Plan Approved by the President, Corresponding Secretary and Treasurer of the National Council of Women, Frames 594–96, Reel 3; Meeting of the Executive Committee, National League of Women Voters, February 18, 1928, Frame 230; Pre-Council Meeting of the Board of Directors, National League of Women Voters, April 22, 1929, Frame 450, Reel 4, Papers of the League of Women Voters, 1918–1972, Part 1, Meetings of the Board of Directors and the Executive Committees: Minutes and Related Documents, 1918–1974; Report of the Sub-Committee to Investigate Attacks Upon Women's Organizations, November 30, 1925, Frame 721, Reel 3, WJCC Records; "Wants World Court Supreme, Mrs. Mead Offers Resolution to National Council of Women, N.Y. Woman Assails Council Chiefs," Detroit, October 29, Reel 10, Lucia Ames Mead, Clippings, 1922–1923–1924–1927, Box 15, Printed Articles, 1922–1936, Mead Papers; Lucia Ames Mead to Gould, December 20, 1925, Folder 8, Box 54, Reel 43, NCPW Collection; Parker to Detzer, December 15, 1928, Frame 504; Balch to Parker, Frame 509, Reel 53, WILPF-U.S. Section, Microfilm version.

128. "War on Radicals Aim of Conference," *New York Times*, May 17, 1924; Miss Margaret DeSilver to Miss Hauswer, May 29, 1924, Frame 242, Reel 8, LWV Papers, 1918–1972, Part 3, Ser. A, National Office Subject Files, 1920–1932.

129. "Council of Women Forget Discord at Farewell Banquet," *Washington Post*, May 14, 1925, 1; "Defends Loyalty of World Council," *New York Times*, May 14, 1925, 3.

130. Mrs. B. L. Robinson, president of the Massachusetts Public Interest League, quoted in "Dangerous Organizations of Women," *National Bulletin*, published by Military Order of the World War, April 1924, Folder: NCPW Attacks on Women's Organizations, Box 498, NCPW Collection.

Chapter 3. "It Takes Women to Fight Women":
The Emergence of Female Anti-Radicalism

1. Mrs. Oliphant, Opening Statement, *Souvenir Edition, First Women's Patriotic Conference on National Defense* (Washington, D.C., February 1925), 23, Minnesota Historical Society, St. Paul.

2. Ibid., 24; Katherine Lewis, "America's Womanhood Declares for Adequate Defense," *American Legion Weekly*, March 20, 1925; "Coolidge, Generals and Weeks Demand National Defense," *Washington Post*, February 24, 1925, 1.

3. Mrs. O. D. Oliphant, "Rallying for National Defense," *American Legion Weekly*, August 21, 1925.

4. Quoted in Lewis, "America's Womanhood Declares for Adequate Defense."

5. The total conference roster, taken from *Souvenir Edition: First Women's Patriotic Conference on National Defense*, 21, was as follows: Daughters of the American Revolution; Women's Relief Corps, G.A.R.; Women's Overseas Service League; Ladies of the G.A.R.; National Society United States Daughters of 1812; National Society of Colonial Dames of America; American Nurses Association; Service Star Legion; American War Mothers; United Daughters of the Confederacy; Women's Club of the Service Flag; American Women's Legion; Women's Auxiliary of the Spanish-American War Veterans; Government Club of New York; American Legion Auxiliary; and Sponsors U.S. Navy. I have not been able to find membership figures for all the organizations participating in the women's national defense conference this first year. For those organizations for which figures are available, the combined membership totals 600,000. This makes their claim to represent one million women credible, although they certainly did not allow for overlap among their organizations. I have compiled membership figures from several sources. See Sophonisba P. Breckinridge, *Women in the Twentieth Century: A Study of Their Political, Social and Economic Activities* (New York: McGraw-Hill, 1933), 42–91; Robert Hunt Lyman, ed., *The World Almanac and Book of Facts for 1925* (New York: New York World, 1925); Ida Clyde Clarke, ed., *Women of Today, 1928–29 Edition* (New York: Women of Today Press, 1928); Lucile Evelyn LaGanke, "The National Society of the Daughters of the American Revolution: Its History, Policies, and Influence, 1890–1949" (Ph.D. dissertation, Western Reserve University, 1951), 498; Frank Ernest Hill, *The American Legion Auxiliary: A History, 1924–34* (Indianapolis: American Legion Auxiliary, 1935), 62, 123, 146; Mrs. Charles B. Gilbert, *The American Legion Auxiliary*, vol. 4 (Indianapolis: American Legion Auxiliary, 1970), 6–28; List of Important Women's Organizations with membership figures from the 1927 World Almanac, File 9835, Box 55, Numerical File, 1921–42, War Department General Staff, RG 165, NARA; National Society United States Daughters of 1812 *News-letter*.

6. "National Defense Is Weeks' Plea to Daughters of 1812," *Washington Post*, April 22, 1924, 12; "Daughters of 1812 Assail Pacifists," *Baltimore Sun*, April 25, 1924, Folder: NCPW Attacks, National Patriotic Council, Mrs. Noble Newport Potts, 1924–1935, Box 496, NCPW Collection; "Peace League Assailed by Daughters of 1812," *Washington Post*, April 25, 1924, 10; "Daughters of 1812 Condemn Women's International League," *Woman Patriot*, May 1, 1924, 1; "Daughters of 1812 Told Women Must Aid Dry Law Work," *Washington Post*, April 23, 1924, 5. Not all members of the Daughters of 1812 were happy with this turn of events. One woman, Edith Edwards, wrote a WILPF representative that during the Daughters of 1812 convention she was "much surprised to learn" that it was "violently and virulently anti-pacifist." Even though she supported

WILPF, she also wanted to continue her membership in the hereditary organization because as a chapter president she was "doing good work for that particular period of American History"; Edith Edwards to Miss A. Marion Holmes, April 29, 1924, Frames 58–60, Reel 39, WILPF-U.S. Section.

7. "For Immediate Release," press release from Mrs. Nobel Newport Potts, Frame 53; "Borah Denies He Will Speak at Peace Meet," *Washington Herald*, April 29, 1924, Frame 63, Reel 39, WILPF-U.S. Section; "Peace Women Cause Row in 1812 Daughters Meeting," *Washington Post*, April 28, 1924, 1; "Women in Uproar over Peace Gathering," *New York Times*, April 28, 1924.

8. Letter to Secretary of War John Weeks, Frame 57, Reel 33; Martha Trimble, WILPF to League of Women Voters, April 24, 1924, Frame 715–16, Reel 41, Series C., Correspondence, WILPF-U.S. Section; "Apology for 'Intolerance' of Opponents," *Washington Daily News*, May 1, 1924, Reel M10-M15, scrapbooks, references to Rosika Schwimmer, vol. 4, European and American Press, Schwimmer-Lloyd Collection; William E. Brigham, "Patriots Gather to Press Cause of Americanization, Mrs. Noble Potts the Leader," July 9, 1924, Folder: Attackers, Daughters of the American Revolution, Clippings About the DAR (1924–29), Box: Attackers, DAR, Material about 1924–38 Blacklists, Virginia Walker Papers, Peace Flag and Peace Policy, 1907–1914, Special Attacks Collection, SCPC.

9. "Peace Flees League Meet; Daughter of 1812 Is Hissed," *Washington Post*, May 4, 1924, 1; "Peace League Stirred Up by 1812 Daughter," *Washington Herald*, May 4, 1924, Reel 40, Vol. X, Scrapbooks, Schwimmer-Lloyd Collection; "International War Ban Is Only Way to Peace, Borah Says," *Washington Post*, May 5, 1924, 2; "What Jane Addams Really Did," *Boston Herald*, March 22, 1925, Folder: Attacks on Jane Addams, Box: Attacks, Attacks on WIL, 1924–39; Brigham, "Patriots Gather to Press Cause"; Anderson to Robins, May 6, 1924, Frame 505–6, Reel 3, Mary Anderson Papers.

10. In addition to working independently, the National Patriotic Council joined the Women's Patriotic Conference on National Defense. National Patriotic Council, Report for 1925–27, and *National Patriotic Councillor* 5, 2 (c. 1931), Folder: NCPW Attacks, National Patriotic Council, Mrs. Noble Newport Potts, 1924–1935, Box 496; Laura Puffer Morgan to Helen Tufts Bailie, Folder: NCPW Attacks, Suspension of Mrs. Helen Tufts Bailie from DAR, 1928, Box 494, NCPW Collection; Brigham, "Patriots Gather to Press Cause"; Julia Emory to Miss Woods, September 23, 1924, Frame 170, Reel 39, WILPF-U.S. Section; "Society May Open D.C. Headquarters, Red Tendencies in America Hit by Founders and Patriots' Body," clipping, no source, Folder: 1925 Research Material Suffrage, Women's Suffrage, Container: D36, La Follette Papers; Tentative Official Program, National Patriotic Conference, Under the Auspices of the National Patriotic Council, March 5–6, 1925, Folder 9, Massachusetts Public Interests League Collection, Massachusetts Historical Society, Boston; Norman Hapgood, ed., *Professional Patriots* (New York: Boni, 1928), 167–69.

11. "Would Add 6,000,000 to Nation's Voters," *New York Times*, April 26, 1924, 8; extract from article in *New York Herald Tribune*, January 22, 1925, Frame 000586, Con-

tainer 27, Reel 17, Catt Papers; Foster, *The Women and the Warriors*, 55; Harriet Hyman
Alonso, *Peace as a Women's Issue: A History of the U.S. Peace Movement for World Peace
and Women's Rights* (Syracuse, N.Y.: Syracuse University Press, 1993), 74–75, 106–9; Joan
M. Jensen, "All Pink Sisters: The War Department and the Feminist Movement in the
1920s," in *Decades of Discontent: The Women's Movement, 1920–1940*, ed. Lois Scharf and
Joan M. Jensen (Boston: Northeastern University Press, 1983), 215–17; Nancy F. Cott,
*The Grounding of Modern Feminism* (New Haven, Conn.: Yale University Press, 1987),
257–58; Dorothy Detzer to Hannah Clothier Hull, January 9, 1925, Folder 4: Correspondence, January 1925, Box 1, Reel 1, Papers of Hannah Clothier Hull, 1889–1958 (Wilmington, Del.: Scholarly Resources, 1991), microfilm (hereafter Hull Papers).

    12. Quoted in Jensen, "All Pink Sisters," 217.

    13. Quoted in Charles DeBenedetti, *Origins of the Modern American Peace Move-
ment, 1915–1929* (Millwood, N.Y.: KTO, 1978), 97. For other accounts of the NCCCW,
see Cott, *The Grounding of Modern Feminism*, 257–58; Jensen, "All Pink Sisters," 215–
17; Jacqueline Van Voris, *Carrie Chapman Catt, A Public Life* (New York: Feminist
Press, 1987), 198–203; Foster, *The Women and the Warriors*, 54–56; Alonso, *Peace as a
Women's Issue*, 106–9.

    14. Van Voris, *Carrie Chapman Catt*, 198.

    15. "Assail Conference of Women on War," *New York Times*, January 25, 1925.

    16. Ibid. For other accounts of this meeting see "Peace Conference Motives Im-
pugned in Hectic Session," *Washington Post*, January 26, 1925, 3; Will Irwin to Frederick J. Libby, January 31, 1925; Associate Secretary to Will Irwin, February 5, 1925; Will
Irwin to Arthur Charles Watkins, February 10, 1925, Folder: NCPW Attacks, Spider
Web Chart, Box 497, DG 23, NCPW Collection; Mary Anderson to Mrs. Robins, February 9, 1925, Frame 510, Reel 3, Mary Anderson Papers.

    17. Van Voris, *Carrie Chapman Catt*, 198.

    18. Cott, *The Grounding of Modern Feminism*, 258.

    19. "New York War Mothers Assail Peace Movement," *Buffalo News*, February 25,
1925, Container 28, Reel 17, Catt Papers.

    20. Oliphant, "Rallying for National Defense."

    21. Cott, *The Grounding of Modern Feminism*, 258.

    22. Alonso, *Peace as a Women's Issue*, 108; Thomas H. Buckley and Edwin B. Strong,
Jr., *American Foreign and National Security Policies, 1914–1945* (Knoxville: University
of Tennessee Press, 1987): 89; Cott, *The Grounding of Modern Feminism*, 265; Robert D.
Schulzinger, *U.S. Diplomacy Since 1900*, 4th ed. (New York: Oxford University Press,
1998), 137–38.

    23. Hill, *American Legion Auxiliary*, 29–30; "Practical Mrs. Oliphant: The New Aux-
iliary Leader and Her Program," *American Legion Weekly*, November 14, 1924, 14. Claire
Oliphant was born in New Jersey and attended Pennington Seminary for high school
and Emerson College in Boston, where she earned a reputation for oratory. She later returned to New Jersey and married O. D. Oliphant, a member of one of New Jersey's oldest families who served for many years in the National Guard. Oliphant's health began

to fail in the late 1930s and she died on May 1, 1939, in Trenton, New Jersey. "Women Leader Dies in Jersey," *New York Times*, May 2, 1939, 21; "Enduring Service for a Secure America," *National News of the American Legion Auxiliary* (April 1940): 10.

24. Mrs. Oliphant, "Dedication of Conference, Pilgrimage to Unknown Soldier's Tomb," *Souvenir Edition, First Women's Patriotic Conference on National Defense*, 21.

25. Oliphant, "Opening Statement," 23.

26. "Introduction," from Margaret Randolph Higonnet, Jane Jensen, Sonya Michel, and Margaret Collins Weitz, eds., *Behind the Lines: Gender and the Two World Wars*, ed. Jane Jensen, Sonya Michel, Margaret Collins Weitz (New Haven, Conn.: Yale University Press, 1987), 2.

27. Ibid.

28. Quoted in Lewis, "America's Womanhood Declares for Adequate Defense." For other descriptions of the first Women's Patriotic Conference on National Defense, see Hill, *The American Legion Auxiliary*, 33–37; "Women's Patriotic Groups to Discuss National Defense," *Washington Post*, February 22, 1925, 12; "Lack of National Defense Criminal, Women Are Told," *Washington Post*, February 23, 1925, 2; "Coolidge, Generals and Weeks Demand National Defense," *Washington Post*, February 24, 1925, 1; "Strong Navy Urged by Admiral Phelps at Defense Session," *Washington Post*, February 25, 1925, 7; "National Defense Act Commended by 16 Patriotic Groups," *Washington Post*, February 26, 1925; "Women's Defense Parley," *New York Times*, February 9, 1925; "Women Open Session for National Defense," *New York Times*, February 23, 1925, 32; "Nation Should Set Arms Cut Example, Coolidge Declares," *New York Times*, February 24, 1925, 1; "Admiral Pictures Clash with Britain," *New York Times*, February 25, 1925, 5; Claire Oliphant, "A Backward Glance: The Story of the First Women's Patriotic Conference Inaugurating a Great Program for Adequate National Defense," *American Legion Auxiliary Bulletin* 9, 8 (August 1935): 4–6.

29. "A Report of the Recommendations Committee as Adopted," *Souvenir Edition: First Women's Patriotic Conference on National Defense*, 79–80.

30. Catherine E. Rymph, *Republican Women: Feminism and Conservatism from Suffrage Through the Rise of the New Right* (Chapel Hill: University of North Carolina Press, 2006), 57–58.

31. Ibid.

32. "Lack of National Defense Criminal, Women Are Told."

33. "Report of the National Committee Woman for Minnesota [1926], Folder 4: American Legion Auxiliary, 1926, Box 3, Subject Files: American Legion Auxiliary, Rose Carolyn Spencer Papers, Minnesota Historical Society, St. Paul.

34. DAR, *Proceedings of the Thirty-Fourth Continental Congress* (April 20–25, 1925): 471–72.

35. Ibid.

36. "The National Defence Committee," Folder 9, Box 1, DAR "Blacklist" Controversy Papers and Palo Alto Chapter of the Daughters of the American Revolution Col-

lection, Department of Special Collections, Stanford University Libraries, Palo Alto, California (hereafter DAR Blacklist Controversy Papers).

37. "Mrs. Brosseau, 87, Ex-Head of D.A.R.," *New York Times*, April 21, 1959, 35; "Mrs. Grace L. H. Brosseau," *National Historical Magazine* (October 1940): 40.

38. LaGanke, "The National Society of the Daughters of the American Revolution," 166.

39. Francesca Morgan, "'Home and Country': Women, Nation and the Daughters of the American Revolution, 1890–1939" (Ph.D. dissertation, Columbia University, 1998), 414.

40. "Mrs. Grace L. H. Brosseau"; LaGanke, "The National Society of the Daughters of the American Revolution," 166–67.

41. Martha Strayer, *The D.A.R.: An Informal History* (Washington, D.C.: Public Affairs Press, 1958), 133, 173–78, 246; Helena Huntington Smith, "Mrs. Brosseau and the D.A.R.," *Outlook and Independent*, March 20, 1929, Folder 13, Box 1, DAR "Blacklist" Controversy Papers; Margaret Gibbs, *The DAR* (New York: Holt, Rinehart and Winston, 1969), 114–15; Judgment number 33099, Divorce Judgment, Alfred C. Baldwin, Judge, Filed in Bridgeport Superior Court, on October 3, 1930, Grace Hall Brosseau vs. Alfred Joseph Brosseau; "Mrs. Brosseau Gets Uncontested Divorce," *New York Times*, October 3, 1930, Container 28, Reel 17, Catt Papers.

42. "State Conferences, Washington State," *Daughters of the American Revolution Magazine* (February 1925).

43. Strayer, *The D.A.R.*, 133, 173–78; "State Conferences, Washington State"; "State Conferences, North Dakota," *Daughters of the American Revolution Magazine* (March 1925).

44. Dana Frank, *Purchasing Power: Consumer Organizing, Gender and the Seattle Labor Movement, 1919–1929* (Cambridge: Cambridge University Press, 1994); Robert L. Friedheim, *The Seattle General Strike* (Seattle: University of Washington Press, 1964); John C. Putman, *Class and Gender Politics in Progressive-Era Seattle* (Reno: University of Nevada Press, 2008): 203–10; C. B. Bagley, "William S. Walker," in *History of Seattle, From the Earliest Settlement to the Present Time*, vol. 3 (Chicago: S. J. Clarke, 1916).

45. Journal of Helen Tufts Bailie, November 19, 1930, Folder: Journal, 1928–33, Box 3, Bailie Papers.

46. Strayer, *The D.A.R.*, 173.

47. Mrs. Alfred J. Brosseau to Mrs. Nellie Nugent Somerville, June 15, 1926, Folder 51: DAR correspondence, Series II, Nellie Nugent Somerville, Microfilm Reel 5, Somerville-Howorth Papers, Schlesinger Library; Morgan, "'Home and Country,'" 429–30. Morgan documents how by 1928, 91 percent of Georgia's DAR chapters contributed money to support National Defense Committee activity. She found that by 1929 83 percent of Michigan's chapters used outlines from the National Defense Committee, and by 1931 only 8.3 percent of chapters in this state claimed to have no activities around National Defense.

48. Mrs. William Sherman Walker, chairman, National Defense Committee,

"The Common Enemy," *Daughters of the American Revolution Magazine* 10, 61 (October 1927): 766. For National Defense work in Michigan, see Morgan, "'Home and Country,'" 400.

49. Quoted in Helen Tufts Bailie, "Perverted Patriotism: A Story of D.A.R. Stewardship," November 11, 1929, Folder: Publications—D.A.R., Box 1, Bailie Collection.

50. DAR *Proceedings of the Thirty-Sixth Continental Congress* (April 18–23, 1927): 393, 419–20.

51. DAR *Proceedings of the Thirty-Seventh Continental Congress* (April 16–21, 1928): 566.

52. DAR *Proceedings of the Thirty-Ninth Continental Congress* (April 14–19, 1930): 600.

53. For membership figures, see LaGanke, "The National Society of the Daughters of the American Revolution," 498.

54. By 1937, the *National Defense News* reported that the National Defense Committee had a full-time staff of five employees, in addition to a full-time messenger, who were paid a total of $7,500 in 1936–37. Mrs. Vinton Earl Sisson, "Annual Report, National Defense Through Patriotic Education," April 1, 1936–March 31, 1937, *National Defense News* 2, 18 (May–June 1937): 3–7, 9.

55. DAR *Proceedings of the Thirty-Sixth Continental Congress*, 390–94; *Proceedings of the Thirty-Seventh Continental Congress*, 308–13; *Proceedings of the Thirty-Eighth Continental Congress* (April 15–20, 1929): 224–27; *Proceedings of the Thirty-Ninth Continental Congress*, 464–68; *Proceedings of the Fortieth Continental Congress* (April 20–25, 1931): 651–59.

56. E. Pendleton Herring, *Group Representation Before Congress* (Baltimore: Johns Hopkins University Press, 1929): 228–32; Statement of Mrs. Sherman D. Walker [sic], U.S. House Committee on Naval Affairs, Bill for the Increase of the Naval Establishment, 70th Cong., 1st sess., February 17, 1928.

57. Mrs. Alfred J. Brosseau to Mrs. Nellie Nugent Somerville, June 15, 1926, Folder 51: DAR correspondence, Series II, Nellie Nugent Somerville, Microfilm Reel 5, Somerville-Howorth Papers. The stationery of the National Defense Committee listed its national officers. For examples of this letterhead, see Adelaide H. Sisson to General Douglas MacArthur, June 16, 1931, File 381, National Defense, Box 2315, Central Files, 1926–1939, RG 407, NA; File 2657–155, 3, Flora A. Walker to Major Simpson, January 19, 1931, MID Correspondence.

58. Shepard also funded the antiradical work of the National Society of New England Women (NSNEW), another member of the Women's Patriotic Conference on National Defense. Report of the President, Cora Pike Stowe, New York City Colony, *National Society of New England Women, Yearbook, 1932–1933*, Papers of the New York City Colony, National Society of New England Women Records, Sophia Smith Collection, Smith College, Northampton, Mass. (hereafter Sophia Smith Collection); Jeanne Fox Weinmann, "Women's Patriotic Conference on National Defense," *National Society United States Daughters of 1812 News-letter* 9, 4 (March 1935); Mrs. Lowell Fletcher

Hobart, National Society Daughters of the American Revolution, to Mrs. Finley J. Shepard, April 9, 1930, Folder: 1930; Helen Gould Shepard to Mrs. Jane Todd, Program Chairman, DAR, May 24, 1928, folder: Helen Gould Shepard, Box 17: Personal correspondence, Helen Gould Shepard Collection, Lyndhurst, Tarrytown, New York (hereafter Helen Gould Shepard Collection); "Shepard, Helen Miller (Gould)," *Who's Who in America* 16 (1930–1931): 2001.

59. "Mrs. F. J. Shepard Dies of a Stroke," *New York Times*, December 22, 1938; "Shepard, Helen Miller (Gould)"; "Helen Gould," newspaper clipping, no source, no date, Folder: unmarked, Box 22: newspaper clippings; Clipping, including line drawing of Helen Gould handing a check to the United States Government for $100,000, no source, no date; "Helen Gould as Philanthropist," no source, no date; "Miss Helen Gould—a study by . . . ," *New York Journal*, Sunday, no date; J. P. Coughlan, "Helen Gould Shepard," *Munsey's Magazine*, no date, Scrapbook, Box 24: newspaper clippings, Helen Gould Shepard Collection.

60. See note 59.

61. Gibbs, *The DAR* , 85.

62. Folder: NCF—Gertrude Beeks Easley—Ltrs. from Mrs. Helen Gould Shepard, 1920–1940 and n.d., Box 147, NCF Collection; Shepard's guestbook shows that she started hosting events having to do with Soviet Russia and National Defense in 1920. Helen Gould Shepard Guestbook, 1913–1924; "Guests" Lyndhurst, 1929–1938, Box 30: Guestbooks, Helen Gould Shepard Collection.

63. "Students Take 'Sex Trips' Radicals' Plans Exposed," *Washington Herald*, April 29, 1931, New York State Scrapbook, United States Daughters of 1812 Library, Washington, D.C.; "Mrs. Shepard Scores Reds, Former Helen Gould Lays Attacks on Religion to Soviet," *New York Times*, May 17, 1931, Section II, 4; "Mrs. Shepard Lists Dangers to Youth, She Assails Atheism, League for Industrial Democracy and Visits to Radical Leaders, Fears Collapse of Ideals," *New York Times*, January 14, 1932, 23; Alan Hynd, "Unrevealed Secrets That Torture Gaston Means," *True Detective Mysteries* (December 1936): 58–61, 99–102, Folder: Gaston Means—Affair of, Box 125; Mrs. Finley J. Shepard, "What Is the Next Step?" Speech at the Executive Committee, Department on Subversive Movements, National Civic Federation, April 13, 1931, Folder: Subversive movements, Dept. on Meeting, 1931, 13 April, Box 104, NCF Collection.

64. Helen Gould Shepard to Mrs. Jane Todd, Program Chairman, DAR, May 24, 1928, Folder: Helen Gould Shepard, Box 17, Helen Gould Shepard Collection.

65. Folder: NCF—Gertrude Beeks Easley—Ltrs. from Mrs. Helen Gould Shepard, 1920–1940 and n.d., Box 147, NCF Collection.

66. Statement by Gertrude Beeks Easley, June 22, 1932, —Means Affair folder, Box 125, NCF Collection; Helen Gould Shepard library booklist, Helen Gould Shepard Collection.

67. Helen Gould Shepard to Gertrude Beeks Easley, July 14, 1930, Folder: NCF— Gertrude Beeks Easley—Ltrs. from Mrs. Helen Gould Shepard, 1920–1940 and n.d.; Miss Vail to Mrs. Helen Gould Shepard, November 27, 1931, Folder: NCF—Gertrude

Beeks Easley—Ltrs. to Mrs. Helen Gould Shepard, 1921–1932, Box 147, NCF Collection; Report of the President, Cora Pike Stowe, New York City Colony, National Society, New England Women, Year book, 1932–1933, Folder: Yearbooks, 1932–1933, 1934–1935. Box: Yearbooks, New York City Colony, National Society, New England Women Collection.

68. Helen Gould Shepard to Gertrude Beeks Easley, Folder: NCF—Gertrude Beeks Easley—Ltrs. from Mrs. Helen Gould Shepard, 1920–1940 and n.d., Box 147, NCF Collection.

69. "Students Take 'Sex Trips' Radicals' Plans Exposed"; "Sensational Charges Made at Medal Rite," no source, no date, Folder: Clippings, D.A.R., Box 1, Bailie Papers; for her fear of publicity, see also Helen Gould Shepard to Mrs. Jane Todd, Daughters of the American Revolution, May 24, 1928, Folder: Helen Gould Shepard, Box 17, Helen Gould Shepard Collection; Shepard, "What Is the Next Step?"; Gertrude Beeks Easley to Mrs. Finley J. Shepard, July 17, 1932, Folder: NCF—Gertrude Beeks Easley—Ltrs. to Mrs. Helen Gould Shepard, 1921–1932, Box 147, NCF Collection.

70. Translations of socialist press, calling card from Mrs. Finley Johnson Shepard, Folder: NCF—Subject File Soviet Russia—Miscellaneous, 1927, Box 126; Memos by Gertrude Beeks Easley on anti-Soviet Investigation; Ralph Easley to Mrs. Helen Gould Shepard, January 30, 1932, Folder: NCF—Gertrude Beeks Easley—Ltrs. to Mrs. Helen Gould Shepard, 1921–1932; Gertrude Beeks Easley to Helen Gould Shepard, June 6, 1933; Gertrude Beeks Easley to Helen Gould Shepard, June 12, 1933; Gertrude Beeks Easley to Helen Gould Shepard, March 4, 1933, Folder: NCF—Gertrude Beeks Easley—Ltrs. to Mrs. Helen Gould Shepard, 1933–40 and misc. memoranda, Box 147, NCF Collection; Hynd, "Unrevealed Secrets That Torture Gaston Means," *True Detective Mysteries*, December, 1936, Folder: Gaston Means, Affair of, Box 125, NCF Collection; "Hints Mrs. Shepard Was Means Victim, Rover Suggests Former Helen Gould Paid 'Large Sums' for Communist Inquiry," *New York Times*, May 11, 1932, 9.

71. Mrs. Edwin C. Gregory, "Report of the North Carolina State Regent," April 21, 1927, DAR *Proceedings of the Thirty-Sixth Continental Congress*, 287–98; John A. Livingstone, "Suggest Mrs. Gregory as Committee Woman," *Raleigh News and Observer*, February 3, 1928, 2.

72. Morgan, "'Home and Country,'" 428–29; Princess Cantacuzene, *Revolutionary Days: Recollections of Romanoffs and Bolsheviki, 1914–1917* (Boston: Small, Maynard, 1919); DAR, *Proceedings of the Thirty-First Continental Congress* (April 1922): 12–16; Hill, *The American Legion Auxiliary*, 227–29; *National Society United States Daughters of 1812 News-letter* 8, 1 (July 1933): 8–9; "Daughters of 1812 Honor First Lady—Mrs. Roosevelt to Be Guest at Annual Banquet of Society Tonight," April 25, 1933, "Scrapbook of the 1812 Society of the District of Columbia, United States Daughters of 1812 Library, Washington, D.C.

73. Hill, *The American Legion Auxiliary*, 122–23, 243–53; Vye Smeigh Thompson, *History, National American Legion Auxiliary* (Pittsburgh: Jackson-Remlinger, 1926), 63.

74. "The Report of the President National at the Thirty-Fifth Associate Council,"

April 24, 1927; *National Society United States Daughters of 1812 News-letter* 5, 3 (March 1928): 27; 1 (June 1927): 12, 18; 14 (December 1930): 8; 11 (March 1930): 18, United States Daughters of 1812 Library.

75. "Mrs. Tucker, Daughter of General Logan, Dies at Home Here," *Washington Sunday Star,* March 17, 1940, from Scrapbook for New York State, 1939–1940, United States Daughters of 1812 Library.

76. *Baltimore: Its History and Its People,* vol. 2 (Chicago: Lewis Historical Publishing, 1912); Florine Josephine Judik file, Obituary, *Baltimore Evening,* March 17, 1961, Dielman-Hayward Files, Maryland Historical Society.

77. For an example of a radical woman alienated by ideologically sympathetic men, see Kathryn Kish Sklar, *Florence Kelley and the Nation's Work: The Rise of Women's Political Culture, 1830–1900* (New Haven, Conn.: Yale University Press, 1995).

78. Flora A. Walker, "Confidential Information Memorandum for DAR Members Only," Folder: Publications—DAR, Box 1, Bailie Papers.

79. Jensen, "All Pink Sisters"; Cott, *The Grounding of Modern Feminism.*

80. " 'Spider-Web' Orator's Charges Aren't Supported by 'Informants,' " *New York World,* June 8, 1924, Frame 395; "Army Fights Women's Societies Because They're in War on War," *New York World,* June 10, 1924, Frame 397, Vol. 4, Reel 2, Maud Wood Park Scrapbooks.

81. "Macnider Condemns Pacifist Agitators," March 19, 1926, unidentified clipping, folder: Attacks, Jane Addams, Box 492, NCPW Collection.

82. Anita Phipps, Director of Women's Relations, United States Army, Memorandum for the Assistant Chief of Staff, G–1, Subject: Report on Meetings of Ultra-Pacifist and Patriotic Organizations, June 25, 1924, File 10314–547, MID Correspondence.

83. The group had been established in 1921 to aid all veterans, especially women, who were not eligible for any government assistance. Breckinridge, *Women in the Twentieth Century,* 48–49.

84. Lena Hitchcock, President, Women's Overseas Service League, to Secretary of War James W. Good, March 30, 1929, Box 2315, "National Defense" 381, Central Files, 1926–1939, RG 407.

85. Phipps, Memorandum for the Assistant Chief of Staff, June 25, 1924.

86. Ibid.

87. Ibid.

88. J. H. Reeves, Memorandum for the Secretary, General Staff. Subject: Report on Meetings of Ultra-Pacifist and Patriotic Organizations, July 17, 1924, File 10314–547, 2, MID Correspondence.

89. G. C. Barnhardt, Memorandum for the Secretary, General Staff, Subject: Report on Meetings of Ultra-Pacifist and Patriotic Organizations, July 21, 1924, File 10314–547, 3, MID Correspondence.

90. Phipps, Memorandum for Assistant Chief of Staff.

91. Roy Talbert, Jr., *Negative Intelligence: The Army and the American Left, 1917–*

*1941* (Jackson: University Press of Mississippi, 1991), 225; Joan Jensen, *Army Surveillance in America, 1775–1980* (New Haven, Conn.: Yale University Press, 1991), 194–200; Jensen, "All Pink Sisters"; Harold Hyman, *To Try Men's Souls: Loyalty Tests in American History* (Westport, Conn.: Greenwood Press, 1959), 323; Frame 515, Investigation of George B. Lockwood, Editor, "The National Republic," part of survey/investigation done by J. N. Stewart, Subject Files: Women's Organizations, attacks on, Container 27, Reel 17, Catt Papers.

92. Reeves, Memorandum for the Secretary, General Staff, 2; Phipps, Memorandum for Assistant Chief of Staff.

93. File 10314–589, 3, Memo by James H. Reeves about inquiry from Charles S. Ryckman, November 11, 1926; File 10314–556/98, Memo by James H. Reeves for the Adjutant General of the Army, February 13, 1926; File 10322–1035, Dr. William B. Reid to Stanley Ford, September 24, 1928; File 10322–1035, 2, Stanley Ford to William B. Reid, October 2, 1928; File 10314–597, 5, Stanley H. Ford to Mrs. Percy V. Pennybacker, July 28, 1927; File 10110–1935, 78, William H. Wilson to Mrs. Paul B. Ryder; File 10314–597, 4, Mrs. Percy V. Pennybacker to War Department, Military Intelligence Division, July 22, 1927; File 10110–1935, 80, 82, Frederick J. Libby to the Secretary of War, June 15, 1931, July 22, 1931, MID Correspondence.

94. Talbert, *Negative Intelligence*, 225; Jensen, *Army Surveillance in America*, 194–200; Jensen, "All Pink Sisters"; Hyman, *To Try Men's Souls*, 323; Frame 515, Investigation of George B. Lockwood, Editor, "The National Republic," part of survey/investigation done by J. N. Stewart.

95. Reports on the Activities of the Communist and Soviet Propaganda in U.S. by the National Society Patriotic Builders of America, File: National Society Patriotic Builders of America, 080 Military Order of Guards to Polar Bear Association, Box 470, Office of the Adjutant General, Central Files, 1926–39, RG 407. The National Society Patriotic Builders of America was another female antiradical group active in the Women's Patriotic Conference on National Defense.

96. Ibid.

97. File 10261–257, O. A. Dickinson to Walter K. Wilson, Washington, D.C., January 9, 1926, MID Correspondence.

98. O. A. Dickinson to Walter K. Wilson; File 10110–2452/135, Report of Agent of Massachusetts Public Interests League on Meeting, Saturday, March 27, 1926; File 10110–2452/135, O. A. Dickinson to Walter O. Boswell; File 10110–2452, 129, O. A. Dickinson to Walter Boswell, March 29, 1926, Boswell to Dickinson, April 5, 1926, MID Correspondence, 1917–41, RG 165.

99. File 10322–1038, 1, W. H. Simpson to Mrs. William S. Walker, DAR, February 3, 1931; File 10322–1038, 2, W. H. Simpson to Mrs. William S. Walker, DAR, February 11, 1931; File 2037–1909, Mrs. Albert J. Brosseau, President General, DAR to Stanley H. Ford; File 10110–2590, 2, W. K. Wilson to Mrs. William Sherman Walker, DAR, November 4, 1927; File 10110–2590, Memo attached to letter from W. K. Wilson, November 4, 1927; File 2657–155, 2, W. H. Simpson to Mrs. William Sherman Walker,

chairman, National Defense Committee, January 12, 1931, MID Correspondence, 1917–41, RG 165.

100. Mary G. Kilbreth to Rossiter Johnson, Postmarked September 24, 1922, Folder: Kilbreth, Mary G., 1919–1922, Box 4, Rossiter Johnson Collection, Rare Books and Manuscripts Division, NYPL.

101. Frame 515, Investigation of George B. Lockwood, Editor, "The National Republic," part of survey/investigation by J. N. Stewart.

102. Memorandum for the Secretary of War from Anita Phipps. Subject: Women's Relations, United States Army, January 8, 1927, Box 55, Numerical File, 1921–42, War Department General Staff, G-1 (Personnel), RG 165.

103. Memorandum by Maude Wetmore, Chairman, National Civic Federation, Women's Department, to Secretary of War Dwight F. Davis, War Department, Washington, D.C., concerning Director of Women's Relations and contact with organized women, May 7, 1927, Box 2316, Classification no. 381, "National Defense," Central files 1926–39, RG 407. For reactions to her proposal, see Colonel John M. Morgan, General Staff, Acting Assistant Chief of Staff, Memorandum for the Chief of Staff: Subject: Comments re study G-1/9835-Status and Duties of the Director of Women's Relations for the United States Army, July 21, 1927; Colonel Stanley H. Ford, General Staff, A.C. of S., Memorandum for the Assistant Chief of Staff, G–1: Subject: Status and duties of the Director of women's relations for the United States Army, July 13, 1927; Colonel John M. Morgan, Memorandum for the Chief of Staff: Subject: Status and duties of the Director, Women's Relations, for the U.S. Army, September 9, 1927, File 9835, Box 55, Numerical File 1921–42, G-1 (Personnel) War Department General Staff, RG 165.

104. Memorandum for the Chief of Staff. Subject: Status and Duties of the Director of Women's Relations for the United States Army by John M. Morgan, Colonel, General Staff, Acting Assistant Chief of Staff, July 6, 1927, File 9835, Box 55, Numerical File, 1921–42, G-1 (Personnel), War Department General Staff, RG 165.

105. Memorandum to the Secretary of War from Anita Phipps, Director of Women's Relations. Subject: Office Space for Director of Women's Relations and War Department Welfare Service, September 21, 1927, File: Women's Relations, Box 195, General Correspondence, 1932–42, RG 107.

106. Secretary of War Dwight Davis, response to Memorandum by Maude Wetmore, Chairman, Woman's Department of the National Civic Federation, concerning Director of Women's Relations and contact with organized women, November 1, 1927, Box 2316, Classification no. 381, "National Defense," Central files 1926–39, RG 407.

Chapter 4. Stopping the "Revolution by Legislation":
Antiradicals Unite Against Social Welfare Reform

1. Alice Bradford Wiles, "Report of the Chairman of Committee on Legislation in U.S. Congress," *Daughters of the American Revolution Magazine* (April 1921): 236.

2. Grace Brosseau, "Address of the President General," April 16, 1928, DAR *Proceedings of the Thirty-Seventh Continental Congress* (April 16–21, 1928): 16.

3. Mrs. William Sherman Walker, DAR Congressional Report of the National Defense Committee, Folder: Publications—D.A.R., Box 1, Bailie Papers.

4. Katherine T. Balch to Alexander Lincoln, December 20, 1926, Folder 9; Mary Kilbreth to Balch, January 22, 1927, Folder 10, Box 2, Alexander Lincoln Papers.

5. DAR *Proceedings of the Seventeenth Continental Congress* (April 20–25, 1908): 542–50; Wiles, Report of the Chairman of Committee on Legislation in U.S. Congress, 236.

6. Robyn Muncy, *Creating a Female Dominion in American Reform, 1890–1935* (New York: Oxford University Press, 1991).

7. Sophonisba P. Breckinridge, *Women in the Twentieth Century: A Study of Their Political, Social and Economic Activities* (New York: McGraw-Hill, 1933), 263.

8. Balch to Lincoln; Kilbreth to Balch; see note 4.

9. Grace Brosseau to Madam State Regent, December 16, 1926, published in Congressional Record, 69th Cong., 2nd sess., January 8, 1927, 1280–81. The Muncie, Indiana, chapter was the first to respond to Brosseau's warnings, preparing a program in December 1926 that explained how "socialists are centralizing in Washington, and working into all kinds of beneficent organizations." Without directly naming women's groups, it claimed that "there is a bloc in Congress now working to carry out the details of the Communist plans, but avoiding the name of Communist party." See "Communism in Government," Prepared for DAR Program in December, 1926 and Presented by the Paul Revere Chapter, Muncie, Indiana, Folder: Publications—DAR, Box 1, Bailie Papers.

10. "Organizing Revolution Through Women and Children," frame 190; "Propaganda Against Our Women's Organizations, Who is Madame Kollontai?" Frames 310–11, Reel 4, Mary Anderson Papers; Summary of Report of Special Committee, Signed by Mrs. John D. Sherman, et al., Frames 1032–1053, Reel 44, Maud May (Wood) Park Papers. Other antiradicals, most notably Mrs. Haviland Lund, lifted wholesale from the piece for their own propaganda. See J. S. Eichelberger to Mr. W. J. Cameron, March 21, 1924, Frames 229–31, Reel 4, Mary Anderson Papers; "Organizing Revolution Through Women and Children," *Woman Patriot*, September 1, 15, 1922.

11. DAR *Proceedings of the Thirty-Sixth Continental Congress*, 420–21.

12. "Our Threatened Heritage," DAR Committee of Protest, Mrs. H. T. Bailie, April 5, 1928, Folder: Publications—Helen Tufts Bailie, Box 1, Bailie Papers.

13. Address of Mrs. William Sherman Walker, "Americanism Versus Internationalism," DAR *Proceedings of the Thirty-Seventh Continental Congress* (April 16–21, 1928): 446. Again, this policy was supported by individual DAR members. Mrs. Lewis Shelton of Leonia, New Jersey, told her chapter in a presentation on "Current Events" that the "Maternity and Infancy Act was a scheme of Soviet Russia" and "seemed to imply that it was part of this plot to 'nationalize' the children of the U.S.," according to Mrs. John L. Houston, Mountain Lakes, New Jersey. Houston to Chief, Children's Bureau, April 15, 1928, Folder: 11-0-11, Box 320, Central File, 1925–28, Records of the Children's Bureau, RG 102, NARA (hereafter Children's Bureau Records).

14. Molly Ladd-Taylor, *Mother-Work: Women, Child Welfare and the State, 1890–1930* (Urbana: University of Illinois Press, 1994), 167–96; J. Stanley Lemons, *The Woman Citizen: Social Feminism in the 1920s*, 2nd ed. (Charlottesville: University of Virginia Press, 1990), 153–80; Muncy, *Creating a Female Dominion*, 93–123.

15. Walter I. Trattner, *Crusade for the Children: A History of the National Child Labor Committee and Child Labor Reform in America* (Chicago: Quadrangle Books, 1970), 40–42.

16. Ibid., 58.

17. Ibid., 119.

18. Ibid., 119–42; "First Federal Child Labor Law" and "Second Federal Child Labor Law," *Congressional Digest* (February 1923): 134–35.

19. "Petition Against Proposed Amendment to the Constitution of the United States Granting Congress Power to Limit, Regulate, and Prohibit the Labor of Persons under 18 Years of Age," Extracts from Congressional Record, 68th Cong., 1st sess., May 31, 1924, 1–16.

20. Ibid.

21. Ibid.

22. "Are Women's Clubs 'Used' by Bolshevists?" *Dearborn Independent*, March 15, 1924.

23. Richard B. Sherman, "The Rejection of the Child Labor Amendment," *Mid-America: An Historical Review* 45, 1 (January 1963): 7.

24. Ibid.

25. "A.F. of L. Backing Child Labor Law," *Boston Post*, October 11, [1924?], Folder 9: Clippings, Industrial Aspect in Favor of Ratification, Child Labor Amendment, Box 8, Henry Lee Shattuck Papers, Massachusetts Historical Society, Boston.

26. Sherman, "The Rejection of the Child Labor Amendment," 12.

27. "The Shame of Massachusetts," Folder 317, Box 20, Papers of the Consumers' League of Massachusetts, 1891–1935, Schlesinger Library; "Miss Smith Announces a Drive," *Springfield Union*, November 20, 1924, Folder 6, Box 8, Henry Lee Shattuck Papers; Trattner, *Crusade for the Children*, 173.

28. "Chicago to Chicago"—Legislative Review, National League of Women Voters, April 29, 1942, Frame 408–9, Reel 44, Maud May (Wood) Park Papers.

29. Quoted in Trattner, *Crusade for the Children*, 169; William Chenery called the popularization of the charges made by the WPPC "a new and significant development in the century-old campaign to protect children from the devastating effects of premature labor." See William L. Chenery, "Child Labor: The New Alignment," *Survey* 53, 7 (1925): 379.

30. Circular letter from Massachusetts Public Interests League to Voters of Massachusetts, Folder 14: "Child Labor Amendment, Important Papers, 1924–25," Box 2, Alexander Lincoln Papers; Mrs. LaRue Brown to Miss Marguerite Owen, December 6, 1924, Folder 58: "Corres.—C.L.A.—Owens, Marguerite," Box 3, Dorothy Kirchwey Brown Collection, Schlesinger Library.

31. "The Massachusetts Public Interests League," Folder 5, Box 1, MPIL Collection; "Statement of Purpose by the Massachusetts Public Interest League," Frame 000540, Reel 17, Subject Files: Women's Organizations, attacks on, Container 27, Catt Papers; Journal of Helen Tufts Bailie, April 12, 1927, Folder: Journal, 1921–1927, Box 3, Bailie Papers; "Statement of Mrs. Henry Preston White," U.S. Senate Committee on Education and Labor, To Create a Department of Education and to Encourage the States in the Promotion and Support of Education, 68th Cong., 1st sess., January 25, 1924, 369–73; Statement of Mrs. H. H. Amsden, U.S. House Committee on Interstate and Foreign Commerce, To Provide a Child Welfare Extension Service and for Other Purposes, 70th Cong., 2nd sess., January 25, 1929, 145–50.

32. "Benjamin Lincoln Robinson," Harvard Class Reports; "Benjamin Lincoln Robinson, Asa Gray Professor of Systematic Botany, and Curator of the Gray Herbarium," Harvard University Gazette, February 29, 1936; "Dr. B. L. Robinson, Botanist, Dead. Curator of Harvard's Gray Herbarium Was on Vacation in New Hampshire," Boston Herald, July 29, 1935, in Robinson, Benjamin Lincoln (1887), Biographical Folder, Harvard University Archives, Pulsey Library, Harvard University; Kim E. Nielsen, "The Security of the Nation: Anti-Radicalism and Gender in the Red Scare of 1918–1928" (Ph.D. dissertation, University of Iowa, 1996), 130–52.

33. Dr. Weatherby, Rough draft of biographical sketch of Benjamin Lincoln Robinson, Folder: Robinson, B. L. Administrative Correspondence Files, Gray Herbarium Library, Harvard University Herbarium, Cambridge, Massachusetts; Mrs. B. L. Robinson, "Christian Socialism—A Contradiction in Terms," Folder: Publications—MPIL, Box 1, Bailie Papers.

34. Margaret C. Robinson, "Suffrage and Socialism," letter to the editor, New York Times, March 21, 1920, sect. 8, 9; Margaret C. Robinson, "Woman Suffrage a Menace to Social Reform," in Anti-Suffrage Essays (Boston: Form Publications, 1916), 98–117.

35. Quoted in Nielsen, "The Security of the Nation," 136.

36. "Aims to Preserve Ideas of Republic," Springfield Union, June 7, 1925, 3, Folder 16, Box 3, Alexander Lincoln Papers.

37. "The Red in Education," MPIL, Folder 5, MPIL Collection.

38. "The Youth Movement," Folder: Publications—Massachusetts Public Interests League, Box 1, Bailie Collection; Margaret Robinson, "The Youth Movement: What Is It?" from "The Truth About the Red Movement," Iron Trade Review, Folder 6, MPIL Collection; "Dangerous Doctrines Being Suggested to Youth"; "Propaganda in Women's Colleges," MPIL, Folder 1, Box 14, Florence Corliss Lamont Collection, Corliss Family Collection, Sophia Smith Collection.

39. "Negroes and Communism," Folder 2, MPIL Collection.

40. Margaret Robinson, "The Responsibility of Being Led," Woman Patriot, July 1, 1925. This was reprinted in pamphlet form and delivered in many venues. See Dearborn Independent, May 23, 1922, and the Women's Patriotic Conference on National Defense, February 1927, Folder 10, MPIL. Slight variations came in the form of "The Need of Americanization Among American Women" and "What Every Woman

Should Know," MPIL, Folder 1, Box 14, Florence Corliss Lamont Collection, Corliss Family Collection.

41. "A Woman's League Worth Joining," *Springfield Union*, April 9, 1923, Folder 14, Box 2, Alexander Lincoln Papers.

42. "Child Labor Amendment," letter to the editor by Felix Rackemann, reprinted by MPIL. For other examples of the propaganda distributed by MPIL, see "Child Labor and the Constitution"; "Federal Council of Churches Wrong on So-Called Child Labor Amendment"; "Child Labor Debate"; "Es ist Verboten"; "The Child Labor Amendment in Massachusetts," Folder: M–28/24, Child Labor Amendment, Chancery Central Subject Files, Archives of the Archdiocese of Boston; Hope Gray, "One Year's Work," MPIL, Folder 16, Box 3, Alexander Lincoln Papers; "The Cat Is Out of the Bag," MPIL, MPIL Collection.

43. Circular Letter from MPIL to the Voters of Massachusetts, Folder 14: "Child Labor Amendment, Important Papers, 1924–1925," Box 2, Alexander Lincoln Papers.

44. "Our Year's Work," 1924, MPIL, Folder 16, Box 3, Alexander Lincoln Papers.

45. Circular Letter from Massachusetts Public Interests League; Mrs. LaRue Brown to Miss Marguerite Owen, December 6, 1924, Folder 58, "corres—C.L.A—Owens, Marguerite. Box 3, Dorothy Kirchwey Brown Collection.

46. "Aims to Preserve Ideas of Republic."

47. Gray, "One Year's Work"; Receipts of "Citizens Committee to Protect Our Homes and Children," Folder 65, Box 3, Dorothy Kirchwey Brown Collection; "Massachusetts Spent $15,522 to Defeat Child Labor Amendment," *American Child* (January 1925), Folder 314: Child Labor Amendment, History, Box 20, Papers of the Consumers' League of Massachusetts.

48. "Limit—Regulate—Prohibit, What It Means," Citizens' Committee to Protect Our Homes and Children, Folder: M–28/24, Child Labor Amendment, Chancery Central Subject Files, Archives of the Archdiocese of Boston.

49. Josephine J. Eschenbrenner, National Child Labor Committee, to Elizabeth Lowell Putnam, Folder 294, Box 16, Putnam Papers.

50. Elizabeth Lowell Putnam, "The Child Labor Amendment," September 13, 1924, Folder 294, Box 16, Putnam Papers.

51. Putnam to Evelyn Sears, June 21, 1920, Folder 455, Box 27, Putnam Papers.

52. Mrs. William Lowell Putnam to Mrs. Proctor, October 31, 1924, Folder 294, Box 16, Putnam Papers.

53. Elizabeth Lowell Putnam to Mr. Leonard, Citizens' Federal Research Bureau, November 14, 1924, Folder 512, Box 31, Putnam Papers.

54. Putnam, "The Child Labor Amendment."

55. Mrs. LaRue Brown to Mrs. Caspar Whitney, December 5, 1924, Folder 61: "Correspondence—C.L.A. campaign, Nov.–Dec. 1924," Box 3, Dorothy Kirchwey Brown Collection.

56. "The Struggle for the Child Labor Amendment, as Revealed by the Massachusetts Referendum," Organizations Associated for Ratification of the Child Labor Amend-

ment," Folder 199: Child Labor Amendment, 1934–1937, Carton 13, Unprocessed papers, Dorothy Kirchwey Brown Collection; "American Men and Women Attention! ... Now All, But Particularly WOMEN Read This!" Folder 65: "Child Labor Amendment Opposition Material," Box 3, Dorothy Kirchwey Brown Collection; Henry S. Pritchett, "The Proposed Child Labor Amendment," Citizens' Committee to Protect Our Homes and Children, Folder 317, Box 20, Papers of the Consumers' League of Massachusetts; "Limit—Regulate—Prohibit, What it Means"; "Facts Are Stubborn Things," Citizens Committee to Protect Our Homes and Children; "If You Love Your Children, Read This Pamphlet," Citizens' Committee to Protect Our Homes and Children; Margaret C. Robinson, "Child Labor Campaign in Massachusetts," MPIL, Folder: M–28/24, Child Labor Amendment, Chancery Central Subject Files, Archives of the Archdiocese of Boston.

57. "A.F. of L. Backing Child Labor Law"; "Child Labor Struggle Comes Next Week," *Boston Evening Transcript*, January 31, 1925, Folder 6, Box 8, Henry Lee Shattuck Papers; Ethel Smith to Dr. Worthy M. Tippy, October 16, 1924, Folder 60: "Corres.—C.L.A. Campaign, Aug.–October, 1924," Box 3, Dorothy Kirchwey Brown Collection.

58. Cardinal O'Connell to Mrs. Thomas W. Proctor, December 15, 1924, Folder: M–28/24, Child Labor Amendment, Chancery Central Subject Files, Archives of the Archdiocese of Boston.

59. Trattner, *Crusade for the Children*, 176; Worth M. Tippy, "Why the Child Labor Referendum Lost in Massachusetts," *Christian Advocate*, December 25, 1924, Folder: M–28/24, Child Labor Amendment, Chancery Central Subject Files, Archives of the Archdiocese of Boston.

60. Sherman, "The Rejection of the Child Labor Amendment," 13–16; Trattner, *Crusade for the Children*, 163–64; printed postcard from William Cardinal O'Connell to Reverend Dear Father, October 1, 1924; Worth M. Tippy, "Why the Child Labor Referendum Lost in Massachusetts," *Christian Advocate*, December 25, 1924; Correspondence from O'Connell, Folder: M–28/24, Child Labor Amendment, Chancery Central Subject Files, Archives of the Archdiocese of Boston.

61. "Urged to Defeat Child Labor Bill, Catholic Women Head Amendment Denounced," Folder 69: "Child Labor Amendment Scrapbook," Box 3, Dorothy Kirchwey Brown Collection.

62. James Kenneally, *The History of American Catholic Women* (New York: Crossroad, 1990), 167–72; "Limit—Regulate—Prohibit: What It Means"; "His Eminence Speaks to Catholic Women," June 22, 1918, Folder 19, Box 3; Report of the Diocesan Council, December 1925, Folder 9, Box 2; Lilian Slattery to Monsignor Haberlin, December 28, 1922, Folder 6, Box 2; "Clarion Call to Catholic Women," *Montreal Gazette*, January 14, 1920, Folder 9, Box 1; Cardinal O'Connell, "Foreword" in grand bazaar program, League of Catholic Women, Folder 4, Box 3, Chancellor's Office, League of Catholic Women Papers, Records of Nondiocesan Agencies, Archives of the Archdiocese of Boston.

63. "League of Catholic Women Lectures," *Framingham News*, November 5, 1926,

Folder 19, Box 3; Mrs. Francis E. Slattery to Miss Mary G. Kilbreth, October 18, 1929, Folder 15, Box 1; Mrs. Francis E. Slattery to Dear Friend, June 5, 1929, Folder 10, Box 2, League of Catholic Women Papers.

64. Peter G. Filene, *Americans and the Soviet Experiment, 1917–1933* (Cambridge, Mass.: Harvard University Press, 1967), 82–84.

65. W. S. Palmer, "Child Labor Amendment: Insidious Attempt to Subvert the Liberties of the People," *Springfield Union*, October 30, 1924, Folder 4, Box 8, Henry Lee Shattuck Papers.

66. "Curley Raps Child Labor Amendment," Folder 69: Child Labor Amendment Scrapbook; Mrs. LaRue Brown to John A. Ryan, October 9, 1924, Folder 60: "Corres.—C.L. A. campaign, Aug-Oct. 1924," Box 3, Dorothy Kirchwey Brown Collection; "Limit—Regulate—Prohibit: What It Means."

67. "The Struggle for the Child Labor Amendment, as Revealed by the Massachusetts Referendum," Folder 11, Carton 13, Unprocessed papers, Dorothy Kirchwey Brown Collection.

68. "Montana Senator Challenged over Child Labor Issue," *Boston Transcript*, February 6, 1925, Folder 7, Box 8, Henry Lee Shattuck Papers.

69. Chenery, "Child Labor: The New Alignment," 425.

70. Margaret C. Robinson, "Why Massachusetts Beat Child Control," *Dearborn Independent*, March 7, 1925, Folder 16, Box 3, Alexander Lincoln Papers.

71. Mary Kilbreth, Letter for Release Thursday Morning, November 13, 1924, Box 8, Folder 11, Henry Lee Shattuck Papers.

72. Editorial Reprint from *Boston Herald*, November 6, 1924, Folder 1: Child Labor, Box 8, Henry Lee Shattuck Papers; Trattner, *Crusade for the Children*, 176.

73. "Patriot Petition Now Public Document," *Woman Patriot*, September 1, 1926, 136.

74. Louis A. Coolidge and Mrs. Benjamin L. Robinson, "Don't Ratify the Child Labor Amendment!" Broadcast from Station WJY on December 30, 1924, Folder 11; Broadside from the Citizens' Committee for Home and Child Protection of New Hampshire, Folder 20, Box 8, Henry Lee Shattuck Papers; B. A. Aughinbaugh to Children's Bureau, February 7, 1925, Folder: 10-9-1(1), Box 306, Central File, 1925–28, Children's Bureau Records; "Charge Reds Back Child Labor Ban," *New York Times*, February 25, 1925, 2; Hermine Schwed, "How They Put It Over in Clubs," and Joseph T. Cashman, "The Child Labor Amendment and Socialism," from "The Truth About the Red Movement," *Iron Trade Review*, Folder 6, MPIL Collection.

75. Lucia Johnson Bing, Ohio League of Women Voters to Grace Abbott, January 15, 1925, Folder: 10-9-1(1), Box 306, Central File, 1925–28, Children's Bureau Records.

76. Report of the Sub-Committee to Investigate Attacks upon Women's Organizations, November 30, 1925, Frame 721, Reel 3, WJCC Records.

77. Quoted in Vance Armentrout, "The Red Brand," a series of articles originally appearing in *Louisville Courier Journal*, March 24–31, 1929.

78. Dorothy E. Johnson, "Organized Women as Lobbyists in the 1920s," *Capitol Studies* 1 (Spring 1972): 51.

79. Effie P. Attwill to Henry Lee Shattuck, 1923, Folder 2, Box 33, Henry Lee Shattuck Papers.

80. Florence V. Watkins to Mrs. Tilton, May 4, 1923, Folder 246, Box 9, Tilton Papers.

81. Elizabeth Tilton to Miss Bottomley, April 13, 1923, Folder 246, Box 9, Tilton Papers.

82. "Shall the United States Recognize Soviet Russia?" issued by General Federation of Women's Clubs, Folder: Pamphlets—D.A.R. and Related Matters, Box 1, Bailie Papers; DAR *Proceedings of the Thirty-Fourth Continental Congress* (April 20–25, 1925): 471–72.

83. Margaret Robinson, "The Responsibility of Being Led," *Woman Patriot*, July 1, 1925. This was reprinted in many different forms. See *Dearborn Independent*, May 23, 1922, and Women's Patriotic Conference on National Defense, February 1927, folder 10, MPIL Collection; see also "The Need of Americanization Among American Women"; "What Every Woman Should Know," MPIL, Folder 1, Box 14, Florence Corliss Lamont Collection, Corliss Family Collection.

84. "Shall the United States Recognize Soviet Russia?"

85. R. M. Whitney, *Reds in America* (New York: Beckwith Press, 1924), 177–82; Belle Sherwin, President of the League of Women Voters to Mrs. John D. Sherman, January 12, 1926, Frame 204; Women's Joint Congressional Committee to Mrs. John D. Sherman, President of the General Federation of Women's Clubs, Part 3, Series A, National Office Subject Files, 1920–1932, Frames 205–9, Reel 9, LWV Papers.

86. Circular letter from the Citizens' Committee for Home and Child Protection of Concord, New Hampshire, Folder 20, Box 8, Henry Lee Shattuck Papers.

87. Martha E. Cook, "George Madden Martin," in *American Women Writers: A Critical Reference Guide from Colonial Times to the Present*, ed. Lina Mainiero (New York: Ungar, 1981); Jacquelyn Dowd Hall, *Revolt Against Chivalry: Jessie Daniel Ames and the Women's Campaign Against Lynching*, rev. ed. (New York: Columbia University Press, 1993), 179, 345. Martin sometimes also used her married name, Mrs. Attwood R. Martin.

88. George Madden Martin, "American Women and Public Affairs," *Atlantic Monthly* (February 1924): 169–71; George Madden Martin, "American Women and Paternalism," *Atlantic Monthly* (June 1924): 744–53; George Madden Martin, "The American Woman and Representative Government," *Atlantic Monthly* (March 1925): 363–71.

89. Martin, "The American Woman and Representative Government."

90. Martin, "American Women and Public Affairs."

91. Martin, "American Women and Paternalism."

92. Martin, "The American Woman and Representative Government."

93. Mrs. George Madden Martin, "The American Woman and the Proposed Twentieth Amendment," Folder 4, MPIL Collection.

94. Dora Arnold continued protesting "federal aid bills" that sought "to bolster communism and socialism" at least until the defeat of Sheppard-Towner in early 1927. "Women's Meeting Pink, Sprinkled with Red," *White Plains Reporter*, March 2, 1925; "Clubwomen Heckle Child Labor Speaker," *New York World*, February 28, 1925; "Local Member Declares Acts Approved to Be Communistic," *White Plains Daily Reporter*, January 25, 1927, Folder 13, MPIL Collection; "Summary of Report of Special Committee," Frames 1032–53, Reel 44, Maud May (Wood) Park Papers.

95. Mrs. Lilla Day Monroe, "Big Business—The Great Magician," *Industry* 16, 8 (October 24, 1925).

96. "Summary of Report of Special Committee"; Address delivered by Mrs. Attwood R. Martin, November 4, 1927, Raleigh, North Carolina, Folder 10, MPIL Collection.

97. Martin address, Raleigh, N.C.

98. "Clubs' Rights Up as Women's Issue," *New York Times*, May 25, 1926, 20; "Calls on Women to Fight for Law," *New York Times*, May 26, 1926, 11; "Clubwomen Facing Internal Struggle," *New York Times*, May 27, 1926, 25; "Clubwomen Favor Child Labor Law," *New York Times*, May 30, 1926, 2; "Clubwomen Assail Movies of Crime," *New York Times*, May 31, 1926, 2; "Insurgents to Get Hearing," *New York Times*, June 1, 1926, 20; "Women's Clubs Get Coolidge Message," *New York Times*, June 2, 1926, 10.

99. Martin address, Raleigh, N.C.; see also Margaret Hinsdale Engelhard, "Shall General Federation Degenerate into Political Machine?" *Woman Patriot*, May 1, 1928, 67.

100. George Madden Martin, *March On* (New York: Appleton, 1921).

101. Mrs. H. H. Amsden, "Political Dictatorship in Women's Clubs," MPIL, Folder 5, MPIL Collection; Martin was also supported by Hannah Schoff, a member of the New Century Club of Philadelphia and one of the first presidents of the National Congress of Mothers and Parent-Teacher Associations. See her letter to *Woman Patriot*, October 15, 1926, 1.

102. *Woman Patriot*, May 1, 1926; "Louisville Women Win Club Aid Here," *New York Times*, October 17, 1926, 24; "Charges Hurled at Club Contradictory," *Courier Journal*, March 29, 1929, Frame 381, Reel 4, Mary Anderson Papers; see also George Madden Martin, "Dangers in the Maternity Bill," *Woman Citizen*, December 1926, 17, 42–43.

103. "Women's Clubs Get Coolidge Message"; "Clubwomen Favor Child Labor Law"; "Women End Session; Stress the Home," *New York Times*, June 5, 1926, 2; "Summary of Report of Special Committee."

104. Breckinridge, *Women in the Twentieth Century*, 51.

105. Martin address, Raleigh, N.C.; Engelhard, "Shall General Federation Degenerate," 67.

106. Alice P. Mulford, Bridgeton, New Jersey, to Mrs. Robbins, March 17, 1928, Folder: 11-0-11, Box 321, Central File, 1925–28, Children's Bureau Records.

107. Copy of letter from Mrs. Craig C. Miller to Mrs. Alfred J. Brosseau, March 21, 1928, Folder: Correspondence, A-Z, Box 2, Bailie Papers.

108. Annual Message of the President-General, Mrs. Alfred J. Brosseau, DAR *Proceedings of the Thirty-Eighth Continental Congress* (April 15–20, 1929): 11.

109. Grace Abbott to Fletcher Swift, May 23, 1927, Folder: 1-6-2, Box 372, Central File, 1929–1932, Children's Bureau Records.

110. Address of Mrs. William Sherman Walker, National Chairman of the Committee for National Defense, DAR at the Ohio State Conference, Columbus, March 16, 1927, Folder: Publications, DAR; Margaret Robinson, "Keep Facts in View, " *Christian Leader*, March 24, 1928, Folder: Magazine Articles, DAR Scandal; Letter from Margaret Robinson, MPIL, 210 Newbury Street, Boston, Massachusetts to Miss Mary L. Allen, 371 Broadway, Cambridge, Massachusetts, December 15, 1927, Folder: Publications, MPIL, Box 1, Bailie Papers; Statement of Mrs. Mary Logan Tucker, National President of Women's Auxiliary of Military Order of the Loyal Legion, U.S. House Committee on the Judiciary, To Prevent Desecration of the Flag and Insignia of the United States and Provide Punishment Therefor, 69th Cong., 2nd sess., January 31, 1927; File 10110–2452, Memo by O. A. Dickinson to War Department, Washington, D.C., March 29, 1926; File 10110–2452/135, Report of Agent of Massachusetts Public Interests League on Meeting, Saturday, March 27, 1926, New International Hall, Waumbeck, Roxbury, Massachusetts, submitted to MID; File 286–8, O. A. Dickinson to Colonel Mark Brooke, Washington, D.C., January 21, 1926, MID Correspondence. For additional citations, see Kirsten Delegard, "Women Patriots: Female Activism and the Politics of American Anti-radicalism" (Ph.D. dissertation, Duke University, 1999), 431–89.

111. Joan M. Jensen, *The Price of Vigilance* (Chicago: Rand McNally, 1969).

112. Mrs. William Lowell Putnam to Mr. Endicott, October 12, 1917, Folder 342, SASAP [Special Aid Society for American Preparedness], New Roster, 1916–1918, Box 19, Putnam Papers.

113. Memo from Mrs. William Lowell Putnam, Chief, Women's Auxiliary Intelligence Bureau to the Adjutant General, State House, Boston, Massachusetts, December 11, 1917; Memo by Jesse F. Stevens, Colonel, Intelligence Bureau, Commonwealth of Massachusetts, Adjutant General's Office, State House, Boston, to Mrs. William L. Putnam, December 11, 1917, Folder 457: Women's Auxiliary Intelligence Bureau, Box 27; Statement, "Preparedness and War Work," Folder 542: Publicity, n.d., Box 32; Mrs. William Lowell Putnam to Mr. Parker, May 4, 1917, Folder 333: SASAP, Department of Home Relief, General, 1916–18, n.d., Box 18; Report of the Home Relief Department of the Special Aid Society for American Preparedness, August 22, 1917, Folder 347, SASAP Reports, 1916–17, Box 19; Mrs. William Lowell Putnam to Endicott, March 4, 1918, Folder 457: Women's Auxiliary Intelligence Bureau, Box 27, Putnam Papers; "Report of the Intelligence Bureau, the Adjutant General's Office, Filed by Robert O. Dalton, Captain in Charge," *Annual Report of the Adjutant General of the Commonwealth of Massachusetts for the Year Ending December 31, 1917* (Boston: Wright and Potter, State Printers, 1918).

114. Report of the Home Relief Department of the Special Aid Society for American Preparedness. August 22, 1917. Folder 347: SASP Reports, 1916–17, Box 19; Elizabeth Lowell Putnam to Mrs. Merrill, February 6, 1918, Folder 457: Women's Auxiliary Intelligence Bureau, Box 27, Putnam Papers; *Annual Report of the Adjutant General of the Commonwealth of Massachusetts for the Year Ending December 31, 1917*, 20–22.

115. Jensen, *The Price of Vigilance.*

116. Flora L. Mason, Women's Liberty Loan Committee of Bristol County, Victory Cottage, Taunton, Massachusetts, to Mrs. Wendell, October 16, 1918, Folder 350, Box 19, Putnam Papers.

117. Robert K. Murray, *Red Scare: A Study in National Hysteria* (New York: McGraw-Hill, 1955); Robert Justin Goldstein, *Political Repression in Modern America: From 1870 to the Present* (Cambridge: Schenkman, 1978), 174–77; Frank J. Donner, *The Age of Surveillance: The Aims and Methods of America's Political Intelligence System* (New York: Knopf, 1980), 42–47; Roy Talbert, Jr., *Negative Intelligence: The Army and the American Left, 1917–1941* (Jackson: University Press of Mississippi, 1991), 221–25; Joan Jensen, *Army Surveillance in America,, 1775–1980* (New Haven, Conn.: Yale University Press, 1991), 194–200; David Williams, "'They Never Stopped Watching Us': FBI Political Surveillance, 1924–1936," *UCLA Historical Journal* 2 (1981): 5–28.

118. Frank Donner, *Protectors of Privilege: Red Squads and Police Repression in Modern America* (Berkeley: University of California Press, 1990); Goldstein, *Political Repression in Modern America*, 177–79. For an example, see Mrs. George H. Root, "Report from Oregon," *National Society U.S. Daughters of 1812 News-letter* 9, 4 (March 1935): 56, United States Daughters of 1812 Library, Washington, D.C.

119. Elizabeth Barney Buel, "Socialist Propaganda in the United States," Connecticut Daughters of the American Revolution, 1925. Reel 40, Vol. X, Scrapbooks, Schwimmer-Lloyd Collection; "D.A.R. Efforts to Aid Security of Nation Told, Explained Defense Aims to Thousands, Officer Tells Congress," *Christian Science Monitor*, April 17, 1929, Folder: Attackers, Daughters of the American Revolution, Box: "Attackers, Daughters of the American Revolution," Special Collection: Attacks, SCPC; Mrs. William Sherman Walker, "D.A.R. Congressional Report of the National Defense Committee, "Folder: Publications, D.A.R, Box 1, Bailie Papers; Frank Ernest Hill, *The American Legion Auxiliary: A History, 1924–34* (Indianapolis: American Legion Auxiliary, 1935); Adelaide Howe Sisson, "Annual Report, National Defense Committee," *National Defense News* 2, 25 (June 1938); *National Defense News* 2, 1 (September 1935); File 10261–257, O. A. Dickinson to Lt. Col. Walter K. Wilson, Washington, D.C., January 9th, 1926, MID Correspondence, 1917–41, RG 165; "Reports on the Activities of the Communist and Soviet Propaganda in U.S. by the National Society Patriotic Builders of America," File: National Society Patriotic Builders of America, 080 Military Order of Guards to Polar Bear Association, Box 470, Office of the Adjutant General, Central Files, 1926–39, RG 407, NARA. For additional citations, see Delegard, "Women Patriots," 431–89.

120. Mrs. William Sherman Walker, National Defense Committee, "The Common Enemy," *Daughters of the American Revolution Magazine* 10, 61 (October 1927): 766.

121. Mrs. William Sherman Walker, National Defense Committee, "International Youth," *Daughters of the American Revolution Magazine* 11, 61 (November 1927): 851–52.

122. These reproductions were funded by wealthy sponsors like Helen Gould Shepard, a prominent member of the DAR. See Gertrude Beeks Easley to Helen Gould Shepard, November 11, 1931, Easley to Mrs. Shepard, April 21, 1932; Gertrude Beeks Easley to Agnes Stebbins, September 14, 1932, Folder: NCF—Gertrude Beeks Easley— Ltrs. to Mrs. Helen Gould Shepard, 1921–32; Memo from Miss Osgood, November 25, 1931, Folder: NCF—Gertrude Beeks Easley—Ltrs. to Mrs. Helen Gould Shepard, 1933–1940 and misc. memorandum, Box 147, NCF Collection. For distribution of anti-radical and radical propaganda, see Margaret Gibbs, *The DAR* (New York: Holt, Rinehart, 1969): 146; Hill, *The American Legion Auxiliary*, 227–28.

123. "Report of Committee on National Defense," *Proceedings of the Fortieth Continental Congress* (April 20–25, 1931), 651–59; Mrs. William Sherman Walker, DAR Congressional Report of the National Defense Committee, Folder: Publications—D.A.R.; "Red Threat to Kill Fish Seen, 'Marked' Because of Anti-Soviet Campaign, D.A.R. Is Informed," *Boston Herald*, December 5, 1930, Folder: Clippings, D.A.R., Box 1, Helen Tufts Bailie Collection; Hill, *The American Legion Auxiliary*, 227–28; "D.A.R. Efforts to Aid Security of Nation Told"; "Jibes and Jabs in Current Magazines Have D.A.R. in Dither," *Washington Daily News*, Thursday, March 25, 1927; "Fish Is Marked for Death by Communists, D.A.R. Told"; "D.A.R. Slaps at Pacifists in Resolution," Folder: NCPW Attacks, the DAR Sees Red, Box 494, NCPW Collection; *Handbook, 1933–1934*, National Defense Embodying Patriotic Education, National Society Daughters of the American Revolution, Memorial Continental Hall, Washington, D.C. Both Helen Gould Shepard and Gertrude Beeks Easley in the National Civic Federation organized exhibits of radical materials that they used as the basis of presentations. Statement by Ralph M. Easley at Executive Council Meeting, April 11, 1935, Box 139, Folder: Executive Council Meeting, April 11, 1935, NCF Collection.

124. DAR *Proceedings of the Thirty-Eighth Continental Congress* (April 15–20, 1929): 224; File 10314–598, Resolutions Adopted by the Women's Patriotic Conference on National Defense, February, 1927, MID Correspondence, 1917–41, RG 165; Hill, *The American Legion Auxiliary*, 227–28; *National Society U.S. Daughters of 1812 News-letter* 6, 1 (June 1931).

125. "D.A.R. Efforts to Aid Security of Nation Told"; *National Defense News*, Bulletin 14 (December 1933); *National Defense News* 11, 9 (May 1936); 2, 22 (January 1938); 2, 24 (April–May 1938); 2, 25 (June 1938); *Handbook, 1933–1934*, National Defense Embodying Patriotic Education, National Society Daughters of the American Revolution.

126. DAR *Proceedings of the Fortieth Continental Congress*, 657.

127. The American Legion Auxiliary also tried to make its headquarters in Indianapolis into a resource center on radicalism, but it seemed to be interested in supplying information primarily to its own members. On a more local level, the DAR in at least one state opened a National Defense Headquarters patterned after the exhibits in Washington, D.C., with the hope of serving people who could not travel to the nation's capital.

See "Report of the National Defense Embodying Patriotic Education Committee, April 1932–April 1933," *National Defense News*, Bulletin 9 (April–May 1933): 2–4.

128. The DAR was the only women's organization whose headquarters rated a visit, according to guidebooks of the time. See David Rankin Barbee, *Washington: City of Mighty Events* (Richmond, Va.: Garrett and Massie, 1930); *The Book of Washington* (Washington, D.C.: Cleland C. McDevitt, 1927).

129. "Report of the National Defense Committee," DAR *Proceedings of the Thirty-Sixth Continental Congress*, 390–94; "Report of the National Defense Committee," *Proceedings of the Thirty-Eighth Continental Congress*, 224–27. When the House of Representatives' Committee on Naval Affairs was considering the so-called "Big Navy" bill, Flora Walker testified that "in my office in the Memorial Continental Hall in this city I have a room, three walls of which are completely covered with exhibits of a similar nature—this radical literature, much of which is strictly against national defense." Statement of Mrs. Sherman D. Walker [*sic*], U.S. House Committee on Naval Affairs, A Bill For the Increase of the Naval Establishment, 70th Cong., 1st sess., February 17, 1928, 1391–1466; "D.A.R. Efforts to Aid Security of Nation Told"; "National Defense Through Patriotic Education," *National Historical Magazine* (October 1940): 80–81.

130. "Soviet Assailed at D.A.R. Congress," *New York Times*, n.d.; "Report of the National Defense Committee, Year 1930," Mrs. William Sherman Walker, Chairman, Folder: NCPW Attacks, D.A.R., Mostly Clippings, Box 494, NCPW Collection; "Report of the National Defense Committee," DAR *Proceedings of the Thirty-Sixth Continental Congress*, 390–94; "Report of the National Defense Committee," *Proceedings of the Thirty-Ninth Continental Congress*, 464–68.

131. Hermine Schwed, *Confessions of a Parlor Socialist, Told by Herself* (Washington, D.C.: National Association for Constitutional Government, 1922), 16.

132. Robinson, "The Responsibility of Being Led."

133. Paul C. Mishler, "The Littlest Proletariat: American Communists and Their Children, 1922–1950" (Ph.D. dissertation, Boston University, 1988). For an example of antiradical warnings about summer camps, see Walker, "International Youth," 853.

134. Testimony of Mrs. Helen K. Stuart, Chicago, Illinois, U.S. House, Hearings Before a Special Committee to Investigate Communist Activities in the United States, 71st Cong., 2nd sess., Part IV, Vol. 2, July 28 1930. The American Legion and Legion Auxiliary encouraged their members to conduct such "investigations." In a contemporaneous incident, Legion members descended on a youth camp in the San Bernardino hills in California because they suspected young people were being indoctrinated with communist ideology. The men were not content to leave with physical evidence of the camp's radical purpose; they made citizen arrests of five young women, presumably camp counselors, and the elderly camp caretaker. They also found a red flag, and secured from young campers the admission that they had been taught every morning to pledge allegiance to this symbol of communism. Charged with violating a never-used red flag law, the camp leaders were given prison sentences ranging from six months to ten years, which were overturned by the Supreme Court in 1931. In seizing the sign, Helen Stuart may have

been hoping to collect evidence that could be used to prosecute the camp leaders. Obviously she was not prepared to mount the same show of force as the men in the California Legion. See Paul Murphy, *The Meaning of the Freedom of Speech: First Amendment Freedoms from Wilson to FDR* (Westport, Conn.: Greenwood., 1972), 245.

135. "Report of the National Defense Embodying Patriotic Education Committee, April, 1932-April, 1933," *National Defense News*, Bulletin 9 (April–May 1933): 2–4, National Society, DAR, Washington, D.C.

136. Benedict Anderson, *Imagined Communities: Reflections on the Origin and Spread of Nationalism* (London: Verso, 1991).

137. Ellen Schrecker, *Many Are the Crimes: McCarthyism in America* (Boston: Little, Brown, 1998), 66. See, for instance, Lillian Carlson, "A California Girlhood," in Judy Kaplan and Linn Shapiro, eds., *Red Diapers: Growing Up in the Communist Left* (Urbana: University of Illinois Press, 1998), 20–26.

138. "A Petition for the Rejection of the Phipps-Parker Bill Proposing an Extension of the Maternity Act," from the Board of Directors of the Woman Patriot Publishing Company, Congressional Record, 69th Cong., 2nd sess., July 3, 1926, 12918–52.

Chapter 5. The "Red Menace" Roils the Grassroots:
"The Conservative Insurgency Reshapes Women's Organizations

1. Frances Cone to Mrs. C. B. Tuttle, n.d., Mitchell, South Dakota, Frame 831, Reel 9, Part 3, Series A, National Office Subject Files, 1920–1932, LWV Papers.

2. Mrs. Feige to Miss Wells, June 29, 1927, Frames 871–72, Reel 9, Part 3, Series A, National Office Subject Files, 1920–1932, LWV Papers; Frances Cone to Hon. Hanford McNider, Washington, D.C., February 7, 1927, National Defense file, 381, Box 2316, Central decimal files, 1926–39, RG 407, Office of the Adjutant General, NARA.

3. Cone to McNider, February 7, 1927; Mrs. Chaffee to Miss Wells, January 21, 1927, Frame 828–29; Mrs. Feige to Miss Wells, June 29, 1927, Frames 871–2; Correspondence between Marguerite Wells, Regional Director, LWV and Mrs. E. W. Feige, Huron, S.D., January 31, 1927, Frames 844–51, Reel 9; Memorandum from Miss Wells Re Propaganda against the League in South Dakota reported October 1926, Frames 744–45, Reel 4; Part 3, Series A, National Office Subject Files, 1920–1932, LWV Papers.

4. Cone to McNider, February 7, 1927; Wells to Feige, January 31, 1927, Frame 844–47; Chaffee to Wells, January 21, 1927; Feige to Wells, June 29, 1927; Memorandum from Miss Wells Re Propaganda.

5. Margaret Robinson, Massachusetts Public Interests League, 210 Newbury Street, Boston, Massachusetts to Miss Mary L. Allen, 371 Broadway, Cambridge, Massachusetts, December 15, 1927, Folder: Publications, MPIL, Box 1, Bailie Papers; Statement of Mrs. Mary Logan Tucker, National President of Women's Auxiliary of Military Order of the Loyal Legion, U.S. House of Representatives, Committee on the Judiciary, To Prevent Desecration of the Flag and Insignia of the United States and Provide Punishment Therefor, 69th Cong., 2nd sess., January 31, 1927; File 10110–2452, Memo by O. A.

Dickinson to War Department, Washington, D.C., March 29, 1926; File 10110–2452/135, Report of Agent of Massachusetts Public Interests League on Meeting, Saturday, March 27, 1926, New International Hall, Waumbeck, Roxbury, Massachusetts submitted to the Military Intelligence Division; File 286–88, O. A. Dickinson to Colonel Mark Brooke, Washington D.C., January 21, 1926, MID Correspondence. For additional citations, see Kirsten Delegard, "Women Patriots: Female Activism and the Politics of American Anti-radicalism" (Ph.D. dissertation, Duke University, 1999), 431–89.

6. Cone to Tuttle; Chaffee to Wells, January 21, 1927, Frame 828–29; Mrs. R. E. Cone, Huron, South Dakota, to Mrs. Fred Hoffman, President PTA Council of Sioux Falls, Frames 888–89, Reel 9, Part 3, Series A, National Office Subject Files, 1920–1932, LWV Papers.

7. Maud Wood Park, "Organized Women and Their Legislative Program," as represented by the Women's Joint Congressional Committee, Frames 999–1005, Reel 44, Maud May (Wood) Park Papers; "Child Labor Amendment Part of Socialist Program"; "The Massachusetts Campaign on Ratifying the So-Called Child Labor Amendment," Issued by the Massachusetts Public Interests League, Folder 11; Mary W. Dewson to Henry L. Shattuck, January 29, 1925, Folder 20, Box 8, Henry Lee Shattuck Papers; "The Amendment's Ancestry," Vol. 11: Notebook and scrapbook, 1932–36, re: American Legion Auxiliary, DAR, Child Labor Amendment, Reel 3, Series II, Nellie Nugent Somerville, Somerville-Howorth Papers, Schlesinger Library.

8. Arthur P. Morley, "Sees Russia's Hand," *Boston Herald*, October 14, 1924, Folder 4, Box 8, Henry Lee Shattuck Papers.

9. Hermine Schwed, "The Strange Case of Mrs. Carrie Chapman Catt," August 1927, Folder: Catt, Carrie C., Box 1, Bailie Papers.

10. Flora A. Walker to the Committee, Lewis and Clark Chapter, D.A.R., Eugene, Oregon, April 8, 1928, Folder 5, Box 1, Daughters of the American Revolution "Blacklist" Controversy papers and the Palo Alto Chapter of the DAR collection; For evidence that the Daughters of 1812 made these same efforts, see "Report from Utah," *National Society United States Daughters of 1812 News-letter* 4, 12 (March 1927), United States Daughters of 1812 Library, Washington, D.C.

11. Molly Ladd-Taylor, *Mother-Work: Women, Child Welfare and the State, 1890–1930* (Urbana: University of Illinois Press, 1994), 185–87; Molly Ladd-Taylor, *Raising a Baby the Government Way: Mothers' Letters to the Children's Bureau, 1915–1932* (New Brunswick, N.J.: Rutgers University Press, 1986).

12. Robyn Muncy, *Creating a Female Dominion in American Reform, 1890–1935* (New York: Oxford University Press, 1991), 125.

13. Quoted in J. Stanley Lemons, *The Woman Citizen: Social Feminism in the 1920s*, 2nd ed. (Charlottesville: University of Virginia Press, 1990), 174.

14. Muncy, *Creating a Female Dominion in American Reform*, 124–57.

15. "American War Mothers Denounce Maternity Act," *Woman Patriot*, May 1, 1927, 71.

16. Mrs. Reuben Ross Holloway, "Correct Use of the Flag," *National Society United*

*States Daughters of 1812 News-letter* 4, 10 (June 1926): 15; 4, 12 (March 1927): 13, United States Daughters of 1812 Library, Washington, D.C.

17. "Statement of Mrs. Francis E. Slattery," U.S. House, Committee on Interstate and Foreign Commerce, Extension of Public Protection of Maternity and Infancy Act, 69th Cong., 1st sess., January 14, 1926, 21–26.

18. U.S. Senate, Committee on Public Health and National Quarantine, Protection of Maternity and Infancy, 66th Cong., 2nd sess., May 12, 1920, 39; Alice Bradford Wiles, "Report of the Chairman of Committee on Legislation in U.S. Congress," *Daughters of the American Revolution Magazine* (April 1921): 236; Ladd-Taylor, *Mother-Work*, 170; Lemons, *Woman Citizen*, 153–80.

19. Mrs. George Madden Martin to President, December 16, 1926, Folder 11-0-11, Box 321, Central File, 1925–28, Records of the Children's Bureau, RG 102; George Madden Martin, "Dangers in the Maternity Bill," *Woman Citizen*, December 1926, 17, 42–43.

20. Mary Kilbreth to Alexander Lincoln, April 23, 1926, Folder 9, Box 2, Alexander Lincoln Papers.

21. Statement of Mrs. B. L. Robinson, U.S., House, Committee on Interstate and Foreign Commerce, Extension of Public Protection of Maternity and Infancy Act, 26–30.

22. Martin, "Dangers in the Maternity Bill"; see "A Petition for the Rejection of the Phipps-Parker Bill Proposing an Extension of the Maternity Act," from the Board of Directors of the Woman Patriot Publishing Company, Congressional Record, 69th Cong., 2nd sess., July 3, 1926, 12919.

23. "Patriot Petition Now Public Document," *Woman Patriot*, September 1, 1926, 136.

24. "Petition for the Rejection of the Phipps-Parker Bill," 12918–52.

25. Ibid.

26. Kathryn Kish Sklar, *Florence Kelley and the Nation's Work: The Rise of Women's Political Culture, 1830–1900* (New Haven, Conn.: Yale University Press, 1995); and "Kelley, Florence," in Mari Jo Buhle, Paul Buhle, and Dan Georgakas, eds., *Encyclopedia of the American Left* (Urbana: University of Illinois Press, 1990): 398–399.

27. "Patriot Petition Now Public Document," *Woman Patriot*, September 1, 1926.

28. Grace Brosseau to Madam State Regent, December 16, 1926, Congressional Record, 69th Cong., 2nd sess., January 8, 1927, 1280–81.

29. Cone to Tuttle.

30. Feige to Wells, June 29, 1927.

31. See Folder 11-0-11, Box 321, Central File, 1925–28, Records of the Children's Bureau, RG 102.

32. Mary Kilbreth to Alexander Lincoln, February 1, 1926, Folder 9, Box 2, Alexander Lincoln Papers.

33. Gladys Harris, Executive Secretary to Miss Helen W. Atwater, June 8, 1927,

Frames 276–78, Reel 15, Part 3, Series A, National Office Subject Files, 1920–1932, LWV Papers.

34. Grace Abbott to Morris Sheppard, U.S. Senate, November 23, 1926; Secretary of Labor James J. Davis to Mary G. Kilbreth, December 13, 1926; Katharine Lenroot to Secretary of Labor, December 23, 1926, Folder 1-7-2, Box 265, Central File, 1925–28, Records of the Children's Bureau, RG 102; Muncy, *Creating a Female Dominion*, 129; Grace Abbott to Morris Sheppard, November 23, 1926, Congressional Record, 69th Cong., 2nd sess., December 11, 1926, 290–92.

35. Grace Abbott to Morris Sheppard, November 23, 1926.

36. See Congressional Record, 69th Cong., 2nd sess., January 8–12, 1927; Speech of Hon. William H. King of Utah, "Abolition of the Children's Bureau," Congressional Record, 69th Cong., 2nd sess., January 11, 1927, Oversized Encapsulated Box, Mrs. Reuben Ross Holloway Collection, Fort McHenry, Baltimore, Maryland.

37. Joseph B. Chepaitis, "Federal Social Welfare Progressivism in the 1920s," *Social Service Review* 46, 2 (1972): 222.

38. "Maternity Act Extended and Repealed," *Woman Patriot*, January 15, 1927, 1.

39. "Federal Maternity and Hygiene," *New York Times*, January 18, 1927, 24.

40. Quoted in Chepaitis, "Federal Social Welfare Progressivism," 223.

41. Ladd-Taylor, *Mother-Work*, 188.

42. "Maternity Act Extended and Repealed."

43. Mary Kilbreth to Mrs. B., January 22, 1927, Folder 10, Box 2, Alexander Lincoln Papers.

44. U.S. Senate, A Bill to Repeal the Act Entitled "An Act to Establish in the Department of Commerce and Labor a Bureau to Be Known as the Children's Bureau," 69th Cong., 2nd sess., February 25, 1927, S.5820; U.S. House, A Bill to Reduce Duplication of Governmental Agencies by Transfer of the Functions of the Children's Bureau, 69th Cong., 2nd sess., March 1, 1927, H.R. 17377; U.S. House, A Bill to Abolish the Children's Bureau, 69th Cong., 2nd sess., March 3, 1927, H.R. 17399.

45. "Resolutions Adopted by the Sentinels of the Republic, February 26, 1927, Folder 10, Box 2, Alexander Lincoln Papers; Petition from the Women's Constitutional League of Virginia, March 31, 1927, Folder: 1-6-2, Box 372, Central File, 1929–1932; "U.S. Children's Bureau Defended As Move for Its Abolition Grows," no source, May 14, 1927, Folder: 1-7-2, Box 265, Central File, 1921–1928, Children's Bureau Records; *National Society United States Daughters of 1812, News-letter*, June 1927, 10; "Daughters of 1812 Ask Abolition of Children's Bureau"; "Women's Constitutional League of Maryland"; "North Carolina D.A.R. for Abolition of Children's Bureau"; "Maryland D.A.R. for Local Self Government"; "New Jersey Society Daughters of the American Revolution"; "The Woman's Constitutional League of Virginia"; "Massachusetts Public Interests League," *Woman Patriot*, May 1, 1927. In 1927, the Good Government Club of Kansas also demanded that its state legislature end its appropriations for Sheppard-Towner and asked Senator Charles Curtis to work for the removal of Grace Abbott as head of the Children's Bureau. Good Government Club to Senator Charles Curtis,

January 31, 1927; Good Government Club, Topeka, Kansas, to Members of the Kansas House of Representatives, February 16, 1927, Folder 11-0-11, Box 321, Central File, 1925–1928, Children's Bureau Records.

46. "Care of Maternity Medical, Not Social, Question," *Woman Patriot*, February 1, 1927, 22–23; Elizabeth Lowell Putnam to Mrs. I. O. Price, May 18, 1927, Folder 310, Box 17, Putnam Papers; Elizabeth Lowell Putnam, "Why the Appropriations for the Extension of the Sheppard-Towner Act Should Not Be Granted"; Memo on Errors in "Why the Appropriations for the Extension of the Sheppard-Towner Act Should Not Be Granted," by Mrs. William Lowell Putnam; Grace Abbott to Mr. Ival McPeak, *Christian Register*, February 28, 1927?; S.J. Crumbine, General Executive, American Child Health Association, to Mr. Herter, January 29, 1929, Folder: 11-0-11, Box 321, Central File, 1925–28, Children's Bureau Records; Mrs. Frederick Schoff, "Children's Bureau 'Absolutely Unnecessary,'" *Woman Patriot*, February 1, 1927, 20–21.

47. Elizabeth Lowell Putnam to Dr. Tagliaferro Clarke, May 6, 1927, Folder 511, Box 30; Elizabeth Lowell Putnam to A. Piatt Andrew, March 8, 1929, Folder 288, Box 16, Putnam Papers.

48. Carrie Chapman Catt, "Lies-At-Large," *Woman Citizen*, June 1927, 10–11, 41.

49. See Mrs. S. M. Covington, State Chairman, Department of Legislation, Mississippi Federation of Women's Clubs, October 6, 1927; Miss Margaret C. Maule, The Girls' Friendly Society in America, to Grace Abbott, October 22, 1927, Folder 11-0-11, Box 321; Letter to Henrietta Roeloss, Young Women's Christian Association, February 14, 1928; Mrs. John L. Houston to Chief of the Children's Bureau, April 15, 1928, Folder: 11-0-11, Box 320, Central File, 1925–28, Children's Bureau Records.

50. Mrs. Robbins Gilman, General Secretary, Women's Cooperative Alliance, Minneapolis, Minnesota, to Grace Abbott, March 21, 1928, Folder 1-7-2, Box 265, Central File, 1921–1928, Children's Bureau Records.

51. Mrs. Jean T. Dillon, Director, Division of Child Hygiene and Public Health Nursing, Department of Health, State of West Virginia, January 29, 1927, Folder 11-0-11, Box 321, Central File 1925–28; See also C. F. Kendall, M.D., Commissioner, State Department of Health, Augusta, Maine to Grace Abbott, January 17, 1928, Folder 1-7-2, Box 265, Central File, 1921–1928, Children's Bureau Records.

52. Grace Brosseau to Madam State Regent, December 16, 1926, Congressional Record, 69th Cong., 2nd sess., January 8, 1927, 1280–81; Katherine T. Balch to Alexander Lincoln, December 20, 1926, Folder 9; Mary Kilbreth to Balch, January 22, 1927, Folder 10, Box 2, Alexander Lincoln Papers; "Communism in Government," Prepared for DAR Program in December, 1926 and Presented by the Paul Revere Chapter, Muncie, Indiana, DAR publications folder, box 1, Bailie Papers.

53. Minutes of the WJCC, April 11, 1927, Frame 757, Reel 3, The Records of the Women's Joint Congressional Committee; Mary Anderson to Mrs. Robins, April 26, 1927, Frame 521, Reel 3, Mary Anderson Papers.

54. Mrs. Edwin C. Gregory, "Report of Committee on Legislation in United

States Congress," DAR *Proceedings of the Thirty-Sixth Continental Congress* (April 18–23, 1927): 380.

55. Annual Message of the President General, Mrs. Alfred J. Brosseau, DAR *Proceedings of the Thirty-Sixth Continental Congress*, 27.

56. Captain George L. Darte, "Subversive Influences," DAR *Proceedings of the Thirty-Sixth Continental Congress*, 406–16; Norman Hapgood, ed., *Professional Patriots* (New York: Albert and Charles Boni, 1928), 172–74.

57. Darte, "Subversive Influences."

58. Mary Anderson to Dr. Parker, April 22, 1927, Frames 310–11, Reel 1; Mary Anderson to Mrs. Robins, April 26, 1927, Frame 521, Reel 3, Mary Anderson Papers.

59. DAR *Proceedings of the Thirty-Sixth Continental Congress*, 420–21.

60. Anderson to Parker, April 22, 1927; Anderson to Robins, April 26, 1927.

61. For example, see Katharine Lenroot to Mrs. H.G. Moore, Charlotte, North Carolina, May 6, 1927, Folder 1-0-11, Box 321; Katharine Lenroot to Mrs. John L. Houston, April 20, 1928, Folder: 11-0-11, Box 320; Grace Abbott to Hon. C. Ellis Moore, Cambridge, Ohio, May 28, 1927; Katharine Lenroot to Aimee Zillmer, March 16, 1928, Folder 1-7-2, Box 265, Central File 1925–28; Grace Abbott to Fletcher Harper Swift, May 23, 1927, Folder 1-6-2, Box 372, Central File, 1929–32, Children's Bureau Records.

62. Press Release from the U.S. Department of Labor Children's Bureau, October 15, 1928, Folder: 11-0-11, Box 320, Central File 1925–28, Children's Bureau Records.

63. Grace Abbott to Fletcher Harper Swift, October 21, 1929, Folder 1-6-2, Box 372, Central File, 1929–32, Children's Bureau Records. In terms of countering the personal attacks made on her, Abbott wrote that she had never issued a public refutation because "I was not willing to assume that a denial was necessary." See Grace Abbott to Mr. Arthur Dunham, Secretary, Child Welfare Division, Public Charities Association of Pennsylvania, December 30, 1927, Folder 11-0-11, Box 321, Central File, 1925–28, Children's Bureau Records.

64. Memorandum concerning the trend in maternal and infant mortality rates 1921 to 1925, May 6, 1927, Folder 11-0-11, Box 321, Central File, 1925–28, Children's Bureau Records; Press Release from the U.S. Department of Labor Children's Bureau, October 15, 1928; "A Study of Patriotic Propaganda," Information Service, Department of Research and Education, Federal Council of the Churches of Christ in America (FCCCA), vol. 7, no. 18, May 5, 1928, Folder: "A Study of Patriotic Propaganda," Box: Attacks, Attacks on WIL, 1924–39, Attacks on Jane Addams et al., Special Attacks Collection, SCPC.

65. Catt, "Lies-At-Large."

66. Ethel Smith to Mrs. Alfred J. Brosseau, April 22, 1927, Frame 606, Reel 1, WJCC Records.

67. Mrs. Alfred J. Brosseau to Ethel Smith, April 28, 1927, Frame 609; Helen Atwater, Chairman, to Mrs. Alfred J. Brosseau, President General, April 29, 1927, Frame 609; Atwater to Brosseau, May 3, 1927, Frame 612; Brosseau to Atwater, May 3, 1927,

Frame 613; Atwater to Brosseau, May 6, 1927, Frame 617; Atwater to Brosseau, June 7, 1927, Frame 631; Brosseau to Atwater, June 8, 1927, Frame 641, Reel 1, WJCC Records.

68. "Measures for Child Welfare Involve State Women Leaders in Lively Exchange of Letters," Newark, New Jersey, July 31, 1927, Frames 000049–51, Reel 18, Container 28, Subject Files: Women's Organizations, attacks on, Catt Papers.

69. Meeting of the Board of Directors, May 2, 1927, Frames 101–2, Reel 4, Part 1, Meetings of the Board of Directors and the Executive Committees, Minutes and Related Documents, 1918–1974, LWV Papers.

70. "Who Are the Patriots?" New Jersey League of Women Voters, August 27, 1927, Folder: 1-7-2, Box 265, Central File, 1921–28, Children's Bureau Records.

71. Marguerite Wells to Belle Sherwin, May 9, 1927, Frames 853–54, Reel 9, Part 3, Series A, National Office Subject Files, 1920–1932, LWV Papers.

72. Belle Sherwin to Miss Marguerite M. Wells, February 11, 1927, Frames 840–841, Reel 9, Part 3, Series A, National Office Subject Files, 1920–1932, LWV Papers.

73. "Statement by Mary W. Miller," June 13, 1928, Folder: Blacklist-Affidavits, Box 2, Bailie Papers; Matter of Charges of Executive Committee of National Society of the Daughters of the American Revolution against Helen Tufts Bailie, Folder: Blacklist Charges—DAR vs. Helen Tufts Bailie, Box 2, Bailie Collection.

74. "Matter of Charges of Executive Committee of National Society of the Daughters of the American Revolution against Helen Tufts Bailie," Folder: Blacklist Charges—D.A.R. vs. Helen Tufts Bailie, Box 2, Bailie Papers.

75. Carrie Chapman Catt, "Lies-At-Large," *Woman Citizen*, June 1927, 10–11, 41.

76. Carrie Chapman Catt, "An Open Letter to the D.A.R.," *Woman Citizen*, July 1927, 11–12, 41–42.

77. "DAR Here in Revolt Against Parent Society," *Boston Herald*, February 22, 1928, Folder: Clippings-DAR, Box 1, Helen Tufts Bailie Collection; "Noted Men Declared Blacklisted by D.A.R.," Folder: NCPW Attacks, D.A.R., Box 494, NCPW Collection.

78. "DAR Accused in Blacklist Expose," *Washington Times*, Monday, April 2, 1928; "Members Get D.A.R. Protest over Blacklist," *New York Herald Tribune*, April 9, 1928, Folder: Clippings, DAR, Box 1, Bailie Papers; see also "DAR Leader Attacks 'Blacklisting' Policy," *Daily Palo Alto Times*, April 2, 1928; "DAR Adds Notables to Its Blacklists," *San Francisco Chronicle*, April 3, 1928; "DAR Rulers Called Dupes of Anti-Reds," April 9, 1928; "Blacklist Was Born in Tiny Hub Office," *Boston Daily Advertiser*, April 5, 1928, 3; "Here Is Entire D.A.R. Blacklist, Women's Secret Roll at Last Made Public," *Boston Daily Advertiser*, April 3, 1928; "D.A.R. Roll of 'Doubtful' Women," *Boston Daily Advertiser*, April 5, 1928, 3, Folder 7, DAR Blacklist Controversy Papers.

79. Helen Tufts Bailie, "Our Threatened Heritage," April 5, 1928, Folder: Publications—Helen Tufts Bailie, Box 1, Bailie Papers.

80. Blacklists. Folder: The "Blacklist"—men, women, organizations, Box 2, Bailie Papers.

81. Emily F. Hurd, State Chairman National Defense, to Mrs. Fiske, April 11, 1927,

Folder: Correspondence, HTB, 1927–30, 1931, 1937, 1947, Box 2, Bailie Papers; see Delegard, "Woman Patriots," chap. 5, "Stopping Words: The Censorship Campaign."

82. "A Study of Patriotic Propaganda," (FCCCA).

83. Elizabeth McCausland, "The Blue Menace," *Springfield Republican*, March 19–27, 1928, Folder: "Magazine Articles, DAR Scandal," Box 1, Bailie Papers.

84. Rene Parks Mackay, "Upholds the DAR," *Boston Daily Advertiser*, May 5, 1928, Frame 342, Reel 46, Maud May (Wood) Park Papers.

85. "Pacifists in the DAR," Washington, April 15, 1928, Folder 7, DAR Blacklist Controversy Papers.

86. Allen F. Davis, *American Heroine: The Life and Legend of Jane Addams* (New York: Oxford University Press, 1973), 252–54; Carrie A. Foster, *The Women and the Warriors: The U.S. Section of the Women's International League for Peace and Freedom, 1915–1940* (Syracuse, N.Y.: Syracuse University Press, 1995), 36.

87. Hurd to Fiske, April 11, 1927.

88. Other organizations distributing blacklists included the Industrial Defense Association, the Massachusetts Public Interests League, the American Legion Auxiliary, and the Daughters of 1812. See McCausland, "The Blue Menace"; "A Study of Patriotic Propaganda" Folder: "Magazine Articles, DAR scandal; "Pastor Root Sounds Alarm of 'Blue Menace' to Free Speech," *Boston Herald*, March 13, 1928, Folder: Clippings, DAR. Box 1. Bailie Papers; Oswald Garrison Villard, "What the Blue Menace Means," *Harper's Magazine*, October 1928, Folder 13, Box 1, DAR Blacklist Controversy papers; *National Society United States Daughters of 1812 News-letter* 5, 2 (December 1927); Cudworth to Tower, December 14, 1927, Folder: Jung, Harry, Box: Attackers—American Coalition, Jung, Harry, Special Attacks Collection, SCPC; "Urge Effort to Check Pacifism, Legion Speakers Find 'Red' Streak in Literature of Two Organizations," *News and Observer*, November 23, 1926, 1; Paul Murphy, *The Meaning of Freedom of Speech: First Amendment Freedoms from Wilson to FDR* (Westport, Conn.: Greenwood., 1972), 200.

89. President General Brosseau asserted at the 1928 DAR national convention that the organization "has no such thing as a 'black list'" but that it does have "a perfect right to say who shall speak before its meetings." See "D.A.R. Backs 'Black Lists' by Inference," *Springfield Weekly Republican*, April 26, 1928, Folder 7, DAR Blacklist Controversy Papers; "DAR President Defends Blacklist," *Boston Daily Advertiser*, April 3, 1928, Frame 338, Reel 46, Maud May (Wood) Park Papers.

90. Remarks by Mrs. George Thatcher Guernsey, Honorary President General, DAR, at the Congress in Washington, D.C., April 17, 1928, reported by Eleanor S. P. St. Omer Roy, Frame 830, Folder 17, Box 5, Reel 42, Series C., Correspondence, WILPF-U.S. Section; "DAR Head Raps Blacklist Critic," April 5, 1928, Folder: clippings-DAR, Box 1; Statement by Mary W. Miller June 13, 1928, Folder: Blacklist—Affidavits; Mrs. J. A. St. Omer Roy to Mrs. William H. Adams, May 28, 1928, Folder: Roy, Eleanor Patterson (Mrs. St. Omer), Correspondence, 1928, Box 2, Bailie Papers; Helena Huntington Smith, "Mrs. Brosseau and the D.A.R.," *Outlook and Independent*, March 20,

1929, Folder 13, Box 1, DAR Blacklist Controversy Papers; Mrs. Edward P. Pendleton, State Chairman Kansas DAR National Defense Committee to Madam Regent, April 11, 1927, reprinted in Statement to the National Board of Management, NSDAR from Mrs. Mary P. Macfarland, September 28, 1928, Folder 6, Box 1, DAR Blacklist Controversy Papers; "New York D.A.R. Has Blacklist, Regent Reveals," April 4, 1928, Folder: NCPW Attacks, D.A.R., Box 494, NCPW Collection.

91. Helen Tufts Bailie, "Perverted Patriotism, a Story of DAR Stewardship," November 11, 1929, Folder: Publications—DAR, Box 1, Bailie Papers.

92. "The 'Blacklist' Again," Information Service, Department of Research and Education, FCCCA, vol. 7, no. 40, November 3, 1928, Microfilm Reel 40, Personal Press Clipping scrapbooks, Schwimmer-Lloyd Collection; Arthur Sears Henning, "Pacifism Kept Alive by Fifty Organizations," Folder: Publications—D.A.R.; "The Common Enemy," Folder: Marvin, Fred R., Box 1, Bailie Papers; Statement by Mary W. Miller, June 13, 1928, Folder: Blacklists-Affidavits, Box 2, Bailie Collection; Petition of the directors of the Woman Patriot Publishing Company, reprinted from Congressional Record, 69th Cong., 1st sess., 12946 (distributed by DAR chapters); McCausland, "The Blue Menace"; Margaret Cobb, "The Soviet of Lady Patriots," *American Mercury* 15, 57 (September 1928); Smith, "Mrs. Brosseau and the D.A.R."

93. See Mrs. Mary P. Macfarland, Statement to the National Board of Management, September 28, 1928, Folder 6; Smith, "Mrs. Brosseau and the D.A.R."; Ellen Starr Brinton, "The DAR Reaches Middle Age," Folder: Ellen Starr Brinton, Unpublished works, DAR, Box 2: Writings and Research," Ellen Starr Brinton Collection, SCPC.

94. Illinois State National Defense Committee to Mrs. C. E. Baldwin, June 14, 1928, Folder: Correspondence, A-Z, Box 2, Bailie Papers; Letter from Mrs. William Sherman Walker, February 25, 1927, quoted in Macfarland, "Statement to the National Board of Management," ; Cobb, "The Soviet of Lady Patriots"; Smith, "Mrs. Brosseau and the D.A.R.," Folder 13, Box 1, DAR Blacklist Controversy Papers.

95. "Dr. Stidger Charges New D.A.R. Blacklist," *Boston Globe*, October 21, 1929, Folder: Clippings, DAR, Box 1, Bailie Papers.

96. Resolution by Abigail Wolcott Ellsworth Chapter, DAR, December 19, 1927, Folder: 1-7-2, Box 265, Central File, 1921–1928, Children's Bureau Records; "A Study of Patriotic Propaganda"; Villard, "What the Blue Menace Means"; Smith, "Mrs. Brosseau and the D.A.R.," Folder 13, Box 1, DAR Blacklist Controversy Papers; Gladys K. Gould Mackenzie, NCPW, to Dear Friend, February 18, 1928, Folder 3: Correspondence, 1926–1929," box 6, reel 3, Mead Papers; "Pacifist's Speech Fought by Jersey D.A.R., Legion"; Bailie, "Perverted Patriotism"; "Windsor, Conn., D.A.R. Rebuked by Chamber of Commerce" and "New Jersey Regent of D.A.R. Protests Address by Frederick J. Libby Before Orange School," *National Council for Prevention of War News Bulletin*, April 1, 1928, Folder: NCPW Attacks, The D.A.R. Sees Red; "Libby's Talk Heard by 125"; "Defies D.A.R. Protest in World Peace Talk", Folder: NCPW Attacks, D.A.R., 1924–1938; "Republican Women Now Protest Libby Lecture in East Orange," Folder: NCPW Attacks, D.A.R., Box 494; "Legion

Won't Oppose Libby, East Orange Post Declines to Support D.A.R.'s Protest," April 16, 1928, Folder: NCPW Attacks, American Legion Clippings, Box 492, NCPW Collection.

97. Darte, "Subversive Influences." See also Address of Mrs. William Sherman Walker, Ohio DAR State Conference, Columbus, March 16, 1927, Folder: Publications—DAR, Box 1, Bailie Papers; "Statement by Mary W. Miller," June 13, 1928; "Charge Jane Addams Silent as U.S. Flag Was Belittled," *Boston Herald*, March 19, 1925, Folder: Attacks on Jane Addams, Box: Attacks, Attacks Collection, SCPC.

98. Mead was prominent in both WILPF and the National Council for Prevention of War, an umbrella organization that included both men's and women's peace groups. "Message of Woman 'Radical' Termed Menace to Student," *Atlanta Constitution*, December 5, 1926, 1.

99. Ida Floyd White, State Regent, Florida DAR, Jacksonville, Florida, to President, Rollins College, August 20, 1926, Folder 3: Correspondence, 1926–29, Box 6, Reel 3, Mead Papers.

100. Joan M. Jensen, "All Pink Sisters: The War Department and the Feminist Movement in the 1920s," in Lois Scharf and Joan M. Jensen, eds., *Decades of Discontent: The Women's Movement, 1920–1940* (Boston: Northeastern University Press, 1983), 201; "Mrs. Lucia Ames Mead," National Publicity Committee of the R.O.A., August 17, 1926; Dossier on Lucia Ames Mead, letter from George Darte, Military Order of the World War, to Mrs. Alfred Brosseau, July 21, 1926, Folder: NCPW, Attacks on Mrs. Lucia Ames Mead by Various Patriotic Groups, 1926–1928, Box 496, NCPW Collection; John M. Craig, "Redbaiting, Pacifism, and Free Speech: Lucia Aimes Mead and Her 1926 Lecture Tour in Atlanta and the Southeast," *Georgia Historical Quarterly* 71 (Winter 1987): 601–22.

101. Craig, "Red-Baiting, Pacifism, and Free Speech," 609.

102. "'1924,' Communication. To the Editor of the Monadnock Breeze," by Lucia Ames Mead. Folder: Lucia Ames Mead, Clippings, 1922–23–24–27, Box 15: Lucia Ames Mead, Printed Articles, 1922–1936, Reel 10, Mead Papers.

103. "Mrs. Lucia Ames Mead"; Dossier on Lucia Ames Mead, Darte to Brosseau, July 21, 1926.

104. Mrs. Edwin C. Gregory, "Report of the North Carolina State Regent," DAR *Proceedings of the Thirty-Sixth Continental Congress*, 287–98; John A. Livingstone, "Suggest Mrs. Gregory as Committee Woman," *Raleigh News and Observer*, February 3, 1928, 2.

105. Villard, "What the Blue Menace Means."

106. Ibid.; Margaret Gibbs, *The DAR* (New York: Holt, Rinehart, and Wilson, 1969), 112–13.

107. "Argument for World Peace Is Presented," *Greensboro Daily News*, November 22, 1926; "Unduly Alarmed?"; "Greensboro College Hears Boston Woman"; "Rumblings Against the Doctrine of Pacifists in This City Include Objections to Anti-War Talk"; "Mrs. Mead Says There Is No Need for War and Law Should Be the Duplicate,"

*High Point Enterprise*, November 24, 1926; "Freedom of Speech in America Discussed by Mrs. Lucia Ames Mead in Connection with Discourtesy Shown Her in Atlanta," *Columbus Enquirer-Sun*, January 9, 1927, Folder: NCPW, Attacks on Mrs. Lucia Ames Mead, Box 496; Lucia Ames Mead to Miss Gould, November 27, 1926, Box 54, Reel 43, NCPW; Craig, "Redbaiting, Pacifism, and Free Speech," 610.

108. "Woman Lecturer Barred as 'Red' at Agnes Scott," *Atlanta Constitution*, December 4, 1926, 1; Office Secretary to Lucia Ames Mead, November 20, 1926, Box 54, Reel 43, NCPW Collection.

109. "Mrs. Lucia A. Mead Spoke at Liberal Christian Sunday," *Atlanta Constitution*, December 6, 1926; "Atlanta Ministers Vote Approval of Mrs. Mead's Views," December 6, 1926, Folder: NCPW, Attacks on Mrs. Lucia Ames Mead, Box 496, NCPW Collection.

110. Murphy, *The Meaning of Freedom of Speech*; Craig, "Redbaiting, Pacifism, and Free Speech."

111. Regional concerns were particularly pronounced in this incident in Greenville, where Landrum organized the usual array of antiradical groups along with the United Daughters of the Confederacy, a rare participant in the censorship campaign, even in the South. These activists cited Mead's views on race as one of the most important reasons to keep her from speaking to the people of Greenville. Representatives of the NCPW responded to the charges against Mead by denying that the organization advocated the "equality of the negro." "Oppose Plans to Allow Woman to Make Talk Here," *Greenville, South Carolina News*, December 11, 1926; Frederick J. Libby to Editor, *Greenville News*, December 20, 1926; Ruth Hanna, Y.W.C.A., Greenville, South Carolina to Miss Gladys Gould, NCPW, December 17, 1926; Libby to Hanna, December 20, 1926, Folder: NCPW, Attacks on Mrs. Lucia Ames Mead by Various Patriotic Groups, 1926–1928, Box 496, NCPW Collection.

112. Other people she named included Mr. Holmes, Mr. Lovett, Mr. Villard, Sherwood Eddy, Rabbi Stephen S. Wise, Mrs. L. K. Elmhirst, Stanley High, and Sarah Bard Field. "New Jersey D.A.R. Surrenders to Blacklist Hysteria," Lucia Ames Mead Clippings, 1919–1928–1929–1930, Box 15 Lucia Ames Mead, Printed Articles, 1922–1936, Reel 10, Mead Papers.

113. "New Jersey D.A.R. Surrenders to Blacklist Hysteria"; "Open Letter to Mrs. Lila M. Houston by Mrs. Helen Brumley Baldwin," *Boonton Times*, Folder 5, Box 17, Mead Papers; Arthur Garfield Hays, *Trial by Prejudice* (New York: Covici, Friede, 1933); "More 'Red' Alarms," *Woman's Journal* 13, 11 (November 28): 27, n.d., typewritten copy, Folder 14; "Heresy Hunters' Blacklist Seen to Cover Wide Range," *New York World*, February 13, 1928, Folder 7, Box 1, DAR "Blacklist" Controversy papers; "The 'Blacklist' Again," Reel 40, Personal Press Clipping scrapbooks, Schwimmer-Lloyd Collection; Craig, "Red-Baiting, Pacifism, and Free Speech," 621; David J. Goldberg, "Passaic Textile Strike of 1926," in Buhle, Buhle, and Georgakas, eds., *Encyclopedia of the American Left*.

114. Bailie, "Our Threatened Heritage"; "Blacklists Spur Patriot Bodies to Bar

Speakers," *New York World*, February 16, 1928, Folder: Schwimmer-Lloyd Collection Scrapbooks, Topic Series, Patrioteers, Box N265, Morgue Files, Schwimmer-Lloyd Collection; Smith, "Mrs. Brosseau and the D.A.R."; Villard, "What the Blue Menace Means."

115. "Woman's Talk Canceled Because She's Pacifist," *Milwaukee Wisconsin News*, November 13, 1929; "Pacifist Flays Legion Here," *Milwaukee Wisconsin News*, November 12, 1929, Folder: American Legion (2) Box: Attackers—American Legion— National—Local Branches, American Legion Material on Peace, Special Collection: Attacks, SCPC; "Peace Worker Cancels Talk," *Milwaukee Journal*, November 10, 1929; "Bar Pacifist from Meeting," *Milwaukee Sentinel*, November 10, 1929; "Pacifist Irked by Talk Ban," *Milwaukee Sentinel*, November 11, 1929; "Woman Pacifist Barred as D.A.R., Legion Protest," November 11, 1929; "Explain Stand on Pacifism," *Milwaukee Journal*, November 11, 1929; "Barred, Says Legion, D.A.R., 'Run County'," *Milwaukee Leader*, November 11, 1929, "Attacks NCPW, Attacks on Eleanor Brannan, 1929," Folder, Box 493, NCPW Collection.

116. "Adequate Defense Plea Is Delivered by Mrs. Brosseau," *Evening Star*, April 16, 1928, Folder: NCPW Attacks, DAR, 1924–1938, Box 494, NCPW Collection. At the same time as Grace Brosseau was fighting the blacklist controversy, she was in the midst of divorce proceedings, which she initiated after her husband struck her in the face. Her divorce was finally granted in 1930 after she had finished her term as DAR president general. "Mrs. Brosseau Gets Uncontested Divorce," *New York Times*, October 3, 1930, Subject files: Women's Organizations, attacks on, Container 28, Reel 17, Catt Papers.

117. "DAR Regents Praise Activity for Defense," *Washington Post*, April 15, 1928; "DAR Backs 'Black Lists' by Inference," April 26, 1928; "Blacklist Sustained by D.A.R.," *Palo Alto Times*, April 20, 1928; "Rebellion Against Blacklist of DAR Breaks in Conclave," unknown, April 19, 1928; "DAR Sess. Names Seven New Leaders," *San Francisco Chronicle*, April 20, 1928, all in Folder 7, DAR Blacklist Controversy Papers; Eleanor S. P. St. Omer Roy to Mrs. Howard A. Steele, May 8, 1928, Frame 943; Eleanor S. P. St. Omer Roy to Molly Foster Berry Chapter, DAR, April 1928, Folder 26, Box 8, Reel 47, Series C., Correspondence, WILPF-U.S. Section; "D.A.R. Chapter Gets Back-Wash on 'Black-Lists,'" *Norwalk, Ohio Reflector Herald*, May 14, 1928, Folder: Clippings-D.A.R. Box 1, Bailie Papers.

118. Macfarland was expelled on October 31, 1928. For both of these expulsions, see "DAR Launches Ouster Move on 'Black List' Foe," April 27, 1928; "D.A.R. Lays Charges Against Mrs. Bailie," *New York Times*, April 28, 1928; "DAR Insurgent Chief Who Bared 'Blacklist' Now Faces Discipline," *Palo Alto Times*, April 28, 1928, all in Folder 7, DAR Blacklist Controversy Papers; "Mrs. Macfarland Expelled from D.A.R. for Criticism"; "Lists 28 Societies on D.A.R. Blacklist," *New York Times*, September 30, 1928; "The Bailie Case," *Springfield Republican*; "DAR Board Seeks to Oust Mrs. Bailie"; "Mrs. Bailie Loses; Expelled by DAR," *New York World*, June 23, 1928; "Calls D.A.R. Report of Trial in Error," *Baltimore Sun*, June 14, 1928; "D.A.R Will Try Mem-

bers Today in Blacklist Case"; "The Trial of Mrs. Bailie," *Springfield Republican*, June 23, 1928; "Mrs. Bailie Renews Blacklist Charges," *New York Times*, June 24, 1928; "DAR Board Sifts 'Black-list' Case," *Washington Star*, June 22, 1928; "DAR Board Hears Testimony in Bailie Case for 7 Hours," *Washington Post*, June 22, 1928; "DAR Board Expels Mrs. Helen T. Bailie in 'Blacklist' Case," June 23, 1928, Folder: Clippings—D.A.R, Box 1; "Insurgent D.A.R. Explains Her Aims in Defying Leaders"; "The 'Black-List' Fight Goes On," *Outlook*, July 4, 1928, Folder: Magazine Articles, D.A.R Scandal, Box 1; "Letter to the National Board of Management," April 21, 1928; Sadie Earle, "Findings of the Executive Committee of the National Society, Daughters of the American Revolution, in the Matter of Charges Filed Against Mrs. Mary P. Macfarland," Folder: Macfarland, Mary Perley; Earle to Bailie, June 16, 1928, Folder: Blacklist Charges—D.A.R vs. Helen Tufts Bailie, Box 2, Bailie Papers; "DAR Expels N.J. Member," *Boston Herald*, November 12, 1928, Frame 343, Reel 46. Maud May (Wood) Park Papers.

119. Sworn statement from Agnes J. Pember, June 16, 1928, Folder: Pember, Agnes Cushing; Statement by Mary W. Miller," June 13, 1928; "DAR Board Sifts 'Black-list' Case"; "Lists 28 Societies on D.A.R. Blacklist"; "The Bailie Case"; Bradley Stone, Letter to the Editor, "Behind the Blacklist," *Springfield Republican*, April 14, 1928; "New Haven D.A.R. Leaders Resign," *N. Star*, May 30, 1928; "D.A.R. Chapter Gets Back-Wash on 'Black-Lists'"; "Mrs. Whitney Criticizes Bailie Trial," Folder: Clippings, DAR, Box 1, Bailie Papers; "DAR News Letter No. III," Northampton, Massachusetts, October 25, 1928, Folder 2; Macfarland, "Statement to the National Board of Management, " Folder 6; Resolution of the Palo Alto Chapter of the DAR, Folder 3; Oregon Lewis and Clark Chapter, DAR, to Mrs. Alfred Brosseau, April 17, 1928, Folder 5, DAR Blacklist Controversy Papers.

120. Mrs. Alfred J. Brosseau to Mrs. J. A. St. Omer Roy, March 3, 1928, Frame 889, Folder 26, Box 8, Reel 47, Series C, WILPF-U.S. Section.

121. Remarks by Mrs. George Thatcher Guernsey of Kansas, reported by Eleanor P. St. Omer Roy, April 17, 1928, Frame 830, Folder 17, Box 5, Reel 42, Series C, Correspondence, WILPF-U.S. Section.

122. Nell Battle Lewis, "Incidentally," *Raleigh News and Observer*, November 13, 1927, 3; Writing before the blacklist controversy, Lewis was an early progressive voice calling for a realignment of women's politics. She declared that "it would be an excellent thing to have a general house-cleaning in the organizations, which would sweep the reactionaries out of the progressive ones and the progressives out of the reactionary."

123. Mary Woolley and Jane Addams, for instance, were DAR members who were blacklisted. The husband of a DAR member in New Haven, Yale economist Irving Fisher, was also blacklisted. See "Daughter's Revolution," *Time*, May 14, 1928, Folder: Clippings, D.A.R., Box 1 Bailie Papers. The DAR did everything to discourage public dissent on the part of its members. See Florence G. Adams to Mrs. Bailie, June 13, 1928, Folder: Correspondence—Adams to H.T.B., 1928–29, Box 2, Bailie Papers.

124. Brinton, "The DAR Reaches Middle Age"; Jane Addams, *The Second Twenty*

*Years at Hull House: September 1909 to September 1929, With a Record of a Growing World Consciousness* (New York: Macmillan, 1930). Other WILPF members who were also members of the DAR included Eleanor St. Omer Roy; Mrs. Lucy Biddle Lewis, a Delaware resident; Mrs. Emma Guffey Miller, of Pennsylvania, who was also prominent in Democratic Party circles; Helen Tufts Bailie had left WILPF before the blacklist controversy began. Another woman prominent in progressive politics who stayed in the DAR until at least 1929 was Catherine Waugh McCulloch. Viola C. Reeling to McCulloch, January 23, 1929, Frame 286, Catherine Waugh McCulloch segment of the Mary Earhart Dillon Collection, Reel E17, Series 1, Part E, Women's Studies Manuscript Collections, Schlesinger Library.

125. Mrs. Raymond Robins to Ethel Smith, May 6, 1927, Frames 161–62, Reel 31, Margaret Dreier Robins Papers, WTUL Papers.

126. Eleanor S. P. St. Omer Roy to Mrs. Howard A. Steele, May 9, 1928, Frames 943–46, Folder 26, Box 8, Reel 47, Series C, Correspondence, WILPF-U.S. Section.

127. "Nationally Prominent Women's Leader Quits D.A.R. Because of Blacklist"; "Dr. Parker Attacks D.A.R. and Resigns," *Washington Herald*, February 10, 1930; "D.A.R. Opposes Peace, Dr. Parker Says, Explaining Why She Quit Order," *New York Telegram*, February 10, 1930, Folder: Clippings, D.A.R., Box 1, Bailie Papers.

128. Elaine Goodale Eastman, "Are DAR Women Exploited?" reprinted from *Christian Century*, September 11, 1929, Folder: Magazine Articles, DAR Scandal, Box 1, Bailie Papers. Kim Nielsen shows how members of both WILPF and the DAR joined the League of Women Voters in Sioux City, Iowa, during the 1920s. By analyzing the battle between antiradicals and progressives for control of the local chapter, Nielsen illuminates the complicated web of overlapping allegiances maintained by many middle-class women. See Kim E. Nielsen, "Dangerous Iowa Women: Pacifism, Patriotism, and the Woman-Citizen in Sioux City, 1920–1927," *Annals of Iowa* 56 (Winter/Spring 1997): 80–98.

129. Evidence about the multiple allegiances of the committee of protest leadership is most plentiful. Eleanor Roy was a staff member for WILPF, the GFWC, and the National Woman's Party. Mary Macfarland was a leading member of the American Association of University Women, the LWV, and the New Jersey Federation of Women's Clubs. Bailie joined WILPF and renewed her membership in the DAR almost simultaneously, although she resigned WILPF before the blacklist controversy. Another protester, Mary Miller, was state president of the LWV and a member of the GFWC. Elaine Eastman, who became responsible for the DAR protest newsletter, was a member of the LWV. See "Statement by Mary W. Miller," June 13, 1928. Georgina Root was an advocate of the Child Labor Amendment and a member of the WCTU. See Statement by Georgina Root to the Members of the Anne Adams-Tufts Chapter, D.A.R., October 10, 1929, Folder: Publications—D.A.R., Box 1, Bailie Papers.

130. For a larger account of the way that progressive women activists absorbed the racial attitudes of American imperialism and Jim Crow, see Louise Newman, *White*

*Women's Rights: The Racial Origins of Feminism in the United States* (New York: Oxford University Press, 1999).

131. "D.A.R. Ignores Black List to Hear Mt. Holyoke Head," *Springfield Republican*, March 14, 1930, Folder: Clippings, D.A.R., Box 1, Bailie Papers.

132. Journal of Helen Tufts Bailie, November 4, 1926, Folder: Journal, 1921–27, Box 3, Bailie Papers.

133. Catt to Burton, April 19, 1926, Frame 213–5, Reel 9, LWV Papers; Mead to Gould, November 27, 1926, Box 54, Reel 43, NCPW Collection.

134. Mrs. Mary P. Macfarland, "To Members of the Daughters of the American Revolution," March 10, 1928, Folder: Publications—D.A.R., Box 1; Mary P. Macfarland, "To the Members of the DAR," April 5, 1928, Folder: Macfarland, Mary Perley, Box 2, Bailie Papers; Mary P. Macfarland, "Statement to the National Board of Management, NSDAR, September 28, 1928, Folder 6, Box 1, DAR Blacklist Controversy Papers.

135. Journal of Helen Tufts Bailie, March 27, 1927,.

136. See, for example, "Mrs. Eastman on Ideals of D.A.R.," Folder: Clippings-D.A.R., Box 1, Bailie Papers; Helen Tufts Bailie, "Perverted Patriotism," *Christian Leader*, July 14, 1928, Folder 13, Box 1, DAR Blacklist Controversy Papers.

137. Eleanor S. P. St. Omer Roy to Mrs. Howard A. Steele, May 9, 1928, Frames 943–46, Folder 26, Box 8, Reel 47, Series C, Correspondence, WILPF-U.S. Section.

138. "D.A.R. Here in Revolt Against Parent Society," *Boston Herald*, February 22, 1928, Folder: Clippings, D.A.R., Box 1, Bailie Papers.

139. Journal of Helen Tufts Bailie, December 21, 1925.

140. When some DAR dissenters left the original organization, they attempted to form a parallel organization also based on hereditary qualifications, but which would be dedicated to progressive rather than antiradical causes. "D.A.R. Dissenters to Form Own Group," Folder: NCPW Attacks, D.A.R., 1924–1938, Box 494, NCPW Collection.

141. Helen Tufts Bailie, for instance, said that she wanted to preserve the DAR work greeting immigrants on Ellis Island and conducting Americanization classes for them, promoting the study of the Constitution, and preserving the "ideals and memory of our ancestors." See Journal of Helen Tufts Bailie, January 4, 1928; "Mrs. Eastman on Ideals of D.A.R.," Folder: Clippings-D.A.R. Box 1, Bailie Papers.

142. Journal of Helen Tufts Bailie, May 19, 1925, April 12, May 15, July 22, 1927.

143. Letter from Helen Tufts Bailie to Hon. Samuel Dickstein, Committee on Immigration and Naturalization, U.S. Congress, House of Representatives, Committee on Immigration and Naturalization, *To Reconcile Naturalization Procedure with the Bill of Rights*, 72nd Cong., 1st sess., January 26, 27, 1932, 234.

144. Helen Tufts Bailie, "My Appeal," April 15, 1929, Folder: Publications-Helen Tufts Bailie. Box 1, Bailie Papers.

145. Journal of Helen Tufts Bailie; "Bailie, William," in *Who's Who in America*, vol. 15, *1928–1929*, ed. Albert Nelson Marquis (Chicago: Marquis, 1929), 211.

146. Journal of Helen Tufts Bailie, March 17, April 7, June 21, September 3, 1927. Bailie seemed aware of her own racism yet not particularly disturbed by it. Her journal of

April 7, 1927, recorded her reaction to an African American poet who read at a meeting of the Arlington Women's Club. "He spoke well, and without the faintest whine, —an upstanding young fellow of 23, an octaroon, or lighter. I think I shall have to abandon all prejudice against negroid features and shape of head. His pointed cranium and broad, flat face hide the brains of a real poet."

147. Ibid., June 20, June 17, October 20, 1925; February 13, 1926; May 19, 1925.

148. Carrie Chapman Catt, "For a Better America," Folder: Speeches, International Woman Suffrage Alliance, 1908–1923, Box 1, Carrie Chapman Catt Collection, Sophia Smith Collection.

149. Haynie Summers, "Opposition That Helped Mrs. Mead," *Christian Leader*, December 25, 1926, Folder 5: Attacks on Mrs. Mead, Box 17, Reel 10, Papers of Edwin Doak and Lucia Ames Mead; Craig, "Redbaiting, Pacifism, and Free Speech," 620.

150. Craig, "Redbaiting, Pacifism, and Free Speech," 610; "Message of Woman 'Radical' Termed Menace to Student," *Atlanta Constitution*, December 5, 1926, 1.

151. Macfarland, "To the Members of the DAR," April 5, 1928.

152. Oregon Lewis and Clark Chapter, DAR, to Mrs. Alfred J. Brosseau, April 17, 1928.

153. "Resolutions Adopted by the Women's Patriotic Conference on National Defense," February 1927, File 10314–598, MID Correspondence.

154. Grace Brosseau to Mrs. Miller, April 3, 1928, Folder: Correspondence, A-Z, Box 2, Helen Tufts Bailie Papers.

155. Florence G. Adams to Helen Bailie, June 13, 1928; "D.A.R. 'Heresy' Trial June 21," *Detroit News*, June 14; "Withdraw from D.A.R. at Crawfordsville," *Indianapolis News*, May 28, 1928; "Mrs. Whitney Criticizes Bailie Trial"; "New Haven D.A.R. Leaders Resign," May 30, 1928, *N.Star*, Folder: Clippings-D.A.R., Box 1, Bailie Papers; "D.A.R. Torn in Blacklist Row; Eleven Resign," Folder 7; "Women, Daughter's Revolution," *Time*, May 14, 1928, 11, Folder 2, Box 1, DAR Blacklist Controversy Papers; "14 Quit D.A.R. in Protest Against 'Blacklist' Policy," *The World*, May 29, 1928; "When Ignorance Is Labeled 'Patriotism,'" *Union Signal*, May 1928, Folder: NCPW Attacks, DAR, Box 494, NCPW Collection.

156. "Mrs. Phelps Leaves D.A.R.," Folder: Clippings, D.A.R., Box 1, Bailie Papers; Mary B. D. Harry, Regent, Valley Forge Chapter, DAR to Miss Virginia Walker, Folder: Attackers, DAR, Virginia Walker Papers. Box: Attackers, DAR, Special Attacks Collection, SCPC; Ethel Jacobsen to Eleanor Patterson Roy, May 9, 1928, frames 936–38, folder 26, box 8, reel 47, series C, Correspondence, WILPF-U.S. Section; Martha Strayer, *The D.A.R.: An Informal History* (Washington, D.C.: Public Affairs Press, 1958), 180–81.

157. Harold Hyman, *To Try Men's Souls: Loyalty Tests in American History* (Westport, Conn.: Greenwood Press, 1959), 323.

158. "DAR May Oust Mrs. Miller, She Says," *Pittsburgh Sun-Telegraph*, April 12, 1930, Folder: Clippings, D.A.R, Bailie Papers; Bailie, "Our Threatened Heritage"; Villard, "What the Blue Menace Means"; Smith, "Mrs. Brosseau and the DAR"; McCausland, "The Blue Menace"; "The Drive Against Liberalism in America," *Unity*, March 7, 1928, 10; "Blacklists Spur Patriot Bodies to Bar Speakers," *New York World*, February 16, 1928;

"Heresy Hunters' Blacklist Seen to Cover Wide Range, Notables in Many Fields Are Included Among Those Held Unpatriotic," *New York World*, February 13, 1928; "Inquiry
Points to Spy System Muzzling U.S.," *New York World*, February 12, 1928. Concomitant
with this repression of political dissenters were the moral purity campaigns to ban "im-
moral" or "indecent" references from the mass media, especially movies. See Alison
M. Parker, *Purifying America: Women, Cultural Reform and Pro-Censorship Activism,
1873–1933* (Urbana: University of Illinois Press, 1997); "Report of the League of Catholic
Women of Lowell, Massachusetts," April 10, 1920, Folder 11, Box 1, League of Catholic
Women Files, Archives of the Archdiocese of Boston.

## Chapter 6. The Legacy of Female Antiradicalism

1. Maud Wood Park, "Organized Women and Their Legislative Program," as represented by the Women's Joint Congressional Committee, Frames 999–1005, Reel 44,
Maud May (Wood) Park Papers.

2. A. N. Hoy, Huron to National PTA, Washington, D.C., December 12, 1926,
Folder 248: Congress of Mothers, correspondence, 1926, Box 9, Tilton Papers.

3. Miss Margaret C. Maule, The Girls' Friendly Society in America, Philadelphia,
to Grace Abbott, October 22, 1927, Folder 11-0-11, Box 321, Children's Bureau Records.

4. Paula Baker, "The Domestication of Politics: Women and American Political
Society, 1780–1920," *AHR* 89, 3 (June 1984): 620–47, 638.

5. Kathryn Kish Sklar, "The Historical Foundations of Women's Power in the
Creation of the American Welfare State, 1830–1930," in Seth Koven and Sonya Michel,
eds., *Mothers of a New World: Maternalist Politics and the Origins of the Welfare States*
(New York: Routledge, 1993), 43–93.

6. See Baker, "The Domestication of Politics"; Karen J. Blair, *The Clubwoman
as Feminist: True Womanhood Redefined, 1868–1914* (New York: Holmes and Meier,
1980); Anne Firor Scott, *Natural Allies: Women's Associations in American History*
(Urbana: University of Illinois Press, 1991); Anne Firor Scott, *The Southern Lady:
From Pedestal to Politics, 1830–1930*, 2nd ed. (Charlottesville: University Press of Vir-
ginia, 1995); Seth Koven and Sonya Michel, "Womanly Duties: Maternalist Politics
and the Origins of the Welfare States in France, Germany, Great Britain, and the
United States, 1880–1920," *AHR* 95, 4 (October 1990): 1076–1108; Nancy A. Hewitt,
"Varieties of Voluntarism: Class, Ethnicity, and Women's Activism in Tampa," in
Louise A. Tilly and Patricia Gurin, eds., *Women, Politics, and Change* (New York:
Russell Sage, 1990), 63–86; Suzanne Lebsock, "Women and American Politics,
1880–1920," in Tilly and Gurin, *Women, Politics, and Change*, 35–62. Mari Jo Buhle
shows how women moved from clubs into socialist activism in *Women and Ameri-
can Socialism, 1870–1920* (Urbana: University of Illinois Press, 1981); see also Deborah Gray White, *Too Heavy a Load: Black Women in Defense of Themselves, 1894–1994*
(New York: Norton, 1999).

7. Mrs. R. E. Cone to Mrs. Fred Hoffman, President PTA Council of Sioux Falls,

Frames 888–89, Reel 9, Part 3, Series A, National Office Subject Files, 1920–1932, LWV Papers.

8. Mrs. F. Hoffman, Sioux Falls, to Mrs. Feige, Huron, South Dakota, November 1927, Frame 887, Reel 9, Part 3, Series A, National Office Subject Files, 1920–1932, LWV Papers.

9. Donald T. Crichtlow, *Phyllis Schafly and Grassroots Conservatism: A Woman's Crusade* (Princeton, N.J.: Princeton University Press, 2005), 71.

10. The committee on attacks was composed of a core group of six women: Ethel Smith, Mary Dickinson Sherman, Maud Wood Park, Mabel Costigan, Emma Bain Swiggett, and Mrs. Henry F. Baker; Minutes, November 29, 1926, Frame 743–44; Minutes, WJCC, January 3, 1927, Frame 751; January 31, 1927, Frame 753; Standing Committee, WJCC, 1926, Frame 749; Standing Committees, WJCC, 1926–27, Frame 760, Reel 3; Annual Report of the Chairman, WJCC, November 26, 1928, Frame 22–23, Reel 4, WJCC Records; Minutes, Special Meeting, WJCC, January 31, 1927, and February 9, 1927, Frames 236–37; Minutes of the Investigating Committee of the WJCC, January 23, 1927, Frames 238–39; Minutes, Special Committee, WJCC, February 24, March 5, March 21, April 11, 1927, Frames 241–45, Reel 1; Minutes, Special Committee, WJCC, Frame 259, Reel 15, Part 3, Series A, National Office Subject Files, 1920–1932, LWV Papers.

11. Helen Atwater, Chairman, WJCC, to Miss Harlean James, April 5, 1927, Frame 599; Atwater to members of the WJCC, July 5, 1927, Frame 652, Reel 1; WJCC, Minutes, April 11, 1927, Frame 757, Reel 3, WJCC Records; To the Members of the WJCC, "Rough Draft—Confidential," Frames 1013–14; "Summary of Report of Special Committee," Frames 1032–1053, Reel 44, Maud May (Wood) Park Papers.

12. "Summary of Report of Special Committee."

13. Ibid.; To the Members of the WJCC, "Rough Draft—Confidential."

14. "Summary of Report of Special Committee"; To the Members of the WJCC, "Rough Draft—Confidential."

15. Helen Atwater to Mrs. Glenn L. Swiggett, November 2, 1927, frames 40–41; Nell Battle Lewis to Atwater, November 5, 1927, Frame 44, Reel 2, WJCC Records; "Brands Women's Bills Socialistic," *Raleigh News and Observer*, November 5, 1927, 1; "Explain Women's Joint Committee," *News and Observer*, November 6, 10; "Ask Correction of Statements," *News and Observer*, November 7, 2; Nell Battle Lewis, "Incidentally," *News and Observer*, November 13, 3; "Mrs. Swift Says She's No Atheist, President of P.T. Congress Replies to Reported Attacks by DAR," *News and Observer*, November 8, 1.

16. Suggested Defense Kit, Frames 866–69, Reel 9; Jesse C. Adkins, Adkins and Nesbit, Attorneys at Law to Miss Gladys Harrison, National League of Women Voters, March 5, 1927, Reel 4, Part 3, Series A, National Office Subject Files, 1920–1932, LWV Papers.

17. Nancy F. Cott, *The Grounding of Modern Feminism* (New Haven, Conn.: Yale University Press, 1987), 259.

18. Circular Letter to State Presidents from Elizabeth Tilton, March 15, 1927, Folder 249, Box 9, Tilton Papers; Mrs. Arthur C. Watkins, Executive Secretary, National Congress of Parents and Teachers, to Aimee Zillmer, March, 1928, Folder: 1-7-2, Box 265, Central File, 1921–1928, Children Bureau Records; quoted in Molly Ladd-Taylor, *Mother-Work: Women, Child Welfare and the State, 1890–1930* (Urbana: University of Illinois Press, 1994), 64.

19. Quoted in Ladd-Taylor, *Mother-Work*, 65.

20. Elizabeth Tilton to Mrs. Moulton, Folder 250, Box 9, Tilton Papers.

21. Mrs. B. L. Robinson, "The Responsibility of Being Led," delivered before the Women's Patriotic Conference on National Defense, February 10, 1927, Folder 10, MPIL Collection.

22. Alice L. Edwards to Dr. Sophonisba P. Breckinridge, March 9, 1933, Frame 488; Margaret C. Maule to Miss Atwater, October 22, 1927, Frame 27; Margaret C. Maule to Helen Atwater, March 21, 1928, Frame 162; Ella A. Boole, President, National Woman's Christian Temperance Union, to WJCC, November 26, 1927, Frame 80, Reel 2, The WJCC Records; "Women's Clubs Ask Congress Inquiry," *New York Times*, May 30, 1928, 21. It is clear that the GFWC continued to be divided over social welfare legislation, even after the expulsion of the Kentucky club. See for example, Alice P. Mulford, Research Club, to Mrs. Robbins, New Jersey Federation of Women's Clubs, March 17, 1927, Folder: 11-0-11, Box 321, Central File, 1925–1928, Children's Bureau Records.

23. "Women's Clubs Get Coolidge Message," *New York Times*, June 2, 1926, 10; "Clubwomen Favor Child Labor Law," *New York Times*, May 30, 1926, 2; "Women End Session; Stress the Home," *New York Times*, June 5, 1926, 2; "Summary of Report of Special Committee," Frames 1032–53, Reel 44, Maud May (Wood) Park Papers.

24. Margaret H. Engelhard, "Honors of Martyrdom," *New York Times*, July 20, 1927, 22.

25. See, for example, Anne E. Rude, Los Angeles, to Abbott, January 26, 1927; Dr. Josephine Pierce, President, Ohio Federation of Women's Clubs, to Grace Abbott, March 6, 1927; Dr. Mary Riggs Noble, Commonwealth of Pennsylvania, to Miss Grace Abbott, September 30, 1927, Folder 11-0-11, Box 321, Central File 1925–28, Children's Bureau Records.

26. Special Meeting, WJCC, February 9, 1927, frames 236–237, reel 1, part 3, series A, National Office Subject Files, 1920–1932, LWV Papers; "Summary of Report of Special Committee"; Report of Greenridge Inn Meeting, Frames 321–23, Reel 4, Mary Anderson Papers.

27. "Shall the United States Recognize Soviet Russia?" issued by the General Federation of Women's Clubs, Folder: Pamphlets—D.A.R. and Related Matters, Box 1, Bailie Papers.

28. An Authoritative Statement of Bolshevik Activities in the United States, Issued by the General Federation of Women's Clubs, Mrs. John Dickinson Sherman, President, December 1927, Bulletin 1, Folder: Pamphlets—D.A.R. and Related Matters, Box 1, Bailie Papers.

29. The Illinois Federation of Women's Clubs included one woman, Mrs. George Thomas Palmer, who was named on the advisory board of the Key Men of America. See "The Advisory Council," in Key Men of America publications folder; and Elaine Goodale Eastman, "Are DAR Women Exploited?" reprinted from *Christian Century*, September 11, 1929, Folder: Magazine Articles, DAR Scandal, Box 1, Bailie Papers; see also Rosika Schwimmer to Professor Paul H. Douglas, May 29, 1935, Folder: Elizabeth Dilling's Red Network, 1934–35, Libel Series, Box F–1, Attacks on Rosika Schwimmer, General Files, 1922–1940, Schwimmer-Lloyd Collection; Resolution from the New York City Federation of Women's Clubs, February 4, 1927, File 10314–598, 2, MID Correspondence; Lucia Ames Mead to Miss Gould, April 5, 8, 1926, f8, Box 54, Reel 43, NCPW Collection. See also a letter from a WILPF agent describing the views of a club leader in Pittsburg, Kansas, November 16, 1926; letter to Mrs. William I. Hull, December 1, 1926, Folder 13, Box 1, Reel 1, Hull Papers.

30. The official program from the conference listed thirty participating organizations: the Colonial Daughters of the Seventeenth Century; the Daughters of Founders and Patriots of America; Disabled American Veterans Auxiliary; National Auxiliary United Spanish War Veterans; Order of First Families of Virginia; Order of the Gold Star; Society of Daughters of Colonial Wars; Women of the Army and Navy Legion of Valor; American War Mothers; American Women's Legion; American Legion Auxiliary; American Woman's Press Association; Auxiliary to Sons of Union Veterans of Civil War; Dames of the Loyal Legion; Daughters of American Colonists; Daughters of the American Revolution; Daughters of Union Veterans of the Civil War; Daughters of the Cincinnati; Ladies of the Grand Army of the Republic; Ladies Auxiliary Veterans of Foreign Wars; National Society Colonial Daughters of America; National Society Patriotic Women of America; National Society Patriotic Builders; National Patriotic Council; National League of American Pen Women; United States Daughters of 1812; Women's Relief Corps, G.A.R.; Women's Overseas Service League; Woman's Naval Service League; and Government Club, Inc. See "Program of Women's Patriotic Conference on National Defense," and "Organizations Participating in Conference with Number of Delegates," File 9650, Box 53, Numerical File 1921–42, War Department General Staff, G–1 (Personnel), RG 165, NARA. The report in the *Daughters of the American Revolution Magazine* asserted that only 27 organizations actually participated. Newspaper accounts claimed 28 or 29 groups took part. See Elisabeth Ellicott Poe, "The Woman's Patriotic Conference on National Defense," *Daughters of the American Revolution Magazine* (April 1927): 270–73; "Longworth Urges Bigger U.S. Navy; Holds Ratio is Cut," *Washington Post*, February 10, 1927, 1; "Pacifists and Reds Assailed Bitterly by Women Patriots," *Washington Post*, February 11, 1927, 2; "Longworth Backs Cruiser Program," *New York Times*, February 10, 1927, 22.

31. "Keeping Step," *American Legion Monthly* (July 1927): 51.

32. Poe, "The Woman's Patriotic Conference."

33. Ibid.; "Longworth Urges Bigger U.S. Navy"; "Pacifists and Reds Assailed Bitterly "; "Longworth Backs Cruiser Program."

34. For instance, Flora Walker and Grace Brosseau were members of the Daughters of 1812 in addition to the DAR. Helen Gould Shepard, known as a widely circulating antiradical speaker, was active in the DAR, Daughters of 1812, and National Society of New England Women. For an example of interlocking memberships and illustrations of how groups worked together on a local level, see Report of the President, Cora Pike Stowe, New York City Colony, *National Society of New England Women Yearbook, 1932–1933*, Papers of the New York City Colony, National Society of New England Women Records, Sophia Smith Collection.

35. Poe, "The Woman's Patriotic Conference"; "Patriotic Women Urge Quick Work on Cruisers," *Washington Post*, February 12, 1927, 1; "The Report of Mrs. Samuel Preston Davis at the Thirty-Fifth Associate Council, National Society Daughter of 1812," April 24–27, 1927, United States Daughters of 1812 Library, Washington D.C.; "Patriotic Conference Board Meeting," *American Legion Auxiliary Bulletin* (July 1927): 6, Folder 5: American Legion Auxiliary, Jan. to July 1927, Subject Files: American Legion Auxiliary, Box 3, Rose Carolyn Spencer Papers, Minnesota Historical Society; Frank Ernest Hill, *The American Legion Auxiliary: A History, 1924–34* (Indianapolis: American Legion Auxiliary, 1935), 161.

36. As far as I can determine, the conference maintained this structure during its entire existence. I believe the budget remained relatively unchanged through the interwar period since participating organizations recorded voting to contribute their "usual" or "normal" payments to the conference. See, for example, *National Society United States Daughters of 1812 News-letter* 5, 2 (December 1927): 17; Minutes of Executive Board Meeting, October 8, 1929, folder 29, National Boards, May 9, 1929–April 8, 1930, Box 16, Series IV, National Boards, National Society of New England Women Records, Sophia Smith Collection.

37. Report of the Chairman of Committee National Defense, Mrs. L. Grant Baldwin, May 5, 1932, New York City Colony, *National Society of New England Women Yearbook, 1932–1933*; Mrs. Edwin C. Gregory, "Report of the North Carolina State Regent," DAR *Proceedings of the Thirty-Seventh Continental Congress* (April 16–21, 1928): 391; Lillian C. O'Neill, "Report from Illinois" and Mrs. George H. Root, "Report from Oregon," *National Society United States Daughters of 1812 News-letter* 7, 4 (March, 1933) Ferne F. Savage, "Report from Michigan," *News-letter* 1, 1 (July 1936): 47.

38. U.S. House, Committee on the Judiciary, To Prevent Desecration of the Flag and Insignia of the United States and Provide Punishment Therefor, 69th Cong., 2nd sess., January 31, 1927; Committee on Immigration and Naturalization, *To Reconcile Naturalization Procedure With the Bill of Rights*, 72nd Cong., 1st sess., January 26–27, 1932; Bill to Permit Oath of Allegiance by Candidates for Citizenship to Be Made with Certain Reservations, 71st Cong., 2nd sess., May 8–9, 1930; Committee on Immigration and Naturalization, Amend the Registration Act (March 2, 1929), 72nd Cong., 1st sess., February 11, 1932; see also Senate, Committee on Immigration, National Origins Provision of Immigration Law: Hearings Before the Committee on Immigration, 70th Cong., 2nd sess., February 4, 6, 9, 11, 13, 1929; House, Committee on Education, Teach-

ers' Oath of Allegiance to the Constitution, 73rd Cong., 2nd sess., May 25, 1934; Committee on Judiciary, Legislation to Make "The Star-Spangled Banner" the National Anthem, 71st Cong., 2nd sess., January 31, February 1, 1930.

39. Report of Chairman of National Defense, March 27, 1930, New York City Colony, *National Society New England Women Yearbook, 1930–1931,* Papers of New York City Colony, National Society of New England Women Records; "Congress Leaders to Address Women," *New York Times,* January 27, 1929, 9; "Women Vote to Urge Stronger Defense Force," February 1, 1933, Folder: W.I.L., Attacks, 1925, Box: Attacks, Attacks on WIL, 1924–39, Attacks on Jane Addams, Lucia Ames Mead, etc., Special Attacks Collection, SCPC; *Summary of Proceedings: The Eighth Women's Patriotic Conference on National Defense,* January 30, 31, February 1, 1933, Annex Stacks, NYPL.

40. Walter Millis, *Arms and Men: A Study in American Military History* (New York: Putnam's, 1956): 246–48; Thomas H. Buckley and Edwin B. Strong, Jr., *American Foreign and National Security Policies, 1914–1945* (Knoxville: University of Tennessee Press, 1987), 65–70.

41. Millis, *Arms and Men,* 246–48; Buckley and Strong, *American Foreign and National Security Policies,* 65–70.

42. "Resolutions Adopted by the Women's Patriotic Conference on National Defense, February 1927, File 10314–598, MID Correspondence.

43. Ibid.

44. Ibid.

45. Linda K. Kerber, *Women of the Republic: Intellect and Ideology in Revolutionary America* (Chapel Hill: University of North Carolina Press, Institute of Early American History and Culture, 1980).

46. Resolutions Adopted by the Women's Patriotic Conference on National Defense.

47. Address of Mrs. Reubel [*sic*] Ross Holloway of Baltimore, Maryland on the Star Spangled Banner before the Women's Patriotic Conference on National Defense, Thursday afternoon, February 10, 1927," FOMC–913, Box 1, Mrs. Reuben Ross Holloway Collection, Fort McHenry National Monument and Historic Shrine, Baltimore; Resolutions Adopted by the Women's Patriotic Conference on National Defense," February 1927.

48. Resolutions Adopted by the Women's Patriotic Conference on National Defense.

49. "Women Support Coolidge on Navy," *New York Times,* February 4, 1928, 25. For complete texts of the resolutions by the 1928 Women's Patriotic Conference on National Defense, see DAR *Proceedings of the Thirty-Seventh Continental Congress* (April 16–21, 1928), 568–76.

50. "Pacifists and Reds Assailed Bitterly by Women Patriots"; Robinson, "The Responsibility of Being Led."

51. Philip Von Blon and Marquis James, "The A.E.F. Comes Home," *American Legion Monthly,* December 1927, 78.

52. "Patriotic Women Urge Quick Work on Cruisers"; U.S. Senate, Senator Tyson introducing resolutions of the Women's Patriotic Conference on National Defense, 69th Cong., 2nd sess., Congressional Record 68, pt. 4 (February 14, 1927): 3632–34; U.S. House, Representative Johnson introducing the resolutions of the Women's Patriotic Conference on National Defense, 70th Cong., 1st sess., Congressional Record 69, pt. 3 (February 10, 1928): 2851–55; Grace Brosseau to Secretary of War, February 1, 1929; Resolutions passed at the Fourth Annual Women's Patriotic Conference on National Defense, February 1, 1929, File 381, National Defense, Box 2315; Faustine Dennis to Harry H. Woodring, February 9, 1935 and Resolutions, File 381, National Defense, Box 2311, Central Files, 1926–39, RG 407, NARA; "Presents Defense Resolutions to President Hoover," *American Legion Auxiliary Bulletin* 40 (April 1930), Folder: American Legion (2), Box: Attackers—American Legion—National—Local Branches, American Legion Material on Peace" Box, Special Attacks Collection, SCPC; Resolutions, Eighth Women's Patriotic Conference on National Defense, 1933, Folder: A16–1 to A16–1/ZZ, Box 682, Office of the Secretary General, Correspondence, 1926–1940, General Records of the Navy Department, RG 80, NARA; Summary of Proceedings, Ninth Women's Patriotic Conference on National Defense, 1934; Eleventh Conference, 1936; Twelfth Conference, 1937; Thirteenth Conference, 1938; Fourteenth Conference, 1939, Annex Stacks, NYPL; U.S. Senate, Extension of Remarks of Senator Johnson, Resolutions Adopted by the Fourteenth Women's Patriotic Conference on National Defense, 76th Cong., Appendix, Congressional Record 84, pt. 11 (March 1, 1939): 795–97.

53. Helen Tufts Bailie, "Dishonoring the D.A.R.," reprinted from the *Nation*, September 25, 1929, Folder 13, Box 1, DAR Blacklist Controversy Papers.

54. Norman Hapgood, ed., *Professional Patriots* (New York: Albert and Charles Boni, 1928), 12.

55. Joan M. Jensen, "All Pink Sisters: The War Department and the Feminist Movement in the 1920s," in Lois Scharf and Joan M. Jensen, eds., *Decades of Discontent: The Women's Movement, 1920–194* (Boston: Northeastern University Press, 1983); Cott, *The Grounding of Modern Feminism.*

56. For an example of a radical woman alienated by ideologically sympathetic men, see Kathryn Kish Sklar, *Florence Kelley and the Nation's Work: The Rise of Women's Political Culture, 1830–1900* (New Haven, Conn.: Yale University Press, 1995).

57. Robyn Muncy, *Creating a Female Dominion in American Reform, 1890–1935* (New York: Oxford University Press, 1991).

58. After moving to Washington, Phipps became a member of the Women's City Club; she was also affiliated with the Colony Club and the Women's National Republican Club, both in New York (Phipps autobiography).

59. Bettie Monroe Sippel to Honorable Dwight F. Davis, Secretary of War, February 27, 1929, File: Women's Relations, Box 195, General Correspondence, 1932–42, RG 107; Chronology of the Proposal of the Department of War to Appoint Women as Civilian Aides; Belle Sherwin to Secretary of War Good, March 15, 1929; Maude

Wetmore, National Civic Federation, to Honorable James Good, Secretary of War, March 15, 1929, File 381, National Defense, Box 2315, Central Files, 1926–1939, RG 407.

60. Dwight Davis, Secretary of War to Miss Mabel Boardman; Mrs. Alfred J. Brosseau; Mrs. Boyce Ficklen; Mrs. Bonnie Busch; Miss Lena Hitchcock; Miss Madeline Phillips; Miss Belle Sherwin; Mrs. Samuel Shope; Mrs. John F. Sippel; Mrs. Thomas Spence; Mrs. Coffin Van Renssealer; Miss Maude Wetmore; Miss Mary E. Wooley, February 15, 1929; Memo for the Chief of Staff by Brigadier General Campbell King, Subject: Invitation to Conference of Secretary of War, February 18, 1929; War Department Press Release, Conference of the Secretary of War, February 25, 1929; Mrs. Thomas Spence, National President, American War Mothers to Mr. James W. Good, Secretary of War, War Department, March 14, 1929; Mrs. William Sherman Walker to Secretary of War, March 29, 1929, File 381, National Defense, Box 2315, Central Files 1926–39, RG 407; Function of Women Civilian Aides; Informal Report of Meeting Held in Office of Director of Women's Relations, to discuss the selection of Women Civilian Aides, February 25, 1929; Informal Report of Meeting Held in Office of the Secretary of War, February 25, 1929, File 9835, Box 55, G–1 (Personnel), Numerical File, 1921–42, RG 165; see also Mattie E. Treadwell, *U.S. Army in World War II: Special Studies—The Women's Army Corps* (Washington, D.C.: Department of the Army, 1954), 11–12.

61. "The Tentative Plan of Organization for Women's Relations, U.S.A. and Women Civilian Aides to the Secretary of War as Developed in Conference with the Secretary of War, May 16, 1928, File 9835, Box 55, Numerical File, 1921–42, G–1 (Personnel), War Department General Staff, RG 165.

62. Informal Report of Meeting Held in Office of Director of Women's Relations; Informal Report of Meeting Held in Office of the Secretary of War; see also Chronology of the Proposal of the Department of War to Appoint Women as Civilian Aides in the Several Army Corps Areas of the United States, 1928–1929, Frames 465–66, Reel 4, Part 1, Meetings of the Board of Directors and the Executive Committees: Minutes and Related Documents, 1918–1974," LWV Papers; Treadwell, *U.S. Army in World War II*, 11–12; "Baltimore Chapter," *Daughters of the American Revolution Magazine*, December 1926, 737–43.

63. Informal Report of Meeting Held in Office of Director of Women's Relations.

64. Sippel to Davis; Chronology of the Proposal of the Department of War to Appoint Women as Civilian Aides; Sherwin to Good; Wetmore, to Good; see note 59.

65. Mrs. John F. Sippel to Hon. James W. Good, March 18, 1929, Women's Relations file, box 195, General Correspondence, 1932–42, RG 107; Memorandum for the Adjutant General, March 12, 1929, by Brigadier General Campbell King, Assistant Chief of Staff, Subject: postponement of conference on women's organizations; Secretary of War James Good to Mrs. John F. Sippel; Miss Lena Hitchcock; miss Belle Sherwin; Mrs. William Sherman Walker; Miss Mabel Boardman, March 15, 1929, File 381, National Defense, Box 2315, Central Files 1926–39, RG 407.

66. "War Department Again After Women," *National Council for Prevention of War News Bulletin* (Washington, D.C., March 1, 1929), 628, Scrapbooks, topic series, Women: militarization of, undated 1916–1930, Box N188, Militarization, n.d. 1916–1941, Morgue Files, Women, Schwimmer-Lloyd Collection.

67. "Women's Clubs Split on Citizens' Camp Aid," *New York Times*, March 15, 1929, Folder: Attacks, General, 1929, Box: Attacks-General, Misc., 1917-date, Clippings, Printed Material, Special Attacks Collection, SCPC; Chronology of the Proposal of the Department of War to Appoint Women as Civilian Aides.

68. Mrs. Boyce Ficklen Jr., American Legion Auxiliary; Mrs. Alfred J. Brosseau, DAR; Mrs. Thomas Spence, American War Mothers, Women's Patriotic Conference on National Defense, to the Secretary of War, March 19, 1929, File 381, National Defense, Box 2315, Central Files 1926–39, RG 407.

69. Mrs. William Sherman Walker to Secretary of War, March 29, 1929, File 381, National Defense, Box 2315, Central Files 1926–39, RG 407.

70. Mrs. Thomas Spence, National President, American War Mothers, to Mr. James W. Good, Secretary of War, March 14, 1929, File 381, National Defense, Box 2315, Central Files 1926–39, RG 407.

71. Ficklen, Brosseau, and Spence, to the Secretary of War, March 19, 1929.

72. Honorable George Wharton Pepper to Secretary of War James Good, March 26, 1929, File 381, National Defense, Box 2315, Central Files 1926–39, RG 407.

73. Wheeler P. Bloodgood, Milwaukee, Wisconsin to Mr. Secretary, April 1, 1929, File 381, National Defense, Box 2315, Central Files 1926–39, RG 407.

74. Telegram from John Holabird, Military Training Camps Association, to Major General Charles P. Summerall, March 22, 1929, File 381, National Defense, Box 2315, Central Files, 1926–1939, RG 407.

75. Bloodgood to Mr. Secretary, April 1, 1929.

76. See, for instance, Mrs. O. D. Oliphant, "We Are Just the Same Women Serving You," January 12, 1925, before the American Legion in Indianapolis, *American Legion Weekly*, January 30, 1925.

77. Calvin Coolidge, "Enemies of the Republic: They Must Be Resisted," *Delineator* (August 1921): 42.

78. Maude R. Cudworth, "What Price Americanism?" *American Legion Auxiliary Bulletin* 7 (July 1927), Indianapolis, Folder 5: American Legion Auxiliary, Jan. to July, 1927, Box 3, Subject Files: American Legion Auxiliary, Rose Carolyn Spencer Papers, Minnesota Historical Society.

79. Report of National Committee Woman for Minnesota, 1926, Folder 4: American Legion Auxiliary, 1926, Box 3, subject Files: American Legion Auxiliary, Rose Carolyn Spencer Papers.

80. Anita Phipps, Memorandum to Chief Welfare Branch, G–1. Subject: Annual Report on Women's Relations Section, May 29, 1929, File 9835, Box 55, Numerical File, 1921–42, War Department General Staff, RG 165.

81. Anita Phipps, Memorandum for the Secretary of War. Subject: Duties of Wom-

en's Relations, October 21, 1930, File 9835, Box 55, Numerical File, 1921–42, War Department General Staff, RG 165.

82. Brigadier General A.J. Bowley, Assistant Chief of Staff, Memorandum for the Chief of Staff, Subject: Status of Director of Women's Relations, November 13, 1930, File 9835, Box 55 (9835 to 9919), Numerical File, 1921–42, War Department General Staff, RG 165; Personnel File of Anita E. Phipps.

83. Memorandum from General Douglas MacArthur, Chief of Staff, March 10, 1931, File 9835, Box 55, Numerical File, 1921–42, War Department General Staff, RG 165; Personnel File of Anita E. Phipps.

84. Personnel File of Anita E. Phipps; Treadwell, *U.S. Army in World War II*, 11–12.

85. Mrs. William Sherman Walker, National Chairman, DAR Congressional Report of the National Defense Committee, Folder: Publications—D.A.R., Box 1, Bailie Papers; "DAR Sets Up U.S. Support for List," *World*, Frame 67, Container 28, Reel 18, Subject Files: Women's Organizations, Attacks on, Catt Papers; Grace Brosseau to Mrs. Miller, April 3, 1928, Folder: Correspondence, A-Z, Box 2, Bailie Papers; "Propaganda Against the League in South Dakota," reported October 1926, written November 1926, Frames 744–45, Reel 4, Part 3, Series A, National Office Subject Files, 1920–1932, LWV Papers. In her testimony before the House of Representatives Naval Affairs Committee, Flora Walker leaped at the chance to conduct an investigation of the finances and activities of the Women's International League for Peace and Freedom, its employees, and the sources for their salaries. Eleanor S. P. St. Omer Roy to Mrs. Alfred J. Brosseau, NSDAR, February 24, 1928, Folder: Correspondence, A-Z, Box 2, Bailie Papers.

86. Sophonisba P. Breckinridge, *Women in the Twentieth Century: A Study of Their Political, Social and Economic Activities* (New York: McGraw-Hill, 1933), 272; Dorothy E. Johnson, "Organized Women as Lobbyists in the 1920's," *Capitol Studies* 1 (Spring 1972): 41–58.

87. Louise M. Young, *In the Public Interest: The League of Women Voters, 1920–1970* (New York: Greenwood Press, 1989), 99.

88. "An Appeal from the Chairman Correct Use of the Flag, Mrs. Reuben Ross Holloway," *National Society United States Daughters of 1812 News-letter* 5, 11 (November 1926).

89. "Oh! Say, Can You Sing," *News American, Maryland Living*, January 5, 1969, Ella Holloway file, Dielman-Hayward Files, Maryland Historical Society, Baltimore, Maryland; Address of Mrs. Reubel [*sic*] Ross Holloway of Baltimore, Maryland, on The Star Spangled Banner Before the Women's Patriotic Conference on National Defense, February 10, 1927, FOMC #913; FOMC 30, "Patriot Raps Anthem Foes," *Baltimore News*, December 14, 1926, FOMC–930, Box 1; Mrs. Reuben Ross Holloway to Charles Linthicum, FOMC–1010, Box 2, Mrs. Reuben Ross Holloway Collection, Fort McHenry National Monument and Historic Shrine, Baltimore, Maryland; Letter to the editor of *Republican* by Lucia Ames Mead, September 28, 1921, Lucia Ames Mead, Clippings, 1920–21, Reel 10, Mead Papers; Carrie Chapman Catt to Mrs. Anna Garland

Spencer, February 11, 1930, Folder: A.G.S. Correspondence, 1930–1931, Box 1, Anna Garlin Spencer Collection, SCPC.

90. "The Committee on National Defense Embodying Patriotic Education," *Daughters of the American Revolution Magazine* 46, 6 (June 1932): 396; Edith Scott Magna, "Keeping the D.A.R. for the D.A.R.," *Daughters of the American Revolution Magazine* 67, 2 (February 1933): 71; 68, 5 (May 1934): 316; DAR *Proceedings of the Forty-Second Continental Congress* (April 17–21, 1933): 701–2; Address of the President General, Mrs. Russell William Magna, DAR *Proceedings of the Forty-Second Continental Congress*, 15.

91. Francesca Morgan, *Women and Patriotism in Jim Crow America* (Chapel Hill: University of North Carolina Press, 2005), 155.

92. Mrs. Charles B. Gilbert, *The American Legion Auxiliary* (Indianapolis: American Legion Auxiliary, 1970): 61–62, 65–66; Marguerite H. White, *American War Mothers, Fifty Year History, 1917–1967*, with update to 1981 (Washington, D.C.: American War Mothers, 1981), 36, 51, 61.

93. Martha Strayer, *The D.A.R.: An Informal History* (Washington, D.C.: Public Affairs Press, 1958), 173; Margaret Gibbs, *The DAR* (New York: Holt, Rinehart and Winston, 1969),146–48.

94. "Red Threat to Kill Fish Seen," *Boston Herald*, December 5, 1930, Folder: Clippings, DAR, Bailie Papers.

95. Report of National Defense Embodying Patriotic Education Committee, Florence Hague Becker, DAR *Proceedings of the Forty-Second Continental Congress*, 595–602.

96. Paul H. Douglas to Mrs. Lloyd, May 24, 1935; Mrs. John L. Whitehurst, "Our Common Cause," National Society Daughters of the American Revolution, *National Defense News* 2, 9 (May 1936): 12, New York Public Library; Elizabeth Dilling, *The Red Network: A "Who's Who" and Handbook of Radicalism for Patriots* (Chicago: the author, 1934); Glen Jeansonne, *Women of the Far Right: The Mothers' Movement and World War II* (Chicago: University of Chicago Press, 1996), 20–23.

97. Strayer, *The D.A.R.*, 173; Gibbs, *The DAR*, 146–48; Dilling, *The Red Network*.

98. Francesca Morgan, "'Home and Country': Women, Nation and the Daughters of the American Revolution, 1890–1939 (Ph.D. dissertation, Columbia University, 1998); Gibbs, *The DAR*, 146–48; Elizabeth Dilling, *The Roosevelt Red Record and Its Background* (Chicago: author, 1936); Leo P. Ribuffo, *The Old Christian Right: The Protestant Far Right from the Great Depression to the Cold War* (Philadelphia: Temple University Press, 1983), 178–224; Jeansonne, *Women of the Far Right*, 152–64.

99. "Hits Church Group as Radicals' Aid," *New York Times*, December 10, 1938, 9; "Mrs. Henry M. Robert., Jr., President General of the Daughters of the American Revolution, today offered the House Committee Investigating Un-American Activities a six-point program to promote Americanism, December 9, 1938, caption from LOC photograph, LC-H22-D–5158, Library of Congress Prints and Photographs Division.

100. American Section of International Committee to Combat the World Menace of Communism, October 19, 1931, Frame 863, Reel 42, Folder 18, Box 5, Series C, Correspondence, WILPF-U.S. Section; *National Society United States Daughters of 1812 Newsletter* 7, 4 (March 1933); Eleanor B. Parks, San Diego County Federation of Women's Clubs, to Upton Sinclair, April 4, 1934, Box 26, Upton Sinclair Papers, Manuscripts Department, Lilly Library, Indiana University, Bloomington. My thanks to Wendy Wall for this letter; Paul H. Douglas to Mrs. Lloyd, May 24, 1935, folder: Elizabeth Dilling's Red Network, 1934–35, Libel Series, Box F–1, Attacks on Rosika Schwimmer, General Files, 1922–1940, Schwimmer-Lloyd Collection; Whitehurst, "Our Common Cause"; Dilling, *The Red Network*; Jeansonne, *Women of the Far Right*, 20–23.

101. Susan Ware, *Beyond Suffrage: Women in the New Deal* (Cambridge, Mass.: Harvard University Press, 1981).

102. Linda Gordon, *Pitied But Not Entitled: Single Mothers and the History of Welfare, 1890–1935* (New York: Free Press, 1981), 257.

103. Muncy, *Creating a Female Dominion in American Reform*, 151–54; Ware, *Beyond Suffrage*, 87–115, 125; Gordon, *Pitied But Not Entitled*, 67–108, 253–85.

104. Clarke A. Chambers, *Seedtime of Reform: American Social Service and Social Action, 1918–1933* (Minneapolis: University of Minnesota Press, 1963); William H. Chafe, "Women's History and Political History: Some Thoughts on Progressivism and the New Deal," in Nancy A. Hewitt and Suzanne Lebsock, eds., *Visible Women: New Essays on American Activism*, ed. (Urbana: University of Illinois Press, 1993).

105. Alan Dawley, *Struggles for Justice: Social Responsibility and the Liberal State* (Cambridge, Mass.: Belknap Press of Harvard University Press, 1991), 371–408.

106. Chambers, *Seedtime of Reform*; Chafe, "Women's History and Political History."

107. Muncy, *Creating a Female Dominion*, 151–54; Ware, *Beyond Suffrage*, 87–117, 125; Gordon, *Pitied But Not Entitled*, 67–108, 253–85.

108. Muncy, *Creating a Female Dominion*; Estelle Freedman, "Separatism as Strategy: Female Institution Building and American Feminism, 1870–1930," *Feminist Studies* 5, 3 (Fall 1979): 512–29; Estelle B. Freedman, "Separatism Revisited: Women's Institutions, Social Reform and the Career of Miriam Van Waters," in Linda K. Kerber, Alice Kessler-Harris, and Kathryn Kish Sklar, eds., *U.S. History as Women's History, New Feminist Essays* (Chapel Hill: University of North Carolina Press, 1995), 170–88.

109. Muncy, *Creating a Female Dominion*; Freedman, "Separatism as Strategy"; Freedman, "Separatism Revisited."

110. Freedman, "Separatism as Strategy"; Freedman, "Separatism Revisited."

Epilogue: From Antiradicalism to Anticommunism

1. Allan J. Lichtman, *White Protestant Nation: The Rise of the American Conservative Movement* (New York: Atlantic Monthly Press, 2008), 151; Catherine E. Rymph, *Republican Women: Feminism and Conservatism from Suffrage Through the Rise of the New Right* (Chapel Hill: University of North Carolina Press, 2006), 104. The WJCC

was not officially dissolved until 1970. See Jan Doolittle Wilson, *The Women's Joint Congressional Committee and the Politics of Maternalism, 1920–30* (Urbana: University of Illinois Press, 2007), 1.

2. Michelle Nickerson, *Mothers of Conservatism: Women and the Post-War Right* (Princeton, N.J.: Princeton University Press, 2012); for a larger discussion of the highly politicized suburban citizenship of the time, see Sylvie Murray, *The Progressive Housewife: Community Activism in Suburban Queens, 1945–1965* (Philadelphia: University of Pennsylvania Press, 2003).

3. Charles M. Payne, *I've Got the Light of Freedom: The Organizing Tradition and the Mississippi Freedom Struggle* (Berkeley: University of California Press, 1995); Chana Kai Lee, *For Freedom's Sake: The Life of Fannie Lou Hamer* (Urbana: University of Illinois Press, 1999); Robert Korstad, *Civil Rights Unionism: Tobacco Workers and the Struggle for Democracy in the Mid-Twentieth Century South* (Chapel Hill: University of North Carolina Press, 2003); Barbara Ransby, *Ella Baker and the Black Freedom Movement: A Radical Democratic Vision* (Chapel Hill: University of North Carolina Press, 2003); Christina Greene, *Our Separate Ways: Women and the Black Freedom Movement in Durham, North Carolina* (Chapel Hill: University of North Carolina Press, 2005); Faith S. Holsaert et al., *Hands on the Freedom Plow: Personal Accounts by Women in SNCC* (Urbana: University of Illinois Press, 2010).

4. Mrs. Charles B. Gilbert, *The American Legion Auxiliary* (Indianapolis: American Legion Auxiliary, 1970), 61–62, 65–66; Marguerite H. White, *American War Mothers, Fifty Year History, 1917–1967*, with update to 1981 (Washington, D.C.: American War Mothers, 1981), 36, 51, 61.

5. Donald T. Critchlow, *Phyllis Schlafly and Grassroots Conservatism: A Woman's Crusade* (Princeton, N.J.: Princeton University Press, 2005).

6. Ibid., 37–38.

7. Rymph, *Republican Women*, 239.

8. Ibid., 174–76, 239–41; Critchlow, *Phyllis Schlafly and Grassroots Conservatism*, 62–88.

9. Biography of Phyllis Schlafly (Eagle Forum, Alton, Illinois), 2010, http://www.eagleforum.org/misc/bio.html, accessed June 4, 2010.

10. Critchlow, *Phyllis Schlafly and Grassroots Conservatism*, 62.

11. Ibid., 62.

12. Ibid., 71–72

13. Ibid., 71, quote 75.

14. Ibid., 71–72; Biography of Phyllis Schlafly.

15. Quoted in Rymph, *Republican Women*, 175.

16. Rymph, *Republican Women*, 174–76; Carol Felsenthal, *The Sweetheart of the Silent Majority: The Biography of Phyllis Schlafly* (Garden City, N.Y.: Doubleday, 1981): 163–78.

17. Rymph, *Republican Women*, 214.

18. Critchlow, *Phyllis Schlafly and Grassroots Conservatism*, 217.

19. Rymph, *Republican Women*, 214–15.

20. Quoted in Rosalind Rosenberg, *Divided Lives: American Women in the Twentieth Century*, rev. ed. (New York: Hill and Wang, 2008), 220.

21. Phyllis Schlafly, "What's Wrong with 'Equal Rights' for Women?" *Phyllis Schlafly Report* 5, 7 (February 1972): 1–4; reprinted in Donald T. Critchlow and Nancy MacLean, *Debating the American Conservative Movement: 1945 to the Present* (Lanham, Md.: Rowman and Littlefield, 2009), 197–200.

22. Ibid.

23. Critchlow, *Phyllis Schlafly and Grassroots Conservatism*, 217.

24. Rosenberg, *Divided Lives*, 224.

25. Critchlow, *Phyllis Schlafly and Grassroots Conservatism*, 221.

26. Ibid.

27. Ibid., 71–72; Biography of Phyllis Schlafly.

28. Critchlow, *Phyllis Schlafly and Grassroots Conservatism*, 223.

29. Rosenberg, *Divided Lives*, 220–27; Critchlow, *Phyllis Schlafly and Grassroots Conservatism*, 243–53.

30. Critchlow, *Phyllis Schlafly and Grassroots Conservatism*, 281.

31. Ibid., 212–69; Lisa McGirr, *Suburban Warriors: The Origins of the New American Right* (Princeton, N.J.: Princeton University Press, 2001).

32. Rymph, *Republican Women*, 114.

# Index

# Acknowledgments

I started thinking about the role that conservative women played in American politics in 1992, at Duke University. The journey from these initial questions to this manuscript was longer than I ever could have imagined. And without the help of friends, colleagues and family, I would have never seen the end of the road. As I gestated babies and endured sleepless nights with young children, learned the rudiments of teaching, moved across the country, worked on other book projects, and tried to figure out how to craft a professional life as a nontraditional historian, my circle of supporters never let me forget my pledge to turn that project into a book. Without their assistance, this endeavor would have been impossible.

This book would not exist without the generous financial aid I received. The National Endowment for the Humanities awarded me a Faculty Research Fellowship that allowed me to devote myself to uninterrupted writing for more than a year, wrestling a sprawling dissertation into something resembling a book. I applied to the NEH at the urging of Marla Miller, who has my eternal gratitude for this suggestion and many others. In its early stages, this project was funded in large part by the Woodrow Wilson National Fellowship Foundation, which awarded me three different grants. I am also grateful for the funding I received from the Schlesinger Library at Radcliffe College and the Duke University History Department.

The research for this book was enhanced by the skill and kindness of innumerable archivists. I am particularly grateful for the guidance I received from Margery Sly at the Sophia Smith Collection at Smith College; Stephen Trent Seames at the Massachusetts National Guard Military Archives and Museum; and Mitch Yockelson and Rick Peuser at the National Archives and Records Administration. I also want to thank the members of the Daughters of 1812 for being so willing to open their headquarters and their records when I contacted them in 1995. These long archival sojourns were made possible by the hospitality of friends. Bill Sherman, Holly Barker, and Laura Edwards welcomed me to Washington, D.C. Ellen and Paul Lazar hosted me during my visit to Baltimore. Rich Warren and Suzanne Cohen opened their home in Philadelphia. Julia Herskowitz and Manny Howard adopted me for two summers in Boston. Before even meeting me, Martha Acklesburg offered me a comfortable berth in Northampton, Massachusetts. All researchers should be so lucky.

The genesis of this book can be found in the phenomenal historical community at Duke University and the University of North Carolina at Chapel Hill. Duke introduced me to an extraordinary group of people. Tami Davis Biddle, Claudia Koonz, and Bill Chafe all challenged, inspired and encouraged me at different times. In commenting on one chapter, Laura Edwards helped me see my project in an entirely new light. Over the last twenty years Steve Lawson has always gone out of his way to mentor me, never missing an opportunity to demand the immediate completion of this book. Jacquelyn Dowd Hall combines brilliance and generosity in ways that have benefited legions of young historians. She touched my life in ways familiar to those who know her well; this manuscript reflects her insights. Susan Thorne taught me how to ask big questions, all the while dazzling me with her rare blend of intellectual rigor and deep compassion. My graduate advisor Nancy Hewitt gave me the creative freedom I needed to begin this quest. Since our first encounter in 1992, she has nurtured me as a scholar, a feminist and a friend, never failing to inspire me with her eloquent writing and socially-engaged vision for history. The good parts of this book are a testament to her boundless dedication as a mentor, her brilliant teaching and unfailing generosity. She will always be my heroine and treasured friend.

I was surrounded by gifted and passionate people who left their mark on me and this book. Most directly, this manuscript reflects the questions, editing and cheerleading provided by David Carter, Jane Mangan, Darcy Buch and Evelyn Sterne. The lovely and talented "Junettes"—Stacy Braukman, Natalie Fousekis, Kathy Newfont, and Ginny Noble—provided both the feminist solidarity and deadlines I needed to craft the first draft of this manuscript. Since leaving Duke I have continued to benefit from the friendship and intellectual acuity of Wayne Lee, Derek Chang and Danna Kostroun. Through word and deed, Rhonda Lee showed me how to combine intellectual vitality with awe-inspiring faith and love. Rhonda read draft after draft of this work over many years and was both an indefatigable champion and exceptional critic.

One of the most difficult parts of leaving North Carolina for my native Minnesota was saying goodbye to the "writing goddesses" Caroline Light, Ginny Noble, Susan Thorne, and Anne Whisnant, who helped me navigate the transition from dissertation to book. Their fingerprints are everywhere on these pages and I cherish the memory of the close fellowship we enjoyed. Over many years, both Michelle Nickerson and Francesca Morgan shared their research and their conviction that it was important for feminists to study conservative women. This book would have been much poorer without their contributions to this field of women's history. Sarah Ball Damberg helped me both survive and flourish. And Nan Enstad and Anne Enke provided both friendship and mentoring in this critical period; I am particularly grateful for their instruction in the art of teaching.

In the home stretch, the fabulous editor Peter Agree was a rock-solid supporter. He never wavered in his enthusiasm, even when the slow pace of my revisions should have raised grave doubts. My narrative was dramatically improved by the advice of Glenda Gilmore, Michael Kazin, Edward J. Blum, and Kate Bjork. Kate also became a dear friend and part of my Minnesota cheering section, which also included Linda Janke and Peter Hennigan. This group provided timely encouragement when I could not see my way forward. When I arrived in Minnesota, Mary Wingerd invited me to join another project, a new history of Minnesota she was writing for the University of Minnesota. Working on *North Country* with Mary and our extraordinary editor Todd Orjala opened up entirely new vistas on the practice and writing of history for me. Even in the thick of this collaboration, Mary never let me forget my own manuscript and pushed me to finish my revisions. Her faith in my abilities lit the way during some dark nights of the soul.

I am fortunate to have the most supportive family on the planet. Edward and Marion Shiffer, my in-laws, have been tireless in their enthusiasm for this endeavor. My father, Curtis Delegard, has made so many things possible. My mother, Dorothy Delegard, has been a constant presence in the life of my children, freeing me to work on this book. She combines a fierce devotion to family with an unflagging faith in the power of ideas and the importance of books, particularly those authored by her daughter. Her love and confidence have always sustained me. My greatest delight and satisfaction in life have come from Annika and Malachi Shiffer-Delegard, who have provided critical perspective on this project since their births. I can't imagine writing—much less living—without the love and faith of James Shiffer, my endlessly optimistic and creative soul-mate. Throughout the life of this project, James taught me the power of narrative and the value of humor. He inspires me every day with his own determination to speak truth to power in the most gorgeous prose possible. I dedicate this project to him.